11-12-00

ENTER THE DRAGON

Also by the Author

A GLORIOUS WAY TO DIE
The Kamikaze Mission of the Battleship Yamato, *April 1945*

ENTER THE DRAGON

CHINA'S UNDECLARED WAR AGAINST THE U.S. IN KOREA, 1950-51

RUSSELL SPURR

Newmarket Press
New York

88 89 90 MV 10 9 8 7 6 5 4 3 2 1 HC

Library of Congress Cataloging-in-Publication Data

Spurr, Russell.
  Enter the dragon: China's undeclared war against the U.S. in Korea, 1950–51 / Russell Spurr.—1st ed.
    p. cm.
    Bibliography: p.
    Includes index.
    ISBN 1-557-04008-7
    1. Korean War, 1950–1953—China. 2. Korean War, 1950–1953—Campaigns. I. Title.
DS919.5.S68 1987
951.9'042—dc19   *87-18436*
                                                                         CIP

Quantity Purchases

Companies, professional groups, clubs and other organizations may qualify for special terms when ordering quantities of this title. For information contact: Special Sales Dept., Newmarket Press, 18 East 48th Street, New York, New York 10017, or call (212) 832-3575.

Manufactured in the United States of America

Maps by David Lindroth, Inc.

First Printing

To Geoff, who urged me on.

Contents

List of Maps

Major Narrative Characters

The Chinese[1]

Chairman Mao Zedong
Ambassador Wu Xiuquan,
    head of special delegation to the United Nations

General Peng Dehuai,
    commander in chief, Chinese Peoples' Volunteers (in Korea)
Major Han Liqun,
    aide to General Peng

Colonel Wong Lichan,
    liaison officer to the North Korean People's Army

The Sharp Swords, a 30-man commando squad attached
    to the 38th Field Army, including:
        Captain Lao Kongcheng
        Big Ears Wong

[1] In Chinese and Korean names, the given name follows the surname—the reverse of Western practice. Thus, as General Douglas MacArthur becomes *MacArthur* in subsequent references, General Peng Dehuai becomes *Peng*, Major Han Liqun becomes *Han*, and so forth.

Little Li
Fat Belly Wu
Opium Li
Young Kung
Deng

Members of the 39th Field Army:
Colonel Yang Shixian
Commissar Wong Wuyi

Members of the 40th Field Army:
Colonel Gu Dehua
Runner Jia Peixing

Members of the 50th Field Army:
Colonel One-Eye Pang
Commissar Pig-Snout Wu
Sergeant Gu Wentu
Trooper Liu

Ah Lo,
a small boy in Andong, Manchuria (China), at the
North Korean border

The Americans

President Harry Truman
Secretary of State Dean Acheson
United Nations Ambassador Warren Austin

General Douglas MacArthur,
Supreme Commander for the Allied Powers, Far East Command;
United Nations commander in Korea (July 7, 1950—April 11, 1951)
General Walton H. "Johnnie" Walker,
Eighth Army commander (June 30, 1950—December 23, 1950)
General Matthew B. Ridgway,
Eighth Army commander (December 23, 1950—April 11, 1951);
UN commander in Korea (April 11, 1951—May 12, 1952)
General Edward M. "Ned" Almond,
X Corps commander

General Laurence B. Keiser,
    2nd Division commander
Colonel Paul L. Freeman, Jr.,
    23rd Infantry Regiment commander (2nd Division)

General Oliver P. Smith,
    First Marine Division commander
Lieutenant Colonel Raymond Murray,
    5th Marine Regiment commander (First Marine Division)

Colonel John H. "Mike" Michaelis,
    27th ("Wolfhounds") Infantry Regiment commander

The North Koreans

Premier Kim Il Sung
General Kim Chaek,
    NKPA front commander before Chinese intervention
Major Kim,
    escort to Colonel Wong Lichan (see *The Chinese*)
General Kim Ung,
    NKPA I Corps commander before Chinese intervention
Comrade Li,
    female guide to the Sharp Swords (see *The Chinese*)

The Soviets

Premier Joseph Stalin
Ambassador Terenty F. Shtykov,
    ambassador to North Korea;
    formerly commander of Soviet occupation troops there

Colonel Andrei Chichirin, and
Captain Sergei Bolganoff,
    members of a military liaison team

Others

President Syngman Rhee,
    South Korean head of state
President Chiang Kai-shek,
    Taiwanese head of state;
    formerly head of the defeated Nationalist government of
    mainland China

Prime Minister Clement Attlee,
    British head of state
Brigadier Basil Coad,
    British 27th Commonwealth Brigade commander

The Correspondents

Stephen Barber, London *News Chronicle*
Homer Bigart, New York *Herald Tribune*
René Cutforth, BBC-TV
Max Desfor, Associated Press
David Douglas Duncan, *Life* magazine
Louis Heron, London *Times*
Marguerite "Maggie" Higgins, New York *Herald Tribune*
Dwight Martin, *Time* magazine
Harold Martin, *Saturday Evening Post*
Reginald "Reggie" Thompson, London *Daily Telegraph*

ABBREVIATIONS

CPV	Chinese Peoples' Volunteers (given name of Chinese troops in Korea)
DPRK	Democratic People's Republic of Korea (North Korea)
NKPA	North Korean People's Army
PLA	People's Liberation Army (China)
PRC	People's Republic of China
ROK	Republic of Korea (South Korea)
UN	United Nations

Chronology

1945   Following the Japanese defeat in World War II, Japanese troops occupying Korea surrender to Allied forces—below the 38th Parallel to American troops, above the 38th Parallel to Soviet troops

1948   Elections are held below the 38th Parallel under the auspices of the United Nations Temporary Commission on Korea, and Syngman Rhee is inaugurated president;

Above the 38th Parallel, under Soviet auspices, the "Democratic People's Republic of Korea" is proclaimed, led by Premier Kim Il Sung

1949   Following years of civil war in mainland China, Chiang Kai-shek, leader of the defeated Nationalist government, flees to the island of Taiwan; he is succeeded on the mainland by the Communist regime of Mao Zedong

1950

June 25   North Korean forces cross the 38th Parallel, attacking numerous South Korean (ROK) positions; the UN Security Council calls for a withdrawal of the attacking North Koreans

June 27   President Truman announces U.S. air and naval assistance to the ROK; UN Security Council calls on UN-member nations to provide aid to the ROK in repelling its attackers

June 29   The North Koreans seize the ROK capital, Seoul; Great Britain orders its Far Eastern Fleet to aid the ROK

June 30   Truman commits U.S. ground troops

July 4   U.S. troops first meet invading North Koreans and are forced to retreat

July 7   U.S. General Douglas MacArthur named commander of all UN forces

August 4   NKPA forces unsuccessfully assault U.S./ROK forces on the Pusan perimeter

August 29   British 27th Commonwealth Brigade arrives from Hong Kong

September 15   U.S. X Corps makes successful amphibious landing at Inchon, allowing UN forces to break out of the Pusan perimeter, heading north and west

September 25   U.S. Joint Chiefs of Staff authorize military operations north of the 38th Parallel

September 26   Seoul falls to U.S. X Corps

October 7   UN adopts a resolution recommending that "all appropriate steps be taken to ensure conditions of stability throughout Korea" including "the establishment of a unified, independent and democratic government"; U.S. troops follow those of the ROK north of the 38th Parallel

October 14   The first troops of the Chinese People's Liberation Army, under the *nom de guerre* of the "Chinese Peoples' Volunteers," cross the Yalu River into North Korea

October 19–20 Pyongyang, capital of North Korea, falls to the U.S. Eighth Army

October 24 MacArthur removes restrictions on the employment of non-ROK troops in North Korean provinces bordering China

October 25 Chinese troops engage the ROK less than 40 miles from the Yalu River

October 27–31 First Chinese offensive halts UN advance; ROK 6th Division, flanking the U.S. Eighth Army, is decimated

November 24 Chinese delegation under Wu Xiuquan arrives at UN headquarters;
MacArthur launches final approach toward Yalu River

November 25–27 Second, major, Chinese offensive launched

December 1 Eighth Army and X Corps start southward retreat

December 5 Chinese occupy Pyongyang following UN troop withdrawal there

December 11 X Corps evacuates Hungnam

December 23 General Walker, Eighth Army commander, killed in accident

December 25 Chinese troops cross south of the 38th Parallel

1951

January 1 Third Chinese offensive launched

January 4 UN forces evacuate Seoul

January 7 Chinese troops enter Wonju

January 8–15 U.S. 2nd Division halts Chinese outside Wonju

February 1 UN condemns China as aggressor

March 15 UN forces retake Seoul

April 11 Truman relieves MacArthur as UN commander

1953

July 27 Armistice signed

Acknowledgments

Volumes have been written from the Western viewpoint on the Korean War, but incredibly little has come from the Chinese. The few snippets they have chosen to release over the years are, for the most part, too skimpy to be taken seriously. Fragments of autobiography by leading Chinese commanders yield little of substance.

But with the rise to power of Deng Xiaoping, following the death of Mao in 1976, many doors once sealed began to open. An international exchange of military views and information blossomed rapidly; senior Chinese officers began to tour the United States, Japan, and Europe; and once-secret facilities in China were thrown open to foreign admirals and generals, who in turn went on to address Peking academy staffs.

This changed political atmosphere, I found, rendered Chinese veterans of many ranks a lot more talkative. The 1980 campaign to rehabilitate the much-loved General Peng Dehuai, the most prominent military victim of the Cultural Revolution (and a major figure in this narrative), undoubtedly helped my researches. So too did emerging new Chinese perceptions about the background of the Korean War. "We are taking an entirely new look at the origins of that war," one Chinese friend told me quite recently. Another acidly observed that "China was conned into a costly struggle for which we got little thanks." Such views have not yet surfaced officially—not while North Korea's durable dictator, Kim Il Sung, continues to play off Peking against Moscow—but this underlying disillusionment, or perhaps simply a new-found urge to put the Chinese viewpoint forward, proved helpful.

Work on this book began five years ago, as an attempt to examine the Chinese military experience in Korea. The first of my more than 40 interviews, carried on both inside and outside China, sprang from contacts with the Red River Brigade, a Chinese Communist guerrilla force which operated on the Pearl River, close to Hong Kong, during World War II. Veterans of this force put me in touch with Colonel Wong Lichan, the former aide to General Peng, in Macao. Colonel Wong shed considerable light on the formation of the Chinese Peoples' Volunteers (CPV)—the given name of the PLA forces in Korea—and on early tactical decisions made at the CPV headquarters. But it took three more years of research, and another two years of writing, before the picture was near completion.

I was able to draw on notes of my own which dated back to the 1950s. (As Far East correspondent for the London *Daily Express*, I had covered the last 14 months of the Korean War, then been stationed in Tokyo, Hong Kong, and Singapore, and had reported on what was then known as the Indochina War, covering Dienbienphu and the French pullout from Hanoi. I was also fortunate during this time to become one of the first Western correspondents to report from Peking following the 1949 establishment of the People's Republic of China.) Moderately revealing tidbits had been picked up in those days from Qiao Guanhua, one of China's most sophisticated diplomats.

This one-time protege of Zhou Enlai, who later fell from grace with the Gang of Four, was in those days a close friend of my old colleague Wilfred Burchett, a left-wing Australian journalist. Wilfred and I occasionally met Qiao in Peking to hear stories of raucous disagreement among the Chinese leaders about the degree to which it was considered advisable to push the Americans. It was Qiao who warned against portraying Chairman Mao as the consistent hawk, and Zhou Enlai as the ever-frustrated dove, in the Korean conflict. Such a view, he warned, ignored the combination of cocky pride and nationalist prejudice that suffused these newly triumphant revolutionaries, shielded in their unworldly enclave by the high, ochre walls of the Forbidden City.

My later research was far from easy. There were talks, spread over some 20 visits to China, with many other soldiers whose reminiscences contributed greatly (though not always for direct attribution) to this book; but the words of these soldiers were hampered by both a degree of soldierly reticence and by an understandable political caution that fluctuated with the waves of debate churned up in the post-Mao power struggle. Even then it was not always easy to establish verifiable facts, owing to a lack of documents and the participants' difficulty in recalling details from half a lifetime ago.

I have taken the liberty throughout this book, as specialists will note, of imposing Western-style ranks upon the Chinese People's Liberation Army (PLA). Ranks as we recognize them were not in fact introduced until shortly after the Korean War. Something comparable to ranks already existed within the PLA, of course, but in a form too cumbersome and confusing to incorporate into this narrative; it is difficult enough for Westerners to keep track of unfamiliar Chinese names without adding such titles as "Squad Leader" and "Unit Commander." I trust that by according the men of the PLA equivalent Western-style ranks, the *dramatis personae* will become more easily identifiable.

I have also struck a compromise between the use of *pinyin*, the official Chinese approximation of the tonal *lingua franca*, and the much older Wade-Giles system once standard for English-speaking writers. Again, to avoid confusion, the most familiar Chinese names, such as Peking, remain unaltered; names of members of the defeated Nationalist government, too, have been left in Wade-Giles because *pinyin*, seen as a Communist aberration, is still not recognized on Taiwan. But Chou En-lai has become Zhou Enlai and Mao Tse-tung is now Mao Zedong. The *pinyin* phonetics are, in most cases, an improvement.

Struggling to keep events in context, I have attempted to balance the portions of the narrative seen through Chinese eyes with the view from our side of the line. Much of this is seen, and seen deliberately, through the eyes of the correspondents. I felt it essential to point up the part played by the media in a highly ideological war.

Korea turned out to be the last *scribes'* war. Television had yet to establish its present dominance—though it was in the process of doing so, as I learned when occasionally shooting TV film for NBC. Returned UN prisoners were brought before press conferences, and our primitive sound cameras were stuffed away on a platform to the rear. My newsreel guru, Ronnie Noble of the British Broadcasting Corporation (BBC), caused an uproar by demanding—successfully— that cameras be re-sited *in front* of the newspaper reporters, to enable us to interview the prisoners in close-up, face to face.

The correspondents were a feisty bunch, and had to be, considering the conditions under which they worked. Most notable was Marguerite Higgins, winner of a Pulitzer Prize for her reportage in Korea and a pioneer feminist if ever there was one. Her treatment at the hands of male chauvinist authorities makes strange reading today.

Others reporting with great distinction include old colleagues such as Robert Guillan of *Le Monde*, Keyes Beech, and Howard Handelman; and old friends, now sadly departed, such as Steve Barber and Dwight Martin. London *Daily Telegraph* correspondent Reginald Thomson and René Cutforth of BBC-TV both produced vivid, disturbing books, as did the distinguished British academic David Rees, whose *Korea: The Limited War* has yet to be surpassed. Other informative works, I found, were Roy Appelman's *South to the Naktong, North to the Yalu*, T. R. Fehrenbach's flamboyant *This Kind of War*, and S.L.A. Marshall's magnificently detailed *The River and the Gauntlet*.

Last touches are being applied to this manuscript in my new home in Australia, following a tour of northern China as a guest of the Beijing International Institute for Strategic Studies. The chairman of the Institute, General Wu Xiuquan, hosted a banquet in my honor in the Great Hall of the People, thus giving me access to fresh material for this book, and also arranged for me a meeting with missile experts in Peking, a visit to the recently formed Defense University in the northwestern part of the Chinese capital, and a tour of the province of Shandong, home of many of the soldiers who figured prominently in the early stages of their country's Korean campaigns. I would like to take this opportunity to thank the Institute, and the Chinese Ministry of Defense, for their untiring support and assistance over the years.

Permit me to conclude with a word of thanks to my publisher, Esther Margolis, and my redoubtable editor and researcher, Jean Highland, for their unflagging support and patience. Especially for their patience. I also could not have asked for more constructive editing than that provided by my in-house editor, Clifford Crouch. A major thank-you to Lt. Colonel Mike Lombardo for supplying so many invaluable documents about the PLA in the early stages of my research. Also to his colleagues, Colonel Tom Roberts of the U.S. Military Attaché's Office, Peking; Colonel Jack Leide, in Tokyo; and Colonel Monty Buller and Major Don Cake in Hong Kong, for their advice and guidance. All these military men have now been re-posted or gone on to new careers. On the Chinese side, my gratitude to the late Colonel Yang Shixian and his family; the now-retired journalist Jia Peixing; and a grown-up Ah Lo, working these days in Bangkok under another, adult, name; and to Colonel Wong Lichan, Major Han Liqun, Captain Lao Kongcheng, and Sergeant Wu Gentu. Thanks finally to my wife, Rosemary, who was not saddled with the typing this time, but had to endure my constant absence while I was in the company of my trusty word processor.

Sydney, Australia
December, 1987

When the enemy is at ease, be able to weary him;
when well fed, to starve him;
when at rest, to make him move.
    Appear at places to which he must hasten;
move swiftly where he does not expect you.

Sun Tze,
The Art of War

Come like the wind, go like the lightning.

Chang Yu,
Sung dynasty
commentator

ENTER THE DRAGON

CHINA'S UNDECLARED WAR AGAINST THE U.S. IN KOREA, 1950–51

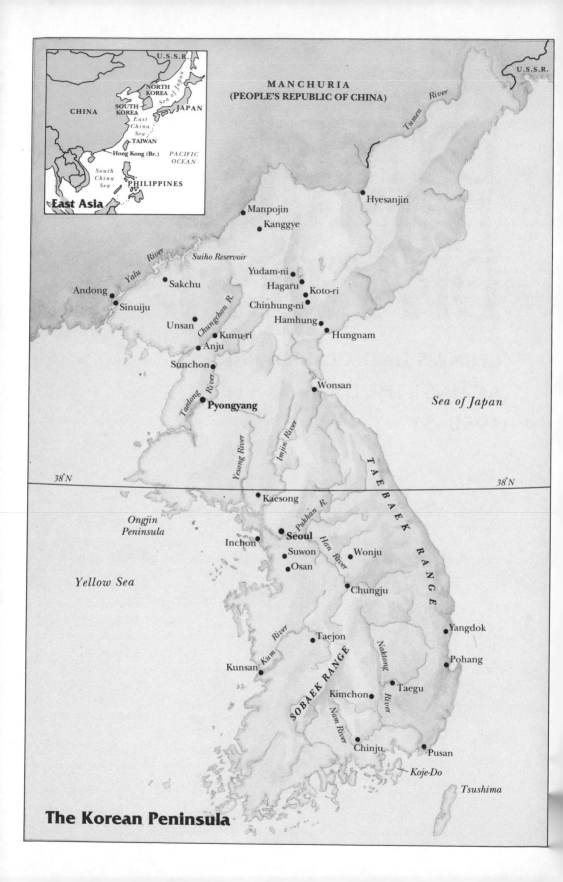

The Korean Peninsula

East Asia

U.S.S.R.

CHINA

NORTH KOREA

SOUTH KOREA

Sea of Japan

JAPAN

East China Sea

TAIWAN

Hong Kong (Br.)

PACIFIC OCEAN

South China Sea

PHILIPPINES

MANCHURIA
(PEOPLE'S REPUBLIC OF CHINA)

U.S.S.R.

Tumen River

Hyesanjin

Manpojin

Kanggye

Yalu River

Suiho Reservoir

Yudam-ni

Sakchu

Hagaru

Koto-ri

Andong

Chinhung-ni

Sinuiju

Chongchon R.

Hamhung

Unsan

Kunu-ri

Hungnam

Anju

Sunchon

Taedong River

Pyongyang

Wonsan

Sea of Japan

Yesong River

Imjin River

38°N   38°N

Kaesong

Pukhan R.

Ongjin Peninsula

Inchon

Seoul

Suwon

Wonju

Han River

Osan

Yellow Sea

Chungju

T A E B A E K   R A N G E

Kum River

Taejon

Yangdok

Pohang

Kunsan

Naktong River

S O B A E K   R A N G E

Kimchon

Taegu

Nam River

Chinju

Pusan

Koje-Do

Tsushima

Prologue

The only Chinese soldier I ever saw in Korea, fully armed and obviously full of fight, was a plump, pimply youth wearing a Soviet-style steel helmet and a swirling waterproof cape. He glowered down at me from a ridgeline overlooking positions held jointly by the U.S. Marines and the British Commonwealth Division north of Seoul, the South Korean capital. The war had ended two days before, on the hot, moonlit night of July 27, 1953, in a marvelous pyrotechnic display by marine gunners determined to fire off any spare ammunition before the cease-fire came into effect.

The war's closing hours had found me holed up in a stuffy forward dugout, waiting to cover the now-forgotten milestone of the armistice for the London *Daily Express*. Loudspeakers from the Chinese positions, on the north side of the valley, blared cheerful music. A female voice appealed to us: "Come out and dance!" At precisely 2200 hours the guns stopped firing, the earth stopped its shuddering, and the night stood eerily still. Hundreds of flares soared up on all sides, bathing the blasted hillscape in a weird silvery light. We hesitated, unused to such tranquillity, before we leaped from our underground burrows onto the trench-tops, shouting and cheering.

A British sergeant toiled up a particularly nasty knoll where snipers had taken their toll in the past. He stood there, king of the castle,

1

and gazed around him in amazement. "I can't believe it!" he exclaimed. And in full view of the enemy he struck a match and lit his pipe.

By the following morning I was back in Seoul filing my story, and it wasn't until two days later that I managed to return to the front and walk nervously out into no-man's-land. Corpses spattered with lime lay rotting close to the British positions. Skulls and bones mingled with the coiled barbed-wire; and, in one place, a skeletal hand still clutched a stick grenade. The Chinese had put in a determined attack shortly before the armistice, in a futile bid to grab as much territory as possible, and the results lay all around me.

Together with a bunch of other correspondents, I picked my way across the tortured valley. We minced through the shell holes, expecting to tread on a land mine at any moment. Voices from the British positions kept calling us to come back. There had been considerable cautious fraternizing between the opposing forces on the morning following the cease-fire; but now, our soldiers warned us, armistice goodwill was gone, and the Chinese were no longer hospitable.

Sure enough, the sentries strung out along the ridgeline were distinctly unfriendly, and the young Chinese soldier in his swirling waterproof cape brusquely ordered us back. More pertinently, he aimed his submachine gun directly at us, with every apparent intention of using it. We waved feebly, shouted friendly greetings, and held out offerings of candy bars and cigarettes, but to absolutely no avail. The Chinese soldier only gestured irritably with his gun. Having survived 14 months reporting on this dreadful war, it seemed ridiculous for me to risk my life now that the official killing was over. We turned back, feeling more than a little foolish, and derided mercilessly by the watching British troops.

The failure of that attempt to mingle with the enemy irritated me more than most because I'd always been intensely curious about the kind of men on the other side of the line. Three and a half years spent in World War II's Burma campaign, while in the service of the Royal Indian Navy, had left me thoroughly fascinated with the anonymous Japanese fighting-men—so seldom seen, so often felt, who gave ground only when slain. (I was so impressed by their extraordinary qualities that long afterward I tried to analyze the Bushido spirit in my first book, *A Glorious Way to Die*, which dealt with the destruction of the super-battleship *Yamato*, pride of the Japanese Imperial Navy, off Okinawa in 1945.)

Now, after over a year in Korea, I found myself impressed by these very different, and unexpected, foes: the Chinese peasant soldiers, whose toughness and tenacity had won renewed respect for their country as an emerging military power. It tends to be forgotten today, but for more than a century Chinese soldiers were a Western barrack-room joke. No one, no matter how friendly to China, would have predicted before the autumn of 1950 that the disciplined armies forged by the Chinese civil war could rout the best that the Americans could muster. Under-estimation of the despised "Chicoms" (Chinese Communists) was responsible for most of the major mistakes made by U.S. field commanders once Mao's forces joined in the Korean conflict.

The war had been underway, of course, for some months before the People's Republic of China threw in with the North Koreans. In a sense, the Korean conflict had begun years earlier—the moment that Korea was divided into two separate nations along the 38th Parallel by the victorious Allied governments, following the surrender of colonizing Japanese forces there in 1945. For five years, North and South Korea—the former under the Soviet-installed Kim Il Sung, the latter under the Western-oriented but authoritarian Syngman Rhee—uneasily respected each other's borders, though both governments claimed sovereignty over the entire Korean peninsula.

Then, on June 25 of 1950, the vastly superior North Korean People's Army (NKPA)—trained and lavishly equipped by the Soviet Union—swept over the Parallel, slashing through the nominal defenses erected by the South Koreans. The United Nations Security Council, in far-off New York, immediately adopted a resolution calling for the withdrawal of the NKPA forces, and two days later recommended that member nations furnish aid to South Korea in repelling the aggressors. Simultaneously, President Harry Truman ordered U.S. ground troops to Korea from their post-World War II occupation bases in Japan. They first met enemy troops, ironically enough, on July 4, and were quickly forced to retreat.

By July 7, U.S. General Douglas MacArthur, serving in Tokyo as Supreme Commander for the Allied Powers (SCAP), Far East Command, was named Supreme UN Commander for the joint defense of South Korea. Ultimately, sixteen nations made offers of military assistance to the Republic of Korea (ROK) and saw combat action there: Australia, Belgium, Canada, Colombia, Ethiopia, France, Greece, Luxembourg, the Netherlands, New Zealand, the Philippines, South Africa, Thailand, Turkey, the United Kingdom, and, of course, the United States—the last supplying the vast bulk of forces and materiel.

Several of these nations also supplied naval and air forces. A number of other countries which did not participate in military operations supported the UN effort by supplying medical and transport facilities.

These United Nations forces succeeded in pushing the NKPA back over the 38th Parallel (thanks to MacArthur's daring amphibious landing at Inchon) and, against the better judgment of some Western leaders, proceeded to "roll back" the Communist North Korean forces on their own territory. By October of 1950 the UN forces occupied the greater part of North Korea; and advance units were within a few miles of some sections of the North Korean-Chinese border when they began to encounter unexpected—and increasing—resistance. Chinese troops had crossed their Yalu River border and joined in on the side of the NKPA.

The entry into Korean territory of the Chinese People's Liberation Army (PLA), under the *nom de guerre* of the Chinese Peoples' Volunteers (CPV), first occurred on October 14, 1950. It was not until the end of November, however, that this large-scale intervention became apparent, to worldwide consternation—and to the horror of American field commanders, who had believed their own approach to the Chinese border to be the final stage of a home-by-Christmas, end-the-war offensive.

Instead, by January 4, 1951, the Chinese had utterly routed the UN forces, which abandoned first the newly captured North Korean capital of Pyongyang, then the South Korean capitol of Seoul, retreating headlong as armies from the north again streamed over the Parallel.

Following these first, breath-taking victories, the entire Communist Chinese establishment fell in with the euphoric belief that the imperialist intruders would forthwith be swept into the sea. Indeed, they made the same mistake Douglas MacArthur had made shortly before their own intervention: the mistake of assuming that they would control the entire Korean peninsula within a few weeks, following that one last end-the-war offensive.

But it was not to be. Instead, U.S. General Matt Ridgway, the newly appointed Eighth Army commander, fell back to ground his technologically superior troops could hold, then in mid-January launched a counterattack upon the overextended Chinese. By March 15, the U.S. Eighth Army had retaken Seoul; a week later it had regained the 38th Parallel.

Heroes do not figure largely in this book, which highlights more mistake than masterstrokes, but Ridgway, America's most underrated military genius, and his great opponent, General Peng Dehuai of the PLA, tower above their peers. Though the war was to grind on for two more years until the armistice of July 27, 1953, Ridgway's counterattack marks a decisive point in the struggle for Korea (there were calls for a cease-fire by June of 1951), and I have therefore chosen it as the cut-off point for this work. The six months from August, 1950 through January, 1951—from China's initial planning of intervention to her challenge of, and stalemate against, America and the United Nations—were months that changed the course of history.

Though this book takes the unusual course of examining the Korean War from the Chinese viewpoint, it is in no way an apologia. It does suggest that, contrary to Western perceptions at the time, the Communist rulers of China, newly triumphant in their own civil war, were dragged reluctantly into a struggle they neither instigated nor welcomed. Diverted from the task of domestic reconstruction, they felt forced to commit ill-equipped troops to prevent the liquidation of a friendly, Communist-ruled buffer state on their Manchurian border.

The Chinese Peoples' Volunteers crossed the Yalu River gingerly at first, its leaders uncertain whether the Americans would resort to use of the atomic bomb—a weapon then still looked on by some as simply a more powerful instrument of destruction, and as a viable option even in limited warfare. Moreover, the Chinese were not only cautious, but deliberately pulled their first punches, hoping the barbarians would get their message and evacuate North Korea. When that failed, they forced the longest, most disgraceful retreat in U.S. military history.

Their intervention—and therefore many of the four million American and UN casualties ultimately inflicted during the course of this three-year war—might never have been necessary had the West been better apprised of the mood in Peking. But the Chinese civil war, in which Nationalist leader Chiang Kai-shek was forced to flee to Taiwan following the triumph of Mao Zedong, had resulted in the severance of diplomatic contacts between China and America, leading to misunderstanding and miscalculation on both sides.

The Communist Chinese leadership, flushed with its success in the civil war, was out of touch with international realities. The Truman administration in Washington, harried by neo-isolationist opposition, could no longer take careful stock of the situation inside China. The British, who might have exercised a restraining influence on America's interest in a Communist rollback, were already a spent force as a world power. Attitudes were therefore struck in a time of crisis which froze relations between the two nations for the next 20 years. The moral, if there is one, would seem to be that confrontations are never quite as irrevocable as they seem. Given a modicum of understanding and communication, yesterday's enemies can yet become tomorrow's allies. The men on the other side of the line are not simply the other country's soldiers, but its leaders as well.

PART ONE

A
DISTANT
THUNDER

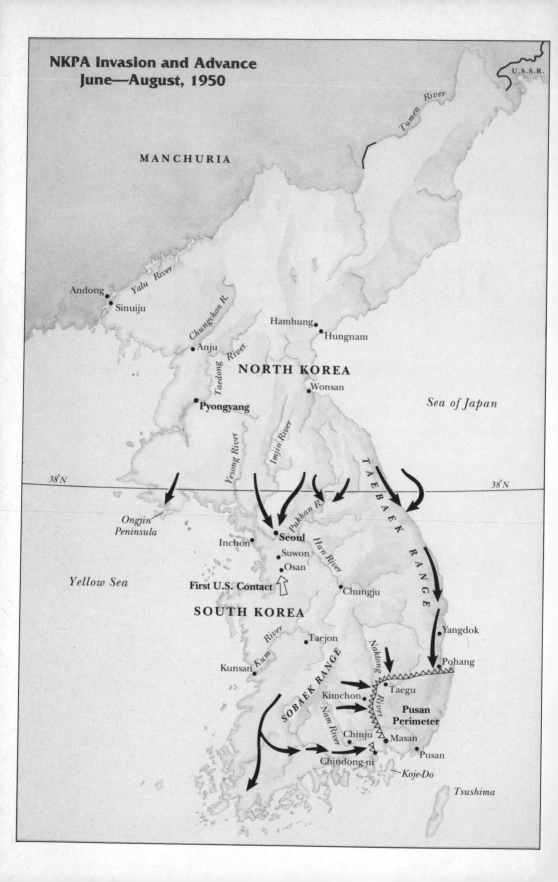

1

Colonel Wong Observes on the North Korean Front.

North Korean Front Headquarters,
Kimchon, occupied South Korea,
August 4, 1950

The Americans never knew how close they came to destroying the command headquarters of the invading North Koreans. U.S. fighter bombers howled in over the tattered rooftops of Kimchon, a modest market town deep in southernmost South Korea, spraying the place with cannon and machine-gun fire. A signaler who had clambered up the steps to watch the raid flopped back headless into the dugout. Medics dragged away the twitching corpse and sprinkled sand upon the concrete floor.

General Kim Chaek, front commander of the North Korean People's Army (NKPA), scarcely glanced up. The first bombs of the raid thudded down nearby, but still he peered over the maps, an unlit cigarette drooping from the corner of his mouth and two days' stubble shadowing his chin. The symbols showed his weary troops pressing upon the Pusan perimeter, only some 20 miles away. They would soon obliterate the last pocket of resistance from troops of the puppet Republic of Korea (ROK) and the United States, which had foolishly joined the losing struggle a month earlier.

The command post took a direct hit a moment later. A 500-pound bomb exploded above the reinforced concrete roof, extinguishing the lights, showering the staff with rubble, and hurling them into breathless heaps.

Colonel Wong Lichan of the People's Republic of China, groping about in the darkness, touched something soft and sticky. It was a body. What part of a body he couldn't quite make out, but his fingers felt tacky with blood. Someone nearby was groaning. The Chinese officer fumbled around in his combat jacket for an emergency field-dressing. He shook his head dazedly, wondering how you applied these bandages blind. The lights had been snuffed out, leaving the place as dark as a demon's dungeon. The crash of the explosion had left him so deaf it took time to realize somebody was yelling. That somebody was the general.

"Lights!" bellowed General Kim. He reeled off a string of soldierly obscenities. A match flared, then another. A staff officer found a flashlight. Others unearthed candles. By flickering, shadowy light the shaken men assessed the damage.

They were fortunate to have survived. The buildings above the shelter had absorbed most of the blast. This abandoned meat-packing plant had been selected by the men directing the final phase of the North Korean drive because of its heavily concreted cellars, once used for refrigeration. Military engineers had worked an entire night adding ceiling reinforcement, piling sandbags onto old rail ties, providing the shielding that stopped the bomb from bursting through the roof. But only just. The concrete ceiling supports bellied down dangerously. Shelves had ripped right off the walls, releasing a shower of papers which swirled about like butterflies in the settling dust.

Colonel Wong found himself following the fluttering paper with faintly hysterical amusement. Never until now had he realized how much paper a fighting army could generate. Requisition forms, pay rosters, ration returns, provost reports, casualty returns . . . all settled around him on top of the dust-coated rubble. He realized with a start that the man next to him was dead. The Korean signals major, whose name he could not remember, had been passing a message to the general when the bomb hit. He now lay face-down in the rubble, a jagged concrete spear in his back. Wong's field-dressing would have done him little good.

General Kim remained unruffled. He must have been the only man in the command post not flattened by the blast. The cigarette, however, was gone from his mouth. The map table lay upended at his feet. His combat fatigues, stained, rumpled, and long unchanged, were frosted with white dust. But he was still very much in command, barking out a stream of orders in the guttural Korean tongue, calling in medics, engineers, and signalers to salvage some order from the chaos.

"Glad to see you're safe," Kim grunted to Wong, slipping into faultless Chinese. It was more than a polite remark. There would have been hell to pay for the death of the sole Chinese officer on the front, this liaison from the People's Republic of China to the North Korean Front Headquarters. Colonel Wong, the assistant military attaché from the PRC embassy in Pyongyang, was a Very Important Person indeed. Even the Soviets had no one so eminent this near to the front.

"That bomb came uncomfortably close," the Chinese said lamely. He wanted to react as calmly as these expressionless North Korean veterans, even if he did not feel it. He had seen more than enough combat since enlisting as a young Red Trooper in 1931, but sustained aerial bombing was unfamiliar—and unnerving.

"Three dead," announced the doctor attending the body of the speared signals major. "The other two are also signalers. Enlisted men. The communications room was worse hit than here."

"How about the radio equipment?" inquired the general. Men were more readily replaceable than machines.

"One transmitter still in working order," someone reported. The entire staff looked relieved. Communication with Supreme Command back in Pyongyang was crucial at this stage.

"Eight wounded," the doctor went on. "Including General Kang."

The North Korean chief of staff, Colonel-General Kang Kon, limped in from the radio room. He had been checking messages at the height of the air raid. Blood now trickled into one of his eyes from a gash on the scalp.

"Nothing serious," he grunted with a self-deprecating grin. The left sleeve of his jacket was ripped up to the elbow. Hours later Kang would realize his forearm was broken. It was a foretaste of grimmer things to come. The next month, on September 8, 1950, the chief of staff would be killed by a land mine.

Kang Kon was unusually tall for a Korean. He towered above everyone else. Born in Kyongsan, not far from the present battlefield, he had been recruiting youthful guerrillas for his old friend Kim Il Sung since the age of 16. Kang's long years of shared exile in China with the future leader of North Korea had helped win him this vital job spearheading the NKPA's southward drive. So far, that drive had been an uninterrupted triumph. At this precise moment, the morning of August 4, 1950, the North Korean People's Army was poised for the kill.

General Kim slapped his chief of staff cheerfully on the shoulder. Kang grimaced with pain. He leaned down for the medic to bandage his bleeding head. The front commander went back to directing the offensive. While the main map table was being repaired he worked from the spidery notations on his field map case. There was little time for delay. Litter parties pattered past, repair gangs hauled in lengths of lumber, and aides scrambled clumsily around in the debris, re-erecting shelves and tables. General Kim worked on, totally absorbed.

Like Kang, Kim had been an intimate of Kim Il Sung from early in the thirties. Their association dated back to the heady days of hit-and-run fighting in mid-thirties Manchuria, when a handful of young Korean Communists had skirmished sporadically against the occupying Japanese. Their puny rebel forays made scant impression on the ruthless Japanese garrisons, though countless official tales have since been spun to support the mythology of massive Korean Communist resistance. It was only after Stalin launched a last-minute assault upon Japan in the closing days of World War II, and Soviet forces temporarily occupied the northern part of the Korean peninsula, that Kim Il Sung and his youthful guerrillas were inexplicably promoted puppet rulers of the Soviet-"liberated" zone. Five years later these same Communist puppets, trained and armed by their Soviet masters, were bursting out of their northern boundaries to seize control of the whole Korean peninsula. But for tens of thousands of them, this would be their last campaign. General Kim was among the many doomed to die within the year.

Colonel Wong needed air. The command post was stuffy at the best of times. With most of the ventilator shafts now blocked by rubble, it had grown positively stifling. The Chinese officer picked his way gingerly through the communications room, where frantic signalmen were righting and repairing their equipment, then clambered across more piled rubble and up onto the ruins of the meat-packing plant by way of the emergency exit. The direct entrance—down which the headless signaler had tumbled at the start of the raid—was choked with debris. The roofless, bomb-scarred plant was well ablaze when the colonel emerged, blinking, into the sunlight. Wooden partitions that once must have formed managerial offices were burning like lucky money at a Chinese funeral. There were few people out to watch. The bombers were gone but the population—what was left of it—stayed underground. The only people visibly active, as far as the colonel could see, were a small group of white-robed elders down the street, vainly spooning half-filled buckets of water over the flames that consumed their small wooden church. The town's solitary fire truck lay upended nearby, pinned beneath a fallen power pole.

It was the first urban air raid Colonel Wong had ever experienced. There had been the haphazard Nationalist attack on Shanghai in late 1948, at the close of China's civil war, but you could hardly call that a raid. The Americans here were much bolder, he noted, resolutely pressing their attacks in face of concentrated ground fire. They took extraordinary risks. Any pilot shot down in this neighborhood could expect little mercy from the North Koreans. The destruction they left, however, was less severe than he expected. A number of buildings were indeed flattened, several fires were obviously out of control, and occasional craters had been gouged from the deserted streets, but it could have been a great deal worse. The bomber was obviously a powerful weapon, but it was not omnipotent.

Out in the field, though, things were different. Colonel Wong had been given a terrifying taste of aerial interdiction on the road journey down here. The NKPA driver who had picked him up in Taejon (in a newly captured American jeep) had been too impatient to wait for nightfall—or else just damned careless. He had insisted on pushing ahead in the late afternoon, four hours before sunset, swearing that the enemy pilots had given up for the day. No such luck, of course: Yankee fighter planes had jumped them like angry hornets along a hilly stretch beyond Yongdong, ripping up the road with bursts of cannon and machine-gun fire as the driver weaved desperately down a narrow stretch of elevated roadway. They couldn't have been caught in a more awkward spot. No room whatsoever to maneuver. When the windshield shattered, the uncontrollable vehicle vaulted into the nearby paddy field, ejecting its occupants into a smelly ditch. The fighters spent a leisurely half hour riddling the jeep. Fortunately they carried neither bombs nor napalm, so the Chinese colonel and his North Korean driver had escaped with only minor cuts and bruises. But both were badly shaken.

All this had occurred less than a week after Colonel Wong's initial arrival in Pyongyang. He had been posted to the North Korean capital as the second most senior member of the military attaché's department in the newly established PRC embassy. His bags were not yet unpacked when, quite unexpectedly, the North Koreans invited him to visit the front. They seemed unusually eager to let Peking learn what was going on. It was a quite uncharacteristic departure because, as the Chinese ambassador wryly remarked, Pyongyang was under Soviet "tutelage." The Chinese felt that the Soviets had excluded them from playing any part in North Korea since the defeat of Japan, though no one put it quite that brutally. World communism still maintained the monolithic facade of socialist solidarity. Speeches, banquet toasts, and editorials in the various "People's Democracies" effectively concealed smoldering international feuds. But anyone who dared burrow beneath the high-flown rhetoric in the Democratic People's Republic of Korea soon struck the bedrock of Soviet power. So complete was China's exclusion that it was not until a month after the outbreak of the Korean hostilities that diplomats from Peking set up shop in Pyongyang.

The Chinese embassy presented its credentials to the government of Premier Kim Il Sung, the man chosen by Moscow to head the North Korean administration. But the real arbiter of affairs in Pyongyang was the former commander of the Soviet occupation forces in North Korea, Colonel-General Terenty F. Shtykov. Shtykov's original mission in 1945, as the *Western* allies understood it, was simply to accept the surrender of Japanese troops in the northern half of the Korean peninsula, while American forces carried out identical duties in the south. After that—the exact plans were a trifle vague—Korea would achieve independence and unification through free democratic elections.

General Shtykov resisted elections until he had installed an un-shakably Soviet-oriented regime in the north. By the beginning of 1948 his occupation role was officially over—and General Shtykov metamorphosed, miraculously, into *Ambassador* Shtykov. Russian forces pulled out of North Korea, as the Soviet delegation never ceased reminding the United Nations; the Soviet Union's *altruistic* policy in Korea contrasted sharply, Stalin's spokesman Andrei Gromyko insisted, with the "machinations of American imperialism intent on shoring up its puppet regime in the south." No mention was made of the hundreds of Soviet "advisers" who remained behind. Jowly, bespectacled Shtykov, a veteran intelligence officer with remarkably sad brown eyes, had merely traded his uniform for a double-breasted serge suit, to stay on as ambassador in his heavily guarded embassy compound—which happened to be next door to Premier Kim's official residence. Koreans still sneeringly referred to the Soviet embassy as "the command post"—provided they were well out of official hearing—and it was here that the Chinese military mission first checked in, on their arrival in Pyongyang.

Colonel Wong had realized, however, as he journeyed south to the war's front lines, that political attitudes were subtly changing. The Democratic People's Republic of Korea had been off limits to China since the end of World War II. Yet suddenly a veil was being parted. The Koreans seemed eager, undoubtedly after Soviet urging, to warn their Chinese neighbors that the time was coming when they might— just might—be needing reinforcement. The message, if there was one, was far from explicit. The tide of war still flowed decisively in North Korea's favor. But it was growing disturbingly obvious that the counterattack against the foreign imperialists and their southern puppets was desperately behind schedule. The Americans were to blame. They were not *supposed* to be defending Korea at all. Policy statements from Secretary of State Dean Acheson had made it clear that South Korea lay outside the U.S. defense perimeter. Yet, thanks to some perverse judgment in Washington, U.S. military forces were being mustered from all over Asia to retain a foothold on this god-forsaken peninsula.

American airpower was already proving fearsome. Aircraft shuttled in from Japan, or from off the U.S. carriers cruising unchallenged around the Korean coast, rained destruction on the advancing NKPA columns. The North Koreans had shrugged off their initial losses philosophically. Just lately, however, with their supply lines critically overstretched, the mounting attrition could no longer be ignored. The enemy airmen were assisted by the unseasonable weather; the summer rains had failed, offering unexpectedly clear flying weather. Colonel Wong passed ample evidence of the outcome on his south-ward journey from Seoul: paralyzed railroads, demolished bridges, gutted towns, and, everywhere, the rusting relics of recent attacks, the burned-out hulks of Soviet-made T-34 tanks, the irreplaceable supply trucks and all those splendid guns reduced to twisted scrap.

The American air offensive had slowed but not stalled the North Korean advance. The Yankees were far less effective on the ground. Their road-bound troops were reluctant to get out of their trucks and slog across the hills. Some gave the impression, rightly, that they'd been given little military training. This weakness could prove decisive, in Wong's opinion, because it was riflemen, not airmen, who seized and held terrain.

But the Americans could no longer be contemptuously brushed aside. Reinforcements were streaming in from occupied Japan. Already a few were arriving, it was said, from the U.S. mainland. No elaborate intelligence network was needed to keep track of these movements. Everything the Americans did was publicized in gushing detail by their press. Strident publicity had accompanied units of the U.S. 24th Division when they were pulverized at Taejon, and had followed the 25th, rushed in to reinforce the shrinking defense line around Pusan. Soon afterward the undistinguished First Cavalry arrived. At any time now, according to *Stars and Stripes*, the first detachments of U.S. Marines would be riding to the rescue.

The North Koreans tended at first to shrug off this rush of reinforcements. They told their Chinese visitor that the caliber of GIs was extremely poor. But they were awestruck by the Americans' superlative equipment. "Enemy firepower would be devastating," General Kim remarked, "if ever they learned how to use it." It would not be long, he reckoned, before they brought in new-type tanks capable of outgunning their own unstoppable armor. To say nothing of artillery . . . Intelligence briefs credited the Americans with a limitless stock of powerful 150-mm guns. And the amount of U.S. transportation devoted to luxuries such as candy bars was an unending puzzle to the intelligence staff of the North Korean Front Headquarters. (Colonel Wong noted that, by Chinese standards, the North Koreans themselves had been magnificently equipped by the Soviets.) Some of this American bounty was being passed down to the puppet South Korean forces as well, briefing officers reported, though the South Koreans had so far played a relatively minor part in the war. The northerners regarded their southern counterparts solely as a source of badly needed American cannon-fodder.

Colonel Wong stood in the rubble outside the North Korean Front Headquarters and watched as a squad of NKPA engineers doubled past to speed repairs. The soldiers wore olive-brown combat smocks of vaguely Soviet design, short black boots, and soft peaked caps. The officer in charge, a chunky, sweaty man with a hard, thin mouth, cursed his men with imaginative invective. He spoke more roughly than the Chinese PLA troops would have tolerated, but, as Wong had already noted, the North Koreans had weird ideas about running a revolutionary army. Military discipline, for instance, was incredibly severe. On the road outside Seoul he had seen an NKPA sergeant beat an enlisted man insensible with a rifle butt for parading with an unbuttoned tunic; that sort of thing went out in China with the warlords. Physical punishment was very much a last resort in the People's Liberation Army.

The Koreans were an entirely different species, Colonel Wong conceded. Born in Kirin, the Manchurian province adjoining Korea, Wong had lived among migrant Korean communities from across the Yalu River, and had acquired both a working knowledge of their strange tongue and a considerable respect for their work ethic. Korea bred the world's most tireless workers, the colonel firmly believed, as well as some of the ruggedest men he had ever seen; the average army instructor's idea of a well-spent afternoon was setting his soldiers to cracking roof tiles over their heads. Fine, perhaps, for the monks of Shaolin, home of the Chinese martial arts, but far beyond anything in the Chinese military training curriculum.

The colonel was predictably condescending toward Korean cuisine. Far too much overspiced food and glutinous rice! He was getting to loathe lunchtimes. For hours afterward the staff officers' pickled breath would swamp the command post. Not that he minded garlic: as a second-generation Manchurian he consumed it by the clove throughout the bleak months of winter. Everyone believed the pungent herb kept out the cold. But the Koreans didn't stop there. To garlic they added fermented cabbage and searing spices, which made them belch and fart abominably. Then they took to *drink*, at their lugubrious celebrations, consuming bottles of a greasy gin alleged to be the national elixir. Even apparently civilized officers would toss back glasses of the filthy stuff, very much in the Russian manner, growing red-faced and raucous before slithering gently to the floor.

Still, it had to be admitted, these North Koreans fought like tigers. Wong had watched their crack 6th Division moving into the attack only a few nights before. He had stood on a hilltop as the troops filed past in the moonlight, column after column of them, spreading out for their final drive on Pusan. Their task was to push the Americans into the sea before the imperialists could organize a coherent defense. The 6th Division had fought a brilliant campaign, overrunning all southwestern Korea, then pivoting east to Pusan, the last enemy foothold, in one of those wide enveloping maneuvers that never failed to keep the enemy off balance. This would be the division's bitterest battle, Colonel Wong had noted prophetically in his diary; for a page or two he waxed poetic, praising the stoic determination of the youthful troops splashing cheerfully past through irrigated fields of ripening rice. It reminded him of an old Soong painting he'd seen at an exhibition in Shanghai. The flooded fields formed silver mosaics beneath the misty moon. Clumps of inky vegetation concealed the occasional village. The only intrusive note here was the tracer ammunition, arching lazily into the sky above the backdrop of distant hills. And the air bursts glowing briefly overhead like bloated fireflies as gunners on both sides checked their range. In real life, unlike the old Soong painting, the last, lethal bayonet thrust was about to enter the soft underbelly of the American perimeter.

It had taken the North Koreans a little over three years to build this marvelously effective army. The NKPA was as powerful, man for man, as any force in Asia. It was ridiculously small by Chinese standards—at this stage of the war little more than 135,000 men—but packed an unrivaled punch. Due credit had to be given to the enormous amount of help they had received from the Soviets. From 1948, when the NKPA was officially activated, hundreds of Soviet advisers had been involved in its training program. (They had departed when the North Koreans began this one-sided war, although Soviet liaison officers still attended important conferences in Pyongyang.)

China, too, had made a significant, if smaller, contribution to the

North Korean military buildup. The men who formed the NKPA's framework were drawn largely from 16,000 repatriated Korean veterans of the Chinese civil war. And just two months before the NKPA crossed the 38th Parallel, the Chinese People's Liberation Army had transferred, at Pyongyang's request, another 12,000 of their veteran soldiers to North Korean control. But although combat-hardened, these troops were not trained to the pitch of mechanized warfare required by the Soviets.

The Koreans had proved avid pupils, the colonel noted approvingly. And, moreover, while they might not be equipped on the American scale, their inventory of Soviet-made materiel left the Chinese army looking like a regular rabble. The T-34 tanks were the biggest Colonel Wong had ever seen. There had been 120 of them in the NKPA's main mechanized unit, the 105th Armored Regiment, when it crossed the 38th Parallel—great armored beasts that shrugged off projectiles like gnat-bites. Each tank weighed 32 tons, crouched low on the ground, and carried massive armor and an 85-mm gun. And every last one of the surviving T-34s was now maneuvering into position on the 6th Division's right flank, ready to exploit the predicted breakthrough at Pusan.

Then there were the guns. You would expect nothing less from the Russians. Their artillery skills dated back to the days of the Tsars. They made sure their North Korean protégés were plentifully supplied with cannon. Each North Korean division was equipped with twelve 122-mm howitzers, the same deadly, dependable weapon that slaughtered the Germans during World War II, plus 24 of the more mobile 76-mm guns, twelve self-propelled SU-76s, and twelve 45-mm antitank guns. Regiments and battalions had their own supporting weapons, including 120-mm and 82-mm heavy mortars, which the North Koreans learned to use with terrible effect. Most of the weaponry was wartime vintage; some of it arrived from Vladivostok aboard Soviet freighters as late as May, 1950.

The supply of trucks, medicines, and radios was equally prolific. Especially radios. Colonel Wong's old outfit, the crack PLA Fourth Army, could never have matched the network of communications the North Koreans flung around their advancing forces. The signals officer at Front Headquarters who had just died in the bombing had told Wong shortly before the raid that, not only did the command post maintain unbroken contact with the Beloved Leader (his voice dropped reverently at the very mention of Kim Il Sung), but that the equipment also kept General Kim directly in touch with selected field commanders down to company level on the battlefield.

But, of course, the late signals officer had added apologetically, that must be routine stuff in the PLA. The Chinese colonel had nodded sagely. Too much face would be lost if he told these Koreans the truth. In his experience Chinese field commanders were lucky to maintain contact at battalion level. Runners, lamps, whistles, and signal flags were still the chief means of their communication. Field radios were a comparative novelty to the Chinese Communists, and were operated mostly by captured Nationalist signalers because their own revolutionary farm lads could hardly flush a toilet, let alone replace a radio tube. Wong hated to admit it, but these Koreans could teach China a thing or two about military modernization. About a lot of things, come to think of it: once reunited under socialism, the Koreans were destined to become a vital force in Asia. . . .

A North Korean staff officer interrupted the colonel's reverie. General Kim expressed felicitations, and would the colonel care to attend the staff conference? Wong returned to the command post. He did not want to miss this briefing. It promised to be historic. Kim Chaek must be about to announce the impending fall of Pusan.

Front Headquarters was wonderfully restored. Heavy timber joists shored up the sagging ceiling. Shelves were back on the walls, and the fugitive paper safely pigeonholed. Most of the desks were repaired. The multicolored operations maps were torn and blotched from the bombing but otherwise quite usable. The fresh doodles that cluttered their protective coverings all converged on the shrunken enemy foothold at the southern tip of the peninsula.

General Kim had shaved and changed into a clean combat jacket. He now hovered before a full-length map of Korea which stood propped against a folding chair. One hand wielded a short white pointer, the other an unlighted cigarette. It occurred to Wong that he had never seen the general actually smoke.

"Making battle is like making love." Kim Chaek spoke quietly, staring intently into his officers' faces. "At some time must come the crucial point on which everything depends. With a woman your virility is at stake. Here in the liberated south the issue is victory."

He looked directly at Wong. "You follow what I am saying?" he asked in Chinese. Wong nodded. The general continued in Korean.

"At this crucial point in battle the commander must call on his men for the ultimate effort. I have already made that call twice since the liberation campaign began, once in the drive on Seoul, once when we faced the Yankees at Taejon. Let us hope I am now making that call for the last time."

He waved the pointer across the map. His sweltering audience craned forward. The temperature in the underground command post hovered around one hundred degrees Fahrenheit. It must have been far worse for the soldiers fighting their way across the hills in this oppressive heat.

"Our 6th Division's offensive has failed." The faces around him betrayed no emotion. The staff had obviously known the news for hours.

"For this I take full responsibility," the general went on quietly. "Our soldiers did their utmost. No, more than that . . . they did better than any commander could have expected. They captured Chinju. They fought their way into the outskirts of Masan. That is less than fifty kilometers [30 miles] from Pusan. But their efforts came too late. The enemy was reinforced and . . . determined. Battles are not won with hindsight. Yet I must freely admit it would have been better if our gallant comrades had driven sooner toward Pusan instead of first mopping up the southwestern coastal areas. That is my mistake. It is now history. But, let me emphasize, the setback is not irretrievable."

General Kim's self-criticism evoked widespread sympathy. His staff saw nothing demeaning about it. The frank and open admission of mistakes, the assumption of total responsibility, was commonplace in Communist armies. Nonetheless Colonel Wong felt a twinge of pity for any commander forced to admit a miscalculation that might cost him his career. But surely things weren't that serious? The general had clearly indicated that all was far from lost.

There followed a more heartening summary of the five-and-a-half-week campaign which had brought the NKPA so tantalizingly close to victory. The main strength of the NKPA had been concentrated in a drive down the western side of the peninsula. Seoul was liberated after only two days' fighting. Two weeks later they were halfway down South Korea. Seven of the 11 available divisions spearheaded the triumphant thrust southward in a classic demonstration of mobile warfare. Neither the Americans nor their puppets had been able to check the tide.

At Taejon the NKPA 3rd and 4th Divisions decimated advance units of the U.S. 24th Division, capturing its commanding general, Major General William F. Dean. Further attempts by the Americans to hold a line somewhere around central South Korea were frustrated with almost contemptuous ease. The NKPA 6th Division dashed off on its remarkable (if ill-directed) outflanking movement through the extreme southwest, while the main body of the army chased the enemy into the far southeastern corner of the country, where the defenders were confined to a rectangular area roughly 130 kilometers [80 miles] from north to south and 80 kilometers [50 miles] from west to east: the Pusan perimeter. It was at the narrow base of this beachhead, directly opposite the supply port of Pusan, that the heaviest North Korean attack was aimed.

The chief intelligence officer—a squat, swarthy man, Soviet-trained, with a mustache like Stalin's—made his contribution to the briefing. The two sides were reaching numerical balance. The NKPA no longer outnumbered its opponents, though it still outfought and outgunned them. Lead divisions had suffered more severely than expected during the advance; available statistics put the present North Korean combat strength at around 70,000 men, compared with an estimated 47,000 Americans and 45,000 South Koreans. The NKPA would soon be outnumbered if the flow of American reinforcements continued. Already the Americans were shipping in M-26 Pershing and M-4 Sherman tanks. Three Pershings had been captured at Chinju, and preliminary reports indicated they were of excellent quality—better than comparable equipment manufactured by the Russians.

"With due respect to our Soviet comrades," the intelligence officer added hurriedly. (It wasn't wise to sound critical, even on the battlefield.)

The Americans were also increasing their already considerable firepower with heavy artillery reinforcements. For instance, a battery of 155-mm guns had helped halt the drive on Masan. Their stock of ammunition was apparently inexhaustible; at the rate the American gunners were firing, the NKPA would have run out two weeks ago. There was also a rising number of air attacks, of which no one needed any reminder. The intelligence officer patted his mustache and glanced at the ceiling. General Kim frowned.

The enemy was commanded by a three-star general named Walton H. Walker, the intelligence officer read from his signals folder. No doubt they all knew that. This Walker was an experienced officer who had served under General George Patton against the Germans during World War II. Korean conditions were very different from those of Western Europe, but as a field commander the man should not be underrated. The liberating forces could take heart from the fact that Walker had not yet come to terms with the Korean terrain. More problematic still was his ability to conduct a successful campaign with such inadequate troops. The intelligence briefing wound up with the habitual tirade against MacArthur. It should also be remembered, the I.O. intoned, that the real brain behind the American aggression in Korea was the old fascist general in Tokyo, Douglas MacArthur. It was this neo-colonialist who had plotted with Truman, the capitalist archreactionary, to prevent the unification of Korea under its rightful leader, Premier Kim Il Sung.

The intelligence officer saluted and stepped smartly into the background. As General Kim resumed his monologue, Colonel Wong realized how tired he looked. It was anyone's guess when he'd last slept.

"On the third of August the lead battalions of the 14th Regiment of the 6th Division were halted eight kilometers [five miles] from Masan," Kim Chaek reported wearily. "The Americans threw in troops of their 25th Division to back up those of the 24th, which were already making a stand at Chindong-ni." He pointed to a small port on the heavily indented coastline. "Our losses were heavy. The combat strength of the 6th Division has been reduced by half in the past week. I have reluctantly ordered the division to fall back and regroup.

"But, as I said, the situation is not irretrievable. We have committed only a portion of our strength. I am therefore ordering the 4th Guards Division to cross the Naktong River north of the present battlefield, capture Yongsan, and drive on to Miryang. This, as you can see from the map, will sever the main supply route between Pusan and U.S. headquarters in Taegu; if we succeed, and I trust we shall, the northern part of the perimeter will collapse. It is defended largely by puppet troops and we know how *they* react when outflanked."

The general ground his unsmoked cigarette under his boot. An aide offered him another. He put it in his mouth, still unlit.

"It is now that I demand the ultimate effort." General Kim's hoarse voice had dropped almost to a whisper. "The counteroffensive was due to be completed in two months' time. Of that, we have little more than two weeks left. Time is running out. The unification of Korea is a sacred task. It cannot be thwarted in the moment of triumph."

Colonel-General Kang called the staff to attention. Stiffly and formally, the chief of staff promised the commander their full support. Then he went off in search of a doctor. His arm was in agony. Kim took a swig from a vodka bottle. He tossed it to the Chinese colonel, who was too polite to refuse. Even though he didn't drink much, it didn't do to let the Koreans know it.

"You understand the situation?" the general asked in Chinese.

Wong nodded. He understood the situation perfectly. Too perfectly. There was no longer the slightest room for doubt. The North Korean offensive was in deep trouble. Protocol prevented him from offering an opinion. Nor was he asked. His role was to observe, to report . . . nothing more. Nonetheless, he was deeply disturbed. The briefing had convinced him of one thing: the North Koreans were not learning from their mistakes. General Kim continued to commit his forces piecemeal against the Pusan perimeter.

The Chinese colonel felt sure his armies would have handled things differently. They had long learned to exploit success, to concentrate, to hit hard and keep on hitting. The People's Liberation Army might never field equipment comparable to that of the Koreans; they might not all be so superbly trained. But the Chinese knew how to hack through the cracks in their enemy's armor. Colonel Wong checked over the battle map. He was almost alone in the command post. The briefing over, all but a handful of duty staff had hurried off for lunch. Only the signalmen and their radios chattered away next door. The dispositions sketched out across the map told a depressing story. Nine NKPA divisions were deployed around the Pusan perimeter. Given the order, they could strike simultaneously. The Americans would never be able to hold them. They must be using their last reserves defending Masan. Now was the time to overwhelm the enemy, to hurl every available unit against those thinly held defenses. A week from now, at the rate reinforcements were pouring into Pusan, it would be too late.

Colonel Wong felt suddenly sick. It must be the aftereffects of the bomb blast. He was still absently holding the vodka bottle. He sneaked another swig from it. A phrase kept running through his head, a quotation from Sun Tze, the Chinese military sage: "When the thunder clap comes, there is no time to cover the ears."

Now he knew why he was here. The breaking storm would spread to China.

2

With Maggie and Mike
Inside the Pusan Perimeter.

**Masan, South Korea,
Inside the Pusan perimeter,
August 3–4, 1950**

The Americans breathed a sigh of relief. They were too tired, too dispirited, to savor the sweetness of victory. From soon after dawn, right through the sweltering morning of August 3, they'd fought a muddled, murderous minibattle not much different from most others during the past two weeks. This once they seemed to have won—an exhilarating change from the current run of humiliating retreats—but they had managed it in fumbling fashion, more by sheer luck than through smart soldiering, and thanks largely to the grit and determination of their commanding officer.

Most were agreed that Colonel John H. "Mike" Michaelis, the handsome ex-paratrooper, onetime aide to Eisenhower, deserved most of the credit. The new regimental commander was the first to rally his startled staff that morning when bullets began ripping the command post apart. Brandishing a pistol, shouting and swearing, shoving and kicking, he dragged cringing clerks from underneath their desks, thrust them against the shattered windows and set them

24

blasting back at the parties of infiltrators fast bearing down the hillside.

The North Korean attack took everyone by surprise. It was par for the course in the opening rounds of this irrational war. The North Koreans were supposed to be miles away. Yet here they were, well behind the American lines, storming the very schoolhouse where the 27th ("Wolfhound") Regiment had set up its rear headquarters. This time there could be no retreat. The Wolfhounds fought with their backs to the sea. They were the southernmost troops of the U.S. 25th Division, rushed from the creaking defenses facing Kimchon to head off a horrifying new North Korean threat to the shrinking bridgehead in South Korea. The Americans did not yet know it, but they had been rushed directly across the path of the same crack NKPA 6th Division that Chinese Colonel Wong Lichan had watched marching away the previous day for the final assault on Pusan. The Americans first knew of the 6th Division's offensive when their outposts began rolling back along the thinly held coastal sector around Chinju. That too was par for the course: minus maps and reliable intelligence and with only the barest minimum of reserves, the defenders of the Pusan perimeter were like smoke-blinded firemen fighting an inextinguishable prairie fire. But although it wasn't obvious at the time, the Americans were overcoming the first major crisis of the Korean War. One savage little skirmish was about to prove a turning point. There would be others, but none so decisive. Had the Wolfhounds not held at Chindong-ni, the enemy would have rolled through nearby Masan and on into Pusan. With the last Korean supply port in enemy hands, the war would have been as good as over.

The 27th Regiment headquarters was ill-prepared for any last-ditch battle. There were plenty of men to defend the place. Exhausted survivors of an abortive battalion-sized sortie launched the previous day were bivouacked inside the schoolhouse yard. Small groups of sweating, grimy soldiers were intermingled with a battery of parked howitzers and four newly arrived tanks. The troops still had a lot to learn, however, about the art of war. Three brief weeks ago (it seemed like years!) these same GIs had been wallowing in the carnal pleasures of occupied Japan. Few were prepared for the shock and strain of a full-scale shoot-out. The four-division army that made up the U.S. occupation force in the Japanese imperial homeland was scandalously unfit, understrength, and undertrained.

The Wolfhounds meandered into Chindong-ni without shielding themselves against direct attack. Why bother? There wasn't a gook in miles. At times it seemed as if the Americans did not want to learn. They still treated this lethal struggle with criminal carelessness. Their executive officer had just managed to sow a scattering of outposts halfway up the hill behind the village school. Nothing more. The climb to the ridgeline was too exhausting in such blazing heat. It was the hottest summer in living memory. The GIs griped like mad. A guy had to be crazy to risk heatstroke sitting on a sunbaked mountaintop! Shortly after dawn, most of the men manning the outposts wandered down in search of chow. The rest dozed in their foxholes. Nobody kept the sentries alert. Officers and NCOs—noncommissioned officers—no longer seemed to care. Discipline throughout the U.S. Army had grown gravely lax since the end of the Pacific war, especially in occupied Japan.

The regimental staff made themselves comfortable in the schoolhouse. Telephone and radio communication was routinely established with neighboring units, as well as with the top brass back at 25th Division headquarters, some 12 miles away, while officers sized up the worsening strategic situation. The most pressing concern of Colonel Michaelis and his immediate entourage was to stem the enemy *blitzkrieg* across the coastal mountains. But their attempts to counterattack on August 2 had run into a bruising ambush.

Officers were still discussing the debacle the following morning over a breakfast of coffee and powdered eggs when bullets began splintering the schoolhouse window frames. The Wolfhounds were playing host to two American correspondents. One was Harold Martin of the *Saturday Evening Post*. The other was a woman. Marguerite "Maggie" Higgins of the New York *Herald Tribune* gaped in disbelief as an incoming burst of machine-gun fire slammed the coffee pot off the mess-hall table. She tried to run outside. Too much lead was flying around. Halfway down the hall she hit the floor and stayed there. The frail wooden walls around her were being shot to kindling. Troops in the yard threw themselves into foxholes, under the guns, or beneath the trucks—any place to escape the gusts of rifle and machine-gun fire. The few who failed to duck for cover were speedily cut down. Seizing the undefended ridgeline, the North Koreans fixed the whole headquarters squarely in their sights. No one down there could move unseen. The stage seemed set for the most appalling slaughter.

The commander of the 1st Battalion, 27th Regiment, Gilbert Check, forced his terrified troops to fight back. Sure, they'd had a bellyful the previous day. The gooks had mauled them badly throughout their fruitless probe into the mountains. But the colonel was not going to take this attack lying down. He heaved protesting men out of hiding, thrust rifles into their hands, and told them which direction to fire. The Communists were executing one of their classic pincer attacks. Assault troops skirting the mountainsides were already entrenched in the adjoining rice field, tossing grenades and firing their machine guns point-blank into the schoolhouse while other fusillades poured in from overhead. Groups of infiltrators were concentrating in ominous strength along the high, steep cliff overlooking the town.

The photogenic fishing village of Chindong-ni nestled beneath the last mountain outcrop in Korea. It was at this spot that those soaring ranges, meandering down the peninsula from the Yalu and beyond, tumbled abruptly into the sea. Eastward beyond this barrier lay the little harbor at Masan. In happier days its deep, azure bay, backed by brooding mountains, had been the favorite retreat of affluent honeymooners. The overload of refugees these past few weeks had reduced the picture-postcard town to a pest-ridden slum. Yet the refugees still kept coming. Thousands upon thousands of South Koreans continued to flee the Communist advance, obstinately spurning all offers of "liberation" by their compatriots from the north. Those with sufficient strength or resources pressed on farther east, beyond Masan, a mere 14 miles by air, double that distance along a spectacular mountain road, to the major supply port of Pusan.

For the North Koreans, Pusan was the ultimate prize. Once they had captured Pusan, the Americans and their South Korean allies would be hopelessly trapped. The loss of the last sizable port in South Korea would prevent any Dunkirk-style evacuation. The defenders could be methodically destroyed inside their imploding perimeter. The Korean War would be over.

Colonel Michaelis knew retreat was out of the question. The northwestern corner of the diminishing allied perimeter—their last surviving toehold on the peninsula—was visibly crumbling under enemy pressure. He had watched important communications centers fall into North Korean hands almost without a fight. The Americans and their South Korean allies had not yet learned to halt the North Korean People's Army. It was indeed remarkable, the colonel kept telling his colleagues, that the United States had chosen to ignore this newborn military power blossoming on the doorstep of Japan. Until the war cloud burst on June 25, Far East Command was largely unaware of the extent of the military buildup in North Korea. Failure to gather or evaluate intelligence constantly hobbled the American war effort.

The first American units to square up to the North Koreans in the defensive battles south of Seoul confidently expected an easy victory over a bunch of Asian peasants. The Americans were rapidly and rudely disabused. The thankless task of salvaging U.S. prestige from the subsequent shambles fell on a tough-talking little Texan who had won a considerable reputation commanding the XX Corps of Patton's Third Army in Europe. Lieutenant General Walton H. "Johnnie"

Walker, commander of the Eighth Army, the American occupation force in Japan, was a spit-and-polish soldier with a lot of the old Patton panache. His talents were wasted in the euphoric environment of the occupation. For two years the diminutive general had been trying to cure his garrison forces of their lotusland lassitude. The U.S. occupation forces in Japan had sunk into slothful neglect. They were abetted in idleness, quite outrageously, by the work-hungry Japanese. American barracks were overrun by teams of shoeshine boys, washers, and cleaners. Ill-fed youngsters eager for a quick buck or a box of candy relieved soldiers of routine chores like furbishing their rifles and equipment, while their sisters offered more intimate services for a box of rations.

The huge wartime draft had profoundly altered the structure of the American armed services. Before World War II, enlisted men were recruited from the poorer sections of society. They were subjected to the cruelest discipline. The slightest misdemeanor landed a GI in the stockade. This provoked protests among the millions of civilians drafted during World War II. Their complaints against overbearing officers and NCOs led to the formation of the Doolittle Board, a congressional investigatory committee convened in Washington in 1945. It recommended an overall relaxation of discipline throughout the armed services. Professionals protested in vain.

The situation grew exceptionally bad in Japan, where the American garrison aimed at maintaining a low, politically acceptable profile. Training exercises were severely restricted, especially in the use of armor. The Japanese farming community, freed from servility toward their own discredited soldiery, and taught by the occupation the value of democratic protest, began complaining vociferously against the damage American tanks inflicted on their fields, roads, and bridges. By the time war broke out in Korea, GIs were spending more time in Japan's proliferating brothels than on the firing range. Their performance upon reaching the battlefront was predictably tragic.

First to arrive in Korea on July 1, 1950, were elements of the 24th Division. They were the most easily and swiftly transportable unit, stationed in nearby Kyushu. Committed piecemeal south of Seoul, the youthful rookies were scattered like chaff before the North Korean onslaught. Persistent American resistance forced the attackers to fan out, however, splitting their concentrated, sledgehammer drive into a multipronged thrust. The Communists were aiming for Pusan in the southeastern heel of the peninsula. The main axis of their advance continued diagonally across country, absorbing the defenders' entire attention, while a single column swept unnoticed through the southwest in a wide enveloping movement. The Communists were on the verge of outflanking the Americans. Victory lay a few days' march away.

The 24th Division commander, Major General William F. Dean, rallied his battered forces across the immediate path of the Communist advance. He made his heroic stand on July 18, 1950, in the road-rail center of Taejon. Through five days of bitter house-to-house fighting, personally led by the bazooka-wielding general, the men of the 24th stalled the enemy advance. The price they paid was high. The general himself was captured; two regiments were badly mauled. But their sacrifice won invaluable time. Two more divisions, the 25th Infantry and the First Cavalry, also from Japan, arrived to join battle by mid-July. Together they linked up with surviving elements of the 24th Division to fend off the increasing weight of enemy offensive power bearing down upon the northeastern corner of the Pusan perimeter. The sudden, unexpected appearance of the outflanking column in the extreme south set Eighth Army commander Lieutenant General "Johnnie" Walker sounding the alarm. These fast-moving Communist forces materialized from nowhere, to the general's complete surprise, slicing through his lightly held southern flank in an unexpected base run to Pusan. Nothing, it seemed, could stop them. The bulk of U.S./ROK—Republic of Korea—strength was irrevocably committed in the north, confronting the main North Korean drive across the Naktong River; few reserves remained to plug this latest gap. The 27th Wolfhounds were rushed south to the area outside of Pusan with orders to stand or die.

Some had already died. Most of the remaining pickets dozing on the hillside were shot or bayoneted by the North Koreans before they could grab their weapons. The rest fled downhill toward the schoolhouse, some without shoes, some in their underpants. Jittery riflemen inside the school yard began aiming dangerously close to their own men. One defending GI suddenly went berserk with a machine gun, spraying the yard with bullets, until an officer brought him down with a well-aimed shot in the shoulder. Medics put the hysterical man under sedation.

Maggie Higgins felt the schoolhouse being shot to bits around her. Bursts of enemy fire peppered its paper-thin walls. Three North Korean prisoners, whimpering in an adjoining room, fell together in one blood-stained heap. The incoming enemy slugs ripped through everything. No one could hope for shelter inside a wooden building. A staff officer finally decided to make a break for it, diving through a window and racing for shelter behind a low stone wall. Maggie followed, together with fellow correspondent Harold Martin. The odd thing was that field telephones were still working. The switchboard had been reinstalled between the wall and a radio truck. The executive officer was on the line to division. "It's a little noisy," he explained apologetically to the general. Harold crouched nearby, methodically capturing the course of the battle in his notebook. What were his chances of living to write the story? Maggie's teeth chattered with fright. The way things looked, this was where she was going to die. The prospect strangely calmed her. By the time Michaelis came round the corner, oblivious to the bullets but solicitous of her safety, the woman war correspondent had regained her nerve. Colonel Mike was determined to impose some semblance of order. "Let's get organized," he shouted. Indiscriminate shooting was quickly brought under control. Riflemen were ordered to provide protective fire as heavy machine-gun squads crept back up the hillside, escorted by companies of infantry. Next came the light mortars. Eventually the howitzer barrels were cranked low enough to belch 155-mm shells into enemy concentrations a few hundred yards away.

"A" Company commander Captain Logan H. Weston led the assault against hilltop positions overlooking the schoolhouse. Enemy domination of the heights posed the gravest immediate danger. The captain wiped out two North Korean machine-gun crews with well-aimed M-1 fire before stopping with a slug in his thigh. He limped down to the aid station, where Maggie Higgins was administering blood plasma. A medic patched him up well enough to get him back into the fight. Half an hour later he was down again, wounded in the shoulder and chest. Calmly he remarked: "I guess I'd better get a shot of morphine now. These last two are beginning to hurt."

Maggie Higgins spent an hour aiding the medics. It was there, she wrote, "that I realized we were going to win after all. Injured after injured came in with reports that the gooks were 'being murdered' and that they were falling back."

The Americans counterattacked with unaccustomed dash. Every one of them hated this war. Every one of them hated being in Korea. An unkind fate condemned them to risk life and limb for a country few pretended to understand. But for the first time since the Wolfhounds came to Korea its soldiers smelled success. The 1st Battalion stormed triumphantly along the ridgeline, sweeping everything before them. It was the North Koreans' turn to be surprised. Prisoner interrogation later established that their scouts had spotted artillery in the school yard the previous afternoon. Nothing else. There were no attendant troops. The NKPA commander must have reckoned that a dawn attack would swiftly overwhelm this unguarded obstacle. After that, little lay between him and Pusan. The enemy plan might very well have succeeded but for the covert overnight arrival of the bedraggled 1st Battalion. Lieutenant Colonel Check's men had gratefully bedded down in the school yard after their fighting retreat from the mountains. The routed battalion had been fruitlessly attempting to launch the first American counterattack of the Korean War.

But, as so often happens, luck took a turn in the battle. No amount of inspired planning can entirely allow for the unexpected. Guderian's drive on Moscow, Xerxes' invasion of Greece, and Pakenham's suicidal assault on New Orleans all cried out for king-sized slices of luck that never quite materialized. Without it, man's best-laid plans are guaranteed to come unstuck. Luck brought Mike Michaelis to Chindong-ni. He was hustled into defending this defenseless sector without really knowing what was going on. Nor was he alone in his confusion. Commanders everywhere floundered through unfamiliar terrain, hampered by creaky communications, outdated maps, unserviceable equipment, and an almost complete lack of reliable intelligence about enemy movements and intentions. The colonel was first ordered to deploy his regiment across the major approach road to Masan. It ran through the valley that correspondents soon dubbed "The Notch." A few miles out front lay the 19th Regiment of the exhausted 24th Division. When it appeared that the 19th was crumbling, opening the door to enemy attack along the alternative coastal road, Michaelis switched his tired troops southward into blocking positions beside the sea. They arrived posthaste to find—nothing. There was no sign of the enemy. Colonel Mike reproached himself for dashing off on a wild-goose chase. "I gambled and lost," he sadly told his officers. "I brought you to the wrong place." Fortunately, he was wrong. Determined to find the elusive North Koreans, the colonel ordered his 1st Battalion to drive westward along the mountain road and flush them out. The Americans ran headlong into powerful NKPA forces advancing toward them across the mountains, their sights set firmly on Pusan.

Where did these columns spring from? The way Maggie Higgins saw it, sneaky North Koreans in traditional white robes mingled unchallenged with the civilian refugees surging along the roads to Pusan. The disguised soldiers then detached themselves, singly or in groups, to gather at mountain assembly points. There they changed into uniform and formed up for battle. Stories like this often circulated whenever a Western army was outwitted by Orientals. During the early stages of World War II the British told similar tales about the Japanese. The evidence suggests, from hindsight, that although a great deal of clandestine activity was mounted by the North Koreans, major assaults were assigned to skillful conventional troops who baffled the truck-bound Americans with their ability to advance speedily across apparently impassable terrain.

The Wolfhounds' 1st Battalion found itself trapped in a narrow valley. Heavy fire swept the road from the surrounding forests.

Lieutenant Colonel Check ordered away all battalion troop transportation. It was an encumbrance, he reckoned; the men would fight better on foot. This time, the hypercritical Michaelis felt he had overreached himself. He wrongly feared heavy losses. He sent off a light plane to drop a personal note to Check ordering immediate withdrawal. A platoon of M-4 medium tanks, newly arrived the previous evening, led the battalion's battling withdrawal to their start-point at Chindong-ni. In spite of Michaelis's gloomy premonitions, no tanks were lost, though two of them completed the hazardous return trip manned by bulldozer drivers who took over the controls from killed or injured crewmen. The shaken, weary troops holed up for the night precisely where they were going to be needed: around the unguarded village schoolhouse.

The North Korean commander redoubled his efforts to overrun the lone howitzer battery below the high cliffs of Chindong-ni. But luck was no longer with him. Ridiculously large forces were being deployed, he must have reckoned, to defend eight miserable guns. There was never anything to suggest that the Communists knew they were attacking the 24th Regiment headquarters. Around noon the North Korean commander called up reinforcements. The advance had to be resumed at all costs. Patrols were already well past this obstinate artillery post, within sight of the port of Masan. But it just wasn't his day. U.S. howitzer gunners blasted the NKPA support battalion as soon as it drove into battle. The North Koreans were disembarking from their trucks about a thousand yards north of the village when American shells began landing in their midst. They scattered into the surrounding mountains, leaving mounds of bodies heaped along the roadside. When the attack was broken off in midafternoon, the North Koreans had lost an estimated 400 dead. American casualties throughout the day were 13 killed and some 60 wounded.

Maggie Higgins moved among the wounded, glancing up at the corpses littering the hillside. The firing had almost died away. Bullets no longer smacked into the nearby wall, forcing doctors and medics to crouch to avoid being hit. The earsplitting crack of mortars had providentially ceased. This one battle, Maggie reckoned, had taught her a great deal. From now on she would carry a carbine whenever she came close to combat. Her marksmanship was wild, but it might make the enemy duck. War correspondents could claim no special immunity in this kind of war. Even when they happened to be women. Maggie felt doubly threatened. Not only was she forced to face the exceptional dangers of her job, but there were constant, maddening confrontations with deep-seated prejudice. Women had won the vote, could even drink and smoke, but traipsing about battlefields was no job for a lady. Ever since war began, and reporters had set out to report it, those reporters invariably were men. The 30-year-old blonde in the sneakers and baggy fatigues had muscled into a man's world. She was the only woman among 131 male correspondents covering the Korean War. Born in Hong Kong of an American businessman and a French mother, she had been educated in both France and the United States, winning her first assignment for the *Tribune* while at Columbia's School of Journalism. She caught the battle-bug in Western Europe toward the end of World War II, but it was here in this unloved peninsula that she sought and relished frontline reporting.

Some thought her suicidal. Breathless Higgins reports of bloody shoot-outs along the fluid battlefront left her less valiant colleagues embarrassed—and envious. Nor did this endear her to the top brass. The situation was tricky enough, harassed generals firmly believed, without having to worry about women. Male correspondents were finding it tough enough to cope with the undeniable dangers and privations. So a determined effort was made, at General Walker's instigation, to confine this pesky news-hen to rear-area Tokyo. And for a few weeks the brass succeeded. But Maggie's stint with the blood plasma, her courage under fire, had won her a new and influential admirer. The glowing letter Colonel Mike Michaelis sent to the editor of the *Herald Tribune* after the action at Chindong-ni helped persuade Douglas MacArthur that this gutsy female should be allowed to continue her coverage. "The Regimental Combat Team considers Miss Higgins' actions on that day heroic . . .," the colonel wrote, "in saving the lives of many grievously wounded men."

Colonel Michaelis did not yet know it, but he had won one of the few decisive battles of an indecisive war. Even Marguerite Higgins failed to grasp quite the full significance of the action in the otherwise vivid account that appeared in her book *War in Korea*. The official U.S. Army historian enjoyed the advantage of hindsight when he wrote, 11 years later, that "never afterward were conditions as critical . . . as in the closing days of July and the first days of August 1950. Never again did the North Koreans come as close to victory."

From now on, their burden would fall increasingly upon the Chinese.

3

INTERLUDE
The Middle Kingdom /
Land of the Morning Calm.

People's Republic of China

The Chinese still call their country *Zhong Guo*, the Middle Kingdom. China remains, in Chinese eyes, the monarch of the civilized world. The Chinese rate themselves a superior people, heirs to an unrivaled historical tradition; a race infinitely more literate, more artistic, and more refined than breeds unblessed by the great Chinese cultural heritage. A handful of neighboring tribes—the Koreans, the Tibetans, the Japanese, and the Vietnamese—might be beneficiaries of that culture, but inferiors they remain, along with all others born in barbarian darkness.

Such unthinking arrogance was inevitable after centuries of isolation at the eastern end of the Asian landmass. The Chinese were undisturbed by outside influences, developing brilliantly in their own cultural vacuum. Buddhism came from India, but little else was imported. Intruders from the peripheral deserts periodically breached the Great Wall, especially during bouts of dynastic weakness, only to be civilized and absorbed. The Chinese went their peculiar way insulated from and largely ignorant of developments in the outside world. Little threat was perceived from the seaborne barbarians who arrived unexpectedly from Europe early in the fifteenth century.

34

The foreign devils, with their big noses and hairy faces, their gawky manners and obscene food, were objects of immediate ridicule. The Chinese had no difficulty humbling them. Portuguese and Dutch emissaries kowtowed before the King of Heaven, awesome in his great palace in Peking, supported by colorful armies and fleets of fighting junks. But unbeknown to the Chinese the balance of world power was changing dramatically; by the beginning of the nineteenth century, when British merchantmen were crowding into the South China Sea, Britannia ruled the waves and a great deal more besides.

China and Britain clashed over commerce. British merchants were eager to purchase Chinese silks, ceramics, and tea. The Chinese were unresponsive. An indifferent administrative class, the mandarins, found the foreigners offered China little it wanted to buy. The odd clock, perhaps . . . nothing more. The crafty British found a more saleable product. They switched to opium, grown in India and supposedly forbidden in China, but smoked by millions of Chinese. Opium addiction spread rapidly. Demand for the drug grew so fast, and trade became so seriously unbalanced, that bullion drained out of China. By the late 1830s the imperial government was forced to stanch the outflow of silver by confiscating illicit opium and suspending trade. News of the Chinese action was received with indignation in London. Free trade, even in narcotics, was sacrosanct. Lord Melbourne's administration refused to be daunted by Peking's pretensions. "The King of Where?" asked one outraged minister. Reports from the China coast spoke disparagingly of the imperial forces. In 1840 the British sent in troops and gunboats. China collapsed exactly as predicted, its military weaknesses apparent to the world. Waves of barbarians poured into the prostrate empire, eager for a share of the spoils. The British grabbed Hong Kong. Tsarist Russia annexed huge chunks of Siberia. The French, the Germans, and finally the despised Japanese also carved out areas of influence. Small foreign enclaves, known as "concessions," sprang up along the China coast, where the barbarians introduced their own legal systems and monopolized much of the commerce. The Chinese became second-class citizens on their own soil. A sign outside a park in the British concession in Shanghai declared: "Dogs and Chinese not admitted."

China sought rejuvenation through emulating the barbarians. The Japanese were modernizing with embarrassing success. Chinese scholars pondered the secrets of the foreigners' extraordinary power. Every aspect of Western industrial technique was explored. But there was opposition, too. It arose from a ruling elite that welcomed the introduction of Western machinery but firmly resisted the spread of Western thought. The emperor and his mandarins owed their positions to a patriarchal society prescribed by the ancient sage

Confucius; their privileges appeared threatened once individual freedom and initiative took precedence over family and the state. Individualism might be essential to the creation of the entrepreneurs and managers needed for the industrial transformation of China, but its dangers were perfectly apparent to the handful who have traditionally manipulated Chinese society.

Reform was effectively blocked by the empress dowager, Cu Xi, a former concubine whose fickle fingers held the threads of power. Alternately she courted, and incited rebellion against, the foreign devils, provoking still more encroachments on Chinese sovereignty. Plots to bring down the empress and her fellow Manchus were formulated in southern and eastern China by republican patriots influenced both by missionaries and by growing contact with the West. The conspirators were loosely led by Doctor Sun Yat Sen, a Westernized physician who spent many years in exile lobbying for revolution. His moment came in 1911, some years after the empress dowager's death, when a military mutiny forced the abdication of the last of the Manchu rulers, the boy emperor Pu Yi.

Dr. Sun and his fellow nationalists tried to establish democratic government, only to be swept aside by a general, Yuan Shih-kai, who declared himself president (and aspired to the imperial title) in Peking. Provincial commanders with their own private armies, the so-called warlords, began parceling out the empire. China lapsed into chaos. Only the encroachments of the foreigners eased off. The outbreak of World War I prevented the Europeans from hacking fresh pieces off the helpless republic. Many Chinese, innocently charmed by Western wartime rhetoric, hoped that when the fighting was over the foreign devils would finally evacuate their enclaves, especially the affluent concessions in Shanghai. First of all, they expected to be given back the former German concessions on the China coast recently occupied (on behalf of the Allies) by the Japanese. But Western leaders, meeting at Versailles to concoct a peace treaty, awarded the German concessions to Japan. The rest remained in colonial hands. Chinese condemnation of this rank injustice erupted in Peking. On May 4, 1919, a wave of youthful protest eddied out from Peking University. The target, ostensibly, was the Versailles Treaty, but Western ideals of freedom and democracy bore the brunt of bitter criticism.

The May 4 movement deepened Chinese disillusion with the West and fostered the growth of Chinese communism. Two years later the Chinese Communist Party was created by a group of frustrated intellectuals who knew next to nothing about Marxism, but thought they saw plenty to admire in the 1917 Bolshevik revolution that had destroyed the nascent democratic government headed by Alexander

Kerensky. The scholars first met in the library of Peking University, marveling at the political coup that had swept Lenin to power in Russia; so tightly organized and disciplined, its formula seemed well-suited to China. Although eager to appear egalitarian in the time-honored tradition of Chinese peasant rebellions, the founders of the Communist party shied away from sharing power with the unwashed masses. Western-style democracy, they unanimously decided, was inapplicable to China. Open government as practiced in the West could not be foisted onto a nation after thousands of years of authoritarianism. Democracy, they now saw, was a sham, so proven by Marxist holy writ. Communism would keep the elite comfortably on top of the pyramid, but acting in the name of the people.

China was ripe for further revolution. The breakdown of centralized power and the consequent political disorders had wrought havoc in the countryside. Irrigation canals silted up. Flood defenses fell into disrepair. Millions died of famine. Intolerable pressures had already been generated on China's farmlands by the population explosion of the eighteenth and nineteenth centuries; by 1949 as many as 40 million peasants were landless. Still more were scratching an inadequate existence from tiny patches of soil. Greedy warlords now drove the peasants to despair. Taxes in some areas were gathered at gunpoint 30 years in advance. First to recognize the revolutionary potential of the peasantry was the young Communist agitator Mao Zedong, eldest son of a modest Hunanese peasant family, and a rebellious schoolmaster later turned guerrilla leader. Mao knew how often rural discontent had destroyed dynasties during China's long and turbulent history. His favorite reading was *Water Margin*, a romantic classic analogous to the Robin Hood tradition, with heroic robbers milking the rich to reimburse the poor.

More orthodox members of the Chinese Communist Party preached the line laid down by Marx (and endorsed by Lenin) that revolution had to be brought about by the urban proletariat. For the Chinese, this proved quite impractical. Genuine industrial workers were rare in China. The small, fragmented urban work-force showed scant enthusiasm for waging an armed rebellion. There were remarkable, if isolated, exceptions in cities such as Shanghai. The peasants, on the other hand, were more numerous and more desperate. Mao toured his home province of Hunan and found unrest reaching such a pitch that "a single spark could start a prairie fire." The peasants had no idea what communism involved, but welcomed its advocates as harbingers of rural reform.

Mao Zedong's heresies were rejected by the scholarly gentlemen controlling the Chinese Communist Party. Throughout the twenties the CCP took its cue diligently from Moscow. The Bolsheviks kept reassuring the malleable Chinese that their path to power was clearly mapped by Marxist prophesy. Peasants played no part in this "scientific" analysis of history. The best Karl Marx had ever expected was an uneasy alliance between revolutionary workers and the invariably conservative peasantry. The Chinese comrades might yet take a convenient shortcut to power, the Bolsheviks suggested, if they rode for a time on the coattails of the Nationalist party, the Kuomintang, of Dr. Sun Yat Sen. The good doctor's fortunes were at an all-time low. The architect of the 1911 revolution and his dwindling, dispirited supporters were holed up, ignominiously, in the southern metropolis of Canton, existing on the sufferance of a local warlord. Sun Yat Sen had been persistently frustrated. He now knew the Nationalists would never win power without guns. But how could they do that? China was already overrun with marauding soldiery. The Nationalists would need to rejuvenate their party and train a dedicated modern army, as the Bolsheviks had done in Russia. Dr. Sun was so elated at Moscow's offer of friendly foreign advisers that he accepted the Chinese Communists as junior partners in a Popular Front coalition.

The deal suited current Bolshevik strategy. Lenin clung to the orthodox belief that the Russian revolution was doomed without a worldwide uprising against capitalism. (The idea of socialism in one country was still a distant, Stalinist heresy.) Orthodox Marxists knew that the proletarian seizure of power, as specified by the Master, should have started in the industrial West; the Bolshevik uprising in Petrograd was an embarrassing aberration. Predominantly peasant societies such as those in Russia (to say nothing of China) were not sufficiently developed industrially to make the "leap" to socialism. But the new occupants of the Kremlin were not inclined to quibble. Any kind of harassment was good enough to destabilize the doomed imperialists. China might very well prove the soft underbelly of capitalism. Bolshevik advisers began arriving in Canton in 1923 saddled with the dual task of rebuilding the Nationalist party along Communist lines and equipping it with a revolutionary army. The Chinese Communists infiltrated wherever they could under the banner of the united front. As junior members of this uneasy menage, they aimed to seize power from within whenever the time was ripe. But first, the coalition would have to sally out of its southern base, crush the warlords in the north, and reunify China by force.

The Nationalists' campaign of conquest, mounted in 1926 and supported by the Communists, was only partially successful. Peking remained in warlord hands. Dr. Sun had died there of cancer, hopelessly negotiating with his opponents, before this northern expedition could be launched. Command of the Nationalist armies passed into the hands of an obscure soldier with an obscurer background. His name was Chiang Kai-shek. Born in Zhejiang, the province bordering Shanghai, this son of a bankrupt tea merchant had been a soldier and, it is said, a hit man for a secret society before he attracted Dr. Sun's patronage. Chiang had his own ambitious plans for the future. No sooner had Nationalist troops reached the Yangtse, capturing Wuhan and Shanghai in the summer of 1927, than the wily general made his peace with the international banking community and turned on the Communists. The slaughter was terrible, especially in Shanghai.

Chiang's act was damaging but indecisive. The decimated Communists survived, swearing eternal vengeance. The Nationalist general had succeeded merely in firing the first shots in a civil war that would drag on, intermittently, over three decades. At the outset the Communists were helpless. Chiang monopolized the military. But mutinies among the infiltrated Nationalist forces gradually brought troops over to the Communist side under the banner of the Workers' and Peasants' Red Army. The mutineers included a burly young peasant called Peng Dehuai. The 30-year-old captain in a warlord army joined the Communists rather than follow orders to suppress the rebellious Hunanese peasantry, according to the official story, although he had been dabbling secretly with communism for years. Peng Dehuai formed a guerrilla band that linked up with Mao Zedong and his military commander, Zhu De, on the slopes of Jingganshan. The heavily wooded mountain in southeast China was traditionally a bandit hideout. It was here that the doctrine of people's war was born.

The concept was scarcely new to China—desperate Chinese peasants had been rebelling against oppression since time immemorial. Rebellion was the patient masses' final resort whenever famine, pestilence, or blatant misrule drove them beyond despair. Their uprisings were usually short-lived.

Mao founded his power base on rural discontent. By 1930 his agitators had created small islands of defiance in the remoter southern areas of China. Their rallying cry was "Land [belongs] to the tiller!" Farms were seized and handed to the landless. The idea was to create rustic utopias in liberated "soviet" areas which would serve as pilot schemes for the rest of China. The plan worked well at first. Some half dozen soviets came into existence north and south of the Yangtse River. The largest was in a distant corner of Jiangxi province, conveniently far from effective government, where Mao set up his headquarters in the village of Ruijin. His efforts were initially condemned by the Chinese Communist Party leadership, hiding in the French enclave in Shanghai.

The Chinese Communist leaders still deferred obsequiously to the Russians, accepting a stream of contradictory and ill-judged instructions that almost destroyed communism in China. They took their orders from Stalin, the ruthless new upstart who had grabbed control of the Kremlin, and an ignoramus when it came to Chinese political realities. Facts that failed to fit his Procrustean theories were summarily discarded. The Soviet dictator stuck to orthodox dogma, insisting that rural revolution was doomed to failure. Power could be won only by seizing cities, in Stalin's view, even when this was plainly impossible in China; throughout the late twenties the dutiful Chinese Communist leadership dissipated its strength (despite private misgivings) by launching hopeless attacks against impregnable urban garrisons.

Chiang Kai-shek had, meanwhile, proclaimed himself president of China. From his immediate, myopic viewpoint, the northern expedition could be judged a modest success. The Nationalists had still to gain direct control of much territory outside the Yangtse valley, but, by a series of deals with the most powerful Chinese warlords, Chiang wheedled enough gestures of allegiance to hoist the Nationalist flag over the entire country. The adventurer-turned-politician married into the wealthy Soong family shortly after the 1927 Shanghai massacre of his Communist rivals; converted, like the Soongs, to Methodism; and borrowed liberally from now-friendly bankers for a military showdown with the Communists. Gradually committing troops trained by some of the former Kaiser's unemployed German generals, he launched a series of "annihilation campaigns" in 1931 against the scattered Communist-held zones. The time had come for a showdown.

The Nationalists found to their discomfort that the Communists had developed a remarkable style of guerrilla warfare. Light-footed Red Troopers brashly dubbed themselves the "biped cavalry." The rebels struck when least expected, using surprise to compensate for their lack of numbers. Some Communist combat units mustered only a single rifle for every seven men—the rest carried spears, swords, and homemade grenades. A battalion was lucky to possess a single machine gun. Artillery was unknown. The ill-equipped defenders of the Jiangxi soviet nevertheless succeeded in throwing the Nationalists back three times with heavy losses. Peng Dehuai was twice wounded in hand-to-hand fighting. Units under his command were regularly destroyed—and re-formed just as regularly with fresh volunteers from the friendly peasantry.

But as Nationalist pressure mounted, Mao Zedong found himself fighting on two fronts. Enemies unexpectedly appeared inside the soviet perimeter: the Stalinist acolytes who still controlled the Chinese

Communist Party suddenly joined Mao's Jiangxi soviet in 1931. (The foreign concessions had become too dangerous for their tastes.)

These newcomers used their authority to oust Mao and take command at a crucial moment in the campaign. Chiang's German-trained troops were modifying their tactics. They built concentric rings of concrete blockhouses that restricted guerrilla mobility. Their economic blockade deprived the defenders of vital supplies, especially salt. The new, Stalin-appointed military adviser, a bespectacled German schoolmaster called Otto Braun (better known by his Chinese alias of Li De), ordered the Communists to switch to Western-style positional warfare. Mao watched fuming from the sidelines—under house arrest, it is said—while the war was lost by these know-nothings appointed by Moscow. The resultant debacle gave the future Chairman endless opportunities to damn his rivals. Writing with hindsight, he claimed well after the event that defeat could have been averted if the Communists had maintained a fluid, guerrilla-style defense. It is extremely doubtful. By the summer of 1934 nothing the Communists could muster stood much chance of holding off the Nationalist war machine.

Heavy reinforcement of men and materiel might have won the defenders a respite, but neither was available. The Communists were trapped, fighting with backs to the wall, with their peasant allies too terrified to support them and the supply of recruits drying up. It was a war of attrition only the Nationalists could win. On October 14, 1934, the Communists abandoned the Jiangxi soviet and started the costly, circuitous 6,000-mile retreat euphemistically known to history as the Long March. A gigantic game of hide-and-seek began across southern and western China, which demonstrated the laxity of Nationalist rule. Much of the countryside was undefended. The Communist columns managed to dodge most of the armies sent against them by Chiang and the regional warlords. At Zunyi in Guizhou province, one of the few towns the retreating Communists temporarily occupied, they paused long enough to stage a Party congress that wrested the reins from Stalin's nominees and handed them to Mao. He kept them firmly in his grip, almost without a break, until he died 41 years later in 1976.

At the time of the Zunyi congress the Chinese Communists seemed more in need of a miracle than of new leadership. The crippled forces staggering to unlikely sanctuary in the northwestern province of Shaanxi later that year, in 1935, were no longer a viable fighting unit. Death and desertion had reduced to a scant 10,000 the force of 100,000 strong which had set out from Jiangxi.

Many of the marchers could hardly remember how they made it. Peng Dehuai had distinct recollections of twice being carried long distances on a litter. He had contracted fever in Sichuan and would have been left behind to die, as many were, if his men had not refused to desert him. Weak as they themselves were, the peasant soldiers transported and nursed their popular commander until he could walk again. It was part-payment, they declared, for his considerate treatment of them.

The Communists were not expected to stay permanently in Shaanxi. Some saw it as a way station on a final line of retreat into the Soviet Union. Far off in Nanking, Chiang Kai-shek urged the Shaanxi garrison to wipe out the exhausted rebels before they could regain their strength. His appeals were sullenly ignored. The Communists had found new and unlikely saviors—the Japanese.

The stunningly successful Japanese campaign against the Russians in 1904–1905 gave Japan its first foothold in Manchuria. After unsuccessfully trying to expand their influence in China during World War I, the Japanese, particularly the imperial army, began extensive penetration of northeast China during the late twenties to preempt the spread of Nationalist influence. Anything that threatened to unify China alarmed the ambitious militarists in Tokyo. When the Manchurian warlord, the "old" marshal, Chang Tso-lin, began to annoy them, his Japanese paymasters ordered his assassination. His son, the "young" marshal, Chang Hseuh-liang, subsequently took over the satrapy and defiantly raised the Nationalist flag. Three years later, in 1931, convinced that young Marshal Chang would never be suborned, the Japanese drove him from Manchuria after a trumped-up bomb attack on the Mukden railroad and proclaimed their own puppet kingdom of Manchuquo under former boy emperor Pu Yi. The Japanese action aroused patriotic ferment throughout China. The Communists sensed the national mood, cleverly appealing for a united front of national resistance—to get the Nationalist armies off their backs—while deriding Chiang's hesitation to challenge the Japanese, the despised "pirate dwarfs." Chiang Kai-shek found himself caught in uncomfortable crossfire. China was not yet strong enough, he felt, to face up to the barbarian aggressors. The country would only be strong once he had cleansed it of domestic enemies. "The Japanese are a disease of the skin," he publicly declared. "The Communists are a disease of the heart."

This view won little sympathy in China. Most patriots, particularly the influential student class, saw no sense in pursuing family squabbles while a far deadlier foe hammered at the gates. Disaffection spread to the army. Young Marshal Chang's Manchurian troops, pushed homeless into Shaanxi by the Japanese, demanded resistance to the invader. They resented Chiang Kai-shek's orders to divert their efforts into attacking their Communist compatriots. The Manchurians' balky behavior so infuriated the president that he rashly flew to the young Marshal Chang's headquarters in Xi'an in December, 1936, to inject new life into the bandit-suppression campaign. Mutinous officers stormed the palatial "guest house" where President Chiang was staying, and although Chiang managed to escape over a back wall they found him (minus his dentures) shivering on the nearby hillside. The rebellious Manchurian troops would have executed Chiang on the spot but for the intervention of the Communists. Mao and his men had plenty of scores to pay off against their old enemy. Right now, however, they preferred to see him preserved as a unifying symbol against Japan. Chiang suffered the galling experience of being bailed out by his bitterest enemies. The delicate task of saving his life was assigned to that suave and elegant patrician, the 36-year-old Zhou Enlai. The ingratiating diplomat pleaded with Marshal Chang to spare Chiang Kai-shek, provided the Nationalist leader call off his anti-Communist campaign and instead form a united front to oppose the Japanese.

The Xi'an mutiny altered the course of Asian history. The Japanese were forced to attack again, and much more forcibly, to forestall Chinese unification. The so-called China Incident lasted eight years. Millions died—and not merely in the fighting, the cruel air raids, and the sack of defenseless cities. Casualties were multiplied by disease, flood, and famine. There had been little peace in China since the turn of the century, but now the wild winds of war engulfed the entire nation, virtually unnoticed by the outside world. A handful of foreign observers conveyed some of the sense of horror. Newsreels occasionally captured the panic and the pain of this frightful war. But the China Incident attracted less attention—and less commitment—than the much smaller conflict in Spain. The Western democracies, deep in economic depression, had more immediate worries than the fate of people so remote and alien. The Chinese might have lived on another planet.

The Japanese had little difficulty smashing Chinese resistance. Most of the eastern seaboard was in their hands by the end of 1938. The Nationalist capital, Nanking, was brutally sacked. Shanghai, Peking, Wuhan, and Canton all fell in quick succession. Chiang Kai-shek retreated to Chungking, deep in Sichuan, safe behind the Yangtse River gorges. From this isolated aerie he proceeded to fight the war that never was. Conserving his main strength for an eventual showdown with the Communists, the self-styled generalissimo sat waiting petulantly for the Americans to bail him out. Even when the Americans found themselves thrust unceremoniously into the war and saddled with this exacting new ally, the generalissimo (or "G'mo," as his admirers now called him) reserved a portion of the military aid poured in by the United States for the postwar day of reckoning. The Communists did likewise. They extended their political influence through guerrilla operations across northern China, but launched only one major offensive against the Japanese.

It has since been called the One Hundred Regiments offensive, unleashed in Shandong in 1943 with encouraging initial results. Fearful reprisals followed. The Japanese commander, Okamura, hit back with the "Three-All" campaign—kill all, burn all, destroy all— which wiped out the Communists' political infrastructure and drove them back into the hills. No further initiatives were attempted until the last year of the war. By that time Japanese troop strength in China had been considerably reduced by the need to reinforce far-flung garrisons confronting the American advance across the Pacific.

The Japanese surrender in 1945 left Chiang undisputed master of China—at least in theory. Nationalist forces totaled more than four million men, some superbly equipped with American arms. The chances for a final showdown with the Communists had never seemed more auspicious. The Communists had also expanded their strength, mustering some one million men in North China, but most of these were atrociously equipped. The Russians' last-minute entry into the war, on August 8, 1945, scattered the run-down Japanese garrisons in Manchuria and brought the Communists a windfall of discarded weapons. This did little to alter the overall military balance. Nationalist forces flew hurriedly into northeast China to reestablish a government presence. A showdown was becoming inevitable. The civil war did not formally resume until July of 1946, when the United States gave up its futile efforts at mediation between the Nationalists and the Communists, but already the battle lines were drawn.

The Nationalists were committed from the start to a strategy that fatally overtaxed their resources. Chiang Kai-shek probably had no alternative. He dared not ignore Manchuria. The northeast was the traditional gateway to northern China. People said "No northeast, no China." Thanks to the Japanese it also housed the country's largest industrial base. The Soviets were busy gutting its factories and shipping the machinery back home. The region had to be secured. Yet defending it was a logistical nightmare. Supplies for the Nationalist armies came all the way from distant bases in the south and west. Shipping was scarce. Rail communication was hazardous. Nationalist garrisons found themselves increasingly reliant on airlifts.

The campaign began encouragingly for the Nationalists with the capture of Mao's old headquarters. The cave complexes at Yan'an, where the Communist leadership had been living since the last stages of the Long March, fell without a shot in March of 1947. Chiang trumpeted that the bandits were finished. But his enemies characteristically counterattacked just when things looked bleakest, striking straight for the Nationalist jugular. They hit the rail corridor funneling all north-south traffic through east-central China. Troops commanded by Chen Yi and Deng Xiaoping "sliced the dumbbell, and the heavy ends began to fall off." It was a dazzling maneuver. Chiang's Nationalist forces never regained the initiative. In early 1948, one of the finest Communist field commanders, Lin Biao, much-acclaimed master of the infantry *blitzkrieg*, swept over the defending garrisons in Manchuria at the start of a drive that would carry him from the Soviet Siberian border to the frontiers of Vietnam. Nearly three million Nationalist troops in North China were killed, wounded, or captured. That same year, on April 21, the Communists forced the Yangtse, capturing Nanking two days later. Wuhan fell on May 17 and Shanghai on May 27. At the beginning of 1949, Peking surrendered without a shot being fired. The Red columns pressed on into the south, the birthplace of the Chinese revolution, to launch the land-reform programs already in progress in the north.

Nationalist catastrophes were amplified by the favoritism, corruption, and inflation that plagued Chiang Kai-shek's regime. Greedy generals stole their troops' pay and rations, padded the payrolls with nonexistent soldiers, and peddled medical supplies and equipment on the black market. Government bureaucrats, eager to make up for the lean years in wartime Chungking, lost no time squeezing contractors and disposing of relief shipments and anything else capable of turning a profit. Money rapidly lost value despite a Draconian currency reform. The G'mo's dreaded son, Chiang Ching-kuo, shot dozens of Shanghai currency dealers. The government had hoped a touch of terror would stampede the financial community into disgorging its valuables in exchange for worthless bank notes. But terror generated an unexpected backlash. Political support for the Nationalists among their chief champions, the urban middle class, now faded faster than the G'mo's armies.

Chiang Kai-shek sought refuge on Taiwan. He flew to the island from his familiar but untenable sanctuary in Sichuan, west China, on an unpublicized "tour of inspection" in August of 1949. The Americans washed their hands of him. The Truman administration was coming round to the British-held view that the Nationalists were no great loss. The Chinese Communists were bound to fall out eventually with the Russians. The "collapse" of China might not prove quite so disastrous as it had at first appeared. It was therefore announced from Washington in January of 1950 that the Nationalists would receive no more U.S. aid. Billions of U.S. dollars had been poured down the Chinese rat hole. All without appreciable result. It was only a matter of time, U.S. State Department officials predicted, before the Communists overran Taiwan. The G'mo would retire to affluent American exile. Red China would receive American diplomatic recognition, taking its place in the United Nations.

History provided an alternative ending . . .

Korea

Korea is known to those who live there as the Land of the Morning Calm. The mountainous 600-mile protrusion from Manchuria forms a convenient stepping stone between China and Japan. Its climate reaches extremes, especially in the north. Its inhabitants are tough, obstinate, and imbued with that determination to preserve national dignity peculiar to people perpetually overshadowed by powerful neighbors. Not for nothing are Koreans known as "the Irish of Asia." Centuries of subjection to foreign cultural influence have never erased their distinct national identity. Men and women still gown themselves in white, instead of the predominant blacks and blues of China. Their peppery diet, built around *kimche,* a national dish of spiced, fermented cabbage, is far more piquant than the blander cuisine of Japan.

By the nineteenth century Korea had become a geopolitical backwater. Westerners called it "the Hermit Kingdom." Things had not always been that way. The glorious Silla dynasty (668–918 A.D.) produced some of the world's greatest ceramics. A phonetic alphabet developed in 1443 for the distinctive Korean language was the first ever extensively printed with movable type. Stagnation set in under hierarchical Confucianism, borrowed from China, which provided the rationale, and little more, for a conservative agrarian patriarchy incompetently dominated by quarrelsome mandarins. Continuity came from the weak but enduring Yi dynasty (1392–1910), which preserved Korea's secluded independence until the emergence of modern Japan.

Victorious Japanese confrontations with imperial China (1898) and Tsarist Russia (1904–1905) established Japan's hegemony over the Korean peninsula. A Japanese-engineered palace coup in 1910 completed the process of annexation. Korea reaped considerably more benefits from Japanese colonialism than its inhabitants would now care to admit. Railroads were built, education was modernized, and industries developed. But the Koreans themselves were treated with utter contempt. The Japanese regarded them as an inferior species, an attitude still discernible today.

Korean nationalists received short shrift. A cruelly efficient police system drove student leaders like Syngman Rhee, known to Koreans as Yi Sung-man (1875–1965), into exile abroad. Christian missionary schools with liberal foreign teachers helped foster a degree of patriotic protest. But the only armed resistance came from the hard handful who took to the hills as guerrillas along the Manchurian frontier. Their efforts made scant impression on the Japanese. World opinion was totally indifferent. The Japanese discouraged visitors to Korea. Foreign newsmen seldom thought to visit the colony except as guided guests of the Japanese authorities. After World War I, self-determination was still not a universally accepted right. Long after dismemberment of the Japanese empire became an official plank of U.S. policy in the wake of Pearl Harbor, the future of Korea remained uncertain. Too little was known about the place. The Cairo summit conference of 1943 between Roosevelt, Churchill, and Stalin (with Chiang Kai-shek hovering on the sidelines) advocated restoration of Korean independence "in due course." Immediate self-government was considered impractical.

Washington planners hoped to limit further casualties in the Pacific war by persuading the Soviet Union to attack Japan; as inducement, Stalin was offered a temporary occupation role in Korea, limited by an arbitrarily chosen geographical line, once the Japanese had surrendered. The 38th Parallel of latitude roughly bisected the Korean peninsula, but politically and economically the division made no practical sense. Existence of a common border a mere 12 miles long with the Soviet Union provided the entry point—and the excuse—for Russian "liberation" of the industrial north. The bulk of the Korean population, living in the agricultural south, became the reluctant responsibility of American forces, eager to be home, but soon embroiled in a quagmire of political intrigue.

Thirty-five years of Japanese repression, following centuries of bureaucratic *diktat*, were poor preparation for a sudden flowering of democratic freedom. The U.S. occupation command met the challenge with frustration and impatience. The planned solution had looked simple enough. The Allies had only to hold free elections throughout Korea. Everyone could then pack up and leave. There was just one snag. The Soviets had other plans. Ambitious plans. The Americans were caught with their options down.

The United States has been unencumbered by foreign policy throughout most of its brief history. The Monroe Doctrine, declaring the New World off limits to the Old, itself underwritten by British sea power, proved adequate for most needs until the American west was won. U.S. intervention in World War I proved a temporary aberration. The Roaring Twenties and the Depression-wracked Thirties ushered in a fresh bout of isolationism broken, traumatically, on December 7, 1941, by Tojo's infamy at Pearl Harbor. But after that war the decline of the European powers, notably Britain, destroyed any comforting hopes of withdrawal to Fortress America. Postwar policies cobbled together in a series of inconclusive summit conclaves were nevertheless based on the optimistic assumption that wartime cooperation with the Soviet Union, the other emergent superpower, would continue unimpaired.

Japan was earmarked for American indoctrination in acknowledgment of the overwhelming U.S. contribution to the Pacific war. China was hailed as the emergent superpower, expected to stay strongly in the Western camp; in little-known borderline cases like Korea, problems were supposed to be solved, automatically, through the ballot box. Korea received so little attention that disembarking American forces, arriving September 8, 1945, to accept the surrender of local Japanese garrisons, did not include a single officer who could speak Korean.

The Russians regarded their occupation of North Korea as a heaven-sent opportunity to continue their advance into Asia. This strategic windfall, once sought by the Tsars, would be sucked into the Soviet sphere of influence. There would be nothing temporary about the Soviet presence. The occupation force that rolled in from neighboring Siberia included several hundred cadres of Korean descent, mostly from families shamelessly uprooted and transported across Soviet Asia on some wartime whim of Stalin. These Sovietized Koreans provided ideal tools for fabricating a puppet state. As its figurehead, the Soviets produced a 36-year-old guerrilla leader, long exiled in Manchuria and possibly in Siberia, known by the name of Kim Il Sung. Mystery still surrounds this man's origins. Official hagiography portrays him as the fighter of an unremitting (if largely unnoticed) campaign against Japanese colonialism throughout the late thirties. Later rewrites of history conveniently omit all mention of Soviet patronage. Legend today depicts an assertive little patriot beating the Japanese forces in Korea to their knees. No clue is offered as to how, when, or why the Soviets chose him—or to confirm stories that he served in the wartime Red Army, notably at Stalingrad. The one clear historical fact is that on October 14, 1945, the Soviet occupation forces staged a mass rally in Pyongyang. Over the platform hung the banner "Welcome General Kim Il Sung." Few, if any, Koreans had ever heard of the man. The slim crew-cut figure in blue double-breasted serge suit, backed by a phalanx of bemedaled Russian officers, was hardly the kind of leader cynical citizens had been led to expect. The crowd of 70,000 was reportedly unimpressed. Age has always commanded considerable respect in Korea. But the northerners had little choice. The youthful-looking upstart was backed by Soviet arms. The opposition was too fragmented to offer an alternative.

Things turned out much the same, ironically, south of the Parallel. Syngman Rhee, now 70 years old, flew in from Hawaii to end 34 years' exile. He reached Seoul two days after Kim's inauspicious debut in Pyongyang. Hailed by the bemused American military, who were delighted at last to meet someone so thoroughly Westernized, the determined old nationalist set about seizing power. Factionalism, always the curse of Korean politics, helped him outwit his squabbling opponents. Within weeks of the end of the Pacific war, two separate Koreas were in the making. Each state ominously claimed sovereignty over the entire peninsula. More ominous still, the Soviets began providing North Korea with a potent army. The South Korean army, haphazardly created by the Americans, looked good on paper. One U.S. adviser described it, with endemic hyperbole, as "the best goddarned shooting army in the world." In truth, its 98,000 men, organized in eight divisions, were disgracefully ill-trained and armed. They might have been better equipped had the Americans not been so uneasy about Syngman Rhee. Fears that the increasingly dictatorial southern leader might try to seize the north prompted the Americans to hold back supplies of tanks, guns, and planes which would have made the South Korean army a match for the north. The United States did not want its cranky ally to reunify Korea by force.

The United States faced problems enough already. The Truman administration was preoccupied, primarily, with the preservation of Western Europe. American military resources were already over-extended. Something had to give. A parsimonious Republican Congress was slashing away at the military budget. Defense allocations for fiscal year 1948 were cut to $11.25 billion, one-fourth less than two years before. Manpower was so short that the last elements of the two U.S. divisions charged with supervising the occupation of South Korea had to be pulled back to Japan. A few weeks later, in January of 1950, U.S. Secretary of State Dean Acheson announced, almost unnoticed, that from now on the United States would be holding a Pacific perimeter stretching from the Aleutians through Japan, Okinawa, and the Philippines. South Korea was pointedly excluded. Critics later accused Acheson of signaling world communism that South Korea was there for the taking. The secretary's policy statement was never meant to be taken that way. Even General MacArthur concurred at the time. But it is possible that Acheson's words were snatched up by the Communist leadership as evidence that the U.S. was writing off South Korea. The truth will never be known. The origins of the Korean conflict are more obscure than those of the Punic, Pyrrhic, or Peloponnesian wars—more is known today of the maneuverings that led up to Alexander's invasion of Persia more than two millennia ago.

Communist historians claim, for what it's worth, that early on Sunday morning, June 25, 1950, South Korean troops attacked across the 38th Parallel from positions on the Ongjin peninsula. If that were true, the southerners could not have chosen a more unlikely jumping-off point for a serious offensive. The artificial border created by the Parallel isolated the Ongjin peninsula from the main part of South Korea, leaving the Regimental Combat Team guarding this isolated spot to be supplied solely by sea from Inchon, the port of Seoul. A full-scale offensive would surely have been launched, one would have thought, along the major west-coast land routes leading direct from Seoul to Pyongyang. The kindest interpretation that can be put on this alleged initiative, if indeed it ever occurred, is that the commander in this inaccessible sector suddenly went completely out of his mind. Observers later confirmed that far from being mobilized for invasion, the bulk of the South Korean forces, sensibly grouped north and west of Seoul, were preparing, according to custom, for a boisterous weekend. It was the Pearl Harbor syndrome all over again. Senior officers were junketing round Seoul, as were many of their men and most of the American advisers. A few of these advisers would undoubtedly have known if something furtive was afoot.

But if the Communist version of history were true and South Korean forces did stage some kind of provocation on a remote stretch of the *de facto* frontier, then the army of the Democratic People's Republic of Korea must be credited with mounting the swiftest and most devastating counterattack in history. The South Koreans never knew what hit them. By dawn that fateful Sunday the alleged aggressors, the outlying forces on the Ongjin peninsula, were being overrun. And two columns of North Korean troops supported by tanks were heading southward toward Seoul. The following day Kim Il Sung broadcast an exhortation to his men to "liquidate the unpatriotic fascist puppet regime of Syngman Rhee." The size and speed of the North Korean assault suggest a great deal more than a reflex to unprovoked aggression. Staff planning must have begun at least a year in advance. The buildup of units destined to carry the first thrust over the border could only have started months before the first shots were fired. When the crunch actually came, seven North Korean divisions were ready and raring to go along a 150-mile front across the 38th Parallel, with five more close behind them. North Korean prisoners afterward confirmed the spate of preparatory detail that went into providing the munitions, fuel, and reinforcements needed to maintain the achieved momentum. The one thing nobody ever revealed was what convinced the Communists they could get away with it.

No leader makes war unless he is confident of victory. The immortal Chinese sage Sun Tze, a strategic thinker who lived in the second millennium B.C., about the time of Philip of Macedon, advised warriors to "know the enemy and know yourself; in a hundred battles you will never be in peril." This demands an infallible perception absent, say, from Napoleon's campaign planning before the march on Moscow, the British defense of Yorktown, and the Confederacy's decision to dare military confrontation with the Union. History is littered with inadequate assessments of the opponent's ability to fight.

The Korean conflict was jointly planned, the West originally assumed, by North Korea, China, and the Soviet Union. The Communists were supposed to have met in secret conclave to plan a new probe against the overextended defenses of the capitalist world—anything to hinder consolidation of Western defense schemes in Europe. The Communist victory in China had undeniably altered the political balance in East Asia. A quick, surgical operation in divided Korea, it could be argued, would browbeat emergent Japan into timely neutrality. America would rage impotently from the sidelines. Blame for this monumental miscalculation can more likely be attributed, today, to the North Koreans and their Soviet advisers. It is extremely doubtful whether China was ever directly involved in planning the war. The possibility of conflict in Korea must have been touched on during Mao's lengthy discussions with Stalin in Moscow, but the Chinese were essentially preoccupied, from the autumn of 1949, with their plans to invade Taiwan. Soviet occupation of the northern half of the peninsula also effectively excluded Korea from the Chinese sphere of influence, no matter how temporarily; events there were no longer China's immediate responsibility. The Chinese may have resented the extent of Soviet influence in Korea—as they resented the privileged position the Soviets had awarded themselves in Manchuria—but at this stage they could do nothing about it. China could not stand alone. Even the looting of Manchurian machinery by Soviet occupation forces had to be swallowed without public protest. One wretched Chinese official who complained too vehemently to visiting Westerners about the Soviets was promptly jailed.

There cannot be the slightest doubt, on the other hand, that Stalin was advised of the North Korean invasion plan. No decisions were taken inside the extended Soviet empire without the suspicious septuagenarian's knowledge. But the Soviet dictator was already a sick man. High blood pressure and hardening arteries left him susceptible to strokes. In addition, he was absorbed, throughout this crucial period, with paranoic witch-hunts. The dying Stalin felt beset by scheming heretics. Events in Asia were of minimal interest—far less engrossing than the inquisitions now terrifying his sycophants in the Kremlin and Eastern Europe. The Soviet dictator may thus have been persuaded to accept without scrutiny the overoptimistic assessments of advisers who had convinced themselves that South Korea would be overrun before the Western world realized what was happening.

President Truman confounded the North Koreans by refusing to bow to the inevitable. He rushed, instead, to the support of South Korea. It was as bold and thankless a decision as the atomic bombing of Hiroshima. First he ordered U.S. aircraft based in Japan to blast the invaders, quieting congressional criticism by simultaneously dispatching the Seventh Fleet to protect Taiwan. As soon as it became obvious that air power alone would never halt the North Korean advance, U.S. troops were detached from the depleted and undertrained garrisons in occupied Japan. The man in charge of the Japanese occupation, five-star General Douglas MacArthur, one of the ablest, oddest soldiers the United States has ever produced, was given overall charge of the defense of Korea. A Soviet boycott of the United Nations, in protest against the exclusion of China from the world body, enabled the Americans to pull off a snap vote that condemned North Korean aggression and supported military intervention in South Korea. A motion along these lines would ordinarily have been floored by the Soviet veto; now it gave legitimacy—the UN's blessing—to MacArthur's efforts to hold the south. The Supreme Commander's headquarters immediately became the UN command, with the South Korean army and token contingents from 15 other nations ultimately under its jurisdiction. The blue and white flag of the United Nations, however, became nothing more than the pennant of successive American commanders, each answerable only to the President of the United States. Yet the near-fiction lives on, perpetuated to this day by a multinational UN honor guard which parades periodically in Seoul. Occasionally in its ranks are a handful of Nepalese Gurkhas seconded from the British garrison in Hong Kong.

4

Conference in the Forbidden City / The Chinese Generals Consider Their Options.

Imperial Palace,
Peking,
August 6, 1950

The newish green Chevrolet swung beneath the Pavilion of the Fragrant Concubine and nearly broke its front suspension. Knee-deep potholes pitted the road around the southern lake. Excavation trucks churned up the surfacing as they groaned out of the drained lake bed where thousands of laborers sweated away in the August heat hacking out heaps of weeds and lotuses. Other equally ragged work teams—political prisoners and war criminals as well as ordinary coolies—were replacing the willows cut down during the Japanese war, clearing overgrown flower beds, and reviving neglected buildings. The parkland of Zhong Nan Hai, home of the newly installed Communist leadership, was getting its biggest face-lift since the heyday of the Manchu emperors.

The driver headed toward the Park of Fruitful Bounty, one of the prettier collections of gardens and curly-roofed pavilions in this part of the imperial pleasure ground. The park lies in the northeastern part of the imperial pleasure ground's parkland, snuggled behind

53

high walls along the flank of the Forbidden City. Emperors and courtiers who spun out their daily rituals inside the adjoining palaces slipped gratefully through the boundary wall whenever possible to frolic in this splendid, secret sanctum where generations of artists, architects, and artisans have conjured up a fantastic world of man-made follies. Nearly half this parkland was painfully dug out during the tenth century to create artificial lakes—the middle and southern "seas," as the park's name implies—whose shores were progressively embellished with rare trees, cunningly eroded rocks, and whimsical deceits designed for contemplation or carousing.

It was here in this oasis of indulgence that Mao Zedong and his fellow revolutionaries ended their arduous odyssey. The Forbidden City next door became a public shrine. Visiting peasants and barbarian tourists were trotted round to be indelibly impressed by China's ancient glories. The eastern park was also opened to the public. A patriarchal state provided theaters and children's playgrounds. Only Zhong Nan Hai remained off limits to the outside world, unmentioned as the nerve center of the Communist regime. Every important meeting in the earlier years of the People's Republic was held behind those concealing walls. Many of the top leaders lived there. Only a handful thought it too claustrophobic. Most ambitious apparatchiks who had reached the dizzying apex of Chinese political power found the final accolade in one of those palatial properties fringing the middle lake.

Chairman Mao settled into the eastern courtyard of the Garden of Abundant Benefaction. Somewhere among its red-pillared courtyards and hidden gardens the Manchu emperors had once staged their symbolic spring seed-sowing. The Study of Chrysanthemum Fragrance, where Mao made his home for 17 years, was formerly the imperial library. It suited his scholarly inclinations. The Chairman's green-carpeted bedroom, lined with books, the plain wood couch raised on blocks impregnated to deter the ants, became a place of pilgrimage after his death, opening and closing according to fluctuations of the Maoist faith. Men like Mao saw nothing paradoxical about this choice of residence. Peking was the capital of China. It had been the capital, with few interruptions, since the Mongol emperor Khubilai settled there in the thirteenth century. Occupation of these venerable palaces invariably legitimized power.

Those who failed to establish themselves in Peking never quite achieved national recognition. The Communists' ousted predecessors, the Nationalist Kuomintang, had to make do with Nanking in the sweltering Yangtse valley. But proclamation of the People's Republic from the Tien An Men, the Gate of Heavenly Peace, overlooking what later became a huge square, on October 1, 1949, assured a tradition-conscious nation that a new dynasty had indeed received the mandate of heaven.

The years of neglect during the long war with Japan reduced Zhong Nan Hai to a weed-grown ruin. Wood-carvers, stonemasons, painters, and landscape gardeners were being brought in from all over China for a thorough renovation—and not a moment too soon. Many of the more delicate buildings were close to collapse. The Pavilion of Musical Water needed total reconstruction. It was here that early Manchu emperors sat beneath a waterfall, floating wine cups around the nine loops of a small artificial stream. More work was needed to save the ornately decorated Study of Spring Lotus Roots, built for emperors who shucked off the cares of state by creating esoteric verse. Extensive restoration had already begun on the Precious Moonlight Tower, the place to ponder the fate of the eighth-century poet Li Tai-po, said to have been drowned while drunkenly embracing the moon's watery reflection. Work was also proceeding on the Porch for Awaiting the Moon, the discreet salon where raunchy rulers prepared to embrace their favorite concubines.

A truck leaking liquid mud almost sideswiped the sedan. The army driver swore. He was proud of his big American car. It drove on real gasoline, unlike most vehicles in present-day Peking, which coughed and spluttered around the capital on wood fuel burned from a device protruding over the rear fender. The American car made big face: there wasn't another like it in the capital. The Chevrolet was one of the many costly presents from Uncle Sam abandoned by the Nationalists during the dying stages of the Chinese civil war. It was seized, still crated, on the dockside at Shanghai. The Communist troops turned their prize over to the garrison command, who in turn presented it, like some captured standard, to the military commander in chief in Peking, Zhu De, who accepted the gift gratefully. Transportation was at a premium in People's China.

This sweltering summer afternoon the car was carrying the second most important member of the Chinese military hierarchy, Peng Dehuai, from the airport to Yiniating, the Hall of Longevity, for important talks with the leadership. Ranks were not to be formally established in the People's Liberation Army (PLA) until September 27, 1955, when Peng would be among ten commanders awarded the Soviet-style rank of Marshal. But even in these egalitarian days a man of his position was referred to as "general." For convenience's sake members of his staff were given equivalent ranks. The general's personal aide, Han Liqun, who sat beside him in the car, for instance, was a major. During the civil war against the Nationalists, before Peng Dehuai co-opted him as confidential aide, the 36-year-old agitator from Wuhan had been a junior commissar in the Northern

Army Group fighting backward and forward across Manchuria. As a former history student and party propagandist, he had earned a reputation for exceptional literacy among his unlettered comrades. He had also proved himself in combat. He sat now beside the army driver, preparing notes for the general's diary. Major Han prided himself on being meticulous. Some people said he overdid it. His uniform was always pressed a shade more carefully than most officers thought necessary in this people's army. His speech was sparing, cautious, and considered. Even the general occasionally joshed him for pomposity.

Nobody ever held that against Peng Dehuai. He overreacted, some maintained, but in a very different way. He cursed and swore with all the poetic imagery of rural Hunan. Friends ignored this veneer of rustic crudity. They saw it as a useful form of defense against the man's illiterate peasant origins, invariably adopted in the company of better-educated colleagues. Critics were less kindly. They felt deflated by these Hunanese who took perverse pride in indulging their nationwide reputation as the most garrulous, rebellious, difficult, and obstinate folk in China. The Hunanese even reckoned themselves the best soldiers, though the men from Shandong and Manchuria might sharply disagree. One boast nobody disputed: Hunan was still the mainspring of the Chinese revolution, with men such as Mao Zedong to prove it. Nearly 30 percent of the PLA's generals in 1950 were Hunanese.

General Peng bounced about in the back seat of the Chevrolet clutching a bundle of files. He looked as if he would have been happier riding a horse. He was 52 years old, small, pert, and cocky. After three months of exhaustive personal surveys he was about to tell the men running China that the PLA was in no shape to invade Taiwan. Peng's report was dated July 30, 1950. It was divided into three parts: Part One was a background preamble, virtually the history of the Chinese civil war leading up to the frantic flight of the defeated Nationalists to their island haven; Part Two examined the present situation, including the status of the PLA and (as an addendum) the impact of the recent U.S. decision to shield Taiwan with the Seventh Fleet. The third part of the report contained recommendations for future action. It was drawn up in consultation with General Su Yu, deputy commander of the Third Army and officer in charge of the proposed invasion.

General Su had conferred with Peng at the assault headquarters in Fujian between bouts of amphibious training. Both generals agreed that the leadership should be urgently advised not to press ahead with plans for the liberation of Taiwan. First there was an urgent need to overhaul the armed forces—the top priority—and to provide more escort ships and air cover. Awaiting the requisite better weather conditions would involve a postponement until the spring of 1951. By then, it was expected, the Korean problem would be satisfactorily solved and the U.S. Navy withdrawn from the Taiwan Strait.

General Peng ordered the car to pause a few hundred meters from the meeting place. The conference was scheduled for 1430. They were eight minutes early. The general was not overly keen on punctuality but well knew the value of a neatly timed entrance. The driver pulled into the bedraggled courtyard. Weeds sprouted thigh-high through the broken flagstones. A door banged forlornly in the stifling breeze. Dust clouds blew up from the lake bed. The mercury must have been way up in the mid-nineties Fahrenheit, and the general wiped his face with a damp towel from his briefcase. He removed his floppy peaked cap and mopped his head, which had been shaven completely bald. Comfortable for campaigning, in Major Han's view, but too stark for peacetime. The aide irritably brushed the accumulated dust off his uniform.

"They must have read the report by now," Peng muttered. He sucked slowly on a cigarette, sourly observing the surrounding reconstruction. The major nodded. It was too hot to argue. The report on the status of forces for the invasion of Taiwan had been handed to the commander in chief for distribution to the main policy-making body, the Revolutionary Military Committee, on August 2, 1950. The leadership would never have had time to digest it.

"Two days isn't enough," Peng admitted, as if reading Han's thoughts. But then he had not expected to be summoned so quickly. It was an important report. He expected it to be thoroughly studied and seriously discussed. The talk could go on for weeks.

The Hall of Longevity is one of the more discreet pavilions inside the Park of Fruitful Bounty. It stands close to what had become Mao's residence. Some of the more outstanding Manchu emperors took a personal interest in this corner of Zhong Nan Hai, supervising the planting and pruning of its mulberry bushes. Few of the bushes had survived the war. Scavengers had cut down everything for kindling. Gardeners were back at work these days preparing the ground for spring replanting.

Sentries patrolled the park. Guards were mounted over all occupied pavilions. Entry passes were required for places with the most exotic names: the Porch of Secret Repose, the Studio of Simple Meditation, and the Tower for Listening to the Wild Geese. These buildings had been used mostly as banquet halls in imperial days. Now they played temporary host to top ministerial cadres awaiting the construction of new offices.

The Park of Fruitful Bounty had an unmistakably military air.

Almost everybody there had been directly engaged in the civil war; most of the cadres had only just changed out of uniform. Some, such as Deng Xiaoping, still held nominal army commands. Others would shuttle for years between civil and military careers. It was a closely knit, cellular community strewn with factional mine fields and labyrinthine personal entanglements.

Sentries outside the Hall of Longevity wore white cotton gloves. It was the latest innovation by Zhu De to smarten up the special unit assigned to guard the top leadership. The guard commander, in high-necked jacket and polished holster belt, led Peng and his aide through the outer entrance into a courtyard paved with hexagonal marble slabs. The main hall was in need of paint, though the interior had recently been elaborately redecorated. Carved-panel walls gleamed with fresh varnish. Silver-gray carpeting stretched from wall to wall. Leather-upholstered armchairs, blue enameled spittoons, and low tables with brimming ashtrays filled out the hall, apparently at random; but were gathered toward a circle of a few dozen chairs where the men who now ran China sat in plenary session. Altogether there must have been 30 to 40 people present, Han recalled years later, and they looked as if they had been locked in debate for a very long time.

The Revolutionary Council governing China mustered 56 members. Some of these were cosmetic, non-Communist appointments artfully designed to preserve the illusion of a united front. These pliable outsiders, however, were seldom invited to important policy discussions. Their largely symbolic function (soon to be abolished) was the endorsement of decisions previously taken by the all-powerful inner circle. This latter body would later take formal shape as the Politburo.

Those present at this meeting included most of the top political and military leadership. Presiding over the deliberations was the burly, tousled figure of Mao Zedong. The Chinese leader was at this time 57 years old, popular at home, admired abroad, and standing at what would later be regarded as the high point of his career. The victory over the Nationalists had been swift and unexpected. The Communists had not dared to hope the civil war would end so soon. By the end of 1949 the PLA had been left with little more than mopping up on the mainland—and Mao was visiting Moscow. The trip, the Chairman's longest and most important foray into foreign affairs, lasted nearly three months. The widely publicized outcome was a friendship treaty between China and the Soviet Union (torn up ten years later), a continued Soviet presence in the Chinese region of Manchuria, and a measly $300 million in economic aid to China spread over five years. But there was more to the visit than that. Two great revolutionary despots were briefly able, this one time, to take each other's measure.

Joseph Stalin was launching his last great purges at the very moment Mao Zedong chose to put in an appearance. Heroes who had organized the wartime defense of Leningrad were being secretly liquidated. A trial was under way in Sofia of the latest batch of Eastern European puppet leaders accused of following the nationalistic, independent line of Marshal Tito of Yugoslavia. The arrival of an unrepentant advocate of peasant revolution who had persistently proved Stalin wrong, as far as China was concerned—and an Asian Tito if ever there was one—could not have been more indelicately timed. A firing squad might have been more appropriate than an honor guard.

Mao, for his part, could never forgive Stalin for his meddling with the Chinese Communist cause in the early thirties, his later indifference to the Chinese Party's interests, and his lack of faith in its eventual triumph. He found himself patronized, lectured, and subjected to such hard bargaining that he thought several times of packing up and returning home. The visit proved a success only because Mao deferred to his host. The Chinese leader had no particular regard for the Georgian dictator—he disliked the man no more and no less than he disliked all foreign devils. But he couldn't help admiring Stalin's style. Those qualities of suspicious ruthlessness, xenophobia, and chauvinism were just the ones to awaken egomaniacal echoes in his deferential guest. When Stalin died in 1953, to the relief of a terrorized nation, Mao was one of the few world figures genuinely sorry. For years, Stalin's portrait was displayed in Peking, alongside those of Marx and Engels, to give legitimacy to Chinese communism.

Mao Zedong was throwing a tantrum when Peng Dehuai and his aide entered the Hall of Longevity. He was arguing with General Ye Jianying, the PLA's master strategist. "I say you are wrong!" the Chairman was shouting. He rushed over to the new arrivals, slapping Peng on the shoulder. "Old Peng," he cried. "Tell him he's wrong!"

Peng looked appropriately pensive. He had no idea what the argument was about. On the other hand, face would be lost if he appeared ignorant. He looked inquiringly toward General Ye. The general was the incarnation of a Chinese movie villain, Major Han privately observed, with his brilliantined hair, toothbrush mustache, and gleaming smile. A member of the rootless Hakka tribe, known to their unwelcoming neighbors as "the guest people," he came from the southern province of Guangdong, where, it was said, people ate anything that moved and a lot that didn't and spoke an unintelligible, multitoned dialect. Ye's lovelife was a source of spicy gossip among the straitlaced leadership.

"I say we'll need four months to move a sizable army into Korea," Ye Jianying patiently explained in his dreadful accent. "The Chairman thinks we can do it in three weeks."

"It'll take longer than three weeks," said Peng, plainly taken aback. Still, he was never one to mince words. Mao stamped his foot in annoyance. "What's come over the army?" he demanded. "Are we recruiting tortoises?"

"It's more complicated than in the old days," Peng started to explain.

"More's the pity," snapped Mao. He caught sight of the aide standing at the general's elbow and signaled to him to withdraw. These exchanges were for important ears only. Han joined the guard commander outside for a ritual glass of chrysanthemum tea. He sat patiently waiting for six hours.

The PLA commander in chief, Zhu De, called his generals together the following day. They met, appropriately, in the Hall for Consummation of the Martial Arts. The green-and-ochre-tiled building, with its handsomely gilded red paint-work, stands in a remote corner of Zhong Nan Hai. From its terrace the Ming emperor Zhengde (1506–1521) reviewed his bodyguard's archery practice.

A duststorm blew up as the first staff cars bumped around the middle lake. The few generals who lived nearby, and did not feel it beneath their dignity to walk to the conference, clapped handkerchiefs over mouth and nose as blinding brown clouds billowed in from the northwest. Such storms had grown worse since wartime tree-felling stripped vital windbreaks from the arid Peking plain. At this time of year, unless unseasonal rains intervened, suffocating grit infiltrated closed windows and crept beneath doors and into books, clothes, and even food. It swirled around the sweating staff officers as they set out files, a blackboard, wall maps, and rows of individual tables inside the main body of the hall. Major Han Liqun was among those cursing the climate. He never could get used to this desiccating weather. The humidity in his native Yangtse valley was infinitely preferable.

Zhu De arrived with a bevy of his generals. A hard-looking lot, every one of them a soldier since his teens. The commander in chief, a onetime warlord officer who claimed to have cured himself of opium addiction, smoked a large Western-style tobacco pipe. It was a habit he had picked up while studying in Weimar, Germany, during the twenties. Now aged 64, he outranked his colleagues in age and military experience. Shortly before the conference began he took Peng to one side for a few minutes' earnest conversation. The two men broke off looking thoughtful.

Proceedings opened with a background briefing from General Nie Rongzhen, 51, commander of the North China Field Army and one of the first Chinese Communists to receive military training in Moscow. The son of a well-to-do landowning family in Sichuan, he had been a schoolmate of diminutive Deng Xiaoping. He now held the appointment of acting chief of staff of the PLA. General Nie reminded his listeners that war had broken out in Korea six weeks before when South Korean puppet troops launched an unprovoked attack across the 38th Parallel upon the Democratic People's Republic of Korea. It was a version of events still to be promulgated in China more than 30 years later (though with less conviction). The general told the meeting he was basing his remarks on briefings given to the military attaché at the Chinese embassy in Pyongyang. A Chinese embassy had been established in the North Korean capital only 11 days before, an indication of the amount of Chinese interest (or lack of it) in that Soviet client state. The military attaché, Colonel Xu Lixu, seemed to have established two disturbing facts.

One was that the North Korean "counterattack"—he stuck strictly to the line that the NKPA invasion was a defensive operation—was running into unexpected difficulties. Nearly six weeks had elapsed, General Nie reminded his audience, since fighting first broke out, and although it was unlikely that the Americans could hold out indefinitely in their Pusan bridgehead, the delays were causing concern.

This brought him to Xu's second point. General Nie adjusted his reading glasses, took another file from an aide, and launched into a detailed analysis of North Korean losses. Any figures given were likely to be outdated, the general warned, because communications between advance units in the extreme south and central command headquarters in Seoul were not always reliable. There was no doubt, however, that U.S. air attacks upon the lengthening North Korean supply lines were becoming more damaging daily. The loss of guns, tanks, fuel, ammunition, and food supplies was greater in transit to the front than in combat action. General Nie paused dramatically over the file. The NKPA had suffered 40 percent casualties, he told the assembled generals; that is, more than fifty thousand killed and wounded in their drive on the Naktong River, at the Pusan perimeter. *Fifty thousand*, he emphasized. Although fresh manpower was being mobilized, this attrition rate could not be sustained for long. The hall buzzed with worried comment. Forty percent casualties? Anything above 30 percent was judged likely, in the PLA, to bring units close to disintegration.

What was China supposed to do about it? The questioner was General Su Yu, commander-designate of the proposed Taiwan invasion force, who had been flown to Peking for the meeting. The reply came from Zhu De.

"The Revolutionary Committee has spent a great deal of time discussing the possibility—and I emphasize the tentative nature of our talks. The Committee feels, after giving the matter lengthy consideration, that we should urgently prepare contingency plans to back up the [North] Korean People's Army if the situation on the Korean battlefront deteriorates. There seems little likelihood of this happening, but I need not remind you of the need for planning for any and every contingency."

There was a lengthy silence. Long afterward, Major Han remembered the growing tension as each general adjusted to the implications. Chinese intervention in Korea meant fighting the Americans. Would the Americans take counteraction against China? One of the toughest-looking men in the hall lumbered to his feet. It was He Long, onetime bandit, at 46 the most experienced guerrilla fighter in the PLA. There was a puzzled frown on his great moon face. "Is there any chance," he asked, "of the Americans using the atomic bomb?"

"They might use it," said General Nie. "But remember that the United States no longer enjoys an atomic monopoly. The Soviet Union completed its first test explosion less than a year ago, much to the Americans' surprise; they hadn't believed the Russians were capable of producing a bomb before 1952. So they may be less eager to use it nowadays."

He Long wasn't satisfied. He wanted to know where the Russians stood. The Democratic People's Republic of Korea was a Soviet responsibility, as he understood it. Why should China become involved?

Zhu De replied with a popular saying. "When the lips are destroyed," he said, "the teeth feel cold."

Everyone laughed. The classic Chinese saying dates back to the Warring States period (475–221 B.C.), when Duke Hsien of Chin picked off the neighboring states of Yu and Kuo. The successful Chin assault on the state of Yu ("the lips") left the state of Kuo ("the teeth") defenseless.

"Are we to cover our ears while stealing the bell?" Nie Rongzhen threw in. This classical quip refers to the looter during the Spring and Autumn period of Chinese history (770–476 B.C.) who thought he could make off unchallenged with a tolling temple bell if he put his fingers in his ears.

"The fact has to be faced that a threat is developing in northeast Asia which China, new China, cannot ignore," General Nie declared.

"Remember, the Chairman said: 'China has stood up.' Well, I ask you, are we to take this threat sitting down?"

"What threat? How serious is it?" asked Su Yu. "The only information is that the [North] Koreans are falling behind schedule."

The danger was that, given time, the Americans would reinforce the Pusan perimeter strongly enough to hang on, the general patiently explained; if that happened it would only be a matter of weeks before they were strong enough to launch a counterattack. "It should be evident," said General Nie, whipping off his spectacles, "that the imperialists and their puppets must be driven into the sea before the [North] Korean People's Army finds itself involved in a prolonged attritional struggle."

An aide handed him a newly arrived signal. The latest news, the general announced, was that the North Koreans had, two nights previously, planned a decisive attack. The information came from the Chinese liaison officer with the North Korean Front Headquarters, the assistant military attaché in Pyongyang. "A certain Colonel Wong, who used to be with the 38th Field Army," Nie remarked. "The attaché, Colonel Xu, speaks of him highly." Several senior members of the audience nodded their agreement. Well, Colonel Wong had just signaled that a divisional attack was being mounted on the night of August 5–6 against the southwestern rim of the Naktong River perimeter. It was confidently expected to produce the required breakthrough. Monitored Tokyo broadcasts reported that the enemy was already blowing up bridges across the Naktong.

There was a general murmur of relief. Major Han felt sure that if a poll were taken at this stage of the proceedings, most commanders would reject involvement in Korea. They would unanimously prefer to continue operations against Taiwan. At least they'd be risking their lives to liberate Chinese soil. Korea was in an entirely different league.

General Ye Jianying seemed eager to have his say. He wanted to relate all this talk about Korea to Peng Dehuai's report on the status of their own People's Liberation Army. This report declared unequivocally that the PLA was in no fit state to take Taiwan. Most interesting. The general spoke slowly and deliberately. There could have been a trace of sarcasm in his voice. But if the PLA were that weak, as General Peng asserted—and at this point Ye rose to his feet—how could it face up to the Americans in Korea? Was Peng suggesting, for instance, that the PLA was inferior to the NKPA? Ye looked around him for support; he had a reputation for stirring things up with his double-edged questions. Others attributed his abrasiveness to an incisive mind.

General Peng leaped to his feet grasping the report, and a trickle of the outdoors dust poured from the file onto He Long's head. "If

Old Ye wants the truth, then the PLA does *not* compare with the [North] Korean People's Army," Peng declared in his usual forthright manner. "Certainly not in terms of organization and equipment. Theirs is a new army, recently created and equipped by our Soviet comrades. It is naturally a more modern army. The PLA has never been the beneficiary of Soviet generosity. The PLA today is equipped with little more than the loot it has managed to pick up over the past five years. But what comparisons does General Ye wish to make? The entire [North] Korean People's Army is no larger than one of our field armies. The PLA's chief strength lies in its size; that is also its weakness."

"I repeat my question," Ye persisted. "In view of the weaknesses General Peng claims to have uncovered, how can the PLA possibly oppose the Americans in Korea?"

Zhu De intervened. The commander in chief made it clear he wanted no one scoring debating points. This morning they were dealing with practicalities.

Peng was not trying to be evasive. But he welcomed the opportunity to coax the assembled brass into debating his report. It contained recommendations very dear to his heart. Chief of these was thorough modernization of the Chinese armed forces. No one present would deny, he said, that an overhaul was urgently required. Ye looked disapproving but kept silent.

"The PLA is ready to attack a tiger with bare hands, to cross a river without a boat." Peng used the classic cautions against rash action. "But our commanders would be still more foolish," he went on, "if they ignored the facts." He dug deeper into the file with Major Han's assistance.

The facts were, he claimed, that on July 15, 1950, PLA strength totaled 5,138,756. Of these, fewer than half could be considered combat-effective. Main force units in the four field armies were at full strength but their quality varied considerably. General He Long's First Army, concentrated mostly in northwestern China, consisted of 34 field armies. (Each Chinese field army was 10,000 to 11,000 strong.) Second Army, with 49 field armies, was poised for the invasion of Tibet. General Chen Yi's Third Army, faced with the task of liberating Taiwan, totaled 72 field armies. The formidable Fourth Army, commanded by the ailing Lin Biao, with 59 field armies, was stationed partly in southern China, partly in the region of Manchuria. Then there was the North China Army, long associated with General Nie Rongzhen, and its 39 field armies. Local defense units and construction corps accounted for another 2.6 million men.

"All together, we have a fat man," Peng declared, "in urgent need of a diet." How did the PLA get into such unhealthy shape? The general referred to recent history. He scarcely needed to remind his audience that victory in the civil war had come faster and more easily than anyone had dared expect. But in their haste to win, the Chinese Communists had recruited anyone willing to bear arms, without paying attention to ideological commitment or professional aptitude. As a result, experienced junior officers and NCOs were in desperately short supply, and the ranks were fleshed out with incompetents.

The collapse of the Nationalist armies came so suddenly that the PLA had picked up 2.25 million prisoners in the last two years of the civil war alone. The surrendered soldiery could not be left to starve, nor could they be allowed to roam free, fomenting trouble; they had to be temporarily absorbed into the PLA forces in some capacity or other. Entire regiments were even now being settled on the land in distant frontier areas such as the northwestern province of Xinjiang, while others had been drafted into railroad and highway construction. A select number of specialists were being given the opportunity to join branches of the service where expertise was in short supply. The overall situation, said General Peng, was far from satisfactory. Mao Zedong had made it clear two months ago in a report to the Revolutionary Council that a reduction in PLA strength was essential. The Chairman specified, of course, that sufficient troops would have to be retained to carry out their national obligations in Tibet and Taiwan, as well as to maintain order throughout the motherland.

"It was partly as a result of this speech that I hurriedly completed the survey you see before you," Peng declared. "I believe there are sound professional reasons for inaugurating a carefully planned demobilization program. There are sound political reasons. There are also economic reasons. You will have seen the speech by Finance Minister Bo Ibo demanding a reduction in military expenditure."

Finance Minister Bo had already warned against trying to wring any more money out of the peasantry. Farm taxes already consumed 21 percent of income in some areas. The Communists would shortly be accused of growing greedier than the banished warlords.

"I'm no financial expert," said Peng. That raised another laugh. Legend had it, quite incorrectly, that he couldn't count beyond his fingers and toes. "But the finance minister claims we are not getting value from the PLA, man for man."

There were a few angry mutterings from the assembled brass. Military men the world over oppose the depredations of civilian cost accountants.

"Sounds like we are dealing in sacks of rice," grumbled He Long.

"The revolution paid up and liked it, as long as we were conquering China," shouted Ye Jianying.

"I am merely suggesting there is room for increased economy, to say nothing of increased efficiency," Peng answered mildly. Major Han held his breath. At any moment Peng's famous temper could burst upon the conference. "I am putting forward the proposition that the PLA is oversized, overpriced, and underequipped."

Everyone looked thoughtful. The equipment problem was well-known. There was no apparent shortage of hardware. The PLA had captured two million rifles, a quarter of a million machine guns, nearly 55,000 artillery pieces, 622 tanks, 561 armored cars, 134 aircraft, and 122 naval vessels from the Nationalists in the last four years of the civil war. They had also picked up useful amounts of materiel from the surrendered Japanese.

But the figures were misleading. Much of this equipment, Peng pointed out, was junk. The bulk of it was worn-out or stalled for lack of spare parts. Technicians were cannibalizing trucks and radios merely to keep services at their present inadequate levels. Military transportation did not even exist in the modern meaning of the term. Logistics, communications, electronics, and medical services were extremely primitive. Ammunition supplies were dangerously low because aging reserve stocks were deteriorating more rapidly than China's few arsenals could replenish them. Machine tools had been ordered from the U.S.S.R. to begin production of Soviet-model small arms. The most limited production could not be expected for two or three years. A nation's armaments industry was only as strong as the general level of development. The manufacture of heavy artillery, for instance, would have to wait until China manufactured enough steel.

"So you agree we are in no fit state to confront the Americans?" Ye Jianying was not going to give up easily.

"This report was not drawn up with the Americans in mind," Peng replied. "The report was not even intended to offer a direct evaluation of the Taiwan operation, although in view of the existing need for modernization of the PLA, I would personally recommend a postponement of the invasion until next spring. There is, of course, an entirely new factor. I am referring to the presence of the Americans' Seventh Fleet in the Taiwan Strait. But even if these intruders were not there, the season has clearly passed this year when we can mount what Su Yu himself has called 'the biggest military operation in modern Chinese history.'"

Su Yu, the deputy commander of Third Army, nodded his agreement from the audience.

"This report was drawn up," Peng continued "to produce a series of recommendations, contained in Section Three. These can best be summarized as a reduction in the PLA to rather more than half its present strength, reorganization of a professional army on Soviet lines, and re-equipment with Soviet weaponry."

Some generals shook their heads. Major Han felt many of them feared for their jobs if such severe cuts were introduced. There seemed to be plenty who disagreed with Peng's proposals.

"Who's going to pay for all this?" asked Third Army Commander Chen Yi. The future foreign minister of China had taken a keen interest in the discussion. "I thought we were trying to achieve economies."

"Demobilization will lead to considerable short-term savings," said Peng, "especially if demobilized troops are directed into reconstruction work. Reorganization and re-equipment must in my opinion be spread over a ten-year period in parallel with plans for national economic development. At this point I would urge you to give closer study to my recommendations."

"All this becomes academic if we get involved in a war with the Americans," complained General Ye. "If a serious threat develops in Korea affecting the security of the motherland, we will be mobilizing, not demobilizing. Since we have all been called upon to consider such a threat, I must again ask Peng Dehuai whether he feels the PLA is capable of meeting it?"

"The answer is yes," Peng replied. "But I would advise against over-hasty action."

"Tell that to Mao," said Ye, breaking into a smile.

"That's exactly what I have done," said Peng.

"And may the dice roll right side up," said Ye, now openly laughing. They all knew what it was like to give the Chairman advice he didn't want to take.

Peng admitted he had urged the Chairman to review the entire range of the PLA's military responsibilities. Their plans for Tibet were still pending; so, of course, was Taiwan. The civil war had officially ended, but widespread banditry persisted in areas of southern China. Some half a million former Nationalist soldiers still held out, as the Communists had once done, in remote mountainous areas of Hunan, Guangdong, Yunnan, and Sichuan. Two hundred thousand PLA troops were tied up in Hunan alone, mainly in the western part of the province, where resistance was proving exceptionally tiresome.

Secret societies dedicated to the overthrow of the state were also staging a comeback. Many of these societies were strongly anti-Communist. Their hit men had regularly been used by the Nationalists in days gone by to liquidate Communists and other potential opponents. The Elder Brothers' Society, for instance, had made a remarkable revival in Sichuan, countered with widespread arrests and executions. Lodges of the 14K Society were also reviving in the southern provinces.

"There are in addition economic questions that require examination by people who specialize in this sort of thing," said Peng. "Taken together, my reaction is cautious. Yes, we can take on the Americans in Korea—and will do, if necessary—but with full recognition of our limitations."

He called over two staff officers carrying a large board between them. It bore a relief map of the Korean peninsula. Major Han stopped his note-taking to watch the reaction. The Martial Arts Hall filled with creaks and shufflings as everyone eased forward in his seat.

"The enemy is bottled up at this moment in the extreme southeast of the puppet state," the general said, pointing to the South Korean port of Pusan. "There is every indication that this bridgehead will be eliminated within the next two weeks. If it is not"—he looked grimly around him—"then the possibility of protracted war in Korea cannot be ruled out. Look carefully at the geography. The Korean peninsula. Long and narrow. Remember the enemy. MacArthur the—what's the word?—the 'island-hopper.' The Korean peninsula lends itself to amphibious operations, though this will require a lot of daring. Our Korean comrades discount the possibility, but remember, whoever makes the first move, wins.

"Remember also that a long and narrow landmass imposes its peculiar limitations on our field armies. In past campaigns we have habitually traded space for time when confronting a better-equipped opponent. Korea has no such space. It could turn out to be a straitjacket. A peninsula presents unusual supply difficulties. This occurred to me when I reviewed the American situation in Pusan. The Americans' problems are considerably eased because distances within the Pusan perimeter are short. Although it is true that the enemy is forced to transport men and materiel great distances by sea, those supply lines are inviolate. They cannot be cut.

"Our Korean comrades, on the other hand, are operating a long way from their supply bases. This is becoming a dreadful disadvantage. American air attacks on those supply lines are causing serious losses. The basic problem of Korea, for either side, is that the farther you advance the slimmer your supplies are likely to become."

General Peng had reached his summing up.

"China will become involved in hostilities in Korea only if the integrity of their Democratic People's Republic is directly threatened. There is no likelihood of any such disaster at present.

"Still, it is our business to cover every contingency, so let us assume that some incredible turn of fortune enables the American imperialists to launch a full-scale invasion north of the 38th Parallel.

"The Chinese response, in my opinion, should be on a limited scale, sufficient to warn the aggressors," Peng Dehuai concluded. "If that fails, we should attack with the full weight of the People's Liberation Army."

5

A Friendly Evening of Drinking With Our Soviet Comrades / General Peng Fights a Cloud / "Only Volunteers."

Shenyang, Manchuria,
People's Republic of China,
Early September, 1950

Major Han and the staff were still hunting spiders. For the past three days they had combed the musty old bomb shelters, dilapidated offices, and barracks of the Shenyang arsenal, the big square hall earmarked for the new operations center. General Peng Dehuai was a peasant born and bred, tough and courageous to a fault, but he could not abide spiders. Nobody knew why. The head of medical services, an elderly American-trained Shanghainese, kept mumbling something about fears deep in their commander's pysche dating possibly back to early childhood, until one of the commissars curtly cut him off. The comrade doctor should be on his guard, the political officer advised, against theories that might be interpreted as "metaphysical bourgeois speculation." Marxists could never swallow that Freudian nonsense. The subject was dropped.

The spider search pressed on, uncovering a revolting assortment of rodents, cockroaches, and such scavengers. Ant beds in the strangest places. Whole ceilings spun full of spiderwebs. Plenty of spiders, too. Along with the bugs, the pest teams unearthed a few forgotten relics of recent history. As General Peng's aide, Major Han had been sent ahead to Shenyang, a 700-kilometer overnight train trip, to help organize things while Peng stayed in Peking, locked in interminable conferences. The major watched with some amusement as work details emerged with rusty Japanese bayonets, stacks of empty ammunition- and ration-boxes, and pocketsful of worthless bank notes depicting the weak, bespectacled face of the traitor Pu Yi, who languished nearby in Fushun jail. This last emperor of China, installed in the early thirties as puppet emperor of Manchuquo (the state carved out of Manchuria by the Japanese), had been abandoned by his sponsors in 1945 during their pell-mell flight from the advancing Soviets.

The remainder of the debris unearthed by the spider-hunt dated only as recently as the Soviet occupation. Empty vodka bottles, worn-out boots, and piles of empty pistol-shells lay strewn around the cellars. Someone jokingly remarked that the liberators must have been playing Russian roulette. Nobody laughed. It was no secret that somewhere around these buildings the Soviet military command had liquidated numerous Chinese war criminals and collaborators. Enlisted men swore the place was haunted.

The staff would have preferred a less depressing location. The arsenal smelled too much of a past everyone was anxious to forget. The Fourth Army headquarters, half a day's drive away in Changchun, was considered much more salubrious. But this rambling old citadel, with its high protective walls and weed-grown moat, was still the best communications center in northeastern China. It had served the Japanese as their northern command headquarters throughout the long years of their aggression. The Soviets had found it equally convenient. They made it their headquarters shortly after seizing the city during their entry into World War II. The building was handed back, gutted, in 1948, when Soviet military occupation of northeastern China officially ended, though several key bases remained in Soviet hands. The last Soviet forces were not to be withdrawn until 1953, as a goodwill gesture by Nikita Khrushchev following Stalin's death.

The Shenyang arsenal had seen better days. Founded by imperial fiat, expanded by warlords, transformed by the Japanese, and looted by the Soviets, the great crumbling complex no longer controlled the operations of vast armies. Nor were its factories spewing out arms, ammunition, and military hardware. Acres of workshops lay stripped of essential equipment. The sophisticated jigs, lathes, and machine tools installed by the Japanese to produce their light artillery, tanks, and aircraft had been carted away in 1945 after the lightning *blitzkrieg* belatedly launched by Stalin in the dying days of the Pacific war.

A monument to the trifling Soviet losses in that conflict dominated the square across from Shenyang's city hall. Anyone seeing such a gross, tasteless assemblage of granite would have been forgiven for thinking that the Soviet invasion of Manchuria had been a hard-fought, heroic conquest instead of a last-minute sledgehammer assault upon a wilting foe. More Russians were killed by drunken driving, Manchurians told each other, than in combat with the demoralized Japanese.

Yet solemn ceremonies were re-enacted every August at the statuary to commemorate the two-week walkover. Soviet and Chinese soldiers goose-stepped around the square, and there were wreaths and promises of undying friendship. The citizens of the old Manchurian capital, those at least who had any say in the matter, kept quietly in the background. They had precious little to celebrate. Manchurians would never forget the sack of Shenyang. The Soviets had treated their city—indeed, the entire region of Manchuria—as little better than enemy territory. The so-called liberators stripped dozens of textile mills, steel plants, and stores in the half dozen main industrial centers founded and developed by the Japanese. Many citizens believed the Soviet barbarians had been seriously intent on destroying China's hopes of economic reconstruction. But it was no longer politic to say so publicly since the Chinese Communists came to power.

The last visible reminders of the postwar Soviet presence had dwindled these days to those Russian bureaucrats who shared operational control of the Manchurian railroad network, a Red Army liaison team, some 20 strong, and occasional parties of sightseeing soldiers and sailors from the scattering of Soviet bases still in Manchuria. The sailors came from Lüta, the most important naval base in northern China, and from Port Arthur, both of which had been seized by Stalin (along with the railroad) as part of his price for entering the war against Japan.

Four days after the arrival of the Chinese headquarters staff at Shenyang, the acting head of the Soviet military liaison team, Colonel Andrei Chichirin, paid a courtesy call. The Russians must have been wondering what was going on. Most people had assumed since the end of the civil war that the arsenal would never again become a military headquarters. The PLA Fourth Army, which garrisoned Manchuria, had maintained its command post in the more provincial surroundings of Changchun. The acting chief of staff, Lieutenant General Xie Fang, on detachment from Changchun, played polite host to the Soviet colonel in one of the dirty, half-furnished offices fronting the main gate of the arsenal. The general spoke fluent Russian, Japanese, and English, and during the thirties had trained, along with his superior, Lin Biao, in the Soviet Union.

Despite these ties, however, General Xie felt no compunction to reveal anything to Chichirin. The PLA's plans lay shrouded in their accustomed secrecy. Painters and carpenters were shooed outside while the general wasted an hour and endless cups of jasmine tea fending off the foreigner's questions. The meeting broke up amid mutual, meaningless protestations of undying friendship.

The phone rang that same evening in the guardroom. Would Major Han take a call? The man on the other end of the line spoke commendably good Chinese. He identified himself as Bolganoff, *Captain* Bolganoff, chief interpreter of the Red Army liaison team in Mukden—in Shenyang, he corrected himself—using the modern Chinese name for the Manchurian capital. Renaming the city supposedly erased bitter memories of dynastic domination. *Captain* Sergei Bolganoff was eager to know whether the major and some of his colleagues would care to drop over for drinks the following evening with the Soviet liaison mission? Nothing special, just a lighthearted get-together. Han Liqun was noncommittal. The staff was genuinely busy. He would check into the situation and advise. General Peng had not yet arrived, so the aide sought permission from Xie Fang.

Xie was in his shirtsleeves, playing cards in an undecorated barrack room. He peered shortsightedly at Han, his eyes watering slightly from the tobacco smoke. No harm in maintaining friendly relations, the general agreed; he personally liked the Russians. Both sides might soon need to get a lot friendlier. But watch it: even if the leadership was keeping Moscow informed of developments (and that he did not doubt for a minute), no one here had permission to breach security. And the Russians drank like camels, he warned.

The general lowered his voice confidentially. Better go along with Lo, that major on the signals staff who spoke Russian, though he should certainly not reveal that fact. And take Captain Tang, the number-three political officer. The man had the constitution of a buffalo. He could be expected to keep an eye on things.

The following evening the three Chinese officers strolled down to the old Pullman Hotel, where most of the Russians were quartered. It was a short, debilitating walk in the end-of-summer heat. Thunder clouds sealed the city beneath a stifling blanket. Everybody was sweating: the men in their ragged dirty singlets propelling their rickshaws, the gangs of coolies glistening under bamboo shoulder poles, the sidewalk food vendors, the astrologers, the conjurers, and the mobs of assorted hawkers . . . All seemed eager to break off whatever they were doing and dash for the nearest bathhouse.

The arsenal rose from this human sea, an antique dreadnought stranded by some forgotten mutiny. Its forbidding bulk brooded over the dark of downtown Shenyang, its watchtowers and wire-topped walls grimly defiant of inquiry. The only sign of activity, Han noted approvingly, was that of a signals squad untangling ropes of telephone wire which meandered through the entrance gate and out across the city.

The hotel inside, by contrast, was ablaze with light, athunder with activity. A Soviet cultural troupe had stopped by on the way to entertain the sailors at Port Arthur and Lüta; the building shook with Russian songs and shouts, and the crash of dancing boots. From upstairs came the sound of breaking glass.

"It isn't usually like this," apologized the slim blonde man who met them in the foyer. Captain Bolganoff obviously knew enough about the Chinese to look faintly sheepish. He had some understanding of the puritanical behavior of PLA officers (and enlisted men). Drinking was not frowned upon in the PLA—far from it—but raucous behavior was too reminiscent of the outrageous way soldiers behaved during the warlord era. "Better use good iron for nails, than turn a son into a soldier." The old saying summed up traditional Chinese contempt for the military profession.

The Soviet captain ushered the three into a reading room out back of the hotel, where the noise was immediately and mercifully muffled. Colonel Andrei Chichirin and two other members of the liaison team rose from a cluster of tattered armchairs. They led their guests straight to a buffet table spread with bread, cake, caviar, sprats, and smoked salmon.

Chichirin, a small, hatchet-faced man, apologized for his sparse knowledge of Chinese. The previous day he had arrived at the Chinese headquarters in a superbly pressed dress uniform literally clanking with medals; but tonight he wore a plain brown combat smock without decorations or epaulets. His companions were similarly attired. It looked like an informal evening. The time was not too distant, Colonel Chichirin declared in a wordy address of welcome, when the Red Army liaison team would have the pleasure of entertaining the great General Peng Dehuai. Their own commander, Colonel-General Antonov, would be back by then from Moscow. He paused to allow Bolganoff to catch up with his translation.

Major Han nodded noncommittally. As far as he knew, Peng's

arrival was still a state secret. Had the Russians been officially informed or were they bluffing? The major replied in suitably flowery language that they looked forward to a great deal of convivial entertainment with their ever-welcome comrades from the Red Army. He tried not to choke as he gagged down the first mouthful of salty salmon and vodka.

The news from Korea was discouraging, Colonel Chichirin rambled on, though no doubt the PLA knew more about it than he did. The new group in the arsenal would naturally be keeping an eye on the situation. The Chinese looked vague. It was a big step, the Soviet colonel persisted, establishing an entirely new command group. What was wrong with Fourth Army HQ in Changchun? Perhaps with Lin Biao sick . . . ?

Captain Tang, the Chinese political officer, said: "I think we're in for a storm." Lightning was flickering through the stained-glass windows of the reading room. Bolganoff translated dutifully. Major Han felt sure that the interpreter knew such clumsy questioning would get them nowhere. The Soviet captain raised his vodka glass.

"To peace and friendship," he announced in Chinese.

"*Mir druzhba*," replied Han, using the only Russian words he knew.

"You speak Russian?" enquired the colonel in faultless Chinese.

"Only a word or two," said Han. "You people appear to be the better linguists."

That seemed to strike the Russians as funny. Major Han could not for the life of him see why. Their hosts began a round of toasts he knew he could never match. Nor could signals officer Lo. But Tang the commissar refused to be outfaced. He apologized to the colonel for his comrades' weak constitutions—"uncured wartime ulcers," he blandly lied—and offered to drink on their behalf. After an hour of munching and gulping he had downed a bottle and a half of vodka without any apparent effect.

Burly old Tang had always been considered one of the more unsociable members of the staff—something of a loner. From this evening on, Major Han would regard him with a new respect. Brusquely ignoring his hosts' questions, Commissar Tang proceeded to drink them to a standstill. One of the Russians passed out on the sofa. Colonel Chichirin turned distinctly pale. And Captain Sergei Bolganoff had to cry off. One more toast, he groaned, and his translation would disintegrate.

"This new headquarters," mumbled the captain. His impeccable Chinese was becoming incomprehensible. "General Peng . . . old friend . . . Korea . . ."

"Time to go," Tang declared. If his speech was the slightest bit impaired his Sichuanese accent concealed it. "Many thanks. Must reciprocate. Good night." The commissar strode smartly out, followed by his queasy colleagues. Back inside the arsenal he fell flat on his face and had to be helped to bed.

Peng Dehuai arrived two days later. He traveled overnight aboard the old Manchurian Express from Peking. Acting Chief of Staff Xie waited at the station, heading a deliberately unobtrusive reception party. The soldiers slipped out through a side door and drove straight to the arsenal. Orders were to keep their activities as low-key as possible. Major Han deposited the general's luggage in his sanitized, bug-free bedroom. A pump-handled insect spray stood on the bedside table. The mosquito net hung tentlike from a ceiling hook just clear of the wheezing wooden paddles of the overhead fan. He flipped the wall calendar over the washstand to the right date: September 4, 1950.

An orderly unstrapped two battered suitcases. Their contents were threadbare and unremarkable, except for a much-thumbed picture book of Chinese butterflies. How could anyone who lived in fear of spiders feel an urge to study butterflies? Maybe the general just liked to look at the pictures. Private jokes circulated among the younger and cheekier officers about their commander's undisguised lack of education.

Things had moved fast since the early meetings in Zhong Nan Hai, though Major Han knew few of the details. All he had been told after three weeks of top-level military meetings was that contingency plans were in preparation for "anything that might happen in Korea." This included, in the last resort, intervention, which meant that a mountain of momentous planning would have to be moved with unaccustomed speed. The gravest problem was the PLA's lack of mobility. The army might be big, but it defied high-speed redeployment. Highways did not even exist. Main roads running northward from Peking were narrow and unsurfaced. Few trucks could be spared to carry riflemen. The already inadequate rail network was still undergoing postwar renovation and repairs. All major routes were single-tracked, which severely limited traffic loads. So the Chinese depended, like the infantrymen of World War I, on over-crowded trains—and their feet.

Staff work was woefully deficient. Chinese commanders had scant experience in handling large armies. The average number of men deployed by any one general at the height of the war against the Nationalists had never exceeded forty thousand. Lack of communi-cations and logistics imposed their own peculiar constraints.

But it was no use trying to explain this to Mao. The Chairman waved his generals' arguments aside irritably. Administrative detail profoundly bored him. "Quibbling," he called it.

Mao Zedong demanded action. The virulent American response to the outbreak of war in Korea aroused gloomy forebodings in Peking. Well before the North Korean advance stalled outside Pusan the Chairman had switched his attention from the problems of Taiwan to the mechanics of Chinese intervention in Korea. Nothing had happened since to ease his fears. More than a month's heavy fighting had failed to produce a breakthrough; the once-invincible army of the DPRK was slowly bleeding to death and there were rumors of a projected American counterattack. Ripples of alarm were spreading all over Peking—and Moscow.

General Peng called an evening staff conference. He appeared, bathed and shaved, his bullet head clipped to baldness, a bulging dispatch case tucked beneath one arm. Major Han knew it contained Peking's operational orders. The details would remain undisclosed until the general received clearance to reveal them; the leadership could never be cured of its obsession with secrecy. The staff stood respectfully to attention while Peng inspected the main operations room. A select handful of staff officers from Fourth Army, together with squads of signalers, pioneers, and construction troops, had been busy restoring this eastern wing of the elderly arsenal. The great square hall was now papered with maps rich in military information. A giant relief model of the area filled the center of the room. The undulating, painted plaster stretched from a simulated Shenyang to the Yalu River border and beyond. In the farthest corner of the model, beyond a succession of pointed peaks, stood Seoul, the captured puppet capital, a few kilometers below the former frontier on the 38th Parallel. It was from Seoul that the Korean Communist leader, Premier Kim Il Sung, planned to rule his united country.

The general made a few minutes' meticulous reconnaissance and grunted with approval. He wiped a clean white handkerchief across the polished stone floor. The handkerchief stayed white. "Not bad," said Peng. Praise indeed from such an unusually demanding man. The chief intelligence officer, a southerner called Zhoi, one of the handful of specialists posted directly from Peking, saluted appreciatively. Most of this work was his. No one mentioned spiders.

The general fished a sheaf of papers from his dispatch case and adjusted his reading glasses.

"The situation in Korea is serious," he began. "The war has entered a new phase. We must expect a prolonged campaign." The staff nodded dutifully. There was nothing new in this. The Chinese press had been saying little else for the past week. "A detailed and careful assessment of the situation has been made in Peking," he went on. "It is the leadership's considered view that things may get a good deal worse. The democratic [North Korean] forces have been gravely weakened. Their ability to conduct the kind of prolonged campaign we anticipate is daily becoming more doubtful." He looked around, as if seeking confirmation. "This is not meant to suggest in any way that our [North] Korean comrades have done anything less than their best. Reports we are receiving confirm that they have performed prodigies of valor." A murmur of agreement came from the staff.

The general's spectacles were steaming up. He wiped them, slowly and deliberately, with the same white pocket handkerchief. "You have no doubt heard that the imperialists are planning a counter-attack," he continued. The staff nodded. Endless rumors were circulating.

"The attack could come from within the Pusan perimeter"—he gestured far out across the plaster model—"or it could come elsewhere, from the sea." His stubby fingers circled the Korean coast. "Put yourselves in the position of the man who is conducting the enemy campaign, the American general, MacArthur." Somebody sniggered derisively. The general shot the sniggerer an angry glance. "Do not underestimate the enemy. Do not underestimate this MacArthur. Examine his career. The Pacific war. Amphibious landings. A different range of experience from Eisenhower, Bradley, Patton, and, I might add, the Soviet marshals as well. At the height of the war in the Pacific, MacArthur boasted one winning tactic. Using his amphibious mobility, MacArthur evolved a most successful means of assault by hitting the enemy where he least expected it. Has anyone given any thought to that?"

"The southwestern coast of Korea?" ventured the intelligence officer in his droll southern drawl. "Somewhere behind the forces besieging Pusan? Someplace where the Americans could cut the Korean supply lines?"

"Possibly," said General Peng. "I wouldn't dare to guess."

"Is there anything we can do about it?" asked General Xie, the acting chief of staff.

Peng shrugged. "Nothing," he murmured. "Not right now. We are not yet involved. But we must prepare for that contingency. My instructions are to intervene if the Americans cross into the Democratic People's Republic [of Korea]."

"No danger of that right now," said Xie. "Not with the Americans tied down in Pusan."

"Not if they stay tied down," Peng replied. "But will they? The indications are that the Americans intend to take the initiative. Given their control of the sea and of the air, you can see what a wide variety of opportunities they have. Of course, we must continue to hope for the best. But our job right here is to prepare for the worst."

The next few days were among the busiest of Han's life. The staff worked as if sleep had been abolished. It was, indeed, impractical. A man could scarcely doze in the banging and yelling bedlam pervading this corner of the arsenal. Signalers loaded with telephones and teleprinters collided, cursing, with carpenters, painters, and electricians. Plumbers on tall ladders fed long iron flues from the heating stoves through gaps in the double-glazed windows. Winter, they warned, was not so far away.

Staff officers still strolled in from Fourth Army headquarters. Most of them were Manchurians, delighted to escape the tedium of Changchun. Their own headquarters, supposedly controlling military operations throughout the region, was being blatantly cannibalized to re-equip this strange new super-HQ in Shenyang. The group being assembled with such unseemly haste had yet to be given an official title. Personnel posted from Changchun carried orders to report to "National Defense Headquarters." Defense against what?, the newcomers demanded. They would learn in good time, Major Han advised. Right at this moment the PLA was forming a new supreme command to meet any possible emergency.

Emergency? So the rumors were true? "Korea, eh?" quizzed the curious ones, with winks and nods. Older men kept their counsel. The major could only look expressionless. He had no idea what they were going to do. Nobody knew, not even General Peng. What they *might* do depended on developments outside their control. The spectrum of possibility was still being debated within the closely guarded confines of the operations room, or late at night, in endless sessions involving General Xie, a host of lesser generals Han had never seen, and unending streams of visitors from Peking. Yet without a burgeoning threat, with nothing to work from beyond scores of theoretical options, it was impossible to do much more than proliferate contingency plans.

"I'm fighting a cloud." Peng Dehuai groped for metaphors. "This is more futile than writing on water."

One piece of heartening news: troop movements were ahead of schedule. The redeployment of army units around China, in readiness for widespread demobilization, had brought three of the Fourth Army's finest units, the 38th, the 40th, and the 42nd Field Armies, back to Manchuria between mid-June and July. These veterans of the Chinese civil war had fought their way across the length of China, from the far northeast to the border of Vietnam.

Western historians would later cite the move of these crack units to Manchuria as evidence of well-laid Chinese plans to intervene in Korea. The Chinese deny this assertion, and say the moves were planned before the Korean War began.

Two more seasoned field armies, the 27th and the 39th, were repatriated over the same period to their home province of Shandong, also in eastern China. They were under orders to entrain for Manchuria on 48 hours' notice. The reserve force, comprising the 50th and 66th Field Armies (now straddling the Yangtse in central China), would shortly be heading north. Part of the proposed Taiwan invasion force, the 20th and 26th Field Armies, was put on standby. No question of peacetime deployment here. These were main force units assigned to eventual confrontation with the Americans.

General Peng ordered a day-long staff exercise for September 10. It began promptly at 0800, around the relief model. The plaster plains and rivers had overnight been interlaced with new-painted railroads and highways. Yellow strips denoted clusters of airfields on both sides of the Yalu River. Someone complained that the model did not extend far enough southward, well below the 38th Parallel. The general shook his head. There was ample space here, he said, for Chinese defense purposes.

Chief of Staff Xie pointed out the small wooden markers, each with a red star bearing a number in its center, which revealed the deployment of the massing Chinese armies. The 38th Field Army was concentrated in the Liaodong peninsula, southeast of Shenyang and conveniently close to the North Korean border. The 40th was gathering around Penqi, an hour from Shenyang on the direct railroad to the North Korean border. A temporary base for the 42nd Field Army had been set up in Tunghua, farther to the east. There were many more to come.

"In war, numbers alone confer no advantage. Do not advance relying on sheer military power." Peng was quoting from the military sage Sun Tze, born 2,775 years before the United States was formed. He paused, frowning thoughtfully. "Manpower alone will not win a war in Korea." He gestured across the model's mountainous spine. "Korea will be a battle of supply."

The general walked over to the three-meter-high wall map, which displayed the entire Korean peninsula and a large segment of adjacent Manchuria. The Pusan perimeter was heavily outlined in colored wax pencil; red stars surmounted by numbers denoted the approximate positions of North Korean divisions. Most of the stars were concentrated deep in the south. There were pitifully few elsewhere: a brigade in Seoul, two or three training divisions inside the DPRK, between Pyongyang and the east-coast industrial center of Hungnam. The North Korean High Command was throwing every available man into its end-the-war assault upon the durable enemy's perimeter.

"Supplies," repeated Peng. He traced the lengthy route south from Pyongyang to Pusan with an instructor's pointer. The elongated geography of Korea would create logistical problems for any advancing army. Yes, even for the Americans, if they ever broke out of their present confinement. Their supplies would dwindle in inverse ratio to the distance they advanced. An American breakthrough was likely at any time, in the general's opinion, now that reinforcements were regularly arriving from the United States. Promises were also coming in of contingents from an assortment of American allies. A British brigade from Hong Kong was reportedly in action on the Naktong River line. The Western capitalists appeared determined to defend their foothold in Korea.

"I have already warned all comrades to expect the worst," the general went on. "It is no more than I have already said in Peking. Some party comrades think you should never anticipate the worst. If you pretend the worst cannot happen, they say, there is a good chance it never will. We soldiers know differently."

No reflection was intended on the brave North Korean comrades, Peng explained apologetically, if—for the purpose of this exercise— the staff today assumed an extraordinarily successful American breakout was threatening Pyongyang. Some of the younger officers considered the proposition farfetched—Major Han could see that from their faces—but everyone was eager to get to grips with the theoretical problems involved.

The general walked back to the relief model. Even the most superficial examination of the terrain, he said, revealed the limitations imposed on both sides. The mountainous country offered PLA footsoldiers a useful degree of mobility. The narrowness of the peninsula, on the other hand, provided little room to maneuver. (The Communists had, in the civil war, relied on maneuverability to offset the Nationalists' superior firepower.) Because of their technology, the Americans would enjoy a distinct advantage on Korea's western plains, where the decisive battles would be fought. And the Chinese troops would be operating not on their own territory but in a foreign country where they could expect little support from the local peasantry.

This was not necessarily a drawback. A note of sarcasm crept into

Peng's voice. "Some military experts, some self-proclaimed authorities on the art of war"—Major Han recognized the allusion to Mao—"Some see the conduct of war in dogmatic terms. The only kind of war fit for revolutionaries to fight, in the opinion of these so-called experts, is guerrilla war. I find myself unable to agree." (There must have been some mighty arguments back in Peking.)

Peng insisted that the Chinese Communists had waged guerrilla war in the opening stages of their campaign against the Nationalists only because they lacked both weapons and organization. There had been no alternative way of fighting. "But given a choice," the general asked, "would anyone of sane mind use a spear against a tank?" He rapidly warmed to his favorite topic. The Communists had entered the higher stage of big unit battles as soon as they had assembled sufficient equipment and manpower. These days, the general said, the PLA must aim higher still—to produce a modern, professional army. For the moment, however, the Chinese had a long way to go before they matched the great military machines of the Soviet Union or the West. This meant approaching the problems of conflict in Korea with considerable caution.

"Our planning must be flexible," Peng emphasized. "In war, there are no constant conditions. We must match our methods to the prevailing circumstances: the terrain, the weather, the state of the enemy. Given the theoretical situation we have here"—he scowled accusingly at the relief model—"knowing our weaknesses as well as our strengths, I would oppose an all-out initial assault. But I would not advocate a purely guerrilla-style campaign." Orderlies installed symbols on the model for hypothetical American divisions closing in on Pyongyang. "Our first response to an American invasion of North Korea should be limited. The PLA has not the equipment, the supplies, or the time to launch large-scale operations deep into Korea. If by some mischance the Americans and their allies ever invade the DPRK, we should halt them north of Pyongyang at the narrow neck of the Korean peninsula."

Senior staff officers echoed their commander's caution, and talked of luring the Americans into the mountainous north in a classic replay of the old defensive campaigns of the thirties. Peng Dehuai doubted whether the Americans would be so stupid as to overreach themselves, especially once they detected large Chinese forces in action. Night-marching and strict camouflage might help inject an element of surprise.

"Surely it will be impossible to avoid American aerial surveillance?" ventured General Xie. The chief of staff shared his commander's concern for U.S. military know-how. Peng reckoned the problem was worth working on. A lot depended on the weather. "But how can we talk about the weather, when we don't even know what time of year we will find ourselves in action?" General Peng complained. "We are still trying to fight a cloud!"

Artillery specialists, signalers, engineers, and supply officers joined the debate. Movement of large quantities of artillery would be difficult over the two or three suitable roads on the Korean side of the Yalu. "This will be an infantryman's war," Peng said grimly. In that case they would need better communications equipment than was now available, objected the senior signals officer. Was there any chance of getting it from the Soviets? "It will take time," said Peng. "We may have to rely on existing equipment." An engineer observed that the North Koreans kept a small army at work repairing road and rail links in the wake of the American air raids; the PLA would need at least three more construction regiments. "I'll instruct Peking," said Peng.

They would need more than three regiments of porters to move food and ammunition, interjected the chief supply officer. They would need four times the number of trucks at present assigned to units. Returns from the Fourth Army showed they possessed eight fuel tankers in various states of disrepair. "Supplies," said Peng. "I must have the supplies." The chief commissar was instructed to organize a meeting with the northeastern revolutionary government to draw up plans to conscript an army of coolies. "And trucks. Search the country for trucks. Carts, too. We will need all the wheels we can get."

From then on, Han recalls, the pace grew frenzied. The two reserve field armies, the 50th and the 66th, arrived by rail from central China and encamped around Shenyang. The three field armies from Shandong would have followed within the week but for the chaos on the railroads. The overworked Manchurian rail system was close to breakdown. Civilian traffic had to be sharply curtailed. The military would have banned civilian trains completely had intelligence not warned against drawing undue attention to the pattern of movement into the region.

General Peng held an emergency meeting early on the morning of September 15 with the chairman of the revolutionary regional government. Gao Gang received the soldiers in his ample secretariat behind the Shenyang city hall. For the past three years this able 48-year-old party official had been managing Manchuria with remarkable pragmatism, fending off interference from the remaining Soviets as well as from his jealous rivals within the Communist court at Peking. Admirers and enemies alike knew him as "Boss of the Northeast." His controversial edicts, especially the decision to introduce efficient one-man factory management in place of cumbersome revolutionary committees, was said to have infuriated Mao Zedong.

Major Han was surprised to meet a quiet-spoken (though obviously self-confident and opinionated) man, whose right cheek twitched with a nervous tic. The provincial administrator seated the general and his staff members with old-fashioned courtesy, fussing over the tall, lidded cups of fragrant chrysanthemum tea and sending out a uniformed woman orderly to fetch candied fruit and cookies.

Outside in the streets, the morning shift-workers were filling the streetcars. Automotive traffic was exclusively military. The buses had been commandeered. Faint honking filtered into the reception room along with the beams of early morning sunlight. The room was bright with flowers. An elegant poem by Premier Zhou Enlai hung beside the door. Scrolls by modern Chinese painters adorned the other walls; white lace antimacassars toned down the vivid velvet-colored armchairs.

"The situation grows still more grave," said Gao. He spoke with authority; nothing went on in this part of China without the regional head of government's full knowledge. Peng nodded. "You've heard the reports this morning?" Gao pursued. "An American task force is reported near the South Korean coast?"

Naturally Peng had heard about it. Now, perhaps, the worthless speculation would be over. His headquarters group could finally work with a definite plan. Two generals would shortly be reporting to him, he explained, prior to the formation of two entirely new army groups destined for Korea.

"Does that mean we can expect to be at war with the United States?" asked Gao. It was the first time Major Han had thought of it that way. China was preparing to take on the greatest military power on earth.

"Not necessarily," said Peng. "Not if China sends only volunteers."

"The Chinese Peoples' Volunteers!" Gao nodded approvingly.

"I think it was Zhou Enlai's idea," said Peng. "The schoolmaster . . ." He paused deliberately. Han felt sure Peng was about to make some unkind remarks about Mao Zedong. The general was openly contemptuous of the Chairman's military pretensions. He often referred scathingly to Mao's academic approach to war. "The schoolmaster has to his credit perceived the dangers in the Korean situation," Peng resumed, with unexpected charity. "I am by no means certain he perceives all the problems involved. We all know he is stronger on strategy than tactics."

General Xie and the older officers laughed, and Gao joined in. Mao Zedong was regarded by his colleagues with affection and respect. Deification was more than a decade away. It was still permissible, for instance, to trade irreverent gossip about his latest wife, Jiang Qing, a former Shanghai movie starlet who seduced him back in Yan'an. There were supposed to be other, less public amours.

"I heard the Chairman is clamoring for action," said Gao. "He never could resist a fight. I sometimes think he's sorry the civil war ended so soon. But here I fully support him. The way things are going in Korea we cannot remain spectators. If the Americans invade the DPRK . . ."

Detailed discussion about additional food supplies, railroad facilities, and the porters needed to maintain a human logistics chain across the Yalu River had been under way less than half an hour when an army messenger burst in with an urgent signal. Peng Dehuai read it gravely. Carefully he folded the paper before stuffing it into his dispatch case. Then he removed his reading spectacles and with due sense of theater announced: "The American counterattack has begun. This morning the imperialists landed on the Korean coast close to Seoul. The place is called Inchon."

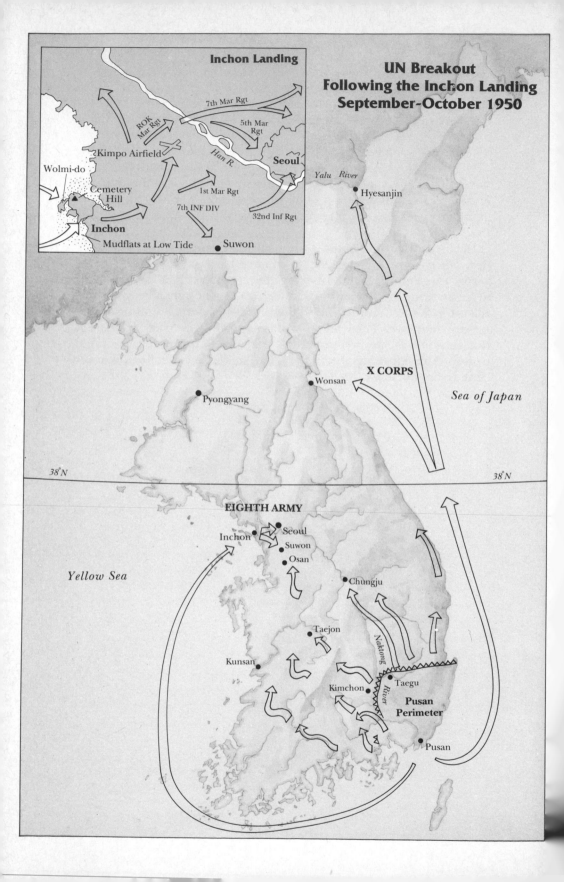

**UN Breakout
Following the Inchon Landing
September-October 1950**

Inchon Landing

7th Mar Rgt

5th Mar Rgt

ROK Mar Rgt

Kimpo Airfield

Han R.

Seoul

Wolmi-do

Cemetery Hill

1st Mar Rgt

7th INF DIV

32nd Inf Rgt

Inchon

Mudflats at Low Tide

Suwon

Yalu River

Hyesanjin

X CORPS

Sea of Japan

Pyongyang

Wonsan

38°N   38°N

EIGHTH ARMY

Inchon

Seoul

Suwon

Osan

Chungju

Yellow Sea

Taejon

Naktong

Kunsan

Kimchon

River

Taegu

Pusan Perimeter

Pusan

6

With Maggie and MacArthur at Inchon / Colonel Wong Gets Strafed in an Embarrassing Position / The Stars and Stripes in Seoul.

Inchon,
South Korea,
September 15, 1950

Marguerite Higgins sat spray-drenched, gripping her typewriter. Crouched around her in the wildly bucking boat were two other war correspondents, a combat cameraman, and 38 marines. The leathernecks, Maggie noted, were elaborately calm. Two had played gin rummy on the engine housing until the boat's pitching at last threw the cards across the dripping deck.

Fear began to flicker only after the group of assault craft ceased nearly an hour of circling the coast and formed a single column for the lengthy dash up the Inchon channel. The men crouched lower, their faces taut with fear, as the straggling line of clumsy, boxlike craft threaded through the bombardment force. The noise on all sides was deafening. Cruisers, destroyers, and rocket ships from half a dozen navies were still raining shells and rockets onto the inner harbor. Warships from Britain, Australia, New Zealand, the Netherlands, and South Korea had contributed their might to this awesome concentration of naval firepower.

The barrage had already pulverized <u>Wolmi-do, or Moontip Island,</u>

which covered the harbor entrance. That one strategically placed bastion capable of blocking access to the port had been neutralized in a matter of minutes. The place seemed to have been swept, in Maggie's words, by "a giant forest fire." The marine assault on the island which followed the bombardment shortly after dawn rapidly overran the defenses, at a cost of only 17 wounded. The 300 shell-shocked NKPA troops were quickly killed off or captured.

The bombardment shifted to the inner harbor. Hours passed before the main landing party headed for the Inchon waterfront. Its designated landing point 2,000 yards away, code-named Red Beach, loomed dimly through the afternoon heat haze. The place could not have looked less inviting. There was, in fact, no beach. The marines were expected to storm ashore upon a 26-foot granite seawall crowned by blazing buildings. Photo reconnaissance had spotted extensive defense works behind the wall, including trenches and pillboxes. Fighters now swooped low over the area, raking its strong points with cannon and machine-gun fire.

There was a further agonizing wait after the landing craft reached the inner harbor. The control ship set the assault group circling yet again while the lead landing waves prepared to make landfall. Perfect timing was essential to avoid a shambles. Each wave of boats was scheduled to hit the seawall six abreast at two-minute intervals. As Maggie Higgins nervously watched, a rocket struck an oil tower, sending up big, ugly smoke rings.

The barrage lifted. Suddenly, there was silence. The first assault wave pulled out of the circle, heading for the seawall. To those few who remembered, Inchon looked ominously like the waterfront at World War II Dieppe. An Allied assault force was decimated in 1943 attempting to land at that French seaside resort. Enfilading machine-gun nests mowed down the landing parties before they could scale the seawall. Here at Inchon a similar towering wall was crowned by an equally formidable network of blockhouses and trenches; other, more substantial fortifications dominated the harbor from the steep cliffs behind the town. It looked impregnable.

Many seasoned staff officers had persistently dismissed the operation as suicide. The odds against success, they claimed, were somewhere around five thousand to one. Their concerted opposition aroused fears in Washington; it came close to scuttling General Douglas MacArthur's daring plan. Amphibious experts who had learned their trade on a dozen dangerous Pacific beaches had only to look at the tide tables to begin lobbying for an alternative beachhead at Kunsan, 100 miles south. Tidal fluctuations were so immense at Inchon, these experts pointed out, that the shallow navigational channel turned regularly—and rapidly—into miles of glistening mud. The initial assault group was likely to be stranded and destroyed before reinforcements and supplies could sail in hours later on the next high tide.

MacArthur refused to be swayed. The port of Inchon lay 18 miles from Seoul. A landing there would both speed the liberation of the South Korean capital—a major psychological boost for the nation he was pledged to defend—and automatically choke off the North Koreans' main supply artery. The general argued that Inchon would not be heavily defended for two very simple reasons: the enemy was fully committed in the south, and would never dream of the Americans landing at such an "impossible" place. The odds against success here were indeed ominous. Yet there would never be a better time to strike. Mid-September offered four days of the highest tides for weeks. In MacArthur's vision the marines would achieve complete surprise, quickly carve out an unexpected foothold, open the gates to an entire army corps, sever the enemy supply line, and end the war.

"Here we go—keep your heads down!" yelled the lieutenant commanding the fifth assault wave. The engine roared, the craft thrust forward, combing the wakes of preceding waves streaming back empty from the beachhead. The correspondents vainly tried to gauge the kind of reception they might expect by studying the faces of returning crewmen. The men manning the emptied craft looked cheerful enough—delighted, maybe, at managing to survive. Spirits soared when an amber signal flare curling up into the smoke-laden sky announced the capture of Cemetery Hill, the marines' first objective. It had taken them all of 22 minutes.

But the defenders had not been completely obliterated. Tracer ammunition began flashing across the bow as the assault wave closed the seawall. A handful of enemy machine gunners had somehow survived the fearful pounding. The defenders were fighting it out to the death. Everyone in the landing craft hunched closer to the deck. They were still hunched there when the bow ground against a dip at the foot of the wall. The ramp crashed down. Nobody moved. A bellowing lieutenant had to push and shove his reluctant squad ashore.

Maggie Higgins found herself floundering in waist-deep water. A grenade burst sent her scrambling for cover in the wall's welcoming hollow. More craft hit the seawall, depositing fresh waves of marines ashore until 60 or more men (and one woman) were crawling around on their bellies at the water's edge. A marine who dared the topside crossfire jumped back so quickly he stepped on Maggie's bottom.

"Hey," she snapped, "it isn't as frantic as all that!" The astounded leatherneck realized he had been treading on a woman. He apologized profusely. The navy brass were usually less polite. Public relations officers had done their utmost to prevent this pesky female from covering the Inchon landing. Sneaked aboard a troopship, she was locked away in a sick bay, chaperoned by a navy nurse. Defying the most dire warnings, she had managed to make it ashore, unrecognizable in camouflaged helmet and shapeless marine combat jacket.

Snuggled against the wet, gray granite, Maggie Higgins found herself admiring a glorious sunset. Its yellow glow splashed across the green-clad marines, creating the kind of Technicolor spectacular, she noted, "that Hollywood could not have matched." But there was no time for reverie. A surge of water heralded the imminent arrival of eight massive tank-landing ships. The cowering group beneath the wall had only a few seconds to choose between being flattened beneath the LSTs' close-packed ramps or leaping over the top to face the ongoing fusillade. Nobody hesitated, though two tail-end marines weren't quite quick enough. Buddies just managed to haul them clear with badly crushed feet. The correspondents threw themselves over the bullet-swept wall, vaulted some empty trenches, and dashed a seemingly endless, open 20 yards to take breathless shelter behind a small earth mound. The marines zigzagged toward a nearby cliff. Not all of them made it. Half a dozen fell before the flying tracer.

The bitterest fighting raged on the left flank of the landing area, where an NKPA squad held out inside a bunker. Eight marines lost their lives before the last North Korean was slain. Elsewhere it was easier. Enemy troops on top of Cemetery Hill threw down their arms and surrendered. The only major delays were caused by the darkness, not by the defense, as the marines pushed on toward their final objective. Not long after midnight, a mile and a half beyond the port, they threw up a roadblock severing the Inchon-to-Seoul highway. Total marine casualties this astounding day were 20 killed, one missing, and 174 wounded.

Douglas MacArthur posed proudly for the photographers on the bridge of the *Mount McKinley*, the command ship anchored a mile offshore. The general swiveled left and right in the admiral's chair, presenting that magnificent profile for posterity—"once more, this way, General"—stared dutifully through binoculars—"General, another shot like that, please"—dictated congratulations to the navy and the marines—they "never shone more brightly than this morning"—and stared with undisguised satisfaction at the distant, smoke-wreathed port.

The 70-year-old hero of Bataan wore the same theatrical cap he had designed for himself as prewar commander in chief in the

Philippines. As far as the U.S. Army was concerned, that cap was strictly nonregulation. But so was the plum-colored tie he habitually wore with his suntans; all other officers were restricted to one strictly specified shade of brown. The flamboyant old patrician had long ago chosen to write his own rule book—and pursue policies he profoundly believed were right. He bridled at the cautious, carping judgments of his political masters back in Washington. Success at Inchon would leave him even less amenable to control, more inclined to press his luck.

Messages continued to pour into the bridge acclaiming the extent and brilliance of the victory. They were passed around the great man's sycophantic staff, ending with that loyal admirer, Major General Edward M. "Ned" Almond, the crusty, steely-eyed chief of staff who would shortly be directing the advance on Seoul. Almond handed selected signals reverently to his commander in chief.

"It's all going just fine," MacArthur told his favored circle of senior newsmen. Indeed it was.

Yet only the night before he had been racked by last-minute doubts about the landing. He aroused his longtime confidant, Major General Courtney Whitney, and paced the cabin deck, weighing and reweighing the odds against him. The risks, he knew, were terrifying. Desperately needed troops had been dragged away from the Pusan perimeter. Not another man was going to be available if this operation bogged down in the Inchon mud. U.S. Far East Command had already scraped the bottom of the barrel. The American garrison in Japan was being stripped. Timorous clerks, snatched from the lotus-life there, had been drafted into the dangers and discomforts of Korea. They had been joined by grumbling reservists plucked from peacetime U.S.A. Nearly half the riflemen of the sadly neglected U.S. 7th Infantry Division, waiting to back up the marines, were untrained South Koreans. These wretched conscripts had only checked into the depots a mere two weeks before in their civilian clothes. None had ever seen a rifle, let alone fired one.

MacArthur refused to be fazed. He had dreamed up the Inchon landing, characteristically enough, in the darkest hours of the war. Late in June, when the North Koreans were rolling irresistibly south, he had stood on a small hillock overlooking the Han River watching the demoralized southerners abandon Seoul. The war looked as good as lost. Yet the sight of so many refugees fleeing communism prompted the Far East commander to plan a dramatic comeback. Two and a half months later, with the world as witness, his unlikely plans were bearing fruit.

This sunset evening, September 15, 1950, Douglas MacArthur was gloriously vindicated. His "impossible" gamble had paid off handsomely. Operation CHROMITE was a massive personal triumph. Last night's fears were laughingly forgotten. The North Koreans were doomed. They too had been gambling. MacArthur had caught them completely off balance. The North Korean People's Army, engrossed in the capture of Pusan far to the south, had little left to throw against this backdoor beachhead. Fewer than 2,000 second-rate enemy troops held Inchon and the road to nearby Seoul, though the North Korean 18th Division, passing through Seoul to the Naktong River front, was thrown hastily into the defense. As soon as the Americans severed the southbound supply lines, the outflanked NKPA could only wither and die.

Within three days of the Inchon landing an armada of 260 ships had put ashore more than 25,000 troops, together with 4,547 vehicles and 14,166 tons of supplies. A week later, two U.S. divisions converged on Seoul. Swinging in from the west, across the Han River, came the cocky, triumphant marines of Inchon; from the east, setting their sights on South Mountain, the great gray peak which forms the backdrop to the capital, came the 7th Infantry. The entire force totaled more than 75,000 men, lavishly equipped with munitions, guns, and tanks, and was backed offshore by an unchallenged fleet and overhead by an unchallengeable air force. Shortly they would bulldoze their way back into Seoul, inflicting a terrible liberation.

North Korean-held Seoul, September 15, 1950

Colonel Wong Lichan sat up, sweating. Something was wrong. An oddly familiar shudder had awakened the Chinese liaison officer. For a brief moment he imagined himself back in the bomb cellar at Kimchon. But no . . . recollection returned and he knew this was Seoul. Two days had passed since he had left NKPA headquarters on the southern front. Shortly after dusk he had checked into this threadbare hotel at the end of an uncomfortable, circuitous jeep journey, snatched a light meal under the suspicious gaze of a group of nameless Soviets, and taken a long, luxurious bath before turning in for the night. The night clerk had received specific instructions. Under no circumstances was the Chinese officer to be disturbed. Come morning he would be heading back to Pyongyang, by train and escorted by a Korean officer, to present a highly confidential report on everything he had seen and heard.

Somebody was now daring to arouse him in defiance of orders. The colonel bristled angrily. He reached irritably for the bedside light. The switch clicked fruitlessly. There was nothing strange about this. The authorities might be conserving power in the early hours of the morning.

Presumably this *was* early morning. Blackout curtains kept the room pitch dark. He was about to strike a match and check his watch when the room shuddered again. An earthquake? Surely not in Korea. Seconds later came the long low rumble of thunder. More shudders followed, gently jolting the hotel until the glass rattled in the windows. Gradually the thunder grew louder. Thunder? That was the sound of guns, heavy guns, dozens of heavy guns mounting the kind of barrage he had recently braved beside the Naktong River. But that was ridiculous. The battlefront was nearly 200 miles from Seoul. Who could be shelling anything around here? Heavy boots clomped down the corridor. People were shouting. Someone was hammering on the door. A shrill, nervous voice (it sounded like the night clerk) squeaked: "The Americans! The Americans!" Colonel Wong rose from his bed and unlocked the door. It was the night clerk, all right. His jacket was unbuttoned, his glasses awry. Scared out of his wits.

"What are you talking about? What Americans?" the colonel demanded.

The man glanced nervously over his shoulder. One of the nameless Soviets dashed past in his underclothes. "The Americans are attacking Seoul," wailed the night clerk, edging off down the corridor. The colonel grabbed hold of his tie.

"Attacking Seoul?" He bellowed so loudly the clerk jumped back, nearly choking himself. His glasses fell off his nose. "The Americans are in Pusan," the colonel declared. "How can they be attacking Seoul?"

"A telephone call from Military Headquarters has ordered the immediate evacuation of all foreigners. The Americans are landing troops at Inchon."

The clerk broke free and dashed away, caroming into a North Korean officer who was running toward them, buttoning his tunic. The officer adjusted his uniform and saluted.

"Colonel Wong? I am Major Kim. It is my duty to escort you immediately to Pyongyang. A most unfortunate situation has arisen. Permit me to help you with your bag, as the hotel porters do not appear to be available." As Wong dressed, the major went on to explain in fluent Chinese that he had originally been assigned to escort the distinguished comrade from the PRC aboard the afternoon train. Rail services were still running to Pyongyang despite sporadic air attacks. Military Headquarters now felt it necessary, in the circumstances, to advance the schedule.

"What exactly are the circumstances?" Colonel Wong inquired. It seemed the most obvious thing to ask. But Major Kim didn't have the answer. "The situation is not yet clear," he replied. "But you must leave without delay." The night clerk had been better informed.

Wong snapped shut his valise. He glowered at his uneasy escort. The strain and fatigue of the past few weeks were gnawing at his nerve-ends. "I came south, to the liberated zone, at the *invitation* of the Korean People's Democratic Republic." It sounded a little heavy-handed, but he was determined to hammer home his point. "My duties are to observe the liberation struggle. If, as you put it, a dangerous situation has unexpectedly arisen, I must insist on being told exactly what is happening."

"But your safety!" groaned the hapless major. "My orders—"

"You will take me to Military Headquarters," Colonel Wong said brusquely. "Those are *my* orders!"

Wong had gained the distinct impression on arrival the previous evening that the hotel was virtually empty. Not so, apparently, for besides the Soviets, now fluttering fully clothed about the oak-lined foyer, more than a score of well-dressed North Korean cadres had materialized, some with wives and families, milling around the reception desk demanding transportation to the north. The cornered night clerk tried to conjure some response from the lifeless telephone.

One of the Soviets yelled something about a truck. The mob made for the door. An old bus stood parked in the empty, unlit street. The Soviets began loading boxes and baggage onto the roof. Two North Korean guards, submachine guns slung around their necks, tried to dissuade their frantic fellow countrymen from stampeding aboard. There were angry shouts and protestations.

Seoul slept on oblivious. Life seemed to have seeped away beneath its sea of gray-tiled roofs. The daily curfew confined civilians to their homes until shortly after dawn; the Chinese colonel wondered whether these invisible citizens had yet heard the news—or whether they even cared? These southerners were a shifty bunch. Sometimes it was difficult to decide which side they supported in the liberation struggle. Once the war was won a determined propaganda campaign would be required to acquaint the South Koreans with *socialist reality*.

Major Kim kept steering the colonel toward the bus. Fistfights were breaking out between the cadres and the guards. Wailing women were beseeching support from the embarrassed driver and trying to stuff bundles and small children through the open windows. The Soviets had tied the last of their packages to the roof and were hollering to leave.

A militia patrol pattered up in ragged brown fatigues. It consisted of three nervous teenagers wearing sneakers and red armbands.

They shared one captured American carbine among them. The youths watched the commotion from the shadows, avoiding involvement with the squabbling VIPs, until one of the bus guards detached himself from the melee and ordered them on their way. Those kids can't be expected to defend Seoul, thought Colonel Wong. Major Kim kept plucking, pleadingly, at his sleeve. "It's time to leave, colonel." The distant guns grew louder. "Time to leave aboard this bus. It is my duty to escort you safely to Pyongyang."

"It is your duty to acquaint me fully with the situation," snapped the colonel. "I repeat my request to be conducted to Military Headquarters."

"But that's a good four kilometers away," moaned the major.

"Then we'll walk," said Colonel Wong. He remembered seeing bicycles in the hotel lobby. "In fact," he added, "we'll ride."

Dawn was dappling the sky when the two officers wobbled into a camouflaged office compound on the western side of town. Fear of air raids had forced the North Korean operational command to move out of the splendid old Yongsong barracks. But there could have been political as well as tactical considerations; the easily targeted Yongsong complex had been built to house the Japanese colonial garrison. Here in the headquarters of a defunct Japanese mining corporation, the colonel caught the first glimpse of military activity: a trigger-happy sentry, alert to the threat of enemy parachutists, came close to shooting the cyclists out of their saddles. He held them several minutes at gunpoint before a furious Major Kim could establish their credentials.

There were still no tanks, trucks, or guns, the colonel later recalled, but a multitude of officers. Most of them seemed to be running aimlessly around. Disheveled staff officers with files and map cases rushed from room to room shouting hoarsely. Switchboard operators shouted too, apparently at the dead lines. The operations room guard glowered suspiciously at Wong's Chinese uniform, but the major thrust his guest past him into the room. The scene was bedlam. Half the staff stood yelling into telephones. The others were feeding files into the stove. The night was already warm and the stove heated the place like an oven. A sweating North Korean colonel grabbed Major Kim by the tunic and started to swear.

"That turtle's ass!" he screamed, pointing at Colonel Wong. "I thought you were escorting him to Pyongyang."

"I refused to go," Wong interjected in perfect Korean, making it clear he understood what the staff officer had said. "As a foreign observer visiting the liberated zones with the permission of Comrade

Kim Il Sung"—the embarrassed officer flinched at mention of the revered name—"I feel it my duty to request a clearer picture of what's happening."

A North Korean general presided coolly over the chaos. He wore full-dress uniform, as if for some ceremonial parade. His boots were mirror-polished. Decorations gleamed across both sides of his chocolate tunic. He strolled across to greet the Chinese colonel, pumping him warmly by the hand. "You should have gone by now," he said, glancing at Major Kim to translate.

"He speaks Korean, sir," Kim interjected.

"Really?" said the general. "How interesting. Where *did* you learn it?"

This was not the time for pleasantries, but Wong politely described his Manchurian upbringing. "You should have gone with the Soviets," the general said reproachfully. "Now you'll have to go by train." He put a friendly arm around Wong's shoulder. "Naturally we cannot allow you to be cut off. I*ma*gine the international implications if you were captured."

"I felt there was time to pay you a courtesy visit," Wong replied. "It is obviously important—"

Heavy explosions rocked the command headquarters. Less than a kilometer away, the colonel thought. He held his breath, wondering whether the bombs would creep closer. One hit here like they'd taken in Kimchon and every one of them would be greeting the King of Heaven. Camouflage alone would not protect this flimsy building.

"Not much time," said the Korean general, cocking his head in the direction of the bombs. "A large enemy fleet is bombarding Inchon. Some enemy troops have already landed. Enemy strength cannot be more than one division, according to our intelligence, but then—" he shrugged sarcastically—"our intelligence also told us it was impossible to launch a full-scale amphibious operation at Inchon."

"The enemy will need more than a division to take Seoul," Wong observed.

"Their big problem will be getting ashore," said the general. "Especially with their heavy equipment. But we must remember what they were able to achieve in the Pacific."

He led Wong and Major Kim over to the wall maps. A big black arrow pierced the heart of Inchon. Other symbols indicated a North Korean division that was holding the port, with three more grouped around Seoul. Another four divisions appeared to be hovering in reserve around Pyongyang.

"Paper divisions," said the general sourly. "A few thousand men at most. All available reinforcements have been sent to the Pusan front. If the Americans win a foothold here—and there is nothing to stop them—we face complete disaster. Only one thing can save us. Chinese military intervention."

Seoul was back to full, bustling life when the colonel and his Korean escort drove to the railroad station. Bicycles were the only available form of transportation. Every last car, bus, and truck had been commandeered overnight to meet the demands of the Inchon front. The two men rode a motorcycle-sidecar combination, courtesy of Military Headquarters—Colonel Wong hugging his valise with its precious notes, and Major Kim perched uneasily on the seat behind a military police driver who plowed indifferently through the city crowds. Many people were stocking up on food. There was frantic haggling around market stalls, with vendors reluctant to accept the newly issued northern currency. Others seemed more intent on fleeing the city. A growing crowd of North Korean officials and their families clustered outside the red brick railroad station beyond the stolid ring of military police.

Air-raid sirens wailed as Wong and his escort walked onto the concourse. Nobody made for the bomb shelters. Passengers in the half-filled train refused to move. Nothing would persuade them to give up their hard-won seats on what would likely be the last train to Pyongyang. The stationmaster ran up and down the cars helplessly blowing his whistle.

"Can't blame people," he grumbled, ushering the VIPs into the first car. An indignant matriarch and her wispy little husband were ordered out of two choice window seats. They retreated, bag and baggage, in high dudgeon.

"I wouldn't expect to leave in daylight," said the stationmaster. "Seems like Inchon is being blown apart. Our signal lines went dead two hours ago." He pulled out his big steel pocket watch. "Correction, two hours and thirty-five minutes ago."

The time was 0935. Still only mid-morning, and Colonel Wong had been up for well over three hours. The first excitement over, he felt grubby, unshaven, and tired. Even a little hungry. The stationmaster produced two bowls of lukewarm rice stinking with pickle. Later he came round with a mug of weak green tea. The all-clear sounded, soon followed by another alert. The two soldiers sat dozing in their seats while more and more civilians squeezed aboard. Some of these passengers seemed very scared indeed. From their accents they sounded like those officials of Korean origin who had once settled in the Soviet Union. Hundreds had been relocated back in Korea by the Soviet forces in 1945 to establish a sympathetic administration there. Many were from families once persecuted by Stalin.

But with a perverse, doglike devotion they loyally helped the dictator plant a Communist dictatorship in their own homeland.

Shortly after three o'clock in the afternoon, while American bombers were pounding Seoul's Kimpo Airfield, the stationmaster reported the train was leaving. It would not go far with all these enemy planes around—the main part of the 240-kilometer journey would be undertaken after dark—but it would be marginally safer out of the downtown area, in a suburban freight yard.

The train slipped furtively out of Seoul, its Japanese-built locomotive gushing clouds of greasy smoke. Colonel Wong, hypersensitive to the air threat, grew quite convinced that the engineer was an enemy agent deliberately signaling overhead marauders. Yet attackers failed to materialize. The Americans were temporarily attracted to meatier targets around Inchon.

The colonel decided to stretch his legs, leaving Major Kim to hold his seat. He strolled up to the locomotive and chatted with the engineer, who kept cautiously scanning the sky. The engineer proved to be a sturdy proletarian, straight off the propaganda posters, who claimed to have belonged to the anti-Japanese underground. He had been driving trains from the day hostilities began and although he had been strafed once or twice, and constantly delayed by track damage, had never failed to complete a journey. Heartening news, indeed. Not many engineers had survived long enough, here in the south, to repeat that kind of boast.

A railroad official walked over from his windowless, bomb-splattered office on the far side of the freight yard. He was eager to be helpful, passing on the scraps of information gleaned from the signal wires. Traffic would move again after dark. A halt had been called after a freight train had been shot up and immobilized between Seoul and Suwon.

"This yard has been bashed before," said the official, casting a speculative eye down the length of the train. "But the bombers mostly fly too high to hit much."

"They aren't very accurate," the engineer agreed, glancing warily at the sunlit sky. "And once we're over the Imjin River and into Kaesong," he added reassuringly, "we'll be as good as home."

The train started off immediately after dark. Passengers held their collective breath, the Korean women stopped their squawking and the infants their ceaseless whining as the engineer inched out of the freight yard, gently easing the throttle to avoid throwing unnecessary sparks. A black canvas hood covered the cab. Lights were switched off in the cars and the blinds pulled down. It was an endless, eyeless journey, punctuated by frequent, unexplained halts. Sound replaced sight as the arbiter of progress. The changed timbre of the sound of the railway car wheels betrayed their cautious escape from the city to the harvest fields, thatched farms, and splendid apple orchards north of Seoul. A bugler blew doleful calls from an invisible trackside camp. A brief echoing roar revealed the passing presence of a country station. Bridges gave off their own peculiar metallic growl. The deepest and longest growl, more than an hour after the start, could only have been the Imjin bridge. Colonel Wong peeped out behind the window screens and glimpsed a latticework of steel girders flitting across the sky. Far away in the direction of Inchon a fiery red glow flickered off the clouds. The tension eased, men lit pipes and cigarettes, and women resumed their nocturnal chatter. Major Kim leaned across the darkness and respectfully touched the colonel's knee. "Soon be in Kaesong," he muttered. "At this rate, only about another half an hour."

Wong was bored. He hated sitting idle in the dark. On journeys like this he liked to read. But reading was impossible. And he still felt too tense to sleep. Besides, his stomach hurt. It must have been those awful Korean pickles.

"I'm going to the lavatory," he told the major. "Hold onto my bag." Major Kim took the valise. It was the last time they ever spoke.

The car was divided into compartments, with a corridor down the right-hand side. On this uncomfortable journey there had been an overflow of passengers and packages into this outside corridor; the colonel found himself maneuvering through an obstacle course that squeaked and complained beneath his feet. The lavatory door at the end of his car was locked and unyielding. He crossed into the second car, an open-aisle model, packed to capacity but with lavatories at both ends. The nearer one was also firmly locked. No amount of banging and shouting could budge the occupants. Forced on by his rumbling stomach he squeezed his way toward the back and leaped thankfully inside the rearmost lavatory as a mother and her small son slipped out.

It stank to high heaven. That was only to be expected with so many people detained for so many hours. He hung his uniform jacket on a wall hook, unbuttoned his pants and squatted down, Asian style, over the shallow flush toilet in the floor. Wong ruefully admitted much later that he could not have been caught in a more embarrassing position. But it undoubtedly saved his life.

The air raid that hit them lasted just over three minutes. It demolished Kaesong station (which they were approaching), pulverized the switching yard, and wrecked their train, derailing the locomotive and four of the eight cars. The train was riddled with deadly splinters. The first car was worst hit. Windows imploded, seats, compartments, and the people in them were torn apart by the blast and fragments. Back in the third car, something chewed off the toilet roof close to the colonel's head. The blast hurled him across the floor. Briefly he blacked out, then struggled to his feet, buckling his pants. Death might be breathing down his neck but he was determined to meet it impeccably dressed. Unfortunately his uniform jacket had vanished. The loss distressed him irrationally. This was no place to go wandering around in shirtsleeves. He remembered the spare jacket in his valise. It became desperately *important* to get to that valise.

The next few hours were relived in Colonel Wong's nightmares for years. Nothing in his wildest imaginings could ever be so horrific, he firmly believed, not even the frozen dead of later in the year, the burned-out ruins of recaptured Seoul. Sixteen years on, under torture by his own country's Red Guards in Nanking, the colonel drew additional strength from the sickening memory. Nothing could be as bad again.

The rail cars had been hurled down a low embankment. They hung there, teetering precariously. The enemy bombers throbbed away into the distance, pursued by ragged flak. Fires were spreading down the train, forcing panic-stricken survivors to leap from doors and windows and run for shelter in the nearby fields. The colonel climbed painfully out of the roofless lavatory, thinking only of the tunic in his valise. To his befuddled brain it was the one remaining scrap of reality. The overriding need to retrieve his uniform insulated him from the surrounding terror.

A screaming girl with shattered arms bumped into him and fell, still screaming, on the ground. He looked at her curiously before tottering back along the track to his old compartment. A blood-stained hand reached from one of the twitching heaps beside the car and grabbed for his ankle. He kicked himself free and staggered on. The door into the corridor sprang open easily, propelled by the tight-wedged bodies pressed against it. Three, possibly four, corpses rolled out onto the grass. The compartment where the colonel had just passed the last 15 uncomfortable hours was reduced to a roofless sieve. Every one of his fellow passengers was dead. Nothing could have survived the shower of bomb fragments that ripped through the car.

The decapitated Major Kim lolled on top of the other bodies, the khaki valise still gripped between his thick peasant fingers. Wong muttered a futile farewell to his late escort before dragging his belongings clear of the wreck. Fires consumed the first two cars as he rummaged stupidly around for a fresh tunic. Rescuers galloped past, but Wong ignored them. Slowly and deliberately he retrieved the jacket from beneath his notebooks; he was slipping his arms into the sleeves when a pistol dug sharply into his ribs. A North Korean soldier was holding the pistol and shouting, his face distorted with rage as he mouthed the Korean word for "looter." Colonel Wong told him not to be so damn stupid and went on buttoning his jacket. The soldier jumped back. Wong realized he had replied in his native Chinese.

"Spy!" screamed the North Korean, blowing a whistle. A squad of NKPA troopers rushed up, eager to impale the alien agent on their bayonets.

"This is absolute nonsense," said the colonel absently. His voice seemed miles away. "Allow me to introduce myself. I am—" He was still speaking Chinese. The man let out a shriek and hit him savagely with the gun butt. The blazing train, the flame-lit faces, the flak-scarred sky spun slowly around until Wong fell face forward into his valise. There was a pleasant smell of shaving soap, starched clothes, and cigarettes before he drifted off into unconsciousness.

It was blazing bright when he awoke. He lay naked on a plain wooden bed. A white-clad man was bent over him with a stethoscope.

"Your spy's awake," he called out in Korean. Another man came into vision.

Colonel Wong looked from one to the other. He struggled to sit up but found himself roped to the bed. Speaking slowly, with distinct effort, he said: "I am no spy. You are mistaken."

The two men looked interested.

"He speaks Korean!" exclaimed the one in white.

Wong was relieved; he had a vague memory of losing his linguistic abilities.

"With a Japanese accent," said the second man. He was tall and lanky, squeezed into a skin-tight khaki uniform with a major's star on the collar. He peered curiously into the colonel's face. "I'd say he was a Japanese spy."

"Then why did the troops tell us he was talking Chinese?" demanded the other. The major impatiently dismissed such quibbling.

"Tell me, doctor, have you ever heard of a Chinese speaking Korean?" He spoke with an air of awesome assurance. Colonel Wong recognized the type. Counterintelligence officers always knew they were right, whatever their nationality.

"You might as well ask who ever heard of a Korean speaking

Chinese," Wong remarked pleasantly. There had obviously been a case of mistaken identity. He would soon have the mistake rectified.

"Don't tell me what to ask," growled the Korean major, vastly unamused.

He shoved his face close to the colonel's and spat out his words on garlic-laden breath: "I ask the questions round here, old man"— Wong prided himself on being a very *youthful*-looking 42—"so listen carefully. Usually we beat our prisoners. Thoroughly. But only when they try to be clever. Don't you try that. We don't want you to die on us." The face went out of focus. The room lurched around and Wong began to vomit.

By the time Wong's vision cleared the doctor was wiping his face with a damp towel. The Korean major came back into view brandishing his valise.

"You were caught looting this bag beside the train," said the major. "How did you get hold of it?"

"It's mine," said the colonel. He felt too weak to argue. If it weren't for the urgent need to reach Pyongyang he would gladly lie here and sleep.

"Well, at least he's honest," said the doctor.

"And dead," said the major with grim delight. "Enemy parachutist, caught assuming foreign uniform, with a bag full of notes on our military dispositions in the south. All we need now are a few more facts, a short painless confession and I'll be able to shoot him. Put him to sleep for a while. We will complete the debriefing after breakfast."

"I am a Chinese officer from the military mission in Pyongyang!" groaned the helpless colonel.

"Then what are you doing here? What are all these notes about the southern front?" snapped the major.

"I have been visiting Front Headquarters at Kimchon," the colonel explained. He wished he did not feel so sick. "Ask General Kim Chaek. Ask the Supreme Command. . . ."

"The next thing you'll be telling me, the Beloved Leader personally signed your movement orders! Very well, where are they? Where's your escort officer?"

Colonel Wong thought of Major Kim, headless among the corpses. He began to vomit again.

"Sedate him quickly," shouted the major.

"You want him to choke?" The doctor sounded anxious.

"Serve the bastard right," said the major.

"But you don't understand. We are wasting time," protested Wong. "I am engaged on a most important mission."

"I'll bet you are," said the doctor as he lunged in with the needle.

* * *

Colonel Wong rose from the depths of a dark, deep river. He floated lazily around in ever-widening circles until it seemed safe to open his eyes. The interrogation cell had vanished. He was tucked into a genuine hospital bed. The sheets were soft and white, and real sunlight streamed through the unbarred window. He sat up, gingerly fingering his bandaged head, and looked around for his valise. It lay open on the floor beside his bed. A nurse came in and darted out again, calling the doctor.

The man who had already treated him hurriedly appeared, followed breathlessly by two older and apparently more senior colleagues. Others filed in while the medics completed their examination. At their head was a Korean general, some high-ranking staff officers, and several civilian cadres. There was no sign of the aggressive major. The general seated himself in the middle of the room. The others grouped themselves around him in a Confucian family cluster. Cued by the doctors at the end of their examination, the general cleared his throat and began to offer apologies on behalf of the Kaesong Military Command for any inconveniences the distinguished Chinese colonel might have suffered. All would agree, no doubt, that conditions at the present time were more than a little unusual. . . .

"Last night's air attack cost over 300 lives," the general said. "Most of the dead were on your train. You were most fortunate to survive."

"In every way," thought Colonel Wong, realizing how close he had come to facing a firing squad.

"The circumstances surrounding your survival and the extensive notes in your valise gave our security officers a dangerously erroneous impression," the general went on. He seemed to be reciting a memorized statement. "The possibility of the appearance of a Chinese officer in this part of Korea struck us as extremely unlikely. Your *laisser passer* [pass] and other credentials had unfortunately been destroyed. When the matter came to my attention I made urgent inquiries to Seoul and Pyongyang. I found plenty of people eager to vouch for you."

The colonel weakly requested permission to complete his journey.

"Tomorrow," said the general. "After nightfall. But not by train." He walked over to shake the patient's hand.

"Soon," he said, "we shall all be moving north."

Outside Seoul,
September 21, 1950

The marines fought their way through a self-made inferno. Their advance firepower, lavished upon the puniest of targets, swiftly reduced Seoul to ashes. First to be gutted were the industrial slums of Yongdungpo, on the southern bank of the Han River.

But their frontal assault made slow headway. Six days after the Inchon landing the marines captured a ferry point on the Han River, still eight miles west of the capital. The North Koreans, reinforced by reserve regiments rushed in from Pyongyang, contested every street and strong point. Each side's attempts to obliterate the opposition ignited whole districts devoted to entertainment, commerce, shopping, and administration, sending up clouds of smoke and swirling sparks that blotted out the watery autumn sun.

Reginald "Reggie" Thompson was appalled. The correspondent of the London *Daily Telegraph* was thoroughly accustomed to mayhem. He had served as a World War II intelligence officer until, once more a newsman, he had been assigned to cover the European campaign from D day to north Germany. The wanton destruction of this helpless city sickened and disheartened him.

The British correspondent walked the streets of Seoul sketching out the scene in his notebook: ". . . inferno of din and destruction with the tearing noise of Corsair dive-bombers blasting right ahead, and the livid flashes of the tank guns, the harsh, fierce crackle of blazing wooden buildings . . . [which] collapse in showers of sparks, puffing masses of smoke and rubble upon us in terrific heat."

Succeeding generations would rely on television to beam such vivid images straight into the living room. But the 16-mm movie cameras, which offered a new portability—and the added dimension of realistic synchronous sound—would not be in battlefield use until 1952. Newsreel was still shot with bulky 35-mm silent cameras (running time: two and a half minutes for each 100-foot roll), which captured little more than dubbed vignettes. For the last time, in Korea, the scribes reigned supreme.

Thompson feared that the destruction of Seoul augured "a new kind of warfare more terrible in its implications than anything that [had] gone before . . . the slayer needs merely to touch a button, and death is on the wing, blindly, blotting out the remote, the unknown people . . . spreading an abysmal desolation over whole communities." Far too much force was being impersonally employed, he believed, to overrun a lightly equipped Communist garrison, fielding neither tanks nor heavy artillery. Its heaviest weapons were 37-mm antitank guns whose shells bounced harmlessly off the American armor, though the North Korean forces contested every blazing building, each sandbagged barricade, until the last lone rifleman slumped dead among the ruins.

By September 24 the marine advance was so far behind schedule that the much-loathed X Corps commander, Major General Ned Almond, the MacArthur protégé with overall command of the land operation, called on the U.S. Army 7th Division to press the assault. The next day, with habitual flamboyance, the Supreme Commander in Tokyo prematurely proclaimed the city's fall. The significance of liberating Seoul on September 25, three months to a day since the outbreak of the Korean War, had not escaped MacArthur's publicity team. Their communiqué claiming the city's capture made headlines all over the world. It did not happen to be true.

Two days after MacArthur's announcement, sniper fire still crackled through the blazing streets of Seoul. The North Koreans had set up street barricades that effectively sealed off scattered sections of the capital. The barricades were painstakingly demolished by flame-throwing tanks or air strikes. The end was obviously in sight, however; hot after the climactic story, Reggie Thompson began working his way downtown. He was determined to witness the final action at the capitol building itself. The shell-torn dome of the national parliament was still capped by a gigantic North Korean flag. For the past week it had mocked the attackers through the haze of heat and smoke shimmering over the city. Removal of that flag, he felt, must surely mark the end of Communist resistance, perhaps the war.

The trick was catching up with the action. Isolated snipers still held out to the rear of the advancing troops. Bullets zipped about the correspondent's ears as he took risky shortcuts through uncleared side streets. People dragged him back into their doorways, pointing out the spots from which the shots were coming. Old men and women and civilians with armbands ran to grasp his hands, "some with tears streaming down their withered walnut faces," sobbing pitiful thanks. . . .

A jubilant crowd surged in procession behind the advancing Americans. The atmosphere was almost like the Fourth of July, complete with bonfires and firecrackers. Thompson sought cover behind a squadron of tanks as they rolled up Mapo Boulevard. This had been a fashionable sycamore-lined thoroughfare before the war, with double-tracked streetcars, a profusion of grocery, tea, and wine shops, and a few expensive homes. The burned and blackened shells of these same buildings now rained soot and ashes on the grimy, red-eyed marines.

The tanks reached the main square of Seoul. A double carriageway divided by grass and shrubs ran directly to the capitol. Squads of marines raced crouching toward the building, its blackened, bullet-pocked shell towering against a mountain backdrop which blazed with napalm. Tracer bullets smacked into the sandbagged windows of surrounding administrative buildings as a few fanatics held out to the bitter end.

Huge portraits of Stalin and Kim Il Sung grinned down upon the city, Thompson wrote, "like massive caricatures of the most cynical benevolence."

The tanks shunted their massive bodies to command the square. A marine sergeant with a bundled flag on his shoulder leaped inside the smoking capitol. He emerged 15 minutes later, high up on the building, climbing toward the dome. Down came the North Korean flag. Up went the Stars and Stripes. Onlookers sheltering in street doorways raised a cheer. The episode might have lacked the visual drama of the marine flag-raising over Iwo Jima; nevertheless it had a certain finality. "[At] precisely three o'clock in the afternoon," Thompson noted, "the battle was won."

But was it? The loose conglomeration of Western nations support-ing the UN/American effort in Korea was far from unanimous about its objectives. The Americans themselves were deeply divided. A limited military intervention to protect a temporary border—the cruelly violated 38th Parallel—had developed, imperceptibly, into a defense of the political *status quo* in South Korea. This was an extraordinary turnaround, overlooked in the heat of battle. Right up to the outbreak of the war, the corrupt and heavy-handed South Korean regime of Syngman Rhee in Seoul had been widely con-demned throughout the West as an affront to freedom. Only now was it being equated with what Americans called "the free world."

The annihilation of the North Korean Communist forces, caught between the now-expanding Pusan perimeter and the conquerors of Seoul, evoked insistent demands to carry the war northward across the Parallel. Conservatives in the United States called for a "rollback" crusade to reunite the Korean peninsula. No one espoused this cause more enthusiastically than General Douglas MacArthur, who loathed communism and loved Asia. As events were to prove, he knew all too little about either. His much-touted knowledge of the Asian mind sprang mainly from postings to the Philippines. As for communism, it was susceptible, in the general's view, to sheer military might. And he selected Asia, not Europe, as the cockpit for the final showdown with the Communist anti-Christ. The fallout from MacArthur's flawed perspectives would help distort American strategic thinking, with humiliating results, throughout the next 20 years.

Right now, however, the victor of Inchon was unassailable. The Joint Chiefs of Staff, his nominal superiors, bowed to his judgment.

And the Truman administration, harassed by congressional opportunists, with midterm elections looming in November, approved the invasion of North Korea. Secret instructions from Washington, drawn up the day Old Glory was raised above the South Korean capitol, in fact urged the general to conduct a limited operation centered on the capture of Pyongyang, the North Korean capital, and the industrial complexes on the eastern coast. The northernmost reaches of the country as far as the Yalu River, the main border with China, would be left strictly to South Korean troops, however, for fear of alarming Peking.

At first light on the morning of September 29, six trucks set out slowly from Seoul's Kimpo Airfield. They crawled down the dusty road, crossed the hastily completed pontoon bridge, and drove through smoldering suburbs to the very steps of the capitol building. One wing of the national parliament was still ablaze, although the worst fires around the city were dying out. There was nothing much left to burn. The last of the untidier wreckage had been bulldozed off the ruined boulevards by the time a triumphant motorcade swept into sight, headed by General MacArthur and his wife in a five-starred Chevrolet. Between them sat the slight, shriveled figure of President Syngman Rhee, the 75-year-old patriot plucked from Hawaiian exile to promote democracy in South Korea.

Silent crowds greeted the liberator with a flutter of paper flags and patriotic banners. The populace was herded well back from the route. Armed guards kept a watchful eye throughout at regular 25-yard intervals. The general started off cheerfully enough from the airfield, waving to schoolchildren and telling Rhee, "This is where I came in," but gradually his face grew grim at the sight of so much devastation.

Seoul, the fifth-largest city in northern Asia, was battered beyond recognition. It must have reminded MacArthur of Manila after its destructive capture six years before. Only the council chamber of the capitol was relatively unscathed. Its heavy mulberry drapes still hung intact, though smoke kept drifting in the doors. At the last minute somebody remembered the Stars and Stripes flying overhead and hurriedly replaced it with the South Korean flag. As the dignitaries stood beneath the elaborate overhead dome, salvos from American heavy artillery pounding the routed enemy shook showers of glass down on their heads. Some retreated to an alcove; others donned steel helmets.

The general was soon in full voice, intoning the Lord's Prayer, the tears streaming down his face. Standing at a lectern draped with U.S., South Korean, and UN flags, he gave thanks for divine intervention. No matter that the majority of Koreans were Buddhists. Reggie Thompson thought MacArthur "curiously human, old and even pitiable without his hat . . . it was difficult to believe that this man with the breaking voice and thinning hair nursed his dreams of the conquest of Asia, and saw himself not only as a superb Mikado, but as a Genghis Khan in reverse. . . ."

The general turned courteously to Syngman Rhee. "Mister President," he said, "my officers and I will now resume our military duties and leave you and your government to the discharge of the civil responsibility."

The disreputable old dictator took his turn at the lectern. He, too, was close to tears. "We admire you," he told the general. "We love you as the savior of our race. How can I ever explain to you my own undying gratitude and that of the Korean people?"

His words moved even the assembled press.

"Let the sons of our sons look backward to this day," the old man declared, "and remember it as the beginning of unity, understanding, and forgiveness. And may it never be remembered as a day of oppression and revenge. . . ."

Despite the fine words, execution squads were busily at work throughout Seoul. They were taking up where the Communists had left off. Thousands of "class enemies" slain by the Communists during the North Korean occupation were being discovered in shallow graves all over South Korea. Now it was the turn of anyone accused of collaboration with the departed enemy. Old scores were paid off. Many an opponent of the Rhee dictatorship was conveniently liquidated inside Seoul's overcrowded prisons.

The remaining populace tried to reconstruct their lives. Crude shacks sprang up among the miles of ruins. With more than a million homeless throughout South Korea, demand always outpaced supply. Public utilities, especially power, took time to restore. Food was in desperately short supply—and prohibitively expensive. The population of Seoul fell to fewer than 300,000 as hungry urbanites sought sustenance in the countryside. Aid and supplies generously donated by the United States fell mostly into the hands of Syngman Rhee's carpetbagging entourage.

On October 1 came the first good news, greeted with headlines in the South Korean press. The previous afternoon, as MacArthur called on the North to surrender, advance patrols of the South Korean (ROK) 3rd Division had crossed the 38th Parallel to light resistance. Many of the advancing troops were poorly equipped and shoeless, but they trudged obstinately north on worn and bloody feet.

PART TWO

ENTER THE DRAGON

7

On the Chinese Home Front / The Dragon Crosses the Yalu River / Commissar Wong Wuyi Inspires His Men.

Andong, Manchuria,
People's Republic of China,
Mid-October, 1950

Soldiers. There'd always been soldiers in Andong. Ah Lo's earliest memories were of men with rifles strolling along the riverbank close to the great steel bridges. The soldiers looked serious and purposeful, and they refused to be pestered by his small-boy questions. Ah Lo asked them how far their guns would shoot and how many class enemies they'd killed, but they only shooed him away. More soldiers arrived during his fifth summer. Gradually their numbers grew until men in uniform outnumbered the townsfolk. Sweating away in their shirtsleeves, soldiers dug trenches on the waterfront, installed long gleaming guns to guard the bridges, and built a bomb shelter for the kindergarten.

The school principal, Miss Wu, blamed all this military activity on the foreign devils. For reasons no one seemed to understand, the barbarians had attacked Korea. Miss Wu insisted that their *real* target was here in China. She claimed the barbarians were planning to conquer the friendly Koreans on the southern side of the Yalu River and then plunder Manchuria, just as the Japanese had before them.

Towns would be sacked and burned and people murdered in their *beds*. She said it with such relish that the little boy had horrific dreams of big-nosed foreigners with great clanking swords battering down the door of their house on the riverfront. He awoke screaming and Mother comforted him, saying Miss Wu should teach the children, not scare them.

But Miss Wu never tired of talking about the war. She was quite an authority. The townsfolk of Andong said she had served in the Red Army during the showdown with the Nationalists. She had been some kind of guerrilla fighter. Mother said the truth was that Miss Wu was bored with peacetime life; she was childless and unmarried, so what could you expect? (Mother was embarrassingly old-fashioned, with the most bourgeois views about the role of women.) Old Wong, the riverfront drunk, swore Miss Wu was a secret weight-lifter. He claimed to have seen her practicing with barbells late one night in her principal's office. During the war, he said, Miss Wu had torn enemy tanks apart with her bare hands. But the children only half-believed him. Old Wong kept laughing when he told the story.

Every day that summer the children crowded the Yalu riverbank to catch a glimpse of the war. Ah Lo sat watching for hours at their front window. For a long time nobody saw anything. The factories at Sinuiju, the Korean town on the other end of the twin bridges, belched out the same amount of smoke as usual. The smoke drifted their way whenever the August winds blew softly from the south. Then one morning air-raid sirens sounded for the first time, wailing and moaning from the top of the fire tower, and sending the people of Andong rushing around in a terrible panic.

Miss Wu kept wonderfully calm. The anti-aircraft guns had no sooner begun barking down at the bridge than she gathered the 50-odd children into an orderly column and led them into their new shelter. Some of the children started crying, but the principal bellowed for silence. Her loud voice sounded louder than ever beneath the sandbagged timber roof. Ah Lo, who had begun to snuffle, decided it best to keep quiet.

Mother was more scared than anyone by the sirens. No bombs had dropped but she expected them to rain down in thousands. She wished Ah Lo was with her. He was their only child, she sobbed to Father, and a boy at that. It wouldn't matter so much losing a girl. Daughters didn't count. You needed a son to take your rightful place among the Ancestors. Father objected mildly to this sort of talk. He was an educated man, an engineer, an underground fighter against the Japanese and a respected member of the Communist party. Mother's superstitious notions exposed him to ridicule. Mother was being impractical as usual, Father pointed out; she couldn't keep Ah

Lo with her all the time. She had to go to work. The child was much safer in the kindergarten bomb shelter.

But, Mother asked, what of the late afternoons when the boy was home and she was still in the cannery? A wife should be in the kitchen, she said, just as her mother and grandmother had been, and not punching out pieces of tin. Father grew quite angry, demanding an end to this reactionary talk, and Mother went off crying, burning sticks of smelly incense at the kitchen altar. Hadn't they seen enough fighting? she wailed. First the Japanese pirate dwarfs, lording over them for years, then the Nationalists, who stole everything they could lay their hands on. Now the big-nosed barbarians with their bombs and airplanes. When would it ever end? She wiped her eyes on her sleeve and lit another batch of incense.

Once a team of women doctors visited the kindergarten to give injections. The children screamed. The doctors quieted them, talking among themselves in a language no one could understand. Pig Face Liu, the joker of the class, followed them into the yard quacking like a duck. One of the women spun quickly around and slapped him across the ear. Pig Face bawled. "Southern barbarians," sniffed Miss Wu of the doctors later. She pointed to the bottom of the map of China where these strange creatures came from. "They eat anything," she told the children. "Mice, monkeys, anything." They all shuddered with disgust. But they were glad to see those southern strangers later that summer.

All the raids so far had concentrated on the Korean side of the river. Now it was smoke from *burning* factories that blew in from Sinuiju. Sometimes the bombers made a determined effort to hit the two bridges. A day came when some of the escorting fighters overflew Chinese territory.

Ah Lo had been home for half an hour when the sirens sounded. Alone in their small wooden house facing the riverfront, he was momentarily afraid. Mother would not be back from work for another hour. She had left a snack for him, as usual, on the big warm *kang*, the low, flat oven (native to northern China) which often served as the family's winter bed. Remembering her constantly repeated instructions, he crawled under the dining table and awaited his parents' return. The gunfire was terrifying. The house shook. Plaster rained down from the ceiling onto the tabletop, filling the room with dust. The front window shattered. Convinced that the house was about to collapse on his head, the five-year-old boy ran screaming into the street.

Something was lying on the sidewalk. It could have been a woman. Or it could have been meat like he'd seen in the market. The roof of his house was punched full of holes. The one where the Liu family lived, a few doors away, had half collapsed, smoke pouring from its splintered timbers. People were rushing around, screaming like himself. Just as he was about to blunder into the river a pair of strong hands scooped him up. It was a great, burly soldier who carried him away from the smoking wreckage, comforting him and asking him his name.

Mother ran up soon afterward. She couldn't stop crying. One of the women doctors put a consoling arm around her shoulder. The doctor took them both home and gave them a drink of some medicine while Father cleared up the wreckage, cursing the Americans. The town had been machine-gunned, he told them, especially the riverfront. The fires had been put out, but the damage would take months to repair. Glass was in short supply and they might have to spend the winter with paper over the window. He did not mention those injured or killed.

Pig Face Liu never came back to the kindergarten. Ah Lo· felt sorry. He regretted calling his friend such a horrid name, even though Pig Face *was* rather ugly. He lit an incense stick when no one was around and wished the Liu family better luck in the next world.

There was talk after the raid of evacuating the children from Andong. Mother and Father argued about it over dinner. Both thought it a worthwhile idea, but where would be safe? Stories were going around about the Americans dropping atomic bombs. Perhaps Ah Lo should go to Second Uncle in Shenyang? Second Uncle had been a shopkeeper, Father protested, and was still full of bourgeois ideas. He might pass his ideas on to their son. Mother said that at least Second Uncle followed the Rites and Principles, as laid down by the venerable Confucius. Father opened his mouth to say something, changed his mind, and went back to his reading. Party members were being inundated with propaganda pamphlets condemning the Americans.

Word came round that the kindergarten pupils were wanted for another demonstration. Ah Lo had already taken part in several. The children enjoyed them thoroughly. Party officials handed out banners the children were unable to read and taught them slogans they could never remember. Still, it was much more fun than class. Once they were led past a man with a big whirring camera. One more time, the man kept pleading, and would they please shake their fists and look angry. Ah Lo also acted in a play, under Miss Wu's watchful eye, carrying a toy rifle and pretending to be a PLA soldier, defeating class enemies and foreign invaders of China. What a shame Pig Face Liu was no longer there; he would have made a wonderfully realistic barbarian.

The demonstrations were connected with something called the

"Hate America" campaign. Ah Lo did not hate America. Not at first, anyway. He had never *heard* of America until Father told him that America was the place the bombers had come from. The people who lived in America were called Yankees. They had big noses and red hair and they ate little boys (and sometimes little girls) for breakfast. Mother told Father not to fill the child's head with scary nonsense.

The day of the "Hate America" demonstration Miss Wu inspected the assembled kindergarten, freshly washed and brushed like little soldiers on parade. The time had come, she said, for the glorious revolutionary army of China to chase the Yankees out of Korea. She formed the children up in line, helped by her two assistants, and led them to the railroad station.

A soldier gave each child a colored paper flag on a bamboo stick. Adults were handed bouquets of flowers tied up with bright silk ribbons. The girls' dance troupe from high school came ready-equipped with bunches of paper streamers. Soldiers were still stringing banners across the station. Ah Lo had no idea what the banners said, and was beginning to feel just a little bit bored when a group of important-looking men in uniform appeared on the concourse. They were accompanied by the man with the whirring camera, the stationmaster in his black-braided uniform, and a military band with gleaming brass instruments.

The children waved their flags, the girls danced, and the adults handed out the bouquets. A locomotive whistled away along the track, the band struck up a cheerful march, and the train, covered with flags and bunting, puffed into Andong. Soldiers leaned out the windows laughing and shouting. The children waved their flags and the high school girls did a most energetic dance.

The train did not cross either bridge. None had crossed for many weeks. Instead, the cars burst open at the station, pouring out a flood of men in padded khaki jackets with backpacks and rifles and all kinds of equipment the children didn't recognize. The soldiers lined up beside the track, shouting and jostling, and eventually set off on foot toward the two great bridges. Ah Lo wondered why they did not take the train. It would have been so much quicker.

The important-looking men in uniform slapped the soldiers on the back as they marched by and wished them the best of luck. Everyone was laughing and joking. The only person not enjoying himself seemed to be the stationmaster, who kept staring nervously at the sky as if the bombers were about to return. He need not have worried. The day was dark and cloudy. The first chill winds were whipping off the Yalu. Long, thin lines of soldiers stretched out over the bridges until the men in front were lost to sight. More and more came up behind them, splitting into files along the worn old footways while the girls danced, the children yelled themselves hoarse, and the band played its cheerful tunes. Miss Wu stood stiffly at the salute in front of her excited children. Ah Lo thought she was crying, though he couldn't for the life of him think why. He bravely waved his little flag, wishing he too could march to war.

Andong,
October 14, 1950

General Peng Dehuai stood watching the marching men long after the children had gone. The band was sent off for a meal. The musicians came back glowing from a few cups of hot rice wine. The wind picked up, whining through the latticed girders of the long parallel bridge spans, but the band played louder and more cheerfully than ever. The stationmaster came over from time to time to offer the staff a drop or two of hospitality; he backed awkwardly away on seeing them so absorbed. General Peng's aide, Major Han Liqun, told the stationmaster that the VIPs would stay out there as long as it was still possible to see. Privately the general's aide prayed their vigil could end more quickly, though knowing the way the old man felt about occasions like this he guessed they would be here for hours.

Han's more pressing worry was the operational signals piling up in Shenyang. There was growing concern at the extraordinary progress the Americans were making in their drive toward Pyong-yang. Besides, the cold here was cutting them all to the bone. It would freeze tonight, without a doubt, although the real winter was supposed to be weeks away. The temperature was dropping faster than the falling sun. A final burst of golden light gilded the sullen waters of the Yalu, twinkling through the endless stream of manpower clattering across the catwalks.

The twin bridges were a superb piece of engineering. Their elegant cantilevers were an intricate legacy of the departed Japanese. The Mikado's late empire makers laid about them with a heavy hand, but they carpeted this corner of Asia with railroads and industries. The 3,000-foot bridges they built at Andong had been the main route between the Japanese colony of Korea and the Japanese puppet kingdom in Manchuria. Although there were seven other main crossing points across the Yalu border, and three across the Tumen River, none rivaled the Andong twins in size and importance. One of the Andong bridges was built for rail traffic, the other for automobiles. But this one auto-bridge would not be enough for the number of vehicles to come. Chinese construction troops were already tackling the formidable task of laying planks upon the rail-ties to take the first convoys of trucks immediately after dark. There was talk of risking a train across the rail bridge, but the Koreans advised against it. Spans in both bridges on the Sinuiju side of the river had twice been severely damaged and twice repaired; it was doubtful whether the structure would carry a train. The smallest trucks would have to cross at 100-meter intervals.

The marching troops belonged to the 334th Regiment, 112th Division of the 38th Field Army. They were Shandong men, tough and assertive, with hard peasant hands and hard soldiers' faces. Their divisional commander, Major General Qiang Yonghui, had once served (like many of the Chinese Communists) in one of the warlord armies. He was at the Andong airfield to greet General Peng when the commander in chief of the Chinese Peoples' Volunteers flew in from Shenyang. Peng much preferred the train to flying, but troop trains were jamming the railroads. Civilian rail traffic was suspended throughout central and northeastern China, from Wuhan and Shanghai through Peking and Tianjin, all the way through Shenyang to eastern Manchuria. The line to Andong was the most heavily burdened. Three reinforced field armies, totaling some 40,000 men, were due to cross here, if the present cloud cover held, by October 20. That gave them six days, marching from noon throughout the night and pausing at dawn. Early mornings were the most favored time, it was noted, for American aerial reconnaissance.

October 14 was the day General Peng started hurrying his troops across the Yalu. Like Caesar's Rubicon, the Yalu River marked an historic boundary, whose crossing created irrevocable commitments. Major Han Liqun recalled the risk-all operation launched by the ruthless and impetuous Xiang Yu (233–202 B.C.), lord chief marshal of the kingdom of Chu. Sending one of his armies across a border river to besiege a neighboring state, he ordered them to smash their cooking pots and scuttle their boats upon reaching the opposite bank. This left them no alternative but to fight, starve, or drown. The Chinese Peoples' Volunteers were not quite so desperately committed in Korea, but their lack of logistics left them with the same limited options as Duke Xiang's ultimately victorious soldiery.

Entry date into Korea was brought forward a week when the enemy imperialists advanced faster than expected across the 38th Parallel. Shortly after the lead units of the Chinese 38th Field Army crossed at Andong, men of the 42nd Field Army began marching across the remoter 450-meter rail-only bridge at Manpojin, 160 kilometers farther east. The Chinese battle plan, finalized on October 12, envisaged a crossing into Korea from Andong by the 38th, 39th, and 40th Field Armies, each reinforced by one division of the 41st Field Army.

This advance force, collectively known as the Thirteenth Army

Group (and commanded by General Li Tianyu), would take up west-coast blocking positions just north of Korea's Chungchon River (some 100 kilometers below the Yalu) to confront the main body of the enemy: the U.S. Eighth Army, which now threatened Pyongyang. The 42nd Field Army would advance beyond Kanggye (the sanctuary of North Korean Premier Kim Il Sung) to the small mountain town of Mupyong-ni, acting as flank guard against a potential enemy advance up the Korean east coast. Indications were that the Americans planned to land a sizable force there to reinforce South Korean units already racing up the coastal road in face of minimal opposition.

Two more Chinese field armies, the 50th and the 66th, would cross into Korea later in the month at Sakchu, 20 kilometers upstream from Andong and near the main dam of the vast Suiho Reservoir system. Troops which had once been earmarked for the invasion of Taiwan, the 20th, 26th, and 27th Field Armies, each reinforced by one division from the 30th Field Army, would enter Korea from Manpojin and Singalpajin in the first week of November. They would form the Ninth Army Group, commanded by the former Shanghai garrison commander, Song Shilun. This would bring Chinese armed strength in North Korea to about 380,000 men.

General Peng emphasized the size and complexity of the operation at his final command briefing. He stressed the desirability of mobility and surprise. The inadequacies of the Chinese Peoples' Volunteers were tactfully ignored, though the general was undoubtedly aware of them. The risks of committing an army of infantrymen, no matter how numerous, against the firepower of the greatest military power on earth were offset by hopes that the Americans would be caught completely off-guard.

The Chinese force that came to the aid of North Korea in the fall of 1950 closely resembled European armies at the start of World War I, with one significant exception: the first detachments of the Chinese Peoples' Volunteers were almost devoid of artillery. No more than three regiments of Soviet 122-mm howitzers and a handful of truck-mounted Katushka (M-13) rocket launchers were assigned to the entire force. Few ever got into action. It would be another year before the Soviets supplied the Chinese with enough artillery to produce any significant increase in firepower. By then it was too late.

Chinese logistics were equally inadequate. Total American air superiority severely restricted use of the North Korean railroads. Traffic was never completely paralyzed, thanks to Herculean efforts by a largely civilian labor force, but rail supplies were erratic to the point of unreliability. The main logistical burdens in the opening months of the campaign fell on a small number of trucks and an army of Manchurian coolies. The Manchurians performed prodigies as long as they were within two or three days' journey of the battlefront. But problems developed as the supply lines stretched farther south.

At this early stage, however, it was a positive advantage to be free of transportation. The Chinese were not tied to the roads. They were adept at fast cross-country night marches practiced throughout the mountainous Manchurian border country. They had also learned a great deal about concealment from air reconnaissance. Tactical emphasis during their extensive field maneuvers was upon infiltration rather than frontal assault. Commanders were confident. The men were going in cheerfully to win.

Standing there at the Andong bridgehead, jollying on his troops, General Peng was himself aroused by their enthusiasm. He said as much to Major Han as they walked back to the station in the darkness. Things had started off well. If they got into position without alerting the Americans, he could guarantee a surprise or two for the unsuspecting foe.

A signaler from the communications unit in the freight yard brought them a message as they thawed out around the railway station stove. The 42nd Field Army was crossing into Korea at Manpojin without detection. Monitored American radio traffic showed no signs of sudden alarm. The general sent congratulations to all units, followed by a brief description, to Zhu De in Peking, of the day's events. There would be sighs of relief in Zhu's headquarters at Zhong Nan Hai, he chuckled, and no doubt a few "told you so's" from the Chairman. He cocked an approving ear at the unseen columns of men clattering on past in the moonless night.

Andong,
October 20, 1950

The Chinese battalion was halfway across the Yalu River when the sirens sounded in Andong. A bugler high up in the girders blew a short warning blast. Everybody froze, faces down, the way they had rehearsed it back in Manchuria. Colonel Yang Shixian waited with bated breath for the growl of airplane engines, the whistle of bombs. Sure enough, he picked up the telltale sound somewhere above the overcast. Any moment now the Americans would be making another attempt on the bridges. Twice in the past week they had dropped bombs while Chinese troops were crossing, each time without result. It would be just his battalion's luck to suffer the first Chinese casualties of the war. The colonel tensed against the cold steel handrail, gaze fixed on the murky river waters swirling 15 meters below. There were shards of ice on the river and a biting breeze that warned of winter. The sound of motors died away. The unseen bugler sounded the all clear.

Colonel Yang shook off the feeling of nausea that always came with danger—a lifetime of campaigning had never quite overcome it— then, squaring his narrow shoulders, stepped out again to the head of his men, careful to avoid even one anxious glance skyward. The 2nd Battalion of the 347th Regiment, 116th Division, 39th Field Army, should have completed this crossing in the dark. The movement schedule set the operation for 2300 on October 20. But it was already past 1600 on October 22, thanks to the snarl-up on the railroads, and the pileup of manpower at the bridge.

The divisional commander, Major General Wang Yang, had considered a morning crossing to make up for lost time, only to be sharply overruled from above. The Americans were flying morning reconnaissance missions over the Yalu River with monotonous regularity these days. Command Headquarters saw no sense in inviting trouble. The colonel remembered the two key words in his operational orders: "concealment" and "surprise." Together, he was told, they offered the formula for victory.

A reception committee awaited them at Sinuiju. The battalion comander was mildly surprised. So many Chinese troops must have passed this way over the last 12 days he had half-expected the Koreans to ignore them. But an NKPA colonel in a spectacular, sweeping cloak was coming toward them across the last, shaky bridge span, followed by some civilian officials, two or three town elders in ballooning gray topcoats, and a deputation of pretty schoolgirls in their voluminous, billowing national dress. Colonel Yang allowed himself to be embraced, kissed on both cheeks, and presented with a bouquet of artificial flowers under the scrutiny of a mob of cameramen. Fortunately there was no time for speeches. Unless a raid alert sounded, no one was allowed to halt on either bridge. The entire group of Chinese and North Koreans, smiling, nodding, making comradely sounds, moved inexorably toward the Korean shore.

The 2nd Battalion was stretched out for at least a couple of kilometers. The rearguard was shuffling along somewhere beyond the Andong freight yards. Two files negotiated the catwalks on each bridge, some laden with metal cook-pots that clanged against the metalwork. Between them, on the road bridge, Manchurian coolies jogged through with handcarts and bamboo shoulder poles. The commanding officer was anxious to get his men across without further alarums. He kept clucking politely to the reception committee, handed his bouquet to his orderly, and strode smartly onto North Korean soil. That first step would be his minor contribution to history. He had been wondering for weeks what it would be like. Surprisingly, the riverbank felt no different from the Chinese side—soggy and half-frozen—although the town itself was badly battered. The American bombers were doing a formidable job. There was no triumphal march down the main street of Sinuiju. North Korean military police diverted the Chinese through the western industrial suburbs. Most of the buildings were bombed or burned or both. Shanties concocted from the wreckage had sprung up among the ruins. Children with dirty faces were playing a wild game with chunks of charred wood. They stopped playing, stood in a row, and bowed as the Chinese marched by.

Colonel Yang was a wiry little Hunanese, 43 years old, a native of Changsha, who had started life as an assistant cook aboard the British-owned steamers that had once plied the Yangtse River. The steamers contained special opium rooms, for those who sought solace with the pipe, and gambling rooms where many a stupid traveler was suckered by marked cards and loaded dice. Britishers and other foreigners maintained a disdainful distance from these quaint native activities, preferring to sit up half the night swilling bottles of intoxicating liquor which left them bloodshot and bemused the following day. A few enjoyed the services of the "flower girls" who came aboard each night at riverside halts to bed down in their cabins.

Then, in 1927, agitators organized a strike among the Yangtse crews, much to the indignation of the owners, who brought in secret-society thugs to beat the strikers back to work. The 20-year-old Yang found himself involved in his first deadly fight—shooting a strikebreaker with the man's own revolver—which forced him to flee, a price on his head, to the nearest guerrilla encampment.

He became a Communist trooper, serving in the civil war under the legendary He Long through four years of hit-and-run attacks upon the Nationalists. The superior forces of Chiang Kai-shek finally forced his unit to retreat. They joined the Long March in Sichuan. The He Long group covered 3,000 miles in eight months, losing half its original force of 8,000 men.

A platoon leader at 29, twice wounded and still largely illiterate, Yang attended the Baoan Military Academy in Yan'an. The Chinese Communists needed new leaders for their coming confrontation with Japan. On September 25, 1937, he was serving with Shaanxi troops who ambushed a Japanese supply column, scoring a notable victory. From August, 1940, through March of the following year he took part in the so-called One Hundred Regiments offensive against the Japanese, which provoked terrible enemy reprisals. During the second phase of the Chinese civil war (1946–1949), he served in the second column of the 343rd Brigade, which became the 39th Field Army, storming Tianjin and fighting all the way to the Vietnam border. Before his outfit moved to Manchuria for operations in Korea, he had been hunting anti-Communist guerrillas in Henan.

The colonel was a modest man, deeply imbued with the traditions of the army. He carried his own pack, ate as often as possible with his men, and worked closely with Wong Wuyi, his political officer or commissar. Yang never underestimated the power of his commissar. They shared equal status within the battalion. According to protocol, which was occasionally ignored, the political officer was expected to countersign all military commanders' orders. The arrangement worked out well in practice. The commissar had no power of veto over military operations, but he exercised enormous influence in this extraordinary army. The huge force of nearly three million men enjoyed exceptional administrative power. Not for nothing was it compared with the evangelical Swedish and Cromwellian English armies of the early seventeenth century. The Chinese had learned from bitter experience that because political power sprang "from the barrel of a gun," that gun had to be strictly *controlled*. Mao Zedong knew his business when he warned that subordinating "the organs of the Red Army's political work to those of its military work . . . may lead to estrangement from the masses, to domination of the government by the army and to a departure from proletarian leadership—in a word, to the same path of warlordism as the Kuomintang [Nationalist] army."

Service in the Red Army—and, as it had since become, the PLA—was a marked improvement over the old warlord armies. An enlisted man's pay in 1950 was still the equivalent of only 41 cents a month. But at least the soldiers received their pittance regularly. They were not "squeezed" by officers who sold their ammunition and stole their rations. No abuse or beating of the men was allowed. Uniforms were regularly and readily replaced. Soap, laundry, and barbershop services were supplied free. Looking back on conditions of a generation before, Colonel Yang admitted there were problems, and it was here that the political officers proved most influential. The army that went to war in Korea was in urgent need of reorganization. There was an urgent need, for instance, to set some limits on military service. Everyone was signed on for an undefined "duration," which led to a constant trickle of desertions. The army was even afraid to allow men leave to get married for fear they would never return.

The expansion of the army during the war against Japan led to a serious dilution of revolutionary fervor. Old-time stalwarts were killed off or promoted. Their replacements lacked the total commitment of the first rebellious peasant guerrillas. Deterioration gathered pace when the civil war was resumed and surrendered Nationalists were recruited to fill the gaps left by heavy initial losses. Their absorption into the PLA was eventually encouraged to keep the mobs of defeated Nationalist soldiers gainfully employed. Otherwise, it was feared, they might be tempted to join the bands of anti-Communist partisans still at large in parts of China.

Commissars had the job of binding together the disparate elements of potentially fragile formations, enforcing their own special form of group discipline. Some foreigners scoffed at the system, calling it internal spying, although there was nothing new about it to the Chinese. Even in the old imperial armies squads were broken down into three-man groups whose members kept an eye on one another. Miscreants were hauled before their peers to make open and often abject confessions of guilt. It was an effective punishment. Loss of face has never been peculiar to the Chinese. But privacy is so rare in China (and Japan) that the exposure of personal frailty can be especially wounding. Shame rather than guilt regulates these Confucian societies. The commissars made use of shame to enforce conformity.

Colonel Yang told Commissar Wong Wuyi he was about to call a halt. They were a good six kilometers beyond Sinuiju and the advance party had found the ideal spot. A bespectacled sergeant was waving them into a farming village surrounded by orchards. A forest of fruit trees stretched on either side of the southbound highway. The last few apples shivered among the branches, blighted by frost. Farmers were busy binding straw around the tree trunks in anticipation of the arctic weather yet to come. The North Koreans nodded incuriously at the oncoming Chinese and silently continued their labors.

"An unfriendly lot," remarked the commissar, contrasting the silent farmers with the ebullient welcomers on the bridge.

"An unfriendly countryside," replied Yang.

Perhaps it was because everything looked so brown. The dusty road, the thatched roofs, and the mud-walled cottages were painted from the same drab palette. So too were the surrounding fields, the distant hills. The farmers' faces could have been cut from old brown leather. The brown-clad Chinese merged perfectly into the dreary monochrome. The troops did not seem to care. They crowded into the orchards chattering and laughing. The excitement of the adventure had not yet worked off. Some smoked, some urinated, some stretched out luxuriously on the ground and munched rice balls saved from breakfast.

The two officers consulted their maps. It would be dark within an hour. Their North Korean guide, who spoke excellent Chinese, was anxious to hit the turn-off trail by dusk. There would still be enough light to help them toward their first encampment. The way things now stood, there must be about 16 kilometers still to go.

The commissar leaned over the colonel's shoulder, smelling strongly of sweat. A seasoned campaigner like Yang was accustomed to the scent of unwashed bodies, but the commissar broadcast an odor of unusual pungency. Commissar Wong Wuyi came from Shandong, like most of the 39th Field Army; to a man they believed themselves the best damn soldiers in China. If only they would be a little more fastidious about their bathing . . .

The men's chatter ceased over the last ten kilometers. The going grew tougher as they groped their way along narrow, stony paths. There was no moon, but the clouds were gone. The sky was bright with stars. North Koreans kept appearing from the shadows to guide them with remarkable efficiency. They ran white tapes between hillside gorse and puny, stunted trees. They stationed men and women with masked lanterns to point the way through the most difficult terrain. Someone always seemed ready to lend a helping hand whenever a cursing soldier slipped and fell. As many as 200 people must have staked out the trail.

Second Battalion reached a shallow pine-clad valley within the foothills. It was getting on toward 2200—ten o'clock at night. Everyone was dead weary, especially Colonel Yang. It had been a long, unnerving day. The cooks greeted them under the trees with a dinner long prepared. A scattering of tents ran up the hillsides swathed in camouflage netting. The signalers were proudly operating their brand-new radio. Transmission was strictly forbidden, but the listening watch had picked up coded orders from division to continue the march, as planned, the following night. The division was due to regroup in the Taeryong River valley northeast of Kusong on the evening of October 24. There was no time to lose, the signal emphasized, because the Americans had taken Pyongyang and were advancing rapidly north. "At this rate," Yang remarked, "we'll be in action in a week." His staff nodded eager assent. Once the dice were rolled they could not wait to get to grips with the Yankees.

Breakfast was served before dawn. It was an unexciting meal. There was rice and steamed bread with a little pork and some stringy vegetables. The cooks apologized. The battalion would soon be down to emergency rations. Each man's pack contained three kilograms of dried millet in a sausage-shaped sock and 12 hard biscuits. They would have to start eating into these unpalatable supplies unless fresh rations arrived within the next two days. The colonel was worried. Supply difficulties were to be expected in this wild country, but a food shortage, developing so soon, sounded ominous. He had often ended a campaign on emergency rations, but it was something new to start on them.

The cooks had begun work at 0300. This way they could conceal their fires beneath heavy tarpaulins. (Cooking by day gave off telltale clouds of smoke.) The fires were out before the first enemy aircraft came wandering across the sky. The American pilots seemed to be scanning the roads. They paid scant attention to these barren foothills, undulating eastward toward the towering peaks of the Taebaek mountain range. The weather was clearing again. That meant ground discipline would have to be tightened up. No one moved around in the open unless it was absolutely essential. The colonel made his way cautiously around the battalion, walking beneath the trees and the netting, while plane spotters with bugles kept watch from the upper slopes. The men stayed under cover cleaning weapons and equipment.

The battalion slept again at noon for three hours. When they awoke the cooks and tents were gone. The advance party had slipped away in small groups, aided by North Korean and Manchurian porters, heading at half-hour intervals across the sunlit hills, for all the world like parties of upland farmers carrying home their harvest. They made the 26-kilometer march to the next bivouac unmolested. Before the battalion followed the cooks, the commissars called routine study meetings. These were held daily, whenever possible, conducted by party activists at squad level.

Commissar Wong Wuyi was notoriously long-winded. More than half a century had passed, he declaimed, since China last came to the aid of her friendly Korean neighbor. On that ill-starred occasion, thanks to the *rottenness* of the imperial regime, the Chinese forces suffered galling defeat at the hands of the pirate dwarfs. The Japanese not only annexed Korea soon afterward, they took advantage of their victory to detach Taiwan from the Middle Kingdom. This ultimate humiliation would never be effaced until the island province was reunited with the socialist *motherland*.

The colonel glanced discreetly at his watch. It was getting dark. The men must take tea and an emergency biscuit before starting their next trek over the hills. It was 12 hours since anyone had eaten. The commissar would surely recognize the need to curtail his speech.

Today, Comrade Wong Wuyi went on, the PLA—or, rather, he corrected himself, the Chinese Peoples' Volunteers—faced a new challenge in Korea. China was marching to the aid of a *fraternal socialist state*. The Democratic People's Republic of Korea faced total *obliteration*. The man who started it all, the American warlord "Marshal" MacArthur, would not stop short at overrunning North Korea. He would not rest content until he had advanced to the Chinese border and *beyond*. This same archreactionary, busy re-arming the Japanese, priming them for fresh adventures, had lately been meeting on Wake Island in the Pacific with his political puppet, the American President Truman, a sworn enemy of China. At that meeting the puppet Truman had approved plans for the *final overthrow* of the Chinese revolution. It should be obvious to *all* of them, the commissar continued, warming to his task, that the CPV were fighting for something more than the liberty of their oppressed Korean brethren. Here in Korea they formed an iron shield—a first line of defense for the Chinese *motherland*. Fighting for Korea was fighting for China. There could be no turning back.

A runner, sweat-sodden and breathless, stumbled in from Sinuiju. He was accompanied by two North Korean guides. Divisional headquarters advised that enemy troops were approaching the Chungchon River line, less than one hundred kilometers to the south.

"Smash the cauldrons, scuttle the boats!" Commissar Wong Wuyi proclaimed, quoting Xiang Yu's do-or-die order at the Rubicon-like river.

"But the nimble foot gets there first," Colonel Yang interjected. It was another ancient maxim, coined to describe the agile self-seeker who eventually destroyed Xiang Yu. The staff chuckled; capping one saying with another promised a witty interchange. But right now, there was no time. Colonel Yang politely wound up political study with a few hasty words of appreciation for the commissar's *penetrating* analysis. Then he ordered plenty of hot tea and one emergency biscuit apiece before embarking on the next exhausting tramp across the hills. The men marched lightheartedly into the Taeryong valley beneath the pallid crescent of a new October moon.

Chairman Mao Zedong addresses the seventh Central Committee of the Chinese Communist Party in this 1949 photo (Eastfoto). Inset: Mao, during his extended visit to Moscow that year, attends the birthday celebrations of Soviet Premier Joseph Stalin, right (Sovfoto).

General Song Shilun, commander of the Chinese Peoples' Volunteers (CPV) Ninth Army Group in Korea (Xinhua).

General Li Tianyu, commander of the CP▮ Thirteenth Army Group in Korea (Xi▮ hua).

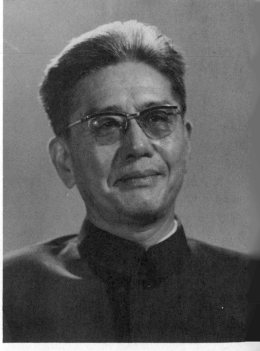

Ambassador Wu Xiuquan, head of the PRC's special delegation to the United Nations in Lake Success, New York. "A documentary film of the [November, 1950] meeting was later shown in China," Wu wrote. "My children said I looked 'ferocious.'" (Xinhua)

Qiao Guanhua, diplomat and head advi▮ to the PRC special delegation to the ▮ (Xinhua).

General Peng Dehuai, commander in chief of the Chinese Peoples' Volunteers in Korea, addresses a rally in Peking (Eastfoto). Inset: In September of 1955, in honor of his distinguished service, Peng became one of ten officers of the People's Liberation Army given the Soviet-style title of Marshal by Chairman Mao Zedong. The recognition would not, however, see him safely through the coming Cultural Revolution (Eastfoto).

The medal-bedecked Premier Kim Il Sung of North Korea mingles at a diplomatic cocktail party, flanked by his Chinese host, Premier Zhou Enlai (China Photo Service/Eastfoto).

May, 1950: U.S. Secretary of State Dean Acheson (left) greets British Prime Minister Clement Attlee at a London social dinner, little more than a month before the outbreak of Korean hostilities. Conservative opposition leader Winston Churchill described Labourite Attlee as a modest man, "with plenty to be modest about." (AP/Wide World Photos).

June 29, 1950: Maggie Higgins of the New York *Herald Tribune* interviews U.S. General Douglas MacArthur, who has flown in from his Tokyo head-quarters to appraise the situation in South Korea. Fighting had broken out four days earlier (AP/Wide World Photos).

July 27, 1950: U.S. Eighth Army commander Walton H. "Johnnie" Walker, defender of the Pusan perimeter, greets MacArthur during one of the UN Supreme Commander's visits (AP/Wide World Photos).

July, 1950: American soldiers disembark from a railroad station in Taejon, South Korea, en route to the battlefront. They were joined, on August 29, 1950, by the British 27th Commonwealth Brigade—the first United Kingdom soldiers to join the UN forces—shown landing at Pusan (AP/Wide World Photos).

September 15, 1950: U.S. Marines pour onshore from landing craft at Inchon, in MacArthur's daring and successful flanking move against the North Koreans (Sgt. W.W. Frank/Official U.S. Marine Corps Photo).

Marines scale the seawall during the amphibious assault at Inchon (Sgt. W.W. Frank/Official U.S. Marine Corps Photo).

September 28, 1950: Tanks lead the way as UN troops march through smoldering rubble to capture Seoul from the NKPA (AP/Wide World Photos).

September 29, 1950: "How can I ever explain to you my own undying gratitude and that of the Korean people?" South Korean President Syngman Rhee clasps MacArthur's hand at an emotion-filled ceremony following a triumphal march through Seoul to the capitol building. The city would see renewed fighting, however, following the entry into the war of the Chinese Peoples' Volunteers (AP/Wide World Photos).

Crowds send off members of the Chinese Peoples' Volunteers as they head to Korea (Xinhua).

The Chinese Peoples' Volunteers cross the Yalu River into Korea (Li Min/Xinhua).

A search party combs through rubble in the border town of Andong, Manchuria, in the People's Republic of China, following a U.S. aerial bombing raid that extended beyond North Korean territory (Eastfoto).

North Korean propaganda posters urge on the production of ammunition against the U.S., whose soldiers are shown as menacing Korean women and children (Sovfoto.)

December 4, 1950: Koreans flee south from Pyongyang, the North Korean capital, even crawling across the girders of this partially sunken bridge spanning the Taedong River, in an effort to escape Chinese and NKPA forces poised to recapture the city from the UN. This picture won photographer Max Desfor a Pulitzer Prize (AP/Wide World Photos).

Life magazine photographer David Douglas Duncan accompanied the U.S. Marines and fellow soldiers in the mountainous trek down to their Hamhung-Hungnam beachhead, capturing the carnage and subarctic conditions they endured while fighting their way out of the Changjin Reservoir area (Associated Press Wirephotos from *Life*).

The CPV's Ninth Army Group sustained heavy losses in an unsuccessful attempt to entrap U.S. Marine troops retreating from the Changjin Reservoir to the coast (Yang Xuzhong and Liu Yunbo/Xinhua).

Explosives destroy a railroad bridge outside Hamhung as UN forces withdraw to a waiting armada of ships. A huge amount of supplies and materiel was destroyed to prevent its use by the foe (Max Desfor; AP/Wide World Photos).

January 4, 1951: UN soliders watch as flames consume one of the dynamited pontoon bridges spanning the Han River south of Seoul. Newly appointed U.S. Eighth Army commander Matt Ridgway ordered his troops back to ground they could hold securely, then consolidated them against the overstretched enemy (AP/Wide World Photos).

January 11, 1951: Ridgway talks with South Korean troops outside Seoul. The hand grenade attached to his shoulder-strap was a Ridgway trademark. (Associated Press Photo from *Life* Magazine)

January 25, 1951: British tanks pass through Osan as UN troops push their way back toward Seoul (AP/Wide World Photos).

February 3, 1951: UN soldiers on a patrol mission slog through heavy snow up a hill on the Korean central front. Despite stalemate conditions, more than two years would elapse before a ceasefire was achieved (AP/Wide World Photos).

Chinese, North Korean, and U.S. soldiers fraternize following the signing of the armistice on July 27, 1953 (Eastfoto).

August 15, 1953: Portraits of Lenin, Stalin, Beloved Leader Kim Il Sung, and others gaze down on a review by the North Korean People's Army through Pyongyang. This parade celebrated the eighth anniversary of the "liberation" of the city from the colonizing Japanese by Soviet troops following World War II. Such displays have continued up through the present day under the northern reign of the Ever-Victorious Captain of the Korean People (Eastfoto).

8

"Grateful As We Are For Chinese Assistance . . ." / The Dragon Strikes At Unsan / The Sharp Swords Visit an American Position.

Kanggye,
Provisional capital of North Korea,
September–October, 1950

Colonel Wong Lichan, survivor of the Seoul train strafing, enjoyed a brief notoriety upon arriving sick and shaken in Pyongyang. His refusal to complain about his mistaken arrest in Kaesong had won him a great deal of unspoken gratitude from North Korean official-dom. Five days after the colonel was deposited at the Chinese embassy and put to bed with a relaxing potion of herbal medicine, the North Korean premier himself, the much-revered Kim Il Sung, dropped by to pin a medal on Wong's chest. Arrangements were being made to send the sorely tried Chinese military observer for a mountain rest cure at the premier's private spa when panic struck again.

The Americans, it seemed, were advancing faster than anticipated. On the afternoon of October 14, when Wong was still not fully recovered from his ordeal, the diplomats of the Chinese embassy were given three hours to leave the city. None of them were surprised. Their personal baggage had stood ready-packed since shortly after the colonel's arrival. There was ample time to burn codebooks and a few sensitive files before throwing their belongings into army trucks. The staff followed (at night) in one large, comfortable bus. It took them just ten hours to reach the mining town of Kanggye, earmarked as the North Korean emergency capital.

The Soviets were not so fortunate. There were so *many* of them. Some lost their baggage on the northern highways. Others lost their *way*. (One group turned up, inexplicably, in Andong, China, without food or funds.) The military advisers hung on perilously long; the last of these were lucky to evade capture when the South Koreans unexpectedly cut their escape route.

Many North Koreans did not get out at all. Most of them did not want to go. Security police rounded up a few thousand and herded them northward up the chilly roads, but a great many slipped away after nightfall to return to their homes. Top Party officials had already taken the precaution of commandeering trucks and drivers to transport their families and belongings to the safety of Manchuria. A farsighted few had established themselves ahead of the rest in Kanggye. Since the emergency capital stood in nearly impassable country, only 70 kilometers or so from the Yalu River, in the remotest mountain region of northernmost Korea, it was considered safe from immediate attack.

No one saw Kim Il Sung for quite some time. The story given the Chinese mission was that The Beloved Leader was out in the field directing operations. But the whisper was that he had been to Peking and, possibly, Moscow. He did not reappear until October 20, almost a week after the refugee North Korean government had moved to its emergency headquarters. On that day a twilight parade was staged through the main street of Kanggye, with a fresh batch of conscripts goose-stepping awkwardly past the reviewing stand. Kim took the salute. Diplomats expecting to see a much-deflated figure were pleasantly disabused. The jovial, prematurely pudgy dictator presented the very picture of confidence. He wallowed in the adoration of his glum-faced retainers, smoking, saluting, chatting, and joking, his long black hair slicked back beneath his braided cap, and apparently unmoved by the recent, rapid destruction of his regime. Such *fortitude*, most observers exclaimed, in Korea's darkest hour! It could equally have been self-delusion.

The North Koreans always put a brave face on things, even in defeat. They had welcomed the incoming Chinese, but not as saviors; no, as new-found recruits to their cause. They concealed their eagerness to continue playing some part in the conduct of the war behind a pretended preoccupation with the defense of their last, shrinking patch of wilderness. They quibbled about attending a conference to plan future operations with the Chinese. They claimed there weren't enough men to spare. Right now, Supreme Command had never been busier. Might it not be simpler for the Chinese

Peoples' Volunteers to hold their first discussions right here in Kanggye? Kim Il Sung would be delighted to preside. . . .

The Chinese were polite but firm. Their ambassador, General Lin, pointed out that the deployment of their Thirteenth Army Group was almost complete. Its final, pre-battle conference would have to be staged much closer to the front—not in the seclusion of this one-horse town—preferably in the rail junction of Pukchin, within easy distance of the troops. But while the Koreans hesitated, the enemy was advancing; and the Pukchin site was shelved in favor of Sakchu, close to the Manchurian border and overlooking the Suiho Reservoir. Kim Il Sung was still most welcome to chair the conference, the North Koreans were told; it was, however, questionable, the Chinese ambassador apologetically added, whether the occasion merited The Beloved Leader's exalted presence. There was sure to be some more impressive future conclave, attended by government ministers from Peking, together with the commander of the Chinese Peoples' Volunteers, General Peng Dehuai . . .

The ambassador had never sounded more diplomatic. Colonel Wong listened admiringly. The ambassador knew how to coat steel with sugar. The Chinese mission had spent nearly a month holed up here in Kanggye, following the North Korean government's undignified flight from Pyongyang. They seemed to have spent most of that month arguing. By now the Chinese were growing impatient. Busy indeed? How could Supreme Command be *busy*? The NKPA would be lucky to muster 80,000 men by year's end, a total of 12 understrength divisions. Never again would it operate in this war above corps level. But the North Koreans would never admit it. Their command meetings still echoed with impressive rhetoric about non-existent troops and imaginary offensives guaranteed to turn the tide of battle. It was rather like visiting a once-rich relative, thought Colonel Wong, remembering Third Cousin in old Shanghai who maintained a desperate facade of gentility without enough money for the next meal.

The Chinese leadership in Peking was insistent, however, that North Korean representatives should attend General Li Tianyu's command briefing in two days' time. The date was set for October 28. Cooperation was essential for all future operations, although the North Koreans could be allowed no part in the decision-making process. The North Koreans, naturally, objected. They could never admit, even to themselves, that the defense of their country had passed to alien hands. But the Chinese had at last found a realist in the North Korean defense minister, Marshal Choe Yong Gun, a veteran of the Chinese civil war who knew China and spoke its language fluently. Unfortunately he was hemmed in by an ultranationalistic faction within Kim Il Sung's entourage who unduly prolonged the proceedings, carping and questioning, in a pitiful effort to save national face. The Chinese prepared to conduct military operations in Korea without appearing to do so. Their problem was persuading the North Koreans to accept the illusion of command without granting them operational control.

"Grateful as we are for Chinese assistance," said one of the North Korean generals, "we must emphasize that the final control of overall operations within the fatherland remains a Korean responsibility."

The Chinese ambassador nodded sympathetically. The Peking leadership fully understood Korean feelings, he smoothly replied, expressed as those feelings were in the spirit of comradely cooperation. On the other hand, it was not asking too much of the Korean comrades to consider the Chinese viewpoint. . . .

Colonel Wong Lichan watched this charade with weary boredom. Events of recent weeks had affected his nerves. He felt like telling these balky North Koreans to cut the semantics and get down to *business*. But that was hardly the job of an assistant military attaché. The ambassador reveled in unspoken nuances and oblique remarks—that's what he was there for—and little matters like the war seemed unusually remote in these dank surroundings. The defense minister's office reflected his government's straitened circumstances. It consisted of boxlike partitions erected in one of the horizontal mine shafts a jeep-ride away from Kanggye. Rusting rail tracks ran underfoot. The air was dusty and foul. All other organs of government had gone similarly underground. The town itself, an unattractive huddle of wooden houses straddling the mountain road, was considered too vulnerable to air attack. A few sticks of incendiary could reduce it to ashes.

North Korean Defense Minister Choe Yong Gun seemed anxious this morning to halt the haggling. He reminded the Chinese that two hours of inconclusive discussion had failed to produce any firm decisions. Kanggye might be inappropriate from the operational point of view, he grudgingly conceded, but national sovereignty required a Korean voice in the country's defense. The Sakchu conference was primarily a command briefing for the newly arrived Chinese Peoples' Volunteers. It was nevertheless a turning point in the campaign to liberate Korea. The North Korean passed around a box of Russian cigarettes. They were mild and fragrant, with long paper filters. The most suitable arrangement, he went on, would be joint deliberations. A senior staff delegation from the Democratic People's Republic of Korea would go to Sakchu, together with representatives of the Chinese mission (he nodded deferentially in the direction of Colonel Wong), to draw up operational orders signed by both allies.

"Provided final decisions are left to the Chinese commander in the field," the ambassador interjected quietly. The North Korean minister sucked hard on his cigarette, staring up at the rough-hewn ceiling. A long pause. "Agreed," he said finally.

Sakchu was full of soldiers. All of them were Chinese. There could be no doubt about the identity of these men in their baggy winter jackets and fur caps. They were the first Chinese troops Colonel Wong Lichan had seen in Korea. After the setbacks of recent weeks he found reassurance in their presence. He knew many of the officers personally—and there were plenty more who had heard of *him*. The commander of Thirteenth Army Group, General Li Tianyu, went out of his way to congratulate Colonel Wong on his frontline reports.

The Korean town of Sakchu supported some minor industry, including a machine-tool factory switched to war production. A few kilometers up the hillside, commanding a spectacular view of the reservoir and another brace of two great river bridges, the colonizing Japanese had developed a hot-spring resort for its hydroelectric employees. A small village of bathhouses, hostelries, and residences with heated floors intermingled with deformed firs, pebble paths, and cunningly landscaped rock. It reminded the colonel of gardens he had seen in Suzhou. This wasn't very surprising, Wong told himself, because Japanese gardeners learned their art, and virtually everything else, from China.

The resort was brimming with senior Chinese officers. The generals in charge of the six field armies so far committed to North Korea were present for the conference, as were many of their divisional commanders. The Korean delegation was led by Lieutenant General Kim Ung, a Korean not only born in Manchuria but a longtime revolutionary in the Chinese ranks as well.

A tall, spare man with a deep, rasping voice, General Kim Ung had until recently commanded the Korean I Corps on the late Pusan front. Just how he had extricated himself from *that* debacle wasn't explained, although his reputation as one of the ablest officers in the NKPA appeared undimmed. He was not a particularly popular figure, however, if rumor was to be believed; soldiers swore he was more feared than loved.

Colonel Wong shared a small room with three fellow Chinese, staff officers from Thirteenth Army Group. Lengthy travel had given him a headache—aided, possibly, by the strains of recent weeks—and he curled up gratefully for an afternoon's nap on the warm polished floor. It was heated from beneath, like the familiar *kang* in a Manchurian home, and he awoke from luxurious sleep to find an orderly inviting him to the bathhouse. There he wallowed in hot water until dinner time, joining his roommates and some of their comrades in a mess hall meal.

The newcomers were full of questions. Why weren't the Soviets here? Because they weren't asked, Wong answered guardedly. As far as he knew, Soviet military and diplomatic representatives played no part in Sino-Korean deliberations in Kanggye. The Chinese ambassador had held several private meetings with his Soviet counterpart, Terenty Shtykov, but kept the details to himself. Shtykov, the one-time "Tsar of Korea," had also treated the Chinese mission to a makeshift banquet, apologizing profusely for the total lack of vodka. The Chinese secretly felt relieved.

The newcomers were full of news. The Chinese volunteers were already in action against South Korean puppet troops. The official convoy from Kanggye had been lucky to get past Chosan. The town had only just been cleared that night of an enemy reconnaissance patrol. "This close to the Yalu?" Colonel Wong was astonished. It was impossible to find out what was going on from their dreamland sanctuary. Did this mean the enemy was heading here—and for the main crossing point at Sinuiju? "Unlikely," one his fellow diners remarked dryly. "You'll learn why tomorrow."

The command briefing was staged in the main dining hall of the largest residence in the spa. The place now swarmed with staff officers; small radio trucks stood parked among the frost-bitten azaleas, and maps filled one end of the hall. General Li Tianyu dominated the proceedings from the start. The swarthy bespectacled southern Chinese looked frailer than his hefty comrades, but there was no doubt who was in command. After reading brief exhortatory messages from the Revolutionary Committee in Peking and Command Headquarters in Shenyang, he introduced "our dear comrade and co-commander" General Kim Ung, a "revolutionary veteran of the highest credentials." The Korean stood up to speak but the Chinese commander cut him short. "First," said General Li, "let us look at the operational situation. It is a matter of some urgency."

The Americans and their South Korean puppets were racing north toward the Yalu. Some columns were advancing rapidly along the west-coast road in the direction of Sinuiju, while others were cutting across country toward the Suiho Reservoir. And a puppet probe of South Koreans had reached Chosan. The situation was fraught with dangers, full of opportunity. The immediate danger had been dealt with by elements of the Chinese 42nd Field Army: the puppets were now out of Chosan. The main force of enemy troops, a regiment of the South Korean 6th Division, was cut off at this moment by a roadblock while trying to escape. Pressure was being mounted by the Chinese 38th and 40th Field Armies against this and other puppet divisions guarding the enemy right flank.

Despite these appearances there was no doubt, the general went on, that the CPV still enjoyed the advantage of surprise. The presence of large Chinese forces south of the Yalu River had so far gone undetected by the enemy. Monitored radio signals of the enemy blamed the unexpected and mounting resistance on the North Korean People's Army, units of which, he hastened to add, were of course assisting the CPV in every phase of the operations.

General Kim Ung smiled bleak acknowledgment.

The enemy was already showing signs of alarm, General Li continued. Intelligence reports from Pyongyang confirmed that the American First Cavalry Division, held there in reserve, was being brought up to reinforce the enemy's right flank. It would be somewhere near the town of Unsan that the crucial challenge would arise.

The Chinese 39th Field Army had been entrusted with the task of capturing Unsan and driving enemy advance units back to the Chungchon River. An enveloping movement would simultaneously be mounted by the 38th and 40th Field Armies, advancing southwest toward the mouth of the Chungchon and the sea. The spearhead of the enemy advance, made up of the U.S. 24th Division and some British units, would be cut off. Too much should not be expected of the operation, the Chinese general warned; his orders were to advance with the utmost caution. The CPV's role at this stage was defensive— and exploratory. There should be no underestimating the Americans' fighting ability or their firepower, General Li concluded, staring severely round the hall, but—given resolute action by the Chinese volunteers—the enemy drive to the Yalu River could and would be halted.

Inside the American perimeter at Unsan, North Korea, November 1, 1950

Captain Jack Bolt of the U.S. 99th Field Artillery felt himself shivering. Maybe it was the cold, maybe the menace of those forest fires. He counted ten separate fires burning in the mountains north of Unsan. A high plume of smoke hovered over the frost-flecked peaks. The bare, bleak territory stretching northward to the Yalu was supposed to be deserted. Who would have set off such a conflagration? An enemy, perhaps—an enemy who wished to remain unseen? Somebody was undoubtedly out there. And in considerable force. The American guns had just been directed against two enemy infantry columns seen marching a few miles to the west. The airborne artillery spotter was gibbering with excitement over the radio. "This is the strangest sight I've ever seen!" he yelled. "Our shells are landing right in their columns and they keep on coming!"

From then on the 99th Field Artillery, whose 105-mm howitzers supported the First Cavalry at Unsan, stood ready for instant action. Throughout that difficult day, Jack Bolt stayed close to Charlie Battery, avoiding the icy wind as much as he could. His men had yet to be issued full winter clothing. There had not seemed much urgency while the war looked as good as won. The battery commander now felt increasingly uneasy. The war was growing grim again, right at the final curtain.

The U.S. First Cavalry Division had so far weathered most of the toughest fighting of Korea. The price had been appalling. General MacArthur inspected a 200-strong detachment of cavalrymen after the fall of Pyongyang and asked those who had taken part in the Pusan battles three months before to step out of the ranks. Only five men came forward. Of these, three had been wounded.

But for weeks now First Cavalry had enjoyed a careless canter through minimal resistance into the northern heartland. Its advance units were among the first into the North Korean capital of Pyong-yang, remaining gratefully in reserve there while the rest of Eighth Army surged on triumphantly toward the Yalu. Once the riverline was secured the war was as good as over. The top brass was equally sanguine. The forward supply position was still admittedly worrisome. But there had been so little resistance until now from the shattered North Koreans, it seemed impossible at this late hour that anything could halt their drive.

What about the Chinese? Staff officers were unimpressed. Complacency paralyzed American thinking from Supreme Headquarters in Tokyo all the way to the fighting front. Everyone, including MacArthur, assumed that the Chinese would have intervened weeks ago if they had really meant business. Today it was just too late.

The motorized horsemen of the 8th Regiment, U.S. First Cavalry Division, prepared for a skirmish. Rifle squads made halfhearted attempts to dig foxholes. Entrenching tools had fallen into disuse since the cavalrymen broke out of the Pusan perimeter in September. No one felt seriously threatened—not at first, anyway—because the enemy no longer offered much threat. The gooks were bound to make a stand somewhere. Those marching columns would turn out to be North Koreans massing for a final *banzai* charge. The first warning signals began chattering on October 26. The four South Korean (ROK) divisions covering the U.S. Army's flank began butting into unexpected opposition in the mountainous central wilderness of northernmost Korea. Whole divisions ceased advancing. For the first time since Inchon, some actually retreated. Almost within walking distance of the Yalu, an inexplicable force was maintaining so much pressure that in certain sectors the ROK retreat quickly turned to *rout*.

The upset was growing so serious by October 28 that First Cavalry was hauled from its peaceful quarters in Pyongyang. An enemy enfilade movement appeared to be developing—unbelievable as this seemed—threatening the main U.S. advance through the west-coast plain. The 8th Regiment, First Cavalry, rushed forward to secure Unsan. This insignificant little market-town became the bastion protecting the entire right flank. Light defensive positions were dug into the foothills north and west of the town. Battalions were spread far too thin, however, to hold a sustained attack. The cavalrymen might be combat-hardened, but they still had a lot to learn about soldiering. The regiment held the head of a valley unusually wide for this mountainous part of the country. It provided direct road access from Unsan to the Chinese border just 45 miles away. First Cavalry should have been rolling unchallenged along that road, were it not for the mysterious hang-ups. Victory was that close.

The Samtan River wandered aimlessly through the valley, between barren, harvested rice terraces, before joining the larger Kuryong River and switching suddenly westward in a series of lazy loops. South Korean troops on the far side of the Samtan were coming under increasing pressure. American tanks and guns had been sent to their support, so far without avail. Word kept seeping in that Chinese forces were involved. Soldiers had been captured during the past few days who understood neither Korean nor Japanese. After a pitched battle northeast of Onjong, the shrewd and experienced South Korean General Paik Sun Yup, who had served in the Japanese army in Manchuria, inspected the enemy dead and declared them all Chinese.

U.S. Eighth Army commander Lieutenant General Walton H. "Johnnie" Walker was under a different kind of pressure from Tokyo. Messages from the Supreme Commander's sanctum in the Dai Ichi building showed no sympathy for the embattled ROKs. MacArthur's sole interest was in a speedier rate of advance. His wall maps made it deceptively clear that most Eighth Army advance units were within a few hours' drive of the Yalu River—and China. So why in hell's name didn't they get off their collective ass? It was just no good offering wild excuses about invading Chinese. Typical of the gooks:

they were always panicking. A few thousand Chicoms at most might be bolstering the morale of their deflated North Korean comrades. Troop movement on a scale that would threaten the UN advance would soon have been spotted by aerial reconnaissance, intelligence officers argued.

It was late on the afternoon of November 1 that the First Cavalry commander, Major General Hobart R. Gay, realized his 8th Regiment was dangerously exposed. The ROK divisions on his flank, the cream of the South Korean army, were rapidly disintegrating. Thousands of panic-stricken troops were fleeing southward, discarding their equipment as they ran. The general, who had served as Patton's chief of staff during the Allied drive through France, had never grown accustomed to retreat. Advancing, he was in his element; when the tide turned, as it had right now, he felt unable to cope. He requested permission to evacuate Unsan. The request was refused. It was too late, anyway. Rescue troops groping toward their beleaguered comrades in Unsan found the approach roads blocked by enemy positions entrenched on the surrounding hills. No amount of artillery or aerial bombardment could shift them. By nightfall the 8th Regiment was enveloped on three sides by huge numbers of enemy forces.

The U.S. 1st Battalion commanded the northern approaches to the town of Unsan. Its foxholes covered the narrowing course of both the Samtan River and the nearby Yalu road. The road disappeared behind the distant village of Maebong-Dong. Fighting could be clearly seen on the far side of the river, where the ROK 15th Regiment was falling apart. Bunches of frantic South Koreans periodically plunged into the shallow waters, wading across to the American side. The U.S. 2nd Battalion occupied low foothills to the left, below Mount Obong, an 1,800-foot peak that dominated the valley. Its treeless upper slopes were already white with snow. Farther south the U.S. 3rd Battalion was drawn up in a semicircular perimeter fronting the Nammyon River (a tributary of the Kuryong), which looped around behind them like a lasso. U.S./UN defensive positions were uniformly skimpy.

At first there had been two escape routes. One lay west across a bridge beneath Mount Obong. It was on this road that the advancing would-be rescuers reported impregnable roadblocks. That left only the southbound road, which forded the river a mile and a half from Unsan and wound away through the foothills.

Winter had at last arrived. The temperature had dropped rapidly as northeast winds drove snow flurries across the valley. Cavalrymen huddled in their shallow foxholes, fending off the cold with blankets and sleeping bags. The Korean campaign was acquiring a new and icy edge. Word went around with the evening meal of an impending withdrawal. The rumor proved premature; back at I Corps headquarters in Anju, worried generals were still trying to make up their minds.

At 1930 on November 1, the unknown enemy struck. The 1st Battalion was instantly overwhelmed. Squads of riflemen—decidedly *not* North Koreans—overran the forward platoons. Engineers and mortar crews hastily armed with carbines were flung into the gaps. The attackers broke through at 2100 when the battalion's ammunition was virtually exhausted. Enemy assault squads fought their way into Unsan and pushed on through the rice fields to block the last U.S. escape route.

The Americans were shaken by the ferocity of the attack. The cavalrymen had never experienced anything quite like it. The enemy moved catlike in the darkness. Infiltrators made good use of cover, probing unerringly for weaknesses in the defense and exploiting each advantage with uncanny speed. It was as if the offensive had been painstakingly researched. The attackers pressed on regardless of losses, although there were few head-on assaults. All this to the blowing of bugles, whistles, and the occasional beating of gongs. One knowledgeable GI thought he recognized the cacophony. "My God," he gasped. "A Chinese funeral."

The 2nd Battalion buckled next. Survivors streamed toward Unsan, mingling with the hundreds of terrified South Koreans fleeing westward across the Samtan River. Cavalrymen from the 1st Battalion joined the rabble, exhausted and weaponless. Their commanding officer, Major John Millikin, rushed around trying to reorganize the defense. But the trap was drawing tighter. Enemy rifle fire from inside Unsan compounded the confusion. The moon was up, and burning trucks and houses already lit the scene like day. Millikin ordered all noncombat vehicles to take the road south. A column of 1st and 2nd Battalion trucks, followed by the first of the guns, negotiated the built-up road through the rice fields and escaped across the shallow ford. They were among the last to get away.

The 3rd Battalion area was oddly quiet. The men stood to at dusk expecting an attack. When nothing happened, most of them grabbed what sleep they could. The sounds of battle did not reach them, and their minds were on staying warm. No patrols were mounted. Sentries dozed. Communications were down—as usual. Signalmen were accustomed to dead batteries and ineffective sets. Much of their equipment, recycled stock dating from World War II, was bug-ridden and underpowered. The sets that did work proved maddeningly ineffectual in the mountainous terrain. No one in the signals section was unduly disturbed by the lack of radio traffic.

The commanding officer of 3rd Battalion, Major Robert J. Ormond, displayed equally little curiosity. At no time during the early evening did he contact regimental headquarters for a situation report. The 3rd Battalion command post had been gouged out of the middle of a plowed field well inside the defense perimeter. Unsan lay behind uneven ground more than a mile away. From where Major Ormond sat little could be heard or seen of the ongoing action. He permitted most of his men to sleep on in their foxholes even when orders came to withdraw the guns.

Baker Battery pulled out first, crawling through frozen rice fields, across the shallow Nammyon River and down the southward road to Sinanju and safety. Charlie Battery was due to follow an hour later.

Captain Bolt limbered up his howitzers around 0200 and started off toward the ford. He could see the fires burning in Unsan. The captain headed the column in his jeep down the raised road. Fallow rice fields fell away on either hand. A full November moon lit the scene like day. About 200 yards down the road, Bolt realized his Charlie Battery convoy was not following. A driver had taken a wrong turn, causing a jam. Glancing left across the moonlit fields, he saw a line of men advancing toward him. He reckoned they must be retreating cavalrymen hoping to hitch a lift on his vehicles. But when the men were less than a hundred yards away they opened fire. Bolt told his driver to beat it, *fast*, and the jeep raced on through two groups of enemy soldiers trying to block the road. He caught up with the tail of the escaping Baker Battery column and tried to persuade a tank commander to turn back and keep the escape route open. The tanker claimed he was out of ammunition. Captain Bolt drove on to the ford. Charlie Battery was beyond saving. Its leading gun limber had swerved and blocked the road. A storm of bullets swept the stalled and helpless vehicles, trapped within sight of safety on the last escape route from Unsan.

A commanding hill inside the U.S. perimeter, Unsan, Around midnight, November 1, 1950

Colonel Yang Shixian of the Chinese Peoples' Volunteers bounded up the final slope and dived beneath the shrubbery. Tracer bullets arced into the sky behind him. Something glowed red inside Unsan; the first trucks must be exploding. His headquarters squad spread out, assuming defensive attitudes around the hilltop, eyeing the narrow ribbon of road below them that wound through the moonlit valley. It was a raised road, topping an embankment two meters high and bisecting a checkerboard of frozen rice fields. A *perfect* killing ground. The Americans would have to retreat this way if they were to break out toward their main forces some 25 kilometers to the southwest. All other exits were firmly sealed. Colonel Yang's job was to cut this road as well. He checked his watch. The time was 0140, the early morning of November 2. A surge of traffic on the road, sometime before midnight, indicated that some of the enemy had gotten away. There were bound to be a few lucky ones. . . .

The Chinese mortar squad was already lining up its lethal tubes on the fragile escape route. A diligent Korean farmer had long ago hacked out a rice terrace halfway down the hillside. His efforts yielded little extra agricultural land, but now made an ideal platform for the mortars. At the foot of the hill, crunching about on the frosted earth, machine gunners and riflemen completed their own ambush preparations. Their weaponry was entirely American, part of the vast loot which had been seized from the vanquished Nationalists during the Chinese civil war. It included some cumbersome but capable M-1 repeating rifles—a great improvement on the worn-out Japanese junk issued to the bulk of the Chinese battalion. Suitable ammunition was in short supply but there would soon be plenty, once the attack plan worked.

The offensive had so far gone incredibly well, so well that Colonel Yang might well have felt elated. But the last dash up the hill had left him winded. He had managed to keep pace with his men over the first kilometer or so, creeping through the rice fields past unsuspecting Unsan. The climb up this miserable hill reminded him, however, that he was no longer the youthful hero of a hundred battles. He was 43 and feeling faintly sick.

Yang recognized the symptoms. He always felt sick before combat. No amount of fighting had ever quite inured him. His hands trembled as he focused his precious binoculars on the empty road, calculating ranges, establishing reference points, and sketching out fields of fire. The terrain was almost exactly as he had imagined it. The crude local maps handed out at the assault briefing revealed a valley full of rivers. On the eastern side of the valley, beyond the stream he identified as the Samtan River, his comrades were completing their destruction of the South Koreans. Distant gun flashes marked the progress of the rout.

The colonel's own quarry, the trapped Americans of the First Cavalry Division, were scattering in some disorder around Unsan. They were a tougher enemy. The 39th Field Army commander, Major General Wu Xinzhan, had made that clear at the briefing. The 39th had been chosen, as the most experienced in China, to launch the first direct strike against the Americans.

"Our task is to check the enemy here," Wu had said, tapping his map at the spot where Yang and his men now lay hidden. "As a warning to the imperialists we shall destroy the most vulnerable American advance unit." There was a wider plan, although the general had not gone into too much detail. The full weight of China's Thirteenth Army Group was to be thrown against the enemy forces advancing up northwestern Korea to block further progress toward the border. Puppet forces on the flank would first be crushed. After that, the Americans.

Someone plonked down in the adjacent bushes. The smell was so distinctive the colonel *knew* it must be Commissar Wong Wuyi. The political officer leaned over to whisper in his commander's ear, still smelling of sweat and now breathing clouds of garlic. The commissar swore by garlic as an antidote to winter chills. Most northern Chinese felt the same. The colonel came from Hunan, where garlic did not have quite the same medicinal value, and he wished the man would try something else: mao tai, herbal medicine, magic charms, acupuncture . . .

"You are too far forward," croaked Wong Wuyi. His voice was hoarse. Was it the excitement, or the garlic? Yang nodded politely and went on studying the valley. The commissar was an experienced soldier and he was speaking the truth. Unfortunately Colonel Yang had little choice. Without sophisticated communications equipment to control his troops he was forced to stick his neck out in the forefront of battle.

Major General Wu had told his officers at their briefing that a classic enveloping movement would destroy the U.S. 8th Cavalry Regiment. It required a massive concentration of force against the weakest link in the enemy line of advance. The 38th and 40th Field Armies should have little difficulty rolling up the South Korean forces which were situated on the American right flank. One division of the 39th Field Army, the 115th, would mop up remaining ROK forces to the east of the Samtan River. Meanwhile, the 117th Division would block any rescue attempts from the west.

The division to which Colonel Yang belonged—the 116th—was given the honor of overwhelming the Americans. The 116th Division's three regiments were instructed to break up, infiltrate, and envelop the enemy defense. Yang could expect some rocket support, but no artillery. Any aircraft must be assumed unfriendly. The 348th Regiment was to launch the initial assault down the Yalu road shortly after nightfall. Taking advantage of the diversion, the 346th Regiment could then surround the western side of the American perimeter. They should dig in against air and artillery attack. The 347th Regiment would move through the 346th at 2230 on November 1 and overrun Unsan. Its lead battalion, the 2nd, commanded by

Colonel Yang, would bypass the town and block the southern escape route. "The enemy will then be caught," the general said, "between the hammer and the anvil."

An explosion from the direction of Unsan sent up a shower of sparks. The men of the 347th Regiment, including the rearmost platoons of Yang's own battalion, were tossing satchel charges into American store dumps. Shooting erupted in all directions. Flares glowed and died in the cold, clear moonlight. Conditions could not have been better for night-fighting. The Chinese were in their element. Surprise, swift and concentrated assault, and the cover of darkness made up for their lack of firepower.

The growl of revving engines rumbled up from behind the hill. The Americans were pulling out. A jeep swung into sight along the empty road. Its windshield was locked down on the hood. The car bulged with armed men. Yang held his breath. The trick was to wait for the main convoy. No one was to fire until he gave the order. Some overzealous idiot could still give the game away. The bugler crouched expectantly at his elbow.

The jeep stopped. It backed up a few meters. An American climbed out and waved at something or someone farther down the road. "He's calling the convoy," whispered Yang. Commissar Wong Wuyi nodded. Despite the cold, Wong's pudgy face was streaked with sweat. "Just as nervous as I am," thought Yang with perverse satisfaction. The American suddenly jumped back into the jeep. He pointed wildly toward the river.

Shots rang out from a line of Chinese riflemen approaching in full view across the rice fields. The jeep shot away round the bend. The roar of many overgunned engines echoed throughout the valley as the convoy came racing in pursuit. The big enemy trucks expected to barrel on through, led by a two-and-a-half-tonner towing a 105-mm howitzer whose dull steel tube gleamed in the moonlight. Colonel Yang gestured to the bugler, who sprang defiantly against the skyline. With one hand on hip, one hand holding the red-tassled bugle to his lips, the bugler blew short blasts that unleashed a hurricane of small arms fire upon the speeding vehicles. Windshields shattered, radiators exploded, and men dived onto the road to escape the fusillade. The lead truck swerved off the embankment and nosedived into the rice field. The howitzer jack-knifed, blocking the road. Farther back, one truck rammed the rear of another. A jeep trying to edge past and sort out the mess slid off the road and overturned.

The Americans sought cover behind their stalled vehicles. But by now they were under heavy fire from both sides of the road. The trapped men fought back gamely. Tracer ammunition came whipping up the hill, finding an occasional Chinese target. A messenger running up from the mortar squad staggered and pitched forward. Whatever word he was carrying would never be relayed.

A U.S. tank ground around the bend, and tried to push the stalled truck off the road. Its main turret gun blasted away at the hillside without doing much damage. Chinese satchel squads crawled across the open rice field and up the protective embankment. They rushed the tank, wedging a charge in the nearest track and clawing their way up its armored sides. The charge exploded. A melee developed on the turret as the crew fought to escape with pistols and bare fists. A grenade dropped down the turret. Slowly the immobile monster began to burn. A lightly armored half-track vehicle sporting four 50-caliber machine guns edged into view. Great gusts of shells cut down those Chinese riflemen nearest the road. This was a type of antiaircraft vehicle of World War II vintage which had found better employment in Korea as an infantry-support weapon. The Chinese colonel had been warned about them in his intelligence briefings. He knew this half-track had to be eliminated. He threw himself down the slope just before the gunner began raking the hillcrest.

Yang slithered into the midst of his mortar squad. A hesitant young officer was uncertain where to direct the fire. Perhaps that stricken messenger had been sent to ask. "Hit that machine-gun carrier!" the colonel yelled. The first mortar bombs began exploding, inaccurately, on the far side of the road. The colonel's personal runner, a pimply farm boy named Pang, rolled off the hilltop. He had been nicked in the left arm. "Machine-gun fire," he whimpered. "It hit Commissar Wong, too." Colonel Yang seized the boy by the scruff of his neck and thrust him down the hill. "Get to our machine gunners at the bottom there," he ordered. "Tell them to knock out that carrier."

It took an agonizingly long time, Yang recalled afterward. A small, spunky group of Americans clustered behind their gun shield blazing away at the brown-clad Chinese troops. One gunner pitched backward, arms spread wide, and toppled onto the open road. Another, heaving boxes of ammunition, slammed against the empty driving cabin clutching his throat. An incendiary bullet finally hit the half-track's fuel tank. The deadly vehicle vanished in a ball of flames. The firing died away as the surviving Americans fled back toward Unsan.

Colonel Yang fought back the urge to inspect the abandoned column. Members of the machine-gun squad were already salvaging big steel boxes of ammunition. They were finding a lot of other things, too, if their delighted yells were any indication; the army's strict rules against looting just *might* have to be waived in this moment of triumph. The battalion commander hauled himself painfully back to the hillcrest. He had not realized the slope was so steep and long. Much of the foliage had vanished. Bursts from the 50-caliber machine guns had sheered off the shrubbery like giant clippers. Medics were moving among the men he had left behind. Not that there was much they could do. The bugler was dead. So were the adjutant and three or four riflemen.

Commissar Wong looked dead, but wasn't. His left ear was virtually shot away. His left wrist was shattered. He lay crumpled behind a rock that had undoubtedly saved his life. Stunned and covered with blood, he sipped weakly from a litter bearer's canteen. "Don't waste your time here," said Wong. His voice was almost inaudible. He appeared to be in deep shock. The farm-boy messenger handed the colonel the bugle. It was dented and splattered with blood. "I can play it a little," he said. "Bring it with you," replied Yang. He gathered up his headquarters squad and stumbled northward across the ridge in the direction of Unsan. The time was 0310, November 2. The anvil of ambush had blocked the American escape. Now the black-smith's hammer would destroy them.

U.S. Army vehicles were backed up along the roads which led from the town and from the American defense positions farther to the west. Many trucks looked abandoned. The enemy were running about in great confusion, under fire from Chinese troops inside the town. Unsan itself was well ablaze, a knocked-out tank blocking the main street. Store dumps exploded sporadically. A single American regiment was trapped down there, Yang was told. He marveled at their prolific transportation. No wonder these foreign devils had trouble defending mountainous terrain. They were road-bound. Prisoners of their own technology. The Chinese avoided roads. They kept to mountain paths. They traveled light and fast, attacking without the aid of artillery.

A few Soviet-made Katushka rockets had hit the American positions early in the attack. There was no other supporting fire. The battle was to be won or lost by foot-soldiers. Colonel Yang sent for his mortar squad, directing fire among the lines of silent trucks. Then he ordered his tired men to dig in deep below the hillcrests. Dawn was less than three hours away and with it would come the avenging American aircraft. Unless the weather changed. Over to the west it had begun to snow.

Outside the Unsan perimeter, Around 0300, November 2, 1950

The Chinese left nothing to chance at Unsan. While regular assault troops were blocking off the U.S. First Cavalry's escape route, a 30-

man commando squad was covertly infiltrating the American position on the quiet western perimeter of the Nammyon River. . . .

The squad marched boldly up in column, three abreast, swinging casually along the highway to Unsan as if they were South Korean troops in search of a quiet night's shelter. The bluff was perfectly believable: thousands of ROKs were milling around the valley. Captured helmets, parkas, and combat fatigues perfected the Chinese disguise. The commandos bunched closer as they approached the bridge. Any moment now there would surely be a shout, an alarm, a burst of gunfire. The men plodded on with bated breath, gripping concealed weapons, ready for instant action. Nothing happened. Undoubtedly it was cold and very late. Close to three o'clock on the morning of November 2. And so with a battle raging a few kilometers away, a single sentry wearily waved the squad across the narrow, slippery bridge which led inside the American defenses. They glimpsed a cold-pinched, unshaven face peeping forlornly over the sandbagged emplacement, a BAR automatic rifle close at hand. Captain Lao Kongcheng of the Sharp Swords could scarcely believe his luck. The ruse was working better than he had dared hope. Cheerfully he shouted "Sixth ROKs" as they passed the sentry post. Mission school had given him a smattering of English.

This kind of raid was greatly encouraged by Chinese commanders, who liked to quote the ancient adage: "It is good to win a battle; better to win it without losing a single man." Specialist squads trained for quick cloak-and-dagger attacks were attached to most regiments. Many of these squads had won distinctive titles for their daredevil activities. The dubbing of Captain Lao's group as "The Sharp Swords" was an honor equivalent to a unit citation. They'd earned it at the height of the civil war against the Nationalists. Posing as the advance party of a nonexistent division, the squad had fooled an entire battalion of Nationalist troops into throwing down their arms.

Reconnaissance patrols of the 1st Battalion, 347th Regiment, discovered the opportunity for a far deadlier antic here in Korea when scouting the American positions southwest of Unsan. By the evening of October 31, Chinese commanders had drawn detailed plans of the semicircular U.S. defense perimeter, which lay within a patch of fairly flat ground between two rivers. It was noted that the defenders were dangerously lax. Scouts reported that the Americans were sitting back in their foxholes relying on air strikes and artillery to do the fighting for them. No effort was being made to mount aggressive patrols to ward off (or warn of) impending attack. Sentries appeared grossly negligent. Defense works were haphazard, ill-sited, and undermanned. The enemy looked like rookies who had never fought a war.

The Sharp Swords were given ten hours to plan and prepare their strike. Three South Korean divisions were disintegrating east of Unsan, so there was no shortage of captured ROK uniforms and equipment for purposes of disguise. A Chinese sergeant rehearsed the squad in column marching, using the short-paced step peculiar to U.S.-trained troops, while his captain climbed into a hilltop observation post and personally checked the lay of the land. It would take 20 minutes, Lao reckoned, to march up to the bridge across the freezing Nammyon River—20 minutes in which the squad would be very vulnerable indeed. Another 20 minutes should see them into the heart of the American encampment. There could be no delays. Timing was crucial. The attack would have to synchronize with the main regimental offensive, creating a panic diversion at a crucial point in the battle.

The bulk of the Chinese assault forces, attacking from the north, would fight their way through Unsan and beyond, leaving enemy troops on the town's western side undisturbed. The battalion of the 347th Regiment now occupying the western side of the Nammyon had originally been scheduled to launch a costly frontal attack directly across the river. Instead it would now block enemy attempts to break through to the rescue of their compatriots along the western high- way—and block the trapped enemy's attempts to break out. If the Sharp Swords succeeded, the battalion assault could still proceed as planned.

One thing puzzled Captain Lao: the unguarded bridge. At the very least, a tank should have been covering this vital entry point, backed up by several well-prepared machine-gun positions. Yet the tanks were herded together inside the perimeter like sheep sheltering from wolves. Weapon pits close to the bridge looked empty. For a time he suspected a trap. But no, the Americans were just plain careless, Captain Lao concluded as the Sharp Swords marched openly through their enemy's camp. He checked his watch. It was 0306. In less than 15 minutes his squad would spring to the attack.

The weather was growing more wintry; snow showers were blotting out the sentry post. The Chinese squad might have been advancing through a smoke screen. Heavy storm clouds cloaked the moon. The Americans slept on, amazingly oblivious to the rout around Unsan. The 3rd Battalion, 8th Regiment of the U.S. First Cavalry was oddly unconcerned by the muffled thumps and bangs, the glow of distant fires, and the sporadic tracer bursts rising above the hidden town. The battalion had been told to prepare to pull out; pending delivery of that order they grabbed themselves more sack time. Attempts to arouse the drowsy defenders were apparently ignored.

The Sharp Swords had marched a kilometer past the sentry post when they spotted a huddle of trucks and tanks near a wood-roofed dugout. Captain Lao called his squad leaders together there for final consultations. He felt desperately exposed, crouching there in the middle of a plowed field. Everyone knew what must be done, he reiterated, but at the end of it they must remember the rendezvous: a Korean burial mound close to the largest American vehicle park, some two kilometers away.

The squad split up. The smaller group was led by Big Ears Wong, a tall, gangling Shandong peasant with enormous muscles. Some said he'd been a flame swallower in a traveling circus. No one else could carry the mortar around with the same careless abandon. His shorter, bowlegged companion, known as Little Li, was almost as powerful, bearing a heavy box of mortar bombs on each shoulder. They were accompanied by, among others, Fat Belly Wu, the cook, who now toted a submachine gun. Big Ears Wong ran to the nearest high ground to set up his mortar. At this point, inside the perimeter, he could bring down fire on any part of the enemy defenses. When all was ready he flashed a signal with a shaded lamp to the Chinese troops waiting across the river.

The men who stayed with Captain Lao carried mostly satchel charges and stick grenades. They included Little Liu, the bugler, an 18-year-old peasant orphaned by the Japanese; and Kung, a bespectacled, serious youth who had been teaching in Tsinan High School. The ex-teacher was qualifying to become a commissar, and was regarded as the squad's political activist. There was also another Li, a former Nationalist soldier, who had once smoked opium. Opium Li still chain-smoked cigarettes, and coughed wheezily from ravaged lungs.

Captain Lao dashed for the vehicle park. The others panted close behind him. He threw his first satchel charge into the nearest truck as Little Liu blew mournful blasts on his bugle. An answering Chinese call came from across the river, followed by heavy fire directed at the Americans' outer defenses. The first truck exploded. Then a second. An American stumbled into the open, his uniform aflame. The bugler cut him down with a burst of automatic fire. Chinese commandos carrying rifles fixed their bayonets and hurled themselves at the surrounding foxholes, skewering the Americans who came scrambling out.

The enemy command post was located in a nearby field. Captain Lao threw a satchel charge down the ramp, but it burst harmlessly against the door. He shot the first man to emerge, and would have fought his way inside were it not for the sudden uproar in the vehicle park. Savage fighting had broken out around the tanks. Lao lobbed a grenade into the command post and ran back to the battle. An

American sergeant in his shirtsleeves sat firing a pistol from the turret of a tank. Several of the Chinese squad went down. Attempts to drop their grenades inside the tanks had failed, as the Americans had climbed up there first. Lao warned his men not to get silhouetted against the fires, but they were too excited to listen and rushed madly around the blazing vehicles still hurling satchel charges. Each new burst of flames was greeted with a whoop of triumph.

A wounded American officer limped past in the firelight. Lao held his fire, covering the officer with his carbine. The man was collapsing from loss of blood. Lao told him in English to go find a medic. The officer nodded vaguely and wandered off across the frozen fields. The Chinese found his body the following day. It was the commanding officer of the 3rd Battalion, Major Robert J. Ormond.

Captain Lao decided to pull back. The Sharp Swords had done their best. They had been in action slightly more than half an hour, though it seemed like half a day. The captain ran off to the rendezvous. Little Liu sounded the recall. About twelve men assembled, breathless but elated, behind the humpbacked burial mound. Another bugle call, and bombs from the mortar of Big Ears Wong began to rain on the vehicle park. Assault troops launched the attack across the Nammyon River. Americans began deserting their riverside positions, streaming past in the direction of Unsan. The Sharp Swords fired steadily and deliberately into the fleeing mob. They counted 30 certain kills, although Lao later found only eight American dead. Big Ears Wong and his men dashed in from their position shortly before dawn. The hilltop would be untenable in full light of day.

The captain tried to calculate casualties. Ten of his men were missing. Some might still be lost out there in the dark. The others need not all be dead, though severely wounded men stood little chance lying on freezing ground. The Sharp Swords were resigned to taking losses. The fate of man was preordained, most Chinese believed, though there was no harm in taking a few precautions. These tough troopers considered themselves indoctrinated Marxists, but remained peasants at heart. Concealed about their persons were amulets, paper prayers, slivers of jade, and good-luck charms. They would make offerings to the gods when the commissars were not watching.

Dawn found the Americans still cut off among their trucks and tanks. An American machine gun was still firing from the nearby command post. Big Ears Wong tried lobbing stick grenades in its direction but they fell short. Captain Lao debated whether to set up the mortar again, but the nearest Americans were 200 meters away. Every move beside the burial mound drew heavy, accurate fire. He decided to wait for nightfall. Something would first have to be done for his men. No one had yet complained but all were tired, cold, and hungry. Foragers were sent slithering out behind the low rice field walls in search of straw. It would help keep them warm—and camouflaged. The last emergency biscuits had been eaten, so Fat Belly Wu crawled off to find food.

The cook came back dragging a large American cardboard box filled with small brown cans, boxes of crackers, and a few candy bars. He opened the cans with his jackknife and heaped up a mixture of beans and stew. The men pecked tentatively at this chilly mess with their chopsticks, exclaimed at the exotic taste, then wolfed it down.

What they now needed, Wu announced, was some hot black tea. The squad thought he was joking. Their canteens were frozen. The only drinking water available was a mouthful of snow. The cook used the same jackknife to hollow out a fireplace in the side of the burial mound, then thawed the canteens over a small fire of straw, twigs, and scraps from the cardboard ration box. The Americans aimed a few bursts in their direction until the smoke died away. The shivering Chinese huddled together beneath a layer of straw, sipping mugs of scalding tea.

A blanket of oily smoke hung over the battlefield. The ground was littered with bodies, discarded equipment, and vehicles, all lightly dusted with the powdery snow. More than 100 jeeps and trucks stood abandoned near the road south of Unsan, along with some eight to ten guns. Men from the U.S. 1st and 2nd Battalions, 8th Regiment, rallying round officers such as Major John Millikin, had split into groups during the small hours of that chaotic morning, making their way southward to safety through the encircling Chinese. But there was little chance of breakout here for the entrapped survivors of the 3rd Battalion.

During the morning a light plane circled overhead and dropped the Americans a large bag. Captain Lao thought it must contain medical supplies. A helicopter swooped down, the first the Chinese had ever seen. It hovered above them like an obscene metallic dragonfly. Captain Lao leaned against the burial mound and fired a light machine gun into the sky. The dragonfly hurriedly flew away. American planes kept up a steady bombardment of the surrounding hills, avoiding Unsan. The enemy pilots did not want to hit their own men. They had no idea who was where. The Chinese captain found it impossible not to admire the skill of these airborne technocrats, totally detached from the cruel reality of earthbound conflict, diving through the lowering clouds, looping and rolling over the hilltops, splattering vast areas of uninhabited real estate with harmless tons of napalm and high explosive. Out here in the frozen rice fields those attacks would be more lethal. His squad had no hope of digging in if the airmen pinpointed their position.

Captain Lao could never cure himself of a chilling sense of vulnerability. It had recurred, regularly, throughout his past ten years of combat: a feeling that the enemy's only object was *his* destruction. Dreams of his first skirmish were still a nightmare. He was running across a field, running for his life, and the Japanese were right behind him. Rifle shots cracked past his head. Something slammed into his thigh. He plunged face forward in the long grass and lay waiting for the enemy to catch him. An officer in polished boots stumbled astride his body, flashing a long, bright sword . . . Sometimes Lao woke like a baby, blubbering for his mother. When he had been sick as a child in Tsingtao, his mother would soothe her son with hot towels, and beg him not to wake the foreign devils. Her husband was houseboy to American missionaries. The Reverend Albert Browne and his wife tried hard to provide their servant's son with a rudimentary education—and to secure his soul for Christ. But at sixteen he stole off to fight the Japanese, despite his mother's tearful pleading. Within a few months he was a runner, then a rifleman, in the Communist 343rd Brigade.

Submissive Chinese peasants were aroused for the first time against the Japanese, and their so-called One Hundred Regiments offensive slaughtered the outlying Japanese Shansi garrisons. Rail tracks were torn up, supply depots looted, and the hated invaders sent reeling back into the cities. But retribution, when it came, was frightful. The Japanese hit back with the "Three-All" campaign—kill all, burn all, destroy all—employing ten divisions to put the countryside to the sword. The 343rd Brigade made a hopeless stand in the foothills. For three days it held off the Japanese until food, ammunition, and the troops themselves were completely exhausted. Then suddenly they were all running, with men falling left and right in the frost-spangled grass. Young Lao fell too, and a sword-wielding Japanese officer was about to finish him off when the man reeled away, clawing at his chest. A Chinese squad leader, also fleeing, had bayoneted the officer in the back. The squad leader discarded his precious rifle, threw the wounded Lao over his shoulder, and maneuvered them both to safety.

Memories of those dreadful moments still haunted the commander of the Sharp Swords. Time and again in combat he felt a freezing terror, convinced that someone had him in his sights. It took a huge effort of will to play the commando leader in face of paralyzing fear. The matter was too personal, however, to discuss with anyone. He would lose face, perhaps be withdrawn from active duty. It was not until years later that he found many comrades shared similar feelings.

Captain Lao's orders were to stay close to the Americans and prevent a breakout. It seemed unlikely they would try anything by daylight. Lao's own increasing unease at his squad's isolated position prompted him to send a runner in search of the nearest regular Chinese unit. The safest direction, he told the runner, was westward toward the Nammyon. The river must by now be frozen over, so there was no need to risk wading across and freezing to death.

Two more men rejoined them, both slightly wounded, dragging a U.S. machine gun and several belts of ammunition. There was no tripod. They wiped off the mud, fed the first shell into the breach, and set the heavy weapon on an earth rampart covering the vehicle park. Test firing was postponed for fear of attracting attention, but they promised themselves that as soon as it was dark, the heavy machine gun would be directed against the holed-up Americans at point-blank range.

The runner returned at dusk, cold and scared. The cook gave him a can of stew warmed over the still-smoldering fire. The message he brought back ordered the Sharp Swords to withdraw as soon as it grew dark. They should make their way through the Chinese assault troops, which had already established themselves in the American foxholes this side of the Nammyon. The password was "Ma Ling," which apparently referred to some ancient battle. The squad should be well clear of the vehicle park by 1830, the message warned, because a major assault was scheduled an hour later, at which time they would eradicate the scattered pockets of American resistance in Unsan, the 3rd Battalion vehicle park, and its nearby command post.

Parachute flares lit the scene like day as the Sharp Swords began their withdrawal. The men froze, face downward, according to standing orders, but Captain Lao urged them to continue their ground-hugging crawl. Big Ears Wong and Little Li stayed behind to provide covering fire with the American machine gun. Their shooting was somewhat inaccurate. The heavy weapon bounced uncontrollably without its tripod. But it set off a deafening racket until something at last jammed. The two Chinese gunners jettisoned the unwieldy weapon and followed their comrades to the river.

Fighting spluttered on for two more days. The Chinese mounted heavy night attacks. The Americans fought back heroically but hopelessly. A message dropped by a U.S. light aircraft urged the marooned regiment to break out. Attempts to rescue them had been abandoned. The Chinese offensive was by this time threatening more than an isolated battalion in Unsan. Soon after dark on November 5, some 200 Americans dashed out of the vehicle park, heading east. Few of them evaded the waiting Chinese.

More than 1,000 men from First Cavalry were at first feared missing, but over the next two weeks some 400 filtered through the enemy lines. Some had been hidden for days by friendly Koreans. American losses finally totaled 600, half of them prisoners. These included the many wounded who had been left behind. Nine tanks, twelve 105-mm howitzers, one tank recovery vehicle, and 150 assorted vehicles also fell into enemy hands.

The day after resistance ceased, the Sharp Swords returned to the battlefield. They picked their way among the frozen corpses to retrieve useful weapons, documents, and communications equipment. Seven of their squad were found among the dead. Thoughts now turned to food. Rations were short again. Everyone felt hungry. The main assault troops who overran Unsan had already looted most of the American stores, but Big Belly Wu found enough discarded cans around the command post to serve his squad sausages and beans. They returned to their old rendezvous, the Korean burial mound, eating, smoking, and listening to the message of congratulations from the regimental commander. "Your efforts," the message declared, "were a major contribution to the destruction of the enemy division." (Their chief victim was a single American battalion but this had not yet been clearly established.) "It was," the message more accurately concluded, "the first imperialist force destroyed by the Chinese Peoples' Volunteers in the defense of Korean soil."

Some of the American prisoners were under guard inside the vehicle park. They looked shocked and frozen. Captain Lao tried out his broken, mission-school English. He was surprised to find himself understood. (It had been ten years since he had spoken a word of the language.) The Americans were curious to know what had hit them. They were astounded to learn their captors were Chinese.

"For God's sake!" one of them burst out. "This isn't your war."

"It is now," said Captain Lao.

9

Jia Peixing at the Chungchon Front / "Scared of a Bunch of Chinese Laundrymen?" / General Peng Plans the Great Chinese Offensive.

On the Chungchon River front,
North Korea,
November 4, 1950

Jia Peixing, the newly recruited regimental runner, could never make out what was going on. His regiment of the Chinese Peoples' Volunteers seldom seemed to stop marching. After a week spent chasing South Korean troops among the central mountains his colonel told them a new battle was imminent, but this time with the Americans. Off they went again on foot, struggling across successive waves of bare, brown hills. The reasons behind these bursts of activity remained unclear to Jia. His commissar said they were resisting an American invasion of Korea. Most of the younger soldiers, though, had never seen an American. Nor did they know much about Korea. It was just barbarian country somewhere to the south of Manchuria.

Korea was as close to China, the commissar said, as lips and teeth. The American invasion of Korea was only one phase of a barbarian campaign of imperialist conquest which threatened China. The arguments were confusing to a city-bred teenager with only four years of schooling. But he couldn't help feeling excited. Soldiers were supposed to fight. This was a wonderful opportunity.

152

Jia Peixing, the 18-year-old son of a coal miner, had joined the PLA in January of 1950 with hopes of becoming a radio operator. But after six weeks' boot camp he had instead been assigned to local defense duties at a steel mill. Rumors began flying in mid-August of momentous happenings in Korea, and on September 2 he was drafted, as a runner, to the headquarters of the 358th Regiment, 120th Division of the 40th Field Army. The understanding was that he would be trained as a signaler as soon as equipment became available. That meant later rather than sooner. There were as yet only two or three old radio sets in the headquarters, all operated by former Nationalist soldiers.

Apart from a telephone line to division, contact was maintained by runners. Boys like Jia stumbled around the combat zone, pistols at their hips and canvas message bags around their necks. It was a lowly but important job. His regimental commander, Colonel Gu Dehua, constantly stressed the need for swift and accurate communication. He practiced it himself by keeping his staff up-to-date with developments. Even the most junior runners were invited to his morning briefing. They did not understand everything their commander said, but they still felt flattered and conspiratorial.

The breakfast-time briefing on November 1 enabled Colonel Gu to review the course of recent operations. Since October 25, he recalled, China's 40th Field Army had been successfully engaging South Korean puppet units in the vicinity of Onjong. The ROK 6th Division had been completely destroyed in less than 48 hours. Further action in the direction of Huichon hurled back the ROK 8th Division, endangering the enemy flank and halting the threatened advance toward the Yalu.

Jia failed to grasp the finer points of tactics, but saw some reason for the past week's exertions in this dreary corner of Korea. Newly recruited runners were kept clear of the fighting, though he'd heard occasional bursts of distant gunfire and seen glum lines of grubby prisoners plodding up the valley roads.

The 119th and 120th Divisions were now being ordered westward, the colonel went on, to head off the enemy's northward advance. The danger point was near the coast, north of the Chungchon River. American forward units along the coastal road were within 60 kilometers of the Chinese border. Colonel Gu traced the enemy dispositions on the map. Getting the regiment into attack positions involved tough marching. They had to cover little more than 30 kilometers as birds fly, but a lot more over the hills.

Some of the officers groaned. Young Jia couldn't think why. To him, the map was meaningless. Its squiggly contour lines looked like globs of colored noodles. The rookie runner still felt out of place in this tough outfit. Most of his comrades were much older men—aged between 27 and 30—who were veterans of countless battles. They told tall stories about their civil war campaign in the far south of China, where people ate dogmeat, the same as these Koreans, the rain was like warm soup, and no one had ever seen snow.

Crossing into Korea had, of course, been fun. The 40th Field Army had groped its way across the two huge steel bridges at Andong in the dead of night. The first day on Korean soil was spent sleeping in farming villages along the highway. Houses and barns were mud-walled, heavily thatched. The peasants were busy salting down huge jars of winter cabbage which they called *kimche*. The Koreans were shabby and aloof, their country sad and unimpressive. Warnings circulated through the ranks of a serious food shortage among the civilian population. Foraging was strictly forbidden. The newly ar-rived troops were told they would be entirely fed through coolies bringing supplies from Manchuria. But the coolies had to be fed as well. There wasn't enough food to go around. Everyone was hungry. Some of the coolies grew so weak they dropped their loads.

American planes roamed harmlessly overhead throughout the day. The Chinese found it easy to fool them. Strict march discipline was observed. On the very rare occasions when they marched by day, the troopers learned to keep still whenever the lookout blew his bugle. Once into the mountains, they carefully concealed themselves beneath trees and camouflage netting.

The approach of winter shrouded the sky with opaque gray clouds. Snow began falling as the regiment left Onjong to confront the Americans. Not heavily, but enough to make the going tough on the treacherous trails. The column climbed to giddy heights in the waning moonlight by grabbing onto icy trees and bushes, slithering and cursing—marching until the legs ached, the lungs burned, and backs seemed near to breaking. One man slipped and fell over a cliff. Luckily he broke only a leg. The litter-bearers had trouble carrying him.

The regiment spent November 2 in Yongsan-dong. The pretty little huddle of gray-tiled roofs and hidden courtyards had recently been occupied by the Americans, who had left the town cruelly battered. The few remaining inhabitants said the Americans always destroyed everything they captured. This was the way they punished resistance. The briefest bursts of sniper fire were enough to invite air strikes and artillery. Here there'd been no resistance, but the Americans shelled the town regardless. The lovely old temple was pitted with shell fragments. Part of its roof was missing.

Jia Peixing explored the damaged buildings. He thought them more stylish than the Buddhist temples in his native Fushun. Long before the Communist victory in China, Jia's mother had tried to enroll him in the priesthood. But the monk in charge of the novices beat him so much that at last he ran back home. Standing before the great gilt Buddha, the boy pondered his fate in the coming battle. The priests preached belief in endless dharma, ensuring ultimate salvation after a cycle of rebirths. The commissars dismissed such priest-talk as superstitious garbage. It was hard to know who was right. There could be no harm, however, in praying for guidance and protection. Furtively he lit a half-burned joss stick in the big brass bowl before the Lord of Compassion. Two Korean women crept out of the shadows. They watched him, but said nothing. They seemed a strangely silent people.

The American bombers came back two days later and blew the temple to bits. The Chinese were already gone. They had marched off again into the snowy night along the complex of roads that forked out of Yongsan-dong—first toward Pakchon, reportedly in enemy hands, then east in the direction of Chonghyon. Trucks accompanied them for the first time. There were no more than a dozen of them, but the Manchurian coolies must have been relieved. The burdens of supply grew heavier the farther south the Chinese moved.

Six kilometers before Pakchon the Chinese left the road, the columns of brown-clad troops meandering into wooded hill country. Their quilted jackets and fur hats blended marvelously with the dappled, bleak terrain. Once again the enemy would be taken by surprise.

The silent offensive began soon after dawn on November 4. Two Chinese divisions struck at enemy forces north of the Chungchon River. The 119th Division trickled across a small tributary river, the Kuryong, easily overrunning initial American resistance. Forward units of the U.S. 19th Infantry Regiment fled without putting up much of a fight. Jia Peixing's own division, the 120th, pushed south to outflank something called the British Commonwealth Brigade. It was composed of non-American barbarians.

The 120th Division of the Chinese Peoples' Volunteers was ordered to exploit a 12-kilometer gap between the American and Commonwealth forces. That involved another terrible climb, much of it in the dark. Fortunately they had found a few mules for the big mortars. Otherwise it was the same grumbling grind up precipitous slopes, frightening the pheasant and deer, negotiating pathways that would have worried a mountain goat. It was still dark when Colonel Gu Dehua established himself on a ridge overlooking the Chungchon River. The Chungchon split at this point into reefs, sandbars, and little tree-crowned islands. Its icy water glistened beneath the waning moon. The river was not yet completely frozen. Another week would see it solid enough to take trucks and troops.

Members of Jia's headquarters staff who were not immediately needed sat back among the rocks resting their aching bodies. Cooks conjured up a carefully shielded fire. They prepared bowls of steaming rice and mugs of tea. The men mixed rice and tea together, slurping it down hungrily. Jia dunked one of his emergency biscuits in the mess, ignoring warnings of the hunger to come.

The first cold streaks of dawn revealed the whole wide valley. Ahead of them lay Anju, said to be the enemy headquarters, a smoky patch among the sandbars. Tall chimneys farther to the west rose from the industrial center of Sinanju. Directly below them columns of enemy vehicles raised dust clouds close to the riverbank. Small American spotter aircraft flitted mothlike through the early sunlight.

Other Chinese forces had attacked at dawn, Colonel Gu told his staff, advancing beyond the British positions and nearly overrunning their supporting guns. The gunners were American, the colonel declared with his hard, grating laugh. The British imperialists were no longer rich. They could not afford their own artillery in Korea. But the attacking Chinese force—the 1st Battalion, 358th Regiment— was in danger of overreaching itself. The battalion must be warned to hold back. Gu called for a runner.

Jia Peixing was given his instructions. He had to find the battalion command post on the edge of the valley, somewhere below him, among the shell bursts. At last he was heading into battle, and the prospect turned him cold with fright. A sympathetic staff officer guided the youngster partway down the ridge, pointed him in the proper direction, and wished him luck.

"When in doubt, throw yourself flat," he said.

Jia ran down the slope, the undergrowth thickening around him as he descended. He found the vegetation strangely comforting. Clumps of bushes reached out to conceal, to shield, to detain him. But soon after he reached the valley floor someone began exploding firecrackers. They were giant crackers, larger than the New Year ones in Fushun, so deafeningly loud he feared they would burst his eardrums. Earth fountained up around him. Invisible demons screamed out of the morning sky, hurling scrub and rock and topsoil high into the air. The boy blundered across a dried-up stream. A group of Chinese soldiers crouched in the surrounding bracken. They yelled and waved, warning him to take cover. He hit the ground seconds before a bursting shell half-buried him in dirt and pebbles.

A sergeant dusted the runner down when the barrage lifted. The sergeant's jacket was torn. A thin trickle of blood ran down his face. Most members of his squad had suffered minor cuts and bruises. They shrugged it off without complaint. The regiment had taken a worse pounding outside Shenyang, they mumbled, back in '47, though it had to be admitted these Yankees mustered extraordinary fire-power. "Go carefully from here on," the sergeant warned, directing Jia toward the battalion command post. "This attack has stirred up a wasp's nest."

It had indeed. The U.S. 61st Field Artillery Battalion, supporting the British 27th Commonwealth Brigade, faced inundation beneath waves of Chinese infantry from the surrounding rice fields. A company of the Argyll & Sutherland Highlanders, sent to the assistance of the 61st, found the American gunners blasting their attackers over open sights. Chinese dead were piled up 30 yards from the howitzer gun shields.

Jia paused at a casualty station to check his directions. An orderly in a blood-stained rubber apron was prodding a groaning man's shattered face. He pointed absently across the fields. "Follow the casualties," he grunted. "Be careful not to join them." An officer staggered in, both arms held stiffly away from his body. Blood poured from his jacket sleeves. "See what I mean?" said the orderly. He looked up and saw the boy's frightened face. His look softened. "Take it carefully, kid. Heaven's full of dead heroes."

The young runner was soon pinned down again. Heavy machine-gun fire trapped him in the open rice fields. He crawled whimpering through the frozen paddy stalks. Up ahead, behind the irrigation wall, fellow Chinese soldiers were taking cover. He scuttled over to join them, clapping the first man heartily on the shoulder. The soldier's head swung round, blood-stained with sightless eyes. Every man huddled here was dead. A mindless panic hurled him forward. The command post lay in a copse 200 meters ahead. He zigzagged over the open ground, stumbled across another heap of corpses, and dived into the shelter of the trees, sobbing with fear and exhaustion.

The 1st Battalion commander was a big man made bigger by his bulky clothing. He called Jia "a young hero," speaking with genuine admiration, then read his message and nodded thoughtfully. With-drawal might prove tricky for an hour or two, he remarked, but when the firing died down he would give the necessary orders. One of the staff pointed out that the runner was wounded. An unnoticed nick in the left arm spread a widening patch of blood across his jacket sleeve. The commander bound the scratch with his own emergency dressing and sat the boy down to rest beneath a friendly fir tree. An air burst showered the command post with cones and twigs, but nobody flinched. Quietly, privately, Jia began to cry. . . .

Colonel Gu looked relieved when Jia got back to regimental headquarters on top of the ridge. The return trip had taken four hours. "We feared for you," the colonel said, calling a medic to check the dressing. He seemed to have been scolding himself for sending a rookie on such a dangerous mission. "You have to learn sometime, I suppose," he added. But there were no more missions into the rice fields for Jia.

Two days later the battle ended. Orders came through to break off and withdraw. The Americans had been duly warned. There was no sense in pressing costly attacks until the Chinese command could gauge the enemy's reaction. The Chinese armies pulled back as silently as they had come. They melted away into the mountain valleys north of Yongsan-dong. The Americans were left wondering what hit them.

Tokyo,
Early November, 1950

General Douglas MacArthur received the reports from Korea with querulous disbelief. Chicom forces south of the Yalu River? It didn't make sense. The Chinese Communists had *forfeited* their chance of influencing events in Korea. Back in August, at the height of the Pusan battle, a mere two divisions of them would have tipped the balance. Now it was too late. The general had said as much to President Truman at their mid-October summit on Wake Island.

Chinese troops were, admittedly, massing in Manchuria. Intelligence reports confirmed a constant buildup of PLA units along the Korean border. But this did not necessarily mean the Chinese were planning to enter the war. And even if they did, their forces would immediately be detected. No one doubted the reconnaissance power of the U.S. Far East Air Force. MacArthur displayed touching faith in airpower, though he knew little enough about it. His operational experience with aircraft was essentially tactical. But he regarded the bomber as the definitive weapon. MacArthur believed, for instance, that bombers could cow the Chinese. Its enormous armies would crumble under air attack. Like most Westerners, he had a low opinion of Chinese soldiers. Aesthetes the Chinese might be, with their 3,000 years of art and literature, but soldiers they certainly were not.

Anyone with experience of Asia knew the kind of rabble the Chinese had historically sent into battle. There had been scant improvement, as far as the general knew, since the days of the warlords. A glance at the history books told the story: not for centuries had a Chinese army defeated a first-class foreign foe. The general actually appeared to hope that the Chinese Communists, the loathsome Chicoms, would blunder into the muzzles of his guns. "I pray nightly that they will," he said to Averell Harriman. At Wake he is reported to have told Truman: "If the Chinese Communists cross the Yalu, I shall make of them the greatest slaughter in the history of mankind."

MacArthur had remained unmoved by Chinese threats to enter the Korean War. The Chicoms were patently bluffing. They would do anything, he pontificated, to avoid a showdown. The tough talk coming from Peking was a typical Communist ploy to scare America's weak-kneed allies in Western Europe or to angle for an advantageous position at some future peace conference. But it could be safely assumed that China would never commit itself to a hopeless war. The general's analysis of Chinese intentions was soldierly and simple. The moment of maximum military advantage to China had passed.

But the situation in early November of 1950 demanded subtler, and civilian, judgments. To Americans, the Korean conflict was a purely military problem. To the Chinese, the imminent liquidation of North Korea was a threat not merely to their internal security but to their bid for leadership in emergent Asia. The decisions reached in Peking were therefore primarily political, and MacArthur's martial acumen did not extend to politics. Chinese attitudes during the critical autumn of 1950 cried out for diplomatic evaluation. But American diplomacy was at a discount in eastern Asia. It had been thrust into the background the moment the military gained control of Japan. That nation's postwar occupation had given MacArthur and his fellow generals an unparalleled influence over regional policy, one which the Korean campaign had only enhanced.

The outbreak of World War II had given generals and admirals a sudden, heady importance. Graduates of West Point and Annapolis blossomed overnight from despised time-servers to heroes. And American taxpayers, who had once shared with the Chinese an aversion to the profession of arms, came to regard every garrulous brass hat as a fount of wisdom. MacArthur grew into the guru of the western Pacific. Such was his reputation at this point in history that no one dared question his most questionable assumptions. President Truman, Secretary of State Dean Acheson, the Joint Chiefs of Staff—none felt inclined to argue with the hero of Bataan, the victor of Inchon.

Roy Appleman's official history of the opening months of the Korean campaign notes that "normally the intelligence evaluation of whether a foreign power has decided to intervene in a war in national force involves political intelligence at the highest level." The author goes on to remark that Washington must have been undecided about Chinese intentions, or concurred with its field commander's judgments. The Truman administration was unfortunately in no position to make an independent appraisal—not while MacArthur dominated the flow of intelligence. In more normal circumstances his pronouncements would have been cross-checked against information from the Central Intelligence Agency. But the agency was weak throughout east Asia. It was actually barred from the general's bailiwick. Not until 1952 were CIA operatives granted permission to work in Japan. Their first emphasis was on cloak-and-dagger work, rather than intelligence gathering, a trend that later distorted (and damaged) the agency's role in Taiwan, the Philippines, and, ultimately, Indochina.

Over the course of what turned out to be its final two years, the Truman administration faced rising opposition. The 1950 congressional elections produced a sharp swing against the Democrats. Large numbers of voters were plainly impatient with the setbacks on the Asian mainland. (Tart-tongued Acheson was already under savage congressional attack for "losing China.") And the man at the wheel, former captain of artillery Harry Truman, refused to question his Far East commander's conduct of the war. "You pick your man . . . you've got to back him up," Truman said years later. "That's the only way a military organization can work. I got the best advice I could and the man on the spot said this was the thing to do . . . so I agreed."

The man on the spot clung to his eccentric routine. Each morning, seven days a week, MacArthur drove out of the embassy residence in Tokyo escorted by military police. Around 1030, his 1941 Cadillac, borrowed from a businessman in Manila, pulled up before the six-story, fortresslike Dai Ichi (Number One) building, overlooking the Japanese imperial palace. The Dai Ichi had been the nerve center of the U.S. occupation from the end of World War II. A small crowd of waiting Japanese bowed reverently as their newfound father-figure bounded across the sidewalk. An elevator stood waiting in the entrance hall. (A humble Japanese carpenter once walked into the same car ahead of the Supreme Commander. The man was graciously allowed to stay. The story made national headlines. High-powered public relations had always helped fertilize the MacArthur cult.) In his modest penthouse office, far from the telephone but surrounded by an adoring staff, the general—now in his seventies—labored until lunchtime handwriting drafts of speeches, correspondence, and memoranda. He loved the sight (and sound) of his own grandiloquent prose. Keeping quiet was an art he never entirely mastered.

Always within call was Major General Courtney Whitney, originally an expatriate attorney in Manila, the investment adviser entrusted with the MacArthur family portfolio. Many heartily detested this fawning courtier. His unique privileges included the right to eavesdrop from the next-door office whenever the Supreme Commander received important visitors.

Another key figure in the inner court was Major General Charles A. Willoughby (formerly Tscheppe-Wiedenbach), the German-born head of intelligence. Blame would soon be placed on Willoughby for misreading the omens, though he was doing no more than matching his master's judgment. A typical Willoughby intelligence forecast described Chinese deployments in Manchuria in the fall of 1950 as "probably in the category of diplomatic blackmail." He suggested that the Chinese and Soviets "have decided against further expensive investment in support of a lost cause." Rather than enter the war as active participants, "the Chinese Communists, if called upon, would furnish replacements through discreet integration with Korean units."

MacArthur, in his eighth decade, laid aside the cares of office only when he returned each day to the residency for lunch and a leisurely nap. For a few hours he could also be the devoted family man. He drove back to the Dai Ichi around 1730, often working until midnight. Correspondents who covered Supreme Headquarters, Tokyo, during the end of the MacArthur era, remember it as a quirky, highly personalized regime. Staff meetings were considered superfluous. There was little interchange of ideas. A similarly complacent atmosphere is said to have paralyzed Pacific Fleet command before the Japanese whirlwind struck Pearl Harbor in 1941.

The first Korean storm signal went up October 25, 1950. South Korean forces reported capturing a Chinese prisoner at Unsan. The man could have come only from China because he spoke neither Korean nor Japanese. He was flown for interrogation to Pyongyang, where his story was that he belonged to a Chinese force of unknown strength which had lately crossed the Yalu River at Andong. From then on, the number of Chinese prisoners mounted. Ten had been taken by October 29. Four days later the total stood at 55. Searching examination, including the use of lie detectors, revealed the apparent existence in Korea of elements of six Chinese field armies—the 38th, 39th, 40th, 42nd, 50th, and 66th—each three or more divisions strong, with every division comprising some 10,000 men.

So as many as 180,000 Chinese troops might *possibly* have entered Korea. But the men charged with investigating this Chinese puzzle took their cue from Tokyo. Eighth Army intelligence officers shared Supreme Headquarters' disbelief that large numbers of Chicom troops could lurk undetected in the wilds of North Korea. There had to be a more rational explanation. Analyses flowing in from Korea all supported the view from the Dai Ichi penthouse. The experts agreed that small numbers of Chinese had reinforced the North Koreans. The facts were undeniable. Exactly why was less certain. One interrogator thought the Chinese were helping their neighbors defend the border region. Another plumped for protection of the Yalu power plants. All were agreed that insignificant numbers of Chicoms were involved. Chinese strength south of the Yalu was initially put at 5,000. Estimates rose to more than 60,000 over the next three weeks. Up to the moment the roof fell in, Eighth Army headquarters in Pyongyang could detect "no indications of open intervention on the part of Chinese Communist Forces in Korea."

Washington was less sanguine. The Joint Chiefs of Staff began worrying the moment reports of Chinese military activity came in from the Korean battlefront. The men charged with overall control of U.S. armed forces throughout the world were themselves being harassed by America's allies, particularly the British, who had always agonized over the advance into North Korea. The Joint Chiefs sharply demanded an explanation.

MacArthur refused at first to be ruffled. The reports did not worry him unduly, though he confessed difficulty in assessing Chinese intentions. A new note of hysteria crept into his pronouncements only after the setback at Unsan. By November 6 he was accusing China of entering the Korean War "in one of the most offensive acts of international lawlessness of historic record." The previous day he had demanded permission to throw his entire force of B-29 bombers against the Andong bridges. The Joint Chiefs of Staff hesitated, then consented. Several hits were registered on the bridge spans, while fire bombs wiped out the adjoining Korean city of Sinuiju. "Men and materiel in large force are pouring across all bridges over the Yalu from Manchuria," MacArthur shrieked to Washington. "This movement not only jeopardizes but threatens the ultimate destruction of the forces under my command." His public communiqué was less hysterical. But it paid tribute to General Walker for avoiding a surreptitious trap "calculated to encompass the destruction of the United Nations forces."

This was a far cry from the easy optimism of October, the confident declaration at the Wake conference: "We are no longer fearful . . . we no longer stand hat in hand." Three weeks later the same general was warning Washington that the formidable United Nations forces assembled in Korea faced imminent defeat. The Joint Chiefs were flabbergasted. Further clarification was urgently requested. The next day's reply was more restrained. MacArthur admitted that organized Chinese units of unknown strength had gone on the offensive in western Korea. They had also slowed his advance in the east. It was possible that if the enemy buildup continued, it could reach a point where his men might be forced to retreat. Only through an offensive could an accurate measure of enemy strength be taken. But two days later, November 9, the general had brightened enormously. The Joint Chiefs were assured that sufficient airpower was available to stop Chinese reinforcements crossing the Yalu while he finished off "those forces now arrayed against me in North Korea."

The Chinese themselves helped revive MacArthur's flagging optimism. At the height of the crisis, their forces completely disappeared. Before dawn on November 6 a division of Chinese Peoples' Volunteers was hammering Australian troops at the exposed tip of the U.S. Eighth Army perimeter north of the Chungchon River. By daybreak the attacks had ceased completely. Columns were seen withdrawing northward through the mountains. Suddenly, mysteriously, inexplicably, the Chinese went to ground.

If their intent through these hit-and-run maneuvers was to warn, it was a failed tactic. Soon MacArthur was urging resumption of the drive toward the Yalu. The Chinese gone, prospects looked good. The Supreme Commander now had four complete army corps, totaling 100,000 men, poised to flush out the last, seemingly defenseless strip of Korean territory skirting Manchuria. The enemy was trapped, he said, in the jaws of a giant pincer.

Landings at the end of October on Korea's east coast, just over 100 miles south of the Chinese border, had locked in place the right jaw of the pincer. Three U.S. X Corps divisions were deposited onto empty beaches. The North Koreans had fled. South Korean forces had already cleared the coast in their advance up the coastal road and, by the time the Americans stormed harmlessly ashore, were well on their way to the tiny North Korean–Soviet border.

Command of X Corps was still assigned to MacArthur's protégé, his chief of staff, Ned Almond. The corps included the First Marine and the 7th Infantry Divisions, conquerors of Inchon, plus the newly arrived 3rd Infantry Division. Both understrength army divisions were heavily fleshed out with South Koreans.

The marines struck out smartly from their Hungnam bridgehead in the direction of the Changjin Reservoir. This narrow inland lake, with its four big hydroelectric plants, lay high on a treeless, windswept plateau less than halfway from the coast to the Yalu. The one-lane approach road climbed through precipitous gorges ideal for ambush. Sure enough, the advancing marines were confronted by Chinese troops entrenched on the surrounding heights. The Chinese clung to Hill 750, the southern end of a long ridge thrusting out from the plateau, and fought a bitter six-day battle there with the marines before abruptly breaking off the action. From that point on, the marines moved with commendable care.

The 7th Division faced only sporadic resistance farther to the east. The first units to land at Iwon on October 29 advanced 50 miles by nightfall. Progress then slowed through treacherous mountainous terrain until the division emerged into the valley of the Ungi River. A brisk firefight developed as assault troops waded through its flooded waters. But the weather proved more irksome than the enemy. The wading men were badly frozen. Eighteen suffered frostbite. The clothes had to be cut off their bodies. Further movement was delayed while engineers built an oil-drum footbridge.

Winter was joining in the war. The mid-November weather suddenly turned to bitter cold. Temperatures dropped overnight from the bearable forties to ten, then twenty degrees below zero. The GIs were ill-equipped for such extremes. Each man had nothing more than threadbare fatigues, worn-out shoes, an old army topcoat, and half a blanket. Commanders appealed for parkas, woollen socks, and heavy underwear—and for heaters and hot food. Riflemen packed K rations under their arms to keep the food from freezing. Marines guzzled candy to maintain their energy levels. Medics rigged warming gear for morphine, blood plasma, and water-based medicines. The heating tent became standard equipment for the revival of cold-stunned men.

But no matter how inclement the weather, Colonel Herbert B. Powell was determined to urinate in the Yalu. The commander of the 17th Infantry Regiment, 7th Division, led his men forward in a column of battalions over the last mountain ridge overlooking the border. On November 21 he performed his historic rite.

The Americans had marched unopposed into the burned-out township of Hyesanjin. Seventy-five yards away, on the opposite bank of the river, rose the bare brown hills of China. The Yalu was almost totally frozen over. A six-foot center channel was rapidly shrinking. Four days later the narrow upper reaches would be solid ice. A Chinese village was clearly visible 300 yards upstream. Sentries patrolling the northern bank pointedly ignored the barbarian intruders. U.S. troops had been forbidden by the Joint Chiefs to advance this far, but the Supreme Commander characteristically ignored the order, pleading operational necessity. A bevy of generals arrived for a formal commemorative photograph; among them the 7th Infantry commander, Major General David G. Barr, former chief of the American Military Mission to China, and a beaming Ned Almond.

The breakthrough delighted General MacArthur. "Heartiest congratulations, Ned," he crowed, "and tell Dave Barr that the 7th Division hit the jackpot." It was better than Barr had seen in China, presiding in 1948 over the disintegration of the Nationalist forces in Manchuria. The UN's advance was now at high tide. Few other American soldiers would ever reach the Yalu.

The Supreme Commander urged the rest of his troops to shake the lead from their shoes, and ordered Ned Almond to the Koto-ri plateau to goose up the marines. The Leathernecks' commander, Major General Oliver P. Smith, refused to be hustled. He feared his troops were already dangerously dispersed. The recent skirmishes with the Chinese had left the marines painfully aware of their vulnerability in this hostile wasteland. "Scared of a bunch of Chinese laundrymen?" sneered Almond. But the mulish marines still delayed their advance, securing the heights, guarding their one escape route to the coast. This entirely professional precaution was to save them from destruction.

General Almond privately worried more about the Chinese threat than he cared to admit. So did many other senior officers. The affair at Unsan, for instance, had never been properly explained. Then there were all those Chinese prisoners. . . . To calm these fears, General Willoughby flew over from Japan. The intelligence chief dismissed the Chinese presence as "no more than a battalion of troops from each of the [Chinese] units identified." As for Unsan, *that* debacle had only occurred because 8th Cavalry allowed themselves to be overrun by a small, sharp surprise assault.

Over on the west coast, the Eighth Army commander, General "Johnnie" Walker, was as wary as the marines. Repeated orders from MacArthur to resume the drive to the Yalu were tactfully postponed. There could be no attempt to advance north of the Chungchon River, he declared, without additional reinforcements and supplies. The date for the resumed offensive, initially set for November 15, was put back to November 24, the day after Thanksgiving. By that time a third corps would have swelled Eighth Army's battle line.

Plans for the final advance still assigned the left flank of Eighth Army to I Corps, including the British Commonwealth Brigade, across the west-coast plain. The U.S. IX Corps, moved up to reinforce the center, was targeted on the farthest reaches of the Suiho Reservoir. The rehabilitated South Korean II Corps, again holding the right flank, would head for Kim Il Sung's hideout at Kanggye and, after that, the border. Beyond the right flank, nothing. A gap yawned between Eighth Army and the nearest X Corps troops to the east: a seemingly impassable wall of mountains, 20 to 35 air miles wide, separated MacArthur's pincers. By mid-November those pincers were slipping out of alignment. Troops of X Corps, pushing far to the north of Eighth Army, were in danger of becoming isolated. But Walker could do nothing to restore the balance because Almond's troops were independent of his command.

Eighth Army was responsible for X Corps' logistics but that was all. Control of its operations lay ultimately with MacArthur. Just why was never satisfactorily explained. The general seemed genuinely eager to promote the career of his old friend Ned Almond. MacArthur might also have been eager to cut Walker down to size. And splitting the field command in Korea prevented any one general besides MacArthur from claiming credit for victory.

Shenyang, Manchuria, People's Republic of China, November 15, 1950

A cruel wind cut through Shenyang. The winter was the worst in living memory. Citizens stayed home beside their stoves unless dragged outdoors by the most impelling business. The handful of hardy hawkers who hunched over their charcoal braziers, peddling chestnuts and roast corn, found few buyers among the trickle of pedestrians hurrying past in fur caps and padded jackets. Icy, dusty gusts cracked the lips and penetrated the heaviest quilted clothes.

Outside the main gate of the arsenal sentries stamped their feet in a hopeless effort to keep warm. General Peng's aide, Major Han Liqun, felt faint twinges of guilt, peering from the double-glazed comfort of the command post. Ranks of icicles suspended from the eaves partially obscured his view. Frost etched leaflike patterns across the grimy glass. A stormy, slate-gray sky threatened early snow. Down in the yard, the thermometer registered a record low for mid-November, with the experts warning of worse to come. It must be far colder in the distant mountains of Korea, the major mused. The simple tasks of washing and defecating became complicated, onerous operations in a wilderness of frozen rock. Major Han's own memories were of constant constipation during the winter battles in Manchuria, when the cold left him loath to unbutton his pants.

The only man who seemed to welcome this weather was General Peng Dehuai himself. The general rose regularly at 0530, performed a few basic *tai chi* exercises beside his bed, then trotted round the yard. Young Shu, Peng's bodyguard, stumbled alongside him swathed in furs. Some 20 minutes later the general would return briskly to his bedroom, breathless and frozen, deaf to the complaints of doctors who predicted imminent pneumonia. (He bathed and shaved in cold water, though hot water was always available, declaring he'd never used anything else for 40 years and had no intention of changing a lifetime's habits.) Promptly at 0630 the general was outdoors again, dressed in his oldest, least presentable winter uniform, ready to lead the entire staff on a stiff jog around the arsenal complex. The column wound through the wind-whistling lanes between workshops. Much of the plant was back in production, making rifles and handguns. Night workers, coming off shift, grinned at the passing soldiers. A two-kilometer circuit led officers and men back to the warmth of their barracks.

General Peng breakfasted quietly in his room, reading telegrams and dispatches over cups of tea and a bowl of rice gruel. The porridgelike congee, laced with slivers of liver or chicken, was specially spiced, Hunan-style, with small red peppers. The general ate slowly, savoring every mouthful; it gave him time, he said, to remember the days "when we all went hungry." His peasant instinct (or, as some would have it, a certain in-built pessimism) convinced him that hunger always hovered close at hand. The first staff conference of the day was called for 0800. The general was at his sharpest, Major Han recalls, first thing in the morning. His main decisions, Peng told his aide, were made "just before dawn." But on November 18, General Peng looked tired and ill. He had flown back to Shenyang the previous evening in an unheated plane, following a final briefing of commanders in Peking. Peng's sleep had been disturbed and feverish, though he stubbornly refused to see a doctor. He insisted on self-cure, chewing on an herbal root thought to clear headaches.

Snow was falling on Shenyang as the staff filed into the main operations room. White flakes frosted the caps and capes of the dispatch riders clumping cheerfully into the signals office. In the corridor outside two sentries proudly cradled brand-new Soviet submachine guns in their arms.

Major Han plied the general with steaming tea. It helped him overcome his irritated cough. Peng seemed strained and unusually harried, standing among his officers beside the big relief model. Over the past few weeks the face of the model had again changed drastically. The plaster peaks and plains were interlaced with yet more information—there were additional airfields in Manchuria, newly developed hill tracks through the wilds of North Korea—and, south of the Yalu River, a fresh forest of red-starred wooden markers revealed the growth of Chinese strength in North Korea.

The most remarkable concentration was in the northwestern corner of Korea, where the Chinese Ninth Army Group was assembling. This new force, 120,000 strong, was targeted mainly against the U.S. Marines. It was led by Lieutenant General Song Shilun, a 43-year-old Hunanese veteran of the Long March. Two of the three field armies under his command, the 20th and 26th, had been detached from forces once earmarked for the Taiwan invasion. The 27th Field Army came from Shandong. Each was supplemented by one division from the 30th Field Army.

Facing the U.S. Eighth Army, and poised to drive down the western coastal plain, was a much-enlarged Thirteenth Army Group. Strength: 180,000 men. The commander was a 40-year-old southerner, Lieutenant General Li Tianyu, who had made a reputation for ruthless, perhaps foolhardy, action by sacrificing his entire division during the Long March. (His troops had been wiped out by encircling Nationalist forces, thus winning time for members of the Communist party leadership to escape entrapment.) The Thirteenth Army Group had already seen action at Unsan, along the Chungchon River, and in the vicinity of the Changjin Reservoir. Its original three field armies, the 38th, 40th, and 42nd, had in the past three weeks been reinforced by the 39th, 50th, and the 66th Field Armies. The 39th came from Shandong, the 50th and 66th from central China. The 50th was made up of former Nationalist troops who had surrendered in Manchuria in 1948. Their commander, Lieutenant General Zeng Zesheng, present at this conference, had spent most of his military career *fighting* the Communists. Only three years before, Zeng had been working closely with the American adviser to the Nationalists, David Barr—who now commanded the U.S. 7th Division on the opposite side of this struggle.

General Peng showed his commanding generals the main features of the relief model. Song Shilun nodded approvingly at the simulated mountains; he had just completed a personal inspection of the terrain around the Changjin Reservoir. Major General Zhang Renchu, known as "Limp" Zhang for his wounded walk, declared he'd rather look at this model than march over the actual ground. He was a popular, cheerful commander, destined to lead the 26th Field Army against the U.S. Marines.

They were interrupted by a late arrival, Major General Liu Fei, who had once launched his own private guerrilla war against the Nationalists with 36 wounded soldiers and two pistols. Liu was now in charge of 20th Field Army. "It's snowing thicker than cowshit on the reservoir," he grunted to the assembled generals. Peng laughed. Coarse language made him feel at ease. The exchange of ribaldry died away as Peng's laughter turned to hoarse coughing. He tried to regain control of his voice as he shuffled through his notes.

"The enemy has learned nothing over the past few weeks. They continue to advance recklessly. To that extent, our first-phase offensive has been a failure," said General Peng. His voice was low and husky, his heavy Hunan accent more impenetrable than ever. There was a murmur of concern. Peng put down his notes, took up a pointer, and began flicking it across the model.

"My strategy may have been overly cautious," he went on, drawing a line along the Chungchon River. "But in an encounter of this nature, with so many unknown possibilities, it seemed essential to get into position and deliver deterrent attacks upon the Americans without provoking a level of retaliation that would escalate the Korean conflict into another world war." He paused to sip his tea. None of this was delivered off-the-cuff, as Major Han well knew. Peng was repeating the rationale worked out by the leadership in Peking.

"But all we seem to have accomplished is to convince the Americans that Chinese troops have not entered Korea in any strength." Peng shook a mournful head. "This is unfortunate, because China now has no alternative but to teach the imperialists a lesson." He brandished the latest intelligence reports. There was no longer any doubt about MacArthur's intentions. Any time now the American commander would launch his final offensive. It could be expected, at the very latest, within a week.

"And when it comes"—Peng paused to stifle a cough—"the Chinese Peoples' Volunteers will counterattack with all available force." Sweat stood out on his forehead. He leaned across the relief model, his audience craning their necks to follow his gestures. "The Ninth Army Group will encircle and exterminate the U.S. Marines around the Changjin Reservoir. Other enemy forces in that area will be mopped up along the coast. This should be possible, bearing in mind the enemy's scattered dispositions across difficult country."

Song Shilun, commander of the Ninth Army Group, nodded thoughtfully. The model made clear the problems he faced. The reservoir looked lost in the northwestern mountains, like a dull filling in old, decaying molars. The single supply road connecting the reservoir to the coast looked exceptionally vulnerable, trickling down plaster slopes to the imitation sea.

Peng Dehuai turned to Li Tianyu of the Thirteenth Army Group. His pointer tapped the narrow stretch of low-lying land, the western coastal plain between the Songchon estuary and the central mountain spine. "The other barrel of our gun will be fired from here. The Thirteenth Army Group will concentrate its main force against the South Korean puppet troops. Given the amount of surprise you will undoubtedly achieve, it might be possible to push the enemy back to Yongyu." He indicated a town halfway between the estuary and Pyongyang.

"No farther?" asked Li.

"We must content ourselves for the moment with establishing a line just beyond the 39th Parallel," Peng replied, waving the pointer across the narrow neck of the peninsula above the North Korean capital. "We do not have the logistic backup to advance much more."

He broke off in a fit of coughing. The dry air was aggravating his throat condition.

While Pen paused to sip his tea, the Chinese chief of staff, Xie Fang, gave his own appraisal of the enemy.

"The South Korean puppets do not want to fight this war," he told the generals. "Nor do the Americans. Most of them do not even know where Korea is. Their soldiers have just fought one major war, and feel that is enough. They would prefer to be home with their families." Xie opened a file containing unit reports. "Our field commanders indicate that the American soldiers panic easily. Their riflemen prefer to ride in trucks. They are afraid to die."

"The Americans are inexperienced and overconfident," Peng interjected. "They are unused to night combat. They depend too much on their tanks, planes, and artillery.

"Nonetheless, a word of caution." Peng Dehuai was on his feet again, sweating profusely, waving his tea cup instead of the pointer. "The enemy has firepower. The enemy has transportation. The enemy has supplies." He turned to General Xie. "Our supplies," he said. "Talk about that."

The soldiers of the People's Liberation Army had never known the luxury of full-scale logistical support, Xie said. They had always relied on their feet and their frugality in winning the civil war. That would not be enough in Korea. Most of their food, and all their ammunition, would have to be carried in from northeast China. It was not even certain whether the Chinese railroad system could carry the load. South of the Yalu River, rail traffic moved erratically, under constant air attack. Therefore most supplies would have to be moved by truck. The two best-equipped transportation units of the PLA had been assigned to Korea: the 42nd Truck Regiment to the Korean west coast, crossing at Andong, and the 5th Truck Regiment to the east, through Manpojin.

"That's only 800 trucks all told," said Xie. "No allowance made for servicing. The Americans have three times that number on the roads each day." Trucks were being rounded up from all over China, the chief of staff went on, but they would be lucky to keep more than three or four hundred of these operational. The breakdown rate was appalling.

The Chinese soldiers would have to lean, as in the past, on the sturdy shoulders of the laboring masses. The Revolutionary Committee of the Northeast had recruited more than half a million coolies to carry food and ammunition south across the Yalu River.

"Much as we welcome the efforts of our fellow laborers, it must be noted that coolie-power has serious limitations," said Xie. "These people have to be housed and fed over considerable distances. It will be an added worry for military commanders." Everything was likely to be in short supply. The soldiers would occasionally go hungry, perhaps even run short of ammunition. In time, however, the situation would gradually improve—as long as supply routes did not become overstretched.

"Supply routes will not be overstretched," Peng interrupted. His voice was hoarser than ever. "Our men face exceptional challenges. They have little artillery. No armor. No air support. They must perform heroically. But no more. They will never be called on to perform the impossible. Trust me. I give my word." He broke off in a spasm of coughing. Major Han brought him a chair and more hot tea. He sat down, shrugging apologetically to the staff.

General Xie brought the meeting to its conclusion, issuing packs of written orders and party directives. The generals filed out, shaking Peng's hand and mumbling sympathetically. Cars waited in the snow to whisk them to the Shenyang airfield for their flights back to Korea. There wasn't even time for lunch.

Peng sat alone beside the relief model, wiping his bloodshot eyes. Major Han went out to find a doctor. In the corridor he bumped into the Western-educated physician from Shanghai.

"All that running about in the cold," groaned the doctor as he checked the general's pulse and temperature. He peered sharply at the thermometer. "Bed," said the doctor. "The general has pneumonia."

10

With the Scots at Chungchon / An American Sacrifice / A Runner in Battle.

**A UN camp
South of the Chungchon River,
November 25, 1950**

The Scottish enlisted men had never heard of Thanksgiving. So that morning, when ration trucks arrived fully loaded with turkeys, their cooks were baffled. Something to do with pilgrims, their colonel said. The birds were hard-frozen, impossible to thaw out in time for this unknown, unscheduled celebration.

The dinner was eaten instead the following day, as the valley echoed to the thud of distant guns. The end-the-war offensive had begun.

"The Yanks canna' fight worth a fuck," the Scotsmen agreed, but man, they fed like fighting cocks. Folks back home bought turkeys only at New Year's Eve—which they called Hogmanay—and then not habitually. "Man, it's tough oot here," they joked. "Only the ice cream unit between me and the enemy." It was indeed a triumph of American logistics: so much specialized food delivered to so many scattered units at the end of overstretched supply lines.

The Scots who formed the 1st Battalion, the Argyll & Sutherland Highlanders, marveled at such provisions. They were resting in reserve near Anju, south of the Chungchon River, in their first break from weeks of desultory fighting.

They had been hurried out of their Hong Kong garrison the previous August to become part of the 27th Commonwealth Brigade. Rushed to the Pusan perimeter as the first British contribution toward the defense of South Korea, their makeshift outfit had gone straight to the Naktong River battlefront. Together with the Middlesex Regiment, made up mostly of Londoners, the Argylls helped hold the crumbling Pusan perimeter until MacArthur's Inchon landing brought the North Koreans to collapse. Joined by the 3rd Battalion, the Royal Australian Regiment, they then spearheaded a gallop up the west coast of North Korea attached to the U.S. I Corps. The advance carried them as far as Chongju, a small manufacturing town only 80 miles south of the Yalu River. After that, though, it was someone else's war. Or so they thought. The buzz was that a British troopship had been waiting to relieve them near Pyongyang since November 21. The advance guard of a fresher, better-equipped Commonwealth brigade was already ashore in the south.

Meanwhile the Yanks were finishing off the North Koreans, driving the last few miles to the Chinese border. On the western side of the peninsula, three entire U.S. divisions were heading for the Yalu River, while a full corps of ROKs marched forward line abreast against the central ranges. The poor bloody ROKs—the much-condemned gooks—were worse bloody soldiers, the Scotsmen swore, than the Yanks themselves. Still, they could scarcely foul up this attack. They were supposed to outnumber the North Koreans by ten to one.

The Argylls felt little affection for any of their allies in this incomprehensible crusade. The ROKs were a rabble, and most of the U.S. troops they'd encountered here were soft, slack, and appallingly ill-disciplined. The Argylls set great store by discipline. First day out of combat their boots were polished and webbing scrubbed. Shaving was mandatory. (None of that dog-faced, macho look favored by GIs.) Saluting was mandatory, too. Traditional class differences reinforced the regimental proprieties. Officers kept a respectable distance from the "other ranks."

Rest time was mainly spent overhauling well-worn weaponry. Bren guns were stripped down, cleaned, and oiled. These Czech-designed light machine guns had proved highly portable in the mountainous Korean terrain, and did not jam as frequently as the American BARs. Riflemen were strangely attached to their trusty Lee Enfields, although that bolt-action magazine loader (long the standard British firearm) was clearly outclassed by the automatic American M-1.

However disciplined they might be, the Argylls also snatched the chance to relax. Scots ale appeared from nowhere—"to hell wi' that iced Yankee piss"—and a drop of the hard stuff went around the sergeants' mess. There were hot showers, Hollywood movies, and hurried letters home. "Dear Mum and Dad, Hope this finds you as well as it finds me. See you soon. Your loving son . . ." SWALK printed across the back of the envelope: "Sealed With A Loving Kiss." For wives and girlfriends, it was NORWICH: "Nickers [panties] Off, Ready When I Come Home." Some of the lads would never make it. Their graves lay all over the peninsula. The pipers played a lament for them, weird and wailing, while the chaplain prayed and the battalion stood bareheaded in the wintry sunshine.

The Scottish troops moved mainly on foot. Their trucks had been worn out even before they left Hong Kong, and the rutted Korean roads were fast finishing them off. The trudging Scotsmen envied the American infantry convoys barreling by in a column of dust. Fortunately there was no shortage of tea. British soldiers depended on their daily brew-ups of "char." No one outside the officers' mess had much taste for coffee. Since the brigade drew only American rations, the British had taken special care to ship three months' supply of tea from Hong Kong, an action which got them front-page treatment in *Stars and Stripes*. Even now GIs leaned out of their trucks, speeding past the plodding Argylls, and piped "Do please have a cup of tea, old chap" in what they fondly believed to be English accents. The Scots laughed back sourly; their own dialect was a thick, nasal Glasgow singsong incomprehensible to the average Englishman, let alone some stinking Yank.

A great orange sun slid down behind the Korean peaks. In its place rose a beaming yellow moon which clothed "the wild, deserted land," one correspondent was moved to write, "in a pale shroud of somber beauty." Artillery rumbled on. Gun flashes lit the northern sky. It might almost have been summer lightning. Yank ordnance was working overtime. A bitter wind whipped up, keening like grieving crofters in some ghostly glen. The temperature dropped ten more degrees. Sentries huddled numbly inside their slit trenches, rifles loaded, bayonets fixed.

Officers crowded around the mess stove listening to the wireless, which was tuned to Tokyo. Broadcasts from the Armed Forces station would spread panic in the weeks to come, but tonight the news was upbeat, featuring General Douglas MacArthur's latest victory communiqué.

"The United Nations' massive compression envelopment in North Korea against the new Red armies operating there is now approaching its decisive effort. The isolating components of the pincer, our air force of all types, have for the past three weeks, in a sustained attack of model coordination and effectiveness . . ." On and on it rolled.

MacArthur was a man of many words. ". . . This morning the western sector of the pincer moves forward in a general assault in an effort to complete the compression and close the vise. If successful, this should for all practical purposes end the war, restore peace and unity to Korea, enable the prompt withdrawal of United Nations military forces" —a small cheer here from the Argyll officers— "and permit the complete assumption by the Korean people and nation of full sovereignty and international equality. It is that for which we fight."

Some of those listening felt a faint unease. Enemy resistance had lately been stiffening. Some suspected the Chinese were getting involved.

Much the same thought struck London *Daily Telegraph* correspondent Reggie Thompson. Reports of Chinese infiltration were growing serious. He found the MacArthur communiqué frankly alarming.

"Seldom in the history of warfare," he wrote afterward, "can any appreciation of a situation have been more wrong . . . [It] revealed an unawareness that was in its way as unique as this strange man himself."

From the start, MacArthur had few admirers among the British correspondents in Korea. The general's photogenic posturing, his contrived air of disdain, his high-flown sermons from the mount all seemed simply ludicrous to the irreverent cynics of Fleet Street. His world strategy sounded equally unattractive. The British could hardly be expected to applaud the general's commitment to Asia when the prize Stalin so obviously sought was their own Western Europe.

But MacArthur still made headlines. The British press turned out in force to greet him at Sinanju when he flew in the morning after Thanksgiving to launch his last offensive. The correspondents clustered around curiously, watching seasoned U.S. generals freeze and stammer in the great man's presence. Even the normally cocky Walton H. "Johnnie" Walker, the Eighth Army commander, appeared completely overawed, "looking like a Michelin tire advertisement in his bulky clothing." No one, not even Field Marshal Lord Montgomery, assumed such airs as did MacArthur. The British preferred the homely Eisenhower any day.

The weather was bright and cloudless, whetted by a wind straight off the Manchurian plains. MacArthur looked the picture of confidence, sporting a colorful checkered scarf at the neck of his fur-lined parka. Gallantly defying the cold, he made a dutiful round of divisional visits in open jeeps. The photographers had a field day. At every predetermined halt they formed a phalanx of Speed Graphics, a few *Life* Leicas clicking in between, immortalizing the obligatory handshakes, the mock-hearty salutations, the staged groupings of senior officers who peered dutifully at maps for the benefit of the cameras.

New story leads were urgently required. The scribes scampered off to file on hearing MacArthur openly tell the IX Corps commander, Major General John B. Coulter, "If this operation is successful, I hope we can get the boys back by Christmas." Rewrite swung into action. Wire agencies switched from the "end-the-war offensive" to the "home-by-Christmas drive."

Thompson studied MacArthur with a certain sympathy. Here was a figure straight from Euripidean tragedy. "There was a pathos in MacArthur that day," he wrote, "for I believe that he knew almost less about the situation than anyone. He had lived for so long in a dream world, isolated and insulated against the facts and general opinions by his clique of sycophants."

There was an unusual detachment about the British view. For the first time in living memory they were diminutive partners in an important international struggle. Many of them, at home and in the field, felt helpless and troubled. Those witnessing events wondered whether the fight for freedom was being mishandled. One of the most outspoken critics was Louis Heron of the London *Times*. His most cutting dispatch protested GI use of the word "gook." It revealed a frightening contempt for the Koreans, Heron claimed, dehumanizing the very people the Americans were there to defend.

Stephen Barber of the *News Chronicle* accused the Americans of outright brutality. People turned out to welcome their liberators at one village in North Korea, he claimed, led by a committee of old men in baggy white robes and tall black hats, only to be mowed down by U.S. tank gunners.

Most scathing of all was Reggie Thompson, whose admiration of Americans was marred by disgust at their overuse of firepower.

> Every enemy shot released a deluge of destruction. Every village and township in the path of war was blotted out. Civilians died in the rubble and ashes of their homes. Soldiers usually escaped. Time and again a handful of men held up a regiment, forcing a few of them [the Americans] at last— but never at first—to get on their feet, off the road and deploy.
>
> There were no clear orders then, or ever. The NCOs were often ineffectual, their authority unrecognizable in their commands, or bearing, and seldom pressed to a conclusion. The officers, speaking in the same voices as their men, in the same idiom, and without the absolute authority of discipline and training, were seldom better.

They dressed like slobs, stuffed themselves with candy, and wore undeserved medals, Thompson complained. "The morale of the United States forces who took part in this war is based on illusion," he maintained. "Their experiences . . . have left them quite unprepared for battle."

It could be argued that the British were jealous. Their country had emerged from World War II in sadly straitened circumstances, but delusions of grandeur remained. The British hung on in southeast Asia, Africa, and the Middle East. Their ships and soldiers were deployed throughout the Mediterranean, the Suez Canal Zone, the Iranian Gulf, around south and eastern Asia as far as Singapore and Hong Kong.

Korea offered the British a heaven-sent chance to compensate for their newfound feelings of inferiority. For now Great Britain was not carrying the burden. Some of the correspondents, especially Stephen Barber (of the massacre report), bitterly recalled American abuse over Palestine. Caught in the cross fire from Jews and Arabs, the British had been hounded out. Memories of the debacle still rankled. Now it was the *Americans* who were across a barrel.

Reggie Thompson set out early on November 25 to see how the offensive was going. He borrowed a jeep from *Time* magazine and drove out of Sinanju toward the battlefront. With him was Homer Bigart of the New York *Herald Tribune*. Refugees were pouring north again across the Chungchon River, picking their way along the broken rail bridge in the wake of the American advance. On the far bank women with wooden bowls combed the frozen fields for grains of unharvested rice. Families took shelter inside hollow stacks of straw.

The correspondents found that lead troops of the U.S. 24th Division had captured half a dozen Chinese near Chongju. The prisoners sat guarded in the thrice-taken town; Thompson later described them as "sturdy, bulbous-bodied, like cottage loaves, and looking as though they could give you a terrific bunt in the midriff with their round bullet heads." The Americans were probing cautiously forward with patrols. Resistance, so far, had been slight, but they were taking no chances.

The two correspondents had promised to pick up a colleague at neighboring IX Corps, so they drove back down the crumbling roads and headed east toward Kunu-ri. The town lay 20 miles farther up the Chungchon valley, hemmed in by high frosted peaks, at a point where the lateral route across the peninsula connected with the north-south network that led, eventually, north to the Yalu or back south to Pyongyang. It was late afternoon by the time they had slogged through the heavy traffic, the dust clouds, and the refugees to reach

IX Corps headquarters. The command post stood in a roadside field, a few miles from the Commonwealth Brigade. There was an air of tension. Something was obviously wrong. Reports coming in from the two U.S. divisions, the 25th and the 2nd, spoke of heavy counterattacks. Mortar shells were falling on Kunu-ri.

ROK II Corps was the real worry. Very little had been heard from them since shortly before dawn. The last garbled messages from the three South Korean divisions on the central front spoke of heavy attacks by thousands upon thousands of Chinese. . . .

Central front, North Korea, November 27, 1950

The first faint flecks of dawn tinged the eastern sky as the bugler climbed slowly up to the crag. He struck the traditional pose, one hand on hip, the other holding the red-tassled bugle to his lips. Below, in the mist-filled valley, the enemy was coming to life. Sentries stirred in their foxholes. Fires glowed like cigarette ends in the gloom as sleepy enemy cooks prepared the morning rice.

Colonel Yang Shixian of the Chinese Peoples' Volunteers tried not to think of food. His gut ached with hunger. The battalion had not eaten a hot meal for two days. They had clambered 60-odd kilometers across these mountains—the last stages overnight, in brilliant moonlight—on nothing more than water from the streams and a few handfuls of dried meat and raw millet. It was all each man could carry. Orders were to move light and fast. They had done just that.

The colonel stared impatiently down into the still-dark valley. The date was November 27. His watch said 0507. Yang was waiting for explosions. When they came he would know the infiltration squads had done their work. He tried peering again through his binoculars. Tents, trucks, and guns were all he could see, blurred by the ground mist. Suddenly, a stir of movement. Men running. A series of flashes in the darkness, followed a few moments later by the dull crump of the satchel charges. A burst of flame as a truck caught fire. An outburst of ragged shooting. He nodded curtly to the bugler.

The call to the charge brayed urgently off the mountain-top. Other, distant buglers took up the sound, spreading their staccato message down the mountain slopes. The sounds had scarcely died away when the mountains moved. Ridges cloaked in rock and scrub swarmed suddenly with Chinese soldiers in bulky padded jackets. An avalanche of soldiers with rifles and fixed bayonets emerged yelling from concealment and gushed into the valley.

Colonel Yang found himself shouting hoarsely as he goat-leaped down the slope. With battle irrevocably joined, he felt the old familiar feelings of relief. Vast trouble had been taken to arrive here unde-tected from the ravine where they had rested for three weeks following the Unsan battle. It was good to be active again after so much cowering under camouflage.

Two bodyguards panted along at Yang's elbow. Behind them puffed the new adjutant, Major Lo, a stout bespectacled man desper-ately in need of exercise. He was the replacement for the officer who had been killed at Unsan. A week ago Lo had been lolling about behind a desk in some small Manchurian town. Farther back came Kim Buk Chu, the newly appointed liaison officer from the NKPA, a tough chunky man who spoke Chinese but seldom said a word. He wielded a Soviet-made submachine gun that was the envy of the battalion.

Someone on the flank was sounding a gong. Others blew whistles. But there was no artillery preparation; the nearest Chinese guns were stuck somewhere near the Yalu. The Chinese surprise attack, mounted purely by unsupported infantry, was reminiscent of the American Civil War. European armies had not fought that way this century.

Someone was cracking a whip! It wasn't a whip, the colonel soon realized, it was the sound of bullets zapping overhead from the puppet troops below. The enemy was firing wildly and without effect. The explosions inside their perimeter must have unnerved them. The colonel was less than a hundred meters from the foremost foxholes when something exploded inside the South Korean camp. The defenders stopped shooting and fled. They leaped from their foxholes and blundered off through the tents and trucks toward the Wawon road. They ran in blind panic, heads down and crouching, leaving a trail of helmets, packs, and rifles.

Then the Chinese were over the perimeter defenses and among tents and trucks. A South Korean ran out of a tent in his underwear, waving his arms and shouting. Colonel Yang shot him through the chest with his American automatic. The kick wrenched his wrist. (The heavy handgun was a souvenir of the recent brush with the Americans, but he had never found enough shells to test-fire it.) As the Korean crashed backward against a truck, one of Yang's body-guards thrust a bayonet through his throat. The colonel dashed on past, firing his pistol until the magazine was empty. He paused, breathless, while the soldiers around him fired furiously into the mob of bewildered ROK soldiers falling over one another in the mad rush to escape. The Chinese formed up and charged again, though some hastily stuffed their pockets with half-cooked rice from overturned pots. The colonel detached a detail to guard the food. Another trotted off to round up all available rations. He sent Adjutant Lo searching the tents, accompanied by the liaison officer, Kim.

In the first tent the two men entered there was a loud burst of automatic fire. A South Korean officer staggered outside spouting blood. He collapsed, coughing and retching. Kim stood over him with his gun. "Resisting arrest," he said. Colonel Yang caught Lo's eye. The adjutant shrugged helplessly. "We need prisoners," said the colonel. Kim looked faintly surprised. "Including officers?" he asked. "Including everyone," said the colonel.

Yang felt tired. He could hardly remember when he had last slept. He signaled the bugler to sound the halt. A long trembling call froze the advance on the far side of the South Korean encampment.

The 2nd Battalion, 347th Regiment, regrouped excitedly in the growing light. The Chinese soldiers were plainly delighted with their initial success. A South Korean regimental headquarters had been overrun in those first few hectic minutes. Losses so far were two dead and less than a dozen wounded. No one had expected things to go this easily. But it was not yet all over. A burst of machine-gun fire from inside the southernmost transport park sent them diving for cover. It was at this spot that a well-placed satchel charge had blown up a fuel truck and panicked the Korean defenders. Most of the other trucks were by now ablaze, but somewhere behind the smoke some holdout was putting up a brave, if hopeless, resistance. The first Chinese squad that tried to rush the invisible gunner was promptly cut down by quick bursts of accurate gunfire.

The leader of the Chinese infiltration squad emerged hurriedly from among the tents to offer his services. His stolen South Korean uniform had been badly singed, but the pockets bulged with canned rations. Given enough covering fire, he said through a mouthful of food, his men could get in among the trucks and flush out the enemy gunner with explosives. Covering fire was ordered from the mortars. The first shells fell wide but a few finally landed among the burning vehicles.

With the last explosion, a man spun out from behind the vehicles into the open, flames spouting from his arms and trunk. He rotated slowly, a human torch, firing blindly with a pistol. A barrage of rifle shots brought him down. The medics who went to inspect the corpse cried out in amazement. The dead man was an American, an officer. Undoubtedly one of the advisers to the puppet army. The colonel examined the body thoughtfully. This was the second time he had seen an American sacrifice himself in combat. Perhaps these people were not so soft?

From the valley came the familiar sound of revving vehicles. The

South Korean regimental staff was trying to escape. The lone American must have hoped to buy them time. The enemy could not know that westward the road was already cut.

Yang ordered his adjutant to make sure the men were fed. He personally split open ration boxes, supervised relighting of the cooking fires, and pocketed a supply of shells for his pistol. The company commanders snatched up cans of rations (some containing the most curious foods), then assembled in the command post of the routed ROK 8th Regiment. The sandbagged tent was lined with wall maps, radios, and field telephones. Chairs and papers littered the floor. A dangling phone screeched. Food lay half-eaten on the tables.

The Chinese were fascinated by the maps. They were of Japanese origin, and dated from the thirties, but remained infinitely superior to the hand-drawn sketches of the Chinese. The position the battalion had just taken was clearly marked, along with the deployment of all adjacent puppet forces. The intelligence officer was already making detailed notes to send off by runner to divisional command.

The battalion had achieved complete surprise, the colonel told his company commanders, because the puppet forces that made up the right flank of the American Eighth Army had been heavily engaged by other units of the Chinese Peoples' Volunteers since November 25. The main Chinese assault had been launched the previous night, around 2100, against the entire ROK corps. This had enabled their particular regiment to infiltrate to an advantageous position while all enemy forward units were fighting for survival.

Pointing to the captured wall maps, Yang showed his commanders how their predawn attack had sliced through the left flank of the ROK 8th Division. The Chinese now occupied the head of a valley ten kilometers east of Tokchon. It led onto the main lateral road that passed through the town before snaking off into the mountains in the direction of Kunu-ri, Sinanju, and the Korean west coast. A full-scale offensive down this road would turn the American flank. The plan was for three Chinese field armies to sweep westward, rolling up any South Koreans in their path, to get *behind* the American forces advancing north to the Yalu.

Commissar Wong Wuyi felt the urge for a harangue, but the colonel begged him to wait. A lot of exhausting work remained to be done. The men needed rest as well as food. Ration stocks were still being doled out by Major Lo, who was trying to make sense of the labels. The adjutant was one of the few officers able to read English. None of the captured supplies, apart from rice and several large pots of *kimche*, appeared to be Korean. American GIs ate the oddest things, the adjutant remarked. There was much more meat than the Chinese were used to, but remarkably few vegetables. Some of the rations proved more popular than others. Everyone clamored for candies and cans containing sliced peaches, though something with an unknown Mexican name appealed to men such as the colonel, who enjoyed spicier food. Most of the other stuff was decidedly tasteless.

Captured ammunition stocks were quickly plundered. Search parties gathered up bundles of abandoned carbines and M-1 rifles. The Chinese disliked the carbine. They felt it packed too little stopping power. It was given to runners and mortar crews. But the M-1 rifle was greatly prized. The few infantrymen still using Japanese- and Chinese-made rifles traded them in for M-1s, with orders to keep foraging for further ammunition supplies. The ammunition shortage was serious. Each man carried only four clips of M-1 shells, with instructions never to fire except close to the enemy. Running down the hillside in the predawn attack the battalion had made plenty of noise but expended relatively few rounds.

A runner came stumbling in from the regimental commander. The man had been slightly wounded in the leg in a brush with puppet troops. Groups of South Koreans were all over the hills, he said, some still ready to fight. The message he carried claimed that the puppet troops were being overwhelmed. The ROK 10th, 21st, 16th, and 2nd Regiments had already disintegrated. The Chinese were warned, however, to watch out for aerial counterstrikes.

Already it was past ten o'clock in the morning. The sun was way up beyond the tallest peaks. The sheltered valley grew warmer. Frost melted off the wizened apple trees clumped along the sunny southern slopes. Water gurgled around the wheels of a jeep abandoned in a half-frozen stream. Distant firing could be heard from the direction of the road. Sounds of the wider struggle going on around them were blanketed out by the mountains.

The runner's warning was promptly heeded. Smoke from the burning truck-park sent up the sort of beacon that would attract attention. The battalion took to the hills again, sleeping under blankets and scraps of foliage, prepared to resume their advance in five hours. Two or three men tinkered with the jeep. They had not managed to get it started by the time the colonel dozed off.

The Chungchon River,
November 27, 1950

The Chinese attacked without the essentials of modern war. They attacked without aircraft, artillery, or tanks. They lacked sophisticated communications and logistics. But they had ample manpower. They threw six field armies—totaling some 180,000 men—into the effort to engulf the U.S. Eighth Army. Three of those field armies blocked the path of three American divisions advancing toward the Chinese border from the Chungchon River. Farther inland, where awesome mountains divide the peninsula, three more Chinese field armies hammered the ill-fated South Koreans. The ROK II Corps crumbled, and the Chinese poured through the gap and launched an outflanking movement that threatened the UN escape route to the south. By the evening of November 26 it became apparent to those in the field that MacArthur's home-by-Christmas drive was no more. Chinese pressure was mounting on all fronts.

The young runner, Jia Peixing, strode to the edge of the ridge. They were back on the same long mountainous bluff, he reckoned, a good 20 kilometers east of the spot from which the regiment had launched its limited offensive three weeks before. The view certainly appeared little different. The Chungchon River glowed bright as ever in the golden sunset. Sinanju and the shell-swept killing ground he had been so scared to cross lay lost downriver in the deepening darkness. The central mountains loomed considerably closer, capped near their peaks with tufts of woolly cloud.

Officers of the regimental staff had taught the runners rudimentary map reading during their temporary hibernation in the northern mountains. Young Jia had memorized most of the main features of the river valley. He now felt confident of finding his way around the forward positions once the night's assault got under way. The last rays of the sunken sun backlit plumes of distant dust rising from the valley roads. Those were the convoys of enemy vehicles over to the west, jammed nose to tail, crawling along the northern bank of the river toward the floating bridges at Anju and Sinanju.

The traffic jams downstream confirmed what the Chinese already knew. The U.S. 24th Division was pulling back its advance columns from Chongju, close to the coast, along the road that headed straight for the Yalu bridges at Anju/Sinanju, as well as from the secondary route to the Manchurian border through Pakchon. The withdrawal was being generated by pressure from three Chinese field armies, including the 40th, of which the 358th Regiment was part. The 40th Field Army planned to hit the Kunu-ri area at the point where two other American divisions, the 2nd and the 25th, also stood poised to advance on the Yalu.

"If we only had a few guns," sighed Colonel Gu Dehua. He handed the binoculars to an aide and tugged down the earflaps of his fur hat. It was lined with dog fur, a present from the Koreans. The staff buttoned up their vast padded jackets; the freezing wind was getting up again.

Guns had certainly been promised, as had more food and ammunition. Several artillery batteries were reported to have crossed from Manchuria around October 20. The soldiers had since heard that the column was heavily bombed by American planes. Rumor had it that among those killed was Major Mao Anying, Chairman Mao's eldest son.

The battalion commanders rechecked their orders and finished off their notes. They joined Colonel Gu for a last look down the valley before darkness erased the scene completely. "Better than a map," the colonel told them. He pointed out enemy deployments on both sides of the river. A few American guns were firing from the far bank. The bulk of them were located close to a village called Kujang-dong. The rice fields had thawed during the past couple of days; the ground was too soft to permit the enemy gunners to move in much closer. Directly below, where hills fell away to the water's edge, there was a string of freshly dug foxholes. It was here that the American advance was being halted.

"Take a good look at Kunu-ri," said the colonel, pointing southwestward across the river. "That town is pivotal to our whole situation. There are two ways out of it. One way runs along the south bank of the Chungchon River as far as Anju, then switches south. The other way heads directly south, through the mountains. By tomorrow night the mountain road will be cut. Our job will be to force the enemy back across the river, down that mountain road, and into a trap."

Fighting had been going on for the past two days as the Chinese contested the American advance. Tonight, at 2130, the 40th Field Army would go over to the offensive. All regiments were to hit the enemy simultaneously. The Chungchon River was fast and shallow at this point, Colonel Gu emphasized. It had not yet frozen. Two nearby fords offered the Americans an escape route for their tanks and vehicles. The combat terrain, on the other hand, was ideal for infiltration. The broken, hilly ground next to the river would isolate enemy units from one another, preventing full use of their tanks and artillery. The battle would be man to man; on such terms no one doubted who would win.

On gloved fingers Colonel Gu ticked off the tactical lessons. "Draw the enemy in deep," he recited. "Hit them with all available force on ground of your own choosing." The commanders nodded dutifully. Like young Jia and the others on the staff, they had heard it all a dozen times before. "Finally, cut the enemy off and destroy them," said Colonel Gu. He glowered back over the valley. "With luck, that's exactly what we will do."

The colonel was a noted theorist on the practice of revolutionary war. He gave frequent staff lectures about the stormtrooper tactics developed by General Erich Ludendorff to trigger the German breakthrough on the Western Front in Europe during March, 1918. Like most Chinese guerrilla fighters, the colonel had also learned to respect Japanese military planning and élan. The so-called Ichi-go offensive of April, 1944, when the Japanese overran the American air bases in eastern China, was the subject of much rueful study in the People's Liberation Army. The Japanese had depended on fast, untiring infantry. The PLA now did likewise. During the latter stages of the Chinese civil war, under the inspired leadership of men like Peng Dehuai and Lin Biao, the Communists' marathon-marching riflemen had scattered the better-equipped, far larger armies of the Nationalists.

Victory came easiest after destabilizing the enemy. Surprise attack by commando squads, for example, helped spread confusion. The main, follow-up assault probed for weaknesses in the defense. No holdups were tolerated. Officers kept their men on the move. Any breakthrough was exploited swiftly and in strength until a wedge had been driven deep into the enemy rear. Roadblocks were then thrown up to inderdict supply lines and harass command units until the defenders fell into disorderly retreat. Stoutly defended positions were speedily bypassed, then mopped up later.

Colonel Gu wished his battalion commanders good luck. They faced a long trudge back to their units. The western sky was smeared a brilliant red. An auspicious color for an auspicious night. The regimental runners ate a bowl of cold cooked rice, brought up from the rear by a thoughtful quartermaster, munched paper-thin strips of sweet, dried meat, and dozed off among the bushes. There would be little sleep the rest of the night.

The moon was up when Jia Peixing awoke. The ridge, the river valley, and the mountain range were painted silver. Sentries paced, ghostlike, round the picket lines. It was cold, but not unbearably so. Colonel Gu conferred with his staff in the tightly sealed command tent. A double flap over the doorway prevented leakage of telltale light. Messages kept arriving from the valley, carried by men who wheezed out their breath in steaming silvery clouds. One of them was a slender goatherd whom Jia had met at boot camp.

"Can't wait for it to start," the former goatherd gasped delightedly. To hear him talk they might have been going to a wedding feast. Jia thought of the firecrackers and shuddered. Fear burned again in the bottom of his stomach. The two runners craned over the lip of the ridge looking down into the valley.

The staff joined them there to catch the start of the battle. Colonel Gu was among them. They cheered softly when a red flare went up from the foothills. Another followed, then another. Red flashes spurted from the direction of the foxholes. Tracer arched through the air. The sound of bugles and of firing rose upon the wind. An officer tapped Jia's arm. "Message for the 1st Battalion," he said. "You know the way?"

Jia knew. He had checked out the ridge path while it was still daylight. The message was written on several sheets of squared rice paper. It was chopped with the colonel's personal seal and wrapped in oil cloth. Jia put the packet in the canvas bag he carried round his shoulder, picked up his carbine, and headed down into the valley at a quick jog. Runners passed him toiling up toward the summit. One man handed him a fistful of carbine shells. "You might need these," he said. Jia had fired his carbine only once, and then none too accurately. He trembled as he ran.

The smell of smoke and spent explosives drifted up the ridge. Shells burst in the trees below him with a hollow, echoing crash. The sounds grew louder as he descended: mortar shells with their strangely muffled crump, bigger guns (tank guns, perhaps?), and the ceaseless chatter of machine guns.

Now he was mortally afraid. His breath grew short, his chest tightened, and everything inside him urged a moment's pause, a rest, anything to avoid running on. Nevertheless he kept moving.

A field dressing station had been set up in an orchard. The dressing station was manned by two white-robed medics. They stooped over a row of prone figures—looking to Jia quite spooky in the moonlight— while a handful of lesser casualties squatted under the trees.

A mortar squad tramped toward the Chungchon, and its leader paused to talk with Jia. There had been heavy fighting just ahead, he said, but as far as he knew the 1st and 3rd Battalions had already crossed the river. Only the 2nd Battalion remained this side, liqui- dating American units cut off by the attack. With Jia following each step of the way, the squad crossed a stony stream bed, and emerged onto hilly grassland studded with small poplars. They pointed the runner toward a fire burning in the trees. "From here on," said the squad leader grimly, "death walks at your elbow."

Jia trotted halfheartedly into a cacophony of gunfire. Bodies lay everywhere. Most of them seemed to be Chinese. A machine-gun crew was shooting wildly across a clearing. A hundred meters away an American tank was thoroughly alight. Flames licked over its turret and upper works, illuminating the glade brightly. The faces of the Chinese, pinned down in the surrounding trees, glowed red.

The runner tried to make out what was blocking the advance. He crouched behind the machine gunner and stared blindly at the blaze. His legs turned weak when he at last spotted a second tank squatting nearby, like some giant toad. This tank seemed to be immobilized, but the men inside were firing every gun they could bring to bear. The main cannon swung quickly round, pointing directly at Jia.

"Get down, you fool!" yelled the machine gunner. As he pressed himself down into the undercarpet of leaves, feeling as obvious and vulnerable as a high brick wall, Jia was stunned and deafened by the air burst. Twigs and branches rained down. "What you trying to do?" snarled the gunner. "Win a medal?"

Jia did not want a medal. He wanted out. He groped inside his jacket for the charm his mother had looped around his neck. Carrying this sliver of white jade might be superstitious nonsense, as the commissar kept saying, but he prayed it would magically remove him a million leagues from all this horror. Two men eased themselves down beside him. Between them they carried a sling containing a mortar shell tied round with sticks of explosive. The machine gunner fired a long covering burst. The men with the explosives rose to their feet and hurled themselves across the clearing. They were instantly cut down by a gunner inside the tank. The charge they were carrying went off with an earsplitting crack. Nothing was left but a smoking hole in the ground.

More Chinese ran from left and right until at last in the melee a package of explosives hit the stranded tank. The turret flipped open and Americans leaped out. Three of them ran off into the night. The fourth caught a burst of machine-gun fire in the back. He seemed to leap in the air before pitching forward into the bushes.

The Chinese charged. The night woods were filled with yelling soldiers. They brushed through the poplars, leaped over abandoned defense works, and were almost at the water's edge before the bugler called a halt. Jia halted too. He had run this far, sobbing with fright, because he felt safer with the crowd. He was also lost again. An American truck, loaded with canned rations, had broken down with its front wheels in the river. A Chinese officer was now handing out the food to the troops. He threw the runner a can when he came up in search of directions.

"First Battalion? They're on the other side," the officer said. "Moved faster than expected. Their command post is on the far bank." He pointed a short distance upstream. "If you keep to this side for another three or four hundred meters you'll find a rear party. They'll show you the way."

Shells whistled in again from the American artillery, and burst harmlessly among the trees. The sharp, rustling sound set Jia's hair bristling. "Ranging shots!" yelled the officer. He blew three blasts on a whistle. The troops took cover, still consuming their captured food; the runner pocketed his ration can and continued on his run. He hoped his message was not urgent; more than an hour must have passed since he had left the ridge.

The rear party from the 1st Battalion, when he found them, were all wounded. Some were in pain. The sergeant in charge was passing round a bottle of *gaoliang*. A few gulps of the powerful grain spirit helped numb the senses. The sergeant limped around on a badly wounded leg. They had gotten as far as the river, he said, with remarkably few casualties. Over the other side the going was getting tougher—as he spoke, a salvo of shells burst in the rice fields directly opposite—and it was best to go carefully.

"Head for the railroad," said the sergeant. "Wherever there's any firing."

Jia felt sick all over again. He wished he were not such a coward. Several shells burst nearby in the river, throwing up showers of water, mud, and rocks. "They can't quite figure out where we are," the sergeant observed. He grimaced with pain and took another gulp of *gaoliang*. "Have a mouthful," he said, handing the bottle to the runner. "The water's cold. You're going to need it."

At the age of 18, Jia had never drunk anything stronger than rice wine. He gagged down the burning liquid and was surprised to feel a welcome warmth spreading through his body. He presented the can of rations to the sergeant, slung carbine and message bag around his neck and splashed off across the Chungchon.

The river was about 25 meters wide and no more than around thigh-deep. But it was icy cold, so cold that after three or four steps the runner found himself struggling to continue. The leg muscles no longer seemed to obey his brain. He was still floundering forward, an obvious target in the moonlight, when shells began to fall. The Americans might not know where the Chinese were, but they were doing their damnedest to find out. Jia screamed with terror. He wanted to throw himself flat, but the water was freezing. He wanted to run toward a poplar grove on the opposite bank, but progress was agonizingly slow. The chill currents gripped his legs. The explosions threatened to knock him down. Water and debris splattered down. He was wailing like a lost infant when a hand reached out and hauled him to safety.

"Take it easy, son." The runner scrambled miserably ashore. "Here, drink this." A mug of hot tea was thrust into his hand. Jia leaned against a tree, sipping, gasping, and shuddering. "We all get scared," said the man with the tea. "Even me." He was an old man. Almost 40. A master sergeant with a lifetime of campaigning behind him. One of the old bores who went on and on about the Long March and all that stuff. A useful man to have around, though, at moments like this. The old sergeant poured more tea from a tall tin vacuum flask. "Never go into combat without her." He stroked the flask affectionately. "Nothing like tea for steadying the nerves."

The battle so far had been a pushover, the veteran explained. A few of the Americans had defended this riverbank with great determination, but most had run for their lives. The 1st Battalion's attack had met so little real resistance that they were a day ahead of schedule. One battery of artillery had been overrun with scarcely a shot fired; the battalion command post now stood among the captured guns.

A column of troops waded across the river as the shelling slackened. They shook out their sodden pants upon reaching the bank, adjusted their packs, and began to march silently off across the rice fields. Jia's sergeant-rescuer pointed them toward a low hill two or three kilometers away. The runner tailed along behind, glad of the company. The only sound as the column approached the railroad was the crunch of dry rice stalks underfoot. A long-derailed freight train rusted on top of the embankment. Rockets had knocked out the locomotive. The cab and boiler were shot through with holes. Cars lay upended or overturned.

Beside the ruined train, sentries guarded a handful of captured soldiers. The runner stared at them curiously. They were the first live Americans Jia had seen at close range. They were dirty and disheveled, and somehow smaller than he had been led to expect from the caricatures in the Chinese press.

The American guns overrun by the 1st Battalion were dug into sandbagged pits beside the river road. Their tubes pointed mutely out across the river, apparently in working order. The Chinese battalion commander now sat astride one of the guns issuing orders. He was small and bespectacled, schoolmasterish in manner. He read the runner's message without comment.

Jia was handed a scribbled acknowledgment. Whatever the contents of his message were, they were not disclosed. His most lasting memory of Korea was of running about battlefields, never knowing what was going on. He headed back toward the river hoping his damp clothes would not freeze.

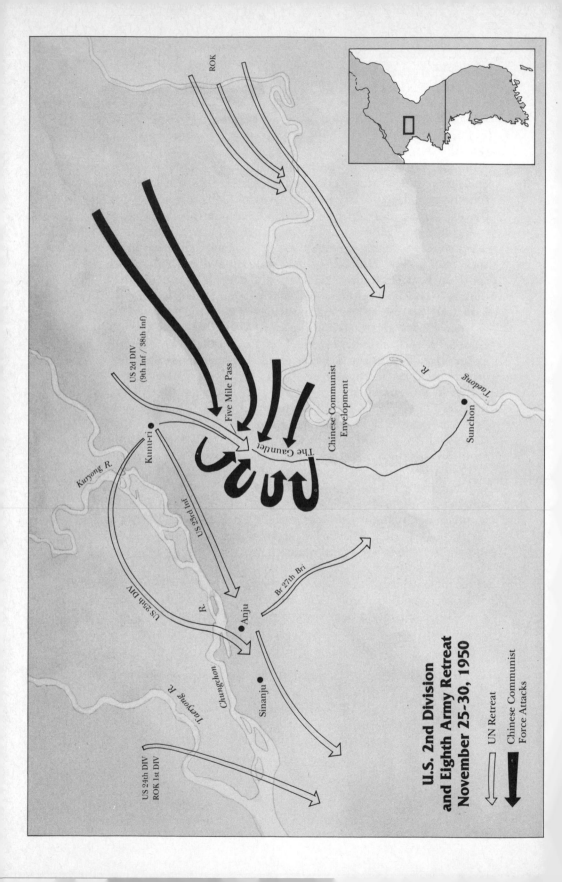

U.S. 2nd Division
and Eighth Army Retreat
November 25-30, 1950

UN Retreat

Chinese Communist
Force Attacks

ROK

US 2d DIV
(9th Inf / 38th Inf)

Five Mile Pass

Kunu-ri

Kuryong R.

US 23rd Inf

US 25th DIV

R.

Changchon

Taeryong R.

Anju

Sinanju

Br 27th Bri

The Gauntlet

Chinese Communist
Envelopment

Taedong R.

Sunchon

US 24th DIV
ROK 1st DIV

11

"Dushman" / The Doomed Retreat Down Sunchon Road of U.S. 2nd Division / The Sharp Swords at the Gauntlet."

Chungchon River,
North Korea.
November 25, 1950

No one was prepared for the Chinese attack. The advancing Americans had shucked off their bayonets, blankets, spare ammunition, and emergency rations for what appeared to be the last and most leisurely effort of the war. Most of them dreamed only of a family Christmas. The top brass was equally euphoric. General Douglas MacArthur issued another sanguine communiqué claiming unresisted advance to the very borders of Manchuria.

But by the evening of November 25 it had become apparent that the twin jaws of the United Nations pincers—Eighth Army in the northwest, and X Corps, including the marines, 150 miles to the east—were engaging armies bigger than North Korea alone could muster. For three more days MacArthur and his staff refused to countenance retreat. At this stage of the war, they argued, the North Koreans were bound to show some spark of defiance. Peremptory demands poured out of Tokyo for resumption of the stalled advance.

Field commanders were brusquely told to stop moaning—and move it.

Eighth Army commander "Johnnie" Walker hated to confront MacArthur. But on the afternoon of November 26 he braved his wrath by confirming that the ROK's II Corps had disintegrated, and that *large* forces of Chinese were charging through the gap. Swiftly the U.S. First Cavalry was moved into blocking positions south of the Taedong River. Hundreds of South Korean troops from the broken ROK corps fled into its safety net. The British 27th Commonwealth Brigade was alerted for battle, its brief rest period permanently aborted. The newly arrived Turkish Brigade was rushed in to shore up the South Koreans.

The Turks, under Brigadier General Tahsin Yazici, were spoiling for a fight. Boldly they headed eastward down the Tokchon road. Very soon they were signaling the destruction of a sizable enemy force. But these formidable soldiers were working in an unfamiliar command environment, with scant command of English, and it was later found they had mistakenly mown down hundreds of fleeing South Korean troops thought to be the enemy, before then blundering into a Chinese ambush less than a third of the way toward Tokchon. The Turkish Brigade fought magnificently. Officers threw their caps on the ground and swore to stand or die. But the Turks were engulfed by the advancing Chinese. Their brigade ceased to exist as a fighting force. A few units managed to hack their way out and escape across the hills.

Walker next withdrew his exposed spearhead north of the Chungchon. First to fall back were the two I Corps divisions, the U.S. 24th and ROK 1st, whose columns of trucks, tanks, and guns jammed the west-coast roads for 50 miles. Past them flowed a tidal wave of refugees, stumbling through the dust, day and night, toward the south and safety.

The Korean winter tightened its chilly grip. Older, weaker refugees died quietly and without complaint beside the roads. On the battlefields, the dead lay as grotesquely as they had fallen. Reggie Thompson found more than a dozen Chinese corpses frozen stiff "like a troop of tumblers" outside Kunu-ri. The once-thriving mining town, with its extensive road network, was now pivotal to the UN position in northwestern Korea. Premature loss of Kunu-ri would put the whole of Eighth Army at risk. The town was defended by the U.S. 2nd Division, deployed along the valley as far as Kujang-dong, a small lumber center some 15 miles up the Chungchon valley. It was there that the commander of the 23rd Infantry Regiment, Colonel Paul L. Freeman, Jr., told Thompson how hard the Chinese were harrying his superbly equipped troops.

"Without air or artillery," he said, "they're making us look a little silly in this godawful country."

Three days before, Freeman had been advancing north. Now he had his hands full fending off the Chinese long enough to permit the two IX Corps divisions, the U.S. 25th and his own U.S. 2nd Division, to pull back across the Chungchon. By nightfall of November 27 the 25th Division was fording the river and starting its long retreat down the valley road westward to Anju. From there, a road branched southward to Pyongyang. The 2nd Division was anxious to follow, before the Chinese closed in completely, but its commander, Major General Laurence B. Keiser, could not get the necessary permission. He had for several days been begging IX Corps headquarters to come up with a coherent operations plan. The corps commander, Major General John B. Coulter, the man MacArthur had urged to "get the boys back by Christmas," seemed incapable of decision. Frequent calls to the command post failed to raise the general, known to his staff as "Nervous John." Coulter was preoccupied, it was said, with operations in the field.

Correspondents covering IX Corps were shocked at the way things were going. The war in Korea had always been conducted with such glaring publicity that it was impossible at this point to conceal the extent of the reverse.

"We're like the meat in a sandwich," a young GI told Reggie Thompson. "And the Chinks are the bread."

"Seems like the Chinese don't want us on that Yalu River," said an American sergeant, leading back his weary squad in search of transportation.

Scare headlines appeared worldwide the evening of November 28, when MacArthur publicly conceded that his plans had gone awry.

"A major segment of the Chinese continental forces in army, corps, and divisional organization of an aggregate strength of over 200,000 men is now arrayed against the United Nations in North Korea," the SCAP communiqué confessed. *Consequently we face an entirely new war.*

This helped compound the fears of 2nd Division, whose exposure was growing more dangerous hourly. The Chinese had been crossing the Chungchon in force, bearing heavily on the exposed 23rd Infantry at Kujang-dong. Still no word from IX Corps. General Keiser radioed in desperation to Major General Frank W. Milburn, commander of nearby I Corps. Milburn asked: "How are things going?" Keiser replied: "Bad, right now. We're getting hit in my command post." Milburn then said: "Well, come out my way."

That meant following the 25th Division and evacuating through Anju. It would have been the safest course. The alternative was retreat down the mountain road that wound southward from Kunu-ri, forded the Taedong River, and ended in Sunchon. No one yet knew it, but this road was already cut. A Turkish supply convoy, bound from Sunchon to Kunu-ri, had just been ambushed and wiped out by Chinese troops.

The worried Keiser drove to IX Corps to request firm instructions. General Coulter was still not there. Nor were certain senior staff officers who had taken off for unexplained reasons in the direction of Anju. (Coulter was later relieved of his command.) The only person the divisional commander could find with any authority was Colonel Louis Kunzig, who was busy redrawing operational boundary lines and withdrawal routes on the wall map. General Keiser copied the notations onto a spare map. No one gave him a specific order. Nor was any particular retreat route mentioned.

Traffic was so heavy on the road back to divisional headquarters that Keiser decided to fly. He took an L-5 communications plane across the dusty valley, scouring the countryside for signs of the advancing Chinese. All he saw, or thought he saw, were long columns of refugees. Later it occurred to him that they might have been the enemy.

The central front, November 29, 1950

The Chinese Peoples' Volunteers rolled down the Tokchon road in swarms. Their columns moved boldly in broad daylight, snaking rapidly westward, the weary riflemen bowed beneath backpacks and supplies, stopping once every second hour and then for no more than five minutes. Commissars passed up and down the ranks encouraging the marchers to maintain their frantic pace. Air alerts were temporarily ignored. American planes flew overhead, some of them quite low, but the men marched on without an upward glance. The endless files of soldiers simply hunched their backs and strode forward through the dust. Often they passed crowds of Korean refugees plodding in the same direction; people of all ages, caked in grime, impeded by their baggy clothes, their canoe-shaped rubber shoes, and the pathetic bundles of private treasures tied in brightly colored blankets.

The presence of so many refugees seemed to be inhibiting the American pilots. The thought occurred to Colonel Yang Shixian. The battalion commander had expected a lot more aerial opposition while moving this brazenly through open countryside. For two days now they had advanced without attack. Several times Yang tried to persuade the refugees to turn back. The wretched people were naturally terrified of enemy bombing, but heading westward led directly to the next combat zone. He told his North Korean liaison officer, Kim, to urge the refugees to go home. Kim yelled and bawled in the refugees' own outlandish tongue. The peasants paused in embarrassed confusion, gawking suspiciously at the foreign troops, their elders looking penitent and distressed. No sooner had the Chinese marched off than they resumed their flight. The colonel hadn't the time to dissuade them. The idea never crossed his mind that these people might be fleeing their own North Korean regime.

Runners reported contact with an enemy force farther down the Tokchon road. A large number of enemy soldiers had been captured. Intelligence officers attempting to interrogate them found they could not speak English. Interesting news. Commissar Wong had heard the Americans were importing troops from yet *other* puppet states to give substance to their claim to represent the United Nations.

"How can they call it the United Nations?" the commissar sneered. "It doesn't even give a seat to China!"

The Chinese 2nd Battalion left the road, taking a more direct route over the hills, up and down steep slopes pockmarked with protruding granite. Everyone laughed when a big iron cook pot broke loose and bounced off down the slope. Half an hour before dusk, the colonel called a halt in a dried-out, rocky valley. A peasant family came out bowing and smiling from a tiny mud-walled hovel thatched with straw. It was the only farm in sight. The women winched up water from their well for them but did not offer to sell them food. The livestock yard where the hay was stacked was bare even of chickens. The exhausted soldiers fell out in the undergrowth, stripping off their packs and boots. Cooks lit fires for a hot meal of soup and rice and salty-tasting American canned meat while the battalion commander and his staff checked out the terrain from the nearest hilltop.

Their newly acquired maps showed the Chinese their current location—three kilometers from the mountain road between Kunuri and Sunchon. It was that road, a vital UN communications vein, the Chinese were determined to sever. They had force-marched the entire way, some 40 kilometers, simply to reach this narrow stretch. Weary as they were, Colonel Yang wanted his battalion settled into blocking positions before dawn. There was no time to lose. The enemy had to be kept off balance. Roadblocks across the supply road would panic them out of Kunu-ri. The Chinese would be waiting in ambush.

The men slept briefly, moving again at midnight. A late moon made the going easy. An old man from the farm led them along a footpath over the last range of low hills overlooking the roadway.

Across the Taedong River, Chinese troops were digging in to protect their flank. Three lines of entrenchments beyond the Taedong were guaranteed to frustrate any moves the enemy might make to relieve the defenders of Kunu-ri. All the way northward in the direction of the town the Chinese were setting up machine guns and mortars to sweep the road.

The colonel deployed the 2nd Battalion astride a cutting in the mountain crest. A pocket in the hillside 200 meters above the road sheltered the mortars and battalion headquarters. The men grumbled but complied when ordered to carve trenches out of the stony, frozen ground. Fire positions were carefully selected along slopes below the hilltops to ease the brunt of air attacks.

The darkness rang with the sound of shovels as the battalion dug in. Soon it would be dawn. The sky was overcast with a hint of snow. Sentries at both ends of the gully rigged crude signal lamps to warn of the enemy's approach. The system was improvised by Major Ma, Yang's second-in-command, a Harbin Muslim who had picked up his technical knowledge in the workshops of the Russian-owned Manchurian railroad. Headlamps salvaged from wrecked trucks were connected to automobile batteries. Flicked on, the lamps shone a beam toward the battalion command post bright enough to give the alert. More sophisticated messages could not be transmitted until enough soldiers had learned the Chinese military equivalent of the Morse code.

The major scrambled across the gully for last-minute consultations. He was a solid, muscular man, with a well-earned reputation as a wrestler. His ungainly padded coat bristled with stick grenades. He listened attentively as Colonel Yang ran through the standard ambush drill. The first ten or more enemy vehicles would be allowed through. They would be dealt with farther up the road. No one was to open fire without the recognized signal. Major Ma nodded. "I've ordered the men to eat," he said.

A dreary place, Yang thought as he looked around, soon to become a valley of the dead. He forced himself to chew a piece of his favorite dried beef, crouching close to the rock face out of the cutting wind.

The warning light flashed from the southern end of the gully at 0735. A convoy of foreign trucks, escorted by Sherman tanks and half-tracks, was fording the Taedong River. It was the supply run to Kunu-ri. Buglers brought the Chinese battalion to combat alert. Colonel Yang tensed himself against the rock, loading his flare pistol.

The convoy thundered into the gully with blazing headlights. The now-familiar half-track vehicle with quadruple machine guns led the column. Behind it, two or three very large utility trucks, then four tanks bunched together, after them another half-track and a string of standard two-and-a-half-tonners. Some of the trucks carried a heavy machine gun mounted over the cab manned by soldiers muffled heavily against the morning cold.

The lead vehicles rumbled far beneath the colonel's feet. It was a relief to get the half-tracks out of the way. The tanks were less worrisome, especially in this gully, but they watched the armor vanish without regret among the frozen rice fields.

The moment he fired his flare, the colonel recalled years later, the action slipped into slow motion. Time seemed to yawn. The rock-hewn gully, the line of roaring trucks, the squad manning the nearby mortars, looked permanently lit by the flare's soaring light. The convoy drivers braked, then surged ahead, but infinitely slowly, as the sudden volleys chewed lazily across their vehicles, shattering windshields, puncturing cabs, tires, and radiators. Trucks swung languidly into the roadsides. Some swerved broadside into the traffic and were rammed, slowly but precisely, by those behind. Enemy soldiers leaped onto the road firing blindly up the slopes. The Chinese mowed them down in heaps. The survivors dove for the ditches. A foolhardy few fixed bayonets and climbed gallantly toward their attackers. None of them got far.

Gradually the firing died down. The Chinese had run out of targets. Enemy dead and wounded lay piled upon the roadsides. Half the 40-odd vehicles of the convoy stood abandoned in the gully. The rest had hurried on along the road to Kunu-ri. The remainder were knocked out before they reached the town. The U.S. military police who drove out to investigate were slaughtered to a man. Garbled reports filtering back to the Americans never established the extent of the threat to the Sunchon road.

Colonel Yang picked his way through the bodies. It wasn't a pretty sight. A black driver lolled dead in his cab with the motor running. Helmeted soldiers in khaki greatcoats still gripped their bayoneted rifles, teeth bared in a snarl of dying defiance. Each truck carried its quota of corpses caught in the storm of Chinese bullets.

Commissar Wong looked sick. He helped the battalion medics carry the least-badly wounded enemy into the several watercourses scoring the walls of the gully. Here at least they would find shelter from the wind. The worst cases were left in the ditches. There was nothing the Chinese could do. The cold would kill them off before nightfall.

Major Ma led a detail collecting rifles, rations, and ammunition;

he beckoned the colonel over when one of the wounded enemy muttered a half-remembered word. The man said something about "dushman." The major spoke a little of the Uighur dialect common to northwestern China. He leaned over the wounded soldier, gave him water from his canteen and gabbled away until the man retched and died. The major covered him with a blanket.

"These soldiers are Turks," Ma told the colonel. " 'Dushman' is their word for enemy."

Kunu-ri,
The morning of November 30, 1950

The Chinese were swamping the U.S. 2nd Division's fragile salient. During the night the 38th Infantry Regiment was overrun east of Kunu-ri; it fought a valiant if ragged action, abandoning its medical aid stations and pulling back toward the town with several hundred wounded. Casualties stacked several deep were evacuated in jeeps and trailers down the Anju road. The ambulances took the westward route the I Corps commander, General Milburn, had originally recommended. They made it to Anju despite the heavy traffic. But harried General Keiser of the 2nd Division, worrying over his maps on the muddled morning of November 30, was against following suit. The last thing he had heard was that the Chinese had established a roadblock four miles west of Kunu-ri.

This did not happen to be true, but in the spreading chaos nobody checked. The 25th Division was withdrawing along this selfsame road, and one call would have established the truth. Radio contact had unfortunately been lost.

Keiser felt impelled to take the shorter, and probably safer, road southward to Sunchon. Yet that also seemed to be cut; a report had come in about an ambushed Turkish convoy, and military policemen sent to find the roadblock had so far failed to check in. But the threat to the rear was not yet considered serious. The Chinese were working around behind the division—this the general knew—but not, he thought, in any numbers. The divisional chief of staff, Colonel Gerald G. Epley, reckoned the enemy roadblock "not more than two companies."

This seemed confirmed after a heartening overnight reconnaissance by the 9th Infantry Regiment. Its well-conducted probe met unexpected resistance a mile or two south of Kunu-ri—alarmingly close to American divisional headquarters—but a determined daylight assault supported by air strikes quickly cleared the dominant hilltops.

The reluctant GIs made no effort thereafter to push on along the ridge lines, as they were worn out from five days of continuous fighting. The regiment's combat strength had shrunk to the equivalent of two battalions. More persistence, however, might have revealed the true strength of the massed Chinese.

The Chinese themselves conspired to reinforce the prevailing UN optimism when at 0800 a platoon of Sherman M-4 medium tanks made an unchallenged run down the threatened road. The Chinese offered no resistance; their line was baited for bigger fish. The tanks made contact with advance patrols of the British Commonwealth Brigade some 12 miles from Kunu-ri. The British and Australians had been called in the previous day to help clear the way for the American withdrawal. The incredible thing is that the tank crews drove blindly past the ambushed Turkish convoy, apparently ignoring the many wounded and dead, without relaying back a word of warning. Communications within the division were breaking down.

General Keiser felt reassured. His aerial glimpse of the countryside the previous day had convinced him that refugees were still moving through the area in large numbers. They would not do that once the Chinese arrived in force. The Communists would feel bound to turn them back.

The general was an old China hand. As a member of the U.S. military mission to Nanking, he had watched the Communists pull off a stunning victory in the last phases of the Chinese civil war. The experience left him with a grudging respect for Mao Zedong's revolutionary army. But his time in China had also taught him enough that he blamed the Nationalist government's collapse on its criminal failures. The common wisdom among China watchers held that inflation had done more to alter the course of Chinese history than incompetence on the battlefield.

Keiser did not denigrate the Chinese fighting man. He simply underestimated him. The Chinese would never prove numerous enough, or mobile enough, the general confidently believed, to prevent his heavily armed GIs from blasting their way out of encirclement.

The divisional train prepared to roll. Tents and equipment were struck and stowed in hundreds of assorted vehicles. Huge quantities of stores were left behind. At the tail of the column the 23rd Infantry, commanded by Colonel Paul L. Freeman, held off the enemy with hard-hitting blasts of artillery.

One final attempt was made to clear the ridge line overlooking the Sunchon Road before 2nd Division began its move. The dirty work was assigned, typically, to the South Koreans. An ROK regiment that had survived the Tokchon debacle swept into attack in splendid style.

Scattered Chinese started like hares before them. American ground-attack planes doused the few visible Chinese with rockets and napalm, and soon the ROKs were through and climbing the next slope. The Chinese broke cover, hurling stick grenades, at the same moment that trigger-happy machine gunners on two American tanks misdirected their fire into their own South Korean lead squads. Too late, the wretched ROKs waved a cerise recognition panel. The Chinese pressed their counterattack, sending the South Koreans reeling back to the start line, some throwing away their weapons in disgust.

Officers of 9th Infantry Regiment urged a *concerted* effort to clear the heights on both sides of the Sunchon Road before beginning the 2nd Division withdrawal. If that seemed too time-consuming, the division should be hauled through piecemeal, escorted by shuttles of tanks.

General Keiser demurred. This was going to be a normal road run. He had made his own on-the-spot assessment. From an artillery-support position close to the road he had watched the failure of the ROK attack. His position, however, had not seen the misdirected U.S. tank fire, and instead believed the half-trained South Koreans had simply fumbled, as usual. The general was equally unimpressed by the Chinese. There was certainly nothing to indicate that they were deployed in any strength. With the British waiting and free a mere mile or two beyond the fire block, Keiser believed, the division would have no trouble pushing through to Sunchon.

Even at this late stage a radio call to the Commonwealth Brigade might have averted disaster. It would have shown that the British were already pinned down, miles away, by massed Chinese mortars and machine guns. The call was not made because nobody knew the British wavelength.

The doomed retreat began soon after noon. Operational orders, drawn up the previous night, put the 9th Infantry Regiment in the vanguard. The 2nd Battalion led off atop Sherman tanks, up to 20 men to each tank, the rest crowded into supply and artillery trucks. Shortly before moving, the tanks were dispersed along the column, one between every ten or a dozen trucks, until 2nd Battalion, and the 3rd and the 1st which followed, were uncontrollably divided.

"The order changed the nature of the operation," according to one officer quoted by the author S.L.A. Marshall. "The regiment dissolved into its individuals . . . they were as scattered as birdshot dropped from a hand."

The commander of the lead tank, Lieutenant James Mace, set off, blazing away at the surrounding peaks with his turret-mounted machine gun; the riflemen riding his tank's upper deck emptied their M-1s as fast as they could reload. Incoming Chinese slugs splattered the hull, missing the riflemen by inches, as the PLA machine gunners, deployed in hillside foxholes, brought the convoy under fire.

Three miles down the road Lieutenant Mace let out a yell. The column ground to an abrupt halt. An empty M-39 utility carrier blocked the crown of the road. Abandoned beside it stood a Sherman tank and a two-and-a-half-ton truck. The men of George Company, led by Lieutenant John Knight, jumped off the tank as bursts of Chinese machine-gun fire poured in from both sides. The Americans took cover in the nearest ditch. Mace fired frantically back while ordering his driver to ram the stalled vehicles out of their path. Another 9th Infantry Regiment officer, Lieutenant Charley Heath, came up trying to help. He stumbled across a wounded Turk. The congealed blood on the man's jacket had turned black: he had been lying there many hours.

"Me Turk! Me Turk!" the soldier gasped.

The lieutenant realized with sudden shock that the Chinese must have been in position for at least the last day and a half, strung out in strength for miles along the Sunchon Road. The 2nd Division had raced into a trap.

Machine-gun fire ripped up and down the mile-long line of thin-skinned vehicles which waited helplessly for someone to remove the obstruction. Trucks died in their tracks, creating more blockages and confusion. Men took shelter wherever they could find it. Soon the roadside ditches were choked with dead and wounded. The few officers still on their feet vainly tried to organize a coherent defense.

Lieutenant Heath leaped into the stalled carrier and released the laterals, then leaped out again as Mace's tank nosed the tracked vehicle into the ditch. An air strike by F-51s hit dangerously close. An exploding rocket temporarily blinded the lieutenant in one eye. He regained the convoy as it moved off again.

Some men were not so fortunate. The tanks they had been riding pulled out without them. The tank crews were safe, but scared. Forsaken soldiers chased down the road, heedless of the shooting, screaming to the drivers to wait. Trucks and jeeps bursting free of the shambles charged madly after the fast-disappearing armor.

Five frightful miles from the departure line the column entered the gully on the highest point of the Sunchon Road. Americans called it "The Gauntlet." Those who entered and lived to tell the tale never forgot what followed. The men riding the lead tank got off lightly. They shot past lines of wrecked Turkish trucks, emptying clip after clip of ammunition at occasional Chinese, expecting bazooka-bursts that somehow failed to materialize. The men of George Company survived, though badly shaken. Splashing through the Taedong River they quailed at the sight of a strange tank approaching from the south. It was American. They had safely run the gauntlet.

Beside the Sunchon Road,
November 30, 1950

The hog cost seven wristwatches. They were American watches, taken from the dead American soldiers at Unsan. The Chinese soldiers were pleased at the purchase-price; there would soon be plenty more watches where those came from. The Korean farmer, too, seemed delighted with the bargain, hastily pocketing his loot before the Chinese soldiers snatched it back.

He drove his squealing animal into a corner of the sty where the squad cook, Fat Belly Wu, expertly slit its throat. Other Koreans watched their Chinese saviors from a wary distance. A group of them peered timidly around the door of the farmhouse. One small boy was at last persuaded to come out and help the cook. He brought a bowl to collect the entrails. A woman, probably his mother, shyly emerged to chop for the squad a bonus helping of spicy cabbage from the large jar standing in the yard. The now-familiar *kimche* pickle took more than an hour to thaw.

A B-25 roared overhead. Its bombs burst close to the road. The Koreans promptly fled. They whipped up their ready-bundled possessions and headed for hideouts up the hill. The children's whimpering died away as the entire family disappeared in the undergrowth. They had made the same faultless exit several times during the past few hours. The Chinese were once more left in lonely occupation of the farm.

The members of the special duties squad, the Sharp Swords, who had marched so boldly into the American camp at Unsan, took little notice of the nearby battle along the Sunchon Road. They clustered hungrily around Fat Belly Wu as he calmly turned his makeshift spit in a sheltered corner of the farmyard. The squad had been poised for action more than 30 hours; by now, drama had turned to tedium. The soldiers found cooked food far more fascinating. Only Young Kung, the would-be commissar, was left following the action. Captain Lao had loaned him the sole pair of binoculars.

Things were peaceful enough when the Sharp Swords had settled into their comfortable quarters early the previous day, November 29, around 0630. There was nothing to see but that empty, insignificant road, winding off into the hills toward Sunchon. Chinese machine gunners from the main body of the 347th Regiment, dug in parallel to the road, were settling down to breakfast when two or three Turkish trucks, survivors of a convoy ambushed some kilometers away, tried to race through to the American base at Kunu-ri. They were halted by the machine gunners, riddled with bullets, their occupants cut down in the ditches.

Then two jeeploads of American military police had come out from Kunu-ri in search of the Turks and were themselves surprised and slaughtered a few hours later. The policeman's bodies still lay slumped and frozen in their seats. The remaining American forces, said to comprise a complete division, the pivot of the entire enemy defense line in northwest Korea, was expected to take to the road under cover of darkness. The Chinese stood expectantly to arms throughout the night. Shortly after dawn a handful of tanks had dashed past unchallenged—there were strict orders to wait for bigger targets—and it was not until midday, that is, until three hours ago, that the head of the American column finally appeared. The stone-filled ditches, the occasional spindly poplar, had offered scant cover from the fire storm unleashed by the waiting Chinese.

But the U.S. air attacks were hurting. As the Chinese fired away at the stalled American column, a small cloud of enemy aircraft circled overhead, seeking the hidden Chinese machine-gun nests, raking the fields with their own murderous weaponry. Napalm exploded in blobs of thick black smoke. The Chinese feared the napalm. Commissars said it was a petrochemical weapon, invented by the Americans for use against Asians. It had been first used against the Japanese on Okinawa.

Already a trickle of Chinese wounded, one or two of them horribly burned, was limping past the farmhouse toward the medical stations deeper in the hills. The wounded men grinned ruefully at the Sharp Swords, safe and cozy beside their sizzling hog barbecue. "Some get it easy!" groaned one Chinese sergeant, half-blinded by a gash across the eyes. He spoke without rancor; the squad's reputation for daring was respected throughout the division.

The wounded sergeant went away munching a crackly slice of hot pork. Cook Wu was slashing off glistening slivers of the skin. Members of the squad burned their fingers and mouths as they gulped it down. None of them had eaten anything this good for months. Captain Lao Kongcheng walked back to the lookout, replete and reinvigorated, wiping the grease off his fingers onto his padded winter coat. Young Kung handed back the binoculars and ran off to claim his share. A single pig did not go far among 30 hearty appetites.

"There won't be many more meals like this," the captain had told his men. This time they had been lucky. All the other farms were bare of livestock. The invaded Koreans had either hidden their animals or killed them off. From now on they would have to rely on seizing more enemy rations, or await the arrival of their own supplies. Something big was being organized. The official word was that huge numbers of coolies had formed a human baggage chain from far inside Manchuria. Thus far the frontline troops had received nothing but ammunition. They had just been given a large consignment of stick grenades. But who could eat grenades?

Captain Lao sought shelter behind a bale of hay. It was strategically placed to ward off the wind. Around him the naked apple trees rattled like skeletons. Snowflakes whirled gently across the hill. Replacements had fleshed out his squad since the Unsan affair. Six of the Sharp Swords had been killed in that skirmish, a remarkably small number considering the risks taken. The wounded included Li, the former Nationalist officer and one-time opium smoker. He was back again, still coughing, from the hospital in Andong. Opium Li crept up beside the captain to examine the fight with professional concern. Behind him came the muscular mortarman, Big Ears Wong, and Little Li, his smaller sidekick, who settled down as unofficial bodyguards, belching luxuriously and picking their teeth with straws. They watched incuriously as the captain studied the Sunchon Road.

The battle was going very well indeed. Come nightfall the Sharp Swords would be down there among the enemy, launching commando raids up and down the column. That would complete the rout. The captain's stomach fluttered at the thought.

An American truck went up in a fist of fire. It must have been carrying gasoline. Opium Li snatched the binoculars and grunted appreciatively. Helmeted figures rolled into the ditches, some with their clothes ablaze. Now the Americans were finding out what napalm was like. "Burn, curse you, burn!" Li wheezed. His shrunken face was flushed with excitement. The cold air set him coughing again.

Captain Lao looked on with a curious compassion. Perhaps these Americans prayed? He remembered kneeling on the cold stone floor of the Tsingtao mission whenever the Reverend Albert Browne invoked his God. The American missionary had spoken humbly, if familiarly, to the deity: the way Chinese do when addressing the Kitchen God, Tsao Wang, before sending him off on his annual trip to heaven. But to young Lao's ears the Reverend's prayers sounded like self-criticism. The missionary seemed obsessed with sin. He constantly craved forgiveness. It was amazing how sinful Christianity made its believers feel. Even their babies were born soiled with sin. This was nonsense, the youngster told himself; everyone knew wicked deeds involved hellfire. Yet, given filial sons, and the right rituals, redemption could always be arranged. The real enemy was not sin.

It was bad luck; a demon who had to be headed off at all costs. If the Americans prayed at all, the captain thought, they ought to be praying right now for better fortune. . . .

The Gauntlet,
Farther down the Sunchon Road,
The afternoon of November 30, 1950

Colonel Yang Shixian did not consider himself superstitious. But the battalion commander cursed his luck when the air attacks began. About five kilometers down the road from the Sharp Swords' position, the first sizable group of American vehicles to get past the Chinese ambush was entering the mouth of the pass. Yang's signal lamps were glowing and his mortars were into their barrage when the blue-black American jets with white stars on their wings came shrieking out of the overcast. They blanketed the commanding hilltops with rockets, machine guns, and napalm. Much of this firepower was wasted—the Chinese 2nd Battalion was well dug in, thanks to its predawn spadework—but the initial impact was terrifying. The Chinese had never been under such direct air attack. The hiss and thud of the rockets, the obscene smoky bursts of the petro-bombs, the showers of liquid, lapping flame, sent soldiers ducking for cover. A few fled their positions. Strafing cannon churned up the ground around him, ripping dust and dirt off the gray rock face. One of the men fell, rolling and sliding like a limp doll until the body dropped into the carpet of corpses covering the floor of the pass.

The Chinese fusillade faltered momentarily, encouraging the American vehicles to weave on through the wreckage, firing blindly as they went. A tank, crowded with men, skidded below them. Colonel Yang leaned over the ledge carefully aiming a borrowed M-1. His beloved pistol was useless at this range. The rifle kicked repeatedly as he squeezed the trigger, but the tank and its topload raced on. The faces of the enemy soldiers as they clung in terror to the turret stayed stamped on Yang's memory. Commissar Wong Wuyi joined in the attack, tossing down stick grenades. They exploded harmlessly in the road and in his rage he threw a hefty rock. It bounced off the hood of a jeep, smashing the strapped-down windshield; the driver swerved, sideswiped a stalled half-track, and shot swaying off around the bend with everyone aboard shooting excitedly upward at the invisible foe.

The air attacks grew worse. The colonel noticed that as the enemy pressed deeper into the pass the supporting jets switched from high explosive to napalm. Experience must have proved it more effective against well-prepared positions. Bombs were likely to start rock slides, which would only seal the trap. For minutes on end the sky seemed to rain napalm. Torrents of flame splattered the hilltops. Two or three machine guns went out as the Chinese crewmen fried in their foxholes. Several squads were driven back to the reverse slopes, where their weapons could no longer be brought to bear. Others were running desperately short of ammunition. The gunners' logistics link to the battalion's main store, one kilometer from the pass, was being gravely disrupted by the aerial strafing. Several supply details had been shot up struggling in with their heavy loads.

A signaler across the pass semaphored a message from Major Ma. The yellow hand-flags stood clearly out against the mottled granite. How much easier it would be, the colonel thought, if they could consult by radio. The major's message made clear that, at present rates of firing, his machine guns had scarcely enough ammunition to last 20 minutes. After that he would be forced to detach riflemen to carry supplies, or send a raiding squad down to the floor of the pass. Ample American supplies lay around below their feet.

Colonel Yang peered over the ledge; it was growing hard to see what was going on down there. Dust, smoke, and exhaust fumes almost concealed the column. A tank was on fire, as were two or three more trucks, and lines of men as well as vehicles could be seen picking their way through the wreckage. It would be unwise, he decided, to allow the major to venture below. If anyone was going down there it would have to be himself. And not merely in search of ammunition.

"Madness!" scoffed Commissar Wong Wuyi when the colonel told him what he planned to do. The adjutant, Major Lo, looked doubtful. The officers crouched beneath an overhanging rock while the colonel explained his plan. Trickles of napalm ran smoking and flaming down the cliffs. None of it reached them.

Quite obviously, the colonel said, large numbers of Americans were still managing to escape. It was his battalion's job to stop them. The enemy column could best be halted, in Yang's opinion, by a small volunteer squad armed with satchel charges that would wreck enough vehicles to create an immovable roadblock. Or perhaps, the colonel reasoned, the Americans would soon try to evacuate their artillery. Nothing was better than a big gun to bar a road. He recalled how the jackknifed gun limber had blocked 8th Cavalry's retreat at Unsan.

Commissar Wong strongly objected to the colonel's leading the assault. Who was going to control the main action? At the present stage there was nothing to control, the colonel argued; the ambush in the pass was becoming a soldiers' battle. The outcome depended from now on upon individual staying power and initiative. Surely

Wong had already set the pattern? The battalion would follow the commissar's example, hurling rocks when it ran out of bullets. The way things were going, that was sure to be soon. The riflemen on the ledge were yelling out for ammunition.

No one was trying to be heroic, the colonel explained years later. Satchel-charge assaults were routine throughout the Korean War. Nor was it unusual for a battalion commander to take personal control of a vital, if dangerous, operation. Poor communications and the divided terrain made it difficult during this particular action to delegate a mission so crucial to the battalion's battle plan.

The signal flags flapped again as Colonel Yang called up covering fire for his mission. Adjutant Lo assembled the assault squad. Including himself and the colonel there were nine of them: two mortarmen, two riflemen, and three sappers carrying high explosives in lightweight canvas bags. They armed themselves with pistols, carbines, and a single BAR machine gun, and mustered on the southern edge of the ledge. Shallow footholds took them 15 meters up the face of the cliff to a path, winding among the boulders, which led down a nearby gully to the road below. Fortunately the enemy was too busy ducking the incoming bursts to notice the tiny figures breasting the rock face.

The colonel paused, puffing, at the summit, amazed to find the landscape so transformed. Since he had last passed this way a few hours before, the straggling tufts of vegetation, the clumps of tall dried grass, and the tiny, stunted trees had been entirely burned away by napalm; the rocks were blackened and in some places still smoking. A fresh flight of jets closed in as the assault party hurried toward the gully, the pilots concentrating their inflammable loads on the farthest end of the pass. A distant pair of signal lamps standing unattended on a craggy outcrop disappeared in clouds of smoke and flame.

Poor bespectacled Lo had lost a lot of weight in the past week, but he was still badly out of condition. Several times he tripped on the downward path, sending small showers of stones clunking off below. The colonel called a halt halfway to check out the locale. The roadside was covered with bodies. Dozens of wounded Americans and Turks had crawled into the roadside gullies seeking refuge from the elements and from the enemy. There they must have frozen to death or died of their wounds. The Chinese continued their cautious descent; anxious not to attract attention, they squeezed themselves behind a big boulder wedged slightly above eye level ten meters from the road.

Following customary procedures, everyone would provide covering fire from their present position while the sappers ran in with the charges to dynamite the first vehicle of large enough size. Two spare satchels full of explosives would be kept in reserve for a second attempt.

The light was beginning to fade. Small groups of Americans trudged by, clamoring for rides off every passing vehicle. The trucks ground grimly past with unwinking headlamps. The colonel counted 15 of them. Too many Americans were getting away. If the big U.S. guns weren't coming—and maybe the Americans had abandoned them?—he could wait no more than another five minutes. He comforted himself with the thought that one or two big supply trucks, properly piled up, would cause as big a jam as an upended 155-mm cannon.

A GI came into the gully systematically searching the bodies and making off with an armful of canteens. A slug hit him as he emerged onto the roadway. It threw him into the path of an oncoming truck. With a hollow crunch the body bounced beneath the front wheels, grinding into the dust. The Chinese watched helplessly. Adjutant Lo vomited where he sat. But the colonel saw only the truck: a familiar half-track vehicle mounting quadruple machine guns, much like the one that had proved so troublesome at Unsan. The driver had braked momentarily. If they could stop him *permanently*, his vehicle would easily block the road; there might even be a chance of grabbing its machine guns and redirecting them, point blank, into the oncoming U.S. column.

Colonel Yang sprang, yelling, to his feet and immediately the sappers were off, charging down the gully swinging their lethal charges. They leaped like acrobats across the bodies while the rifleman with the BAR and everyone else fired frantically at the driving cab and the three men manning the machine guns. A front tire blew, the windshield went out, and the driver slithered down behind the wheel. The half-track slewed broadside to the road, shedding one of its gun crew. The other two gunners were trying frantically to bring the machine guns to bear when the first charge blew out the engine. Another exploded prematurely at the mouth of the gully, killing one of the sappers and showering the other Chinese with rocks. Colonel Yang was still firing wildly with his pistol when something hit him on the head and blacked out everything.

On the Sunchon Road,
Late afternoon,
November 30, 1950

The retreat was agony for Major General Laurence B. Keiser. Throughout the preceding week the U.S. 2nd Division commander had been under intolerable strain. Like his own troops, he was exhausted and bewildered. Surrounded, it seemed, by an innumerable enemy, left on a limb by his corps commander, and confronted hourly with crucial, solitary decisions, the sorely tried general was having trouble maintaining a hold on events. The worst of his problems was readjusting to this new-style war. As one of several veterans of the WW II European campaign holding field commands in Korea, he had learned to fight along modern lines. But here in the Chungchon valley Keiser's foe refused to follow the book.

There was marked relief among divisional staff when General Keiser ordered the retreat on November 29. Many officers were beginning to fear that further dithering would mean annihilation. Now at last a decision had been made. A road-march was something everyone understood. Barreling through was Eighth Army's kind of warfare.

The 2nd Division certainly looked impressive. Mile upon mile of trucks, tanks, jeeps, and guns snaked off across the winter landscape. High hills to the north behind them tangled with the clouds. The freezing Taedong River, start-point for their now-forgotten offensive, meandered through its wide brown bowl of dormant farmland. Crawling through this farmland, raising proud plumes of dust, the column flaunted an awesome array of weaponry.

The general drove confidently out of Kunu-ri in the direction of Sunchon, unfazed by the Chinese fire, expecting at any moment to bump into the British Commonwealth Brigade. The farther he drove the greater grew his concern. Large numbers of trucks were halted. His men made disturbingly little effort to fight. Formations of the 38th and 9th Infantry Regiments, charged with defending the column, were too fragmented to respond to regular commands. The extent of the crisis became horribly apparent at the pass, where he found the exit blocked by the Chinese and jammed with stalled traffic.

The general went into the pass on foot, determined to organize a breakthrough. U.S. support planes were strafing the embankments on either side of the road. Trickles of napalm seared the rock walls. The noise was deafening. Surrounding ditches were heaped with dead and wounded. Troops of the 38th Infantry, clustered in dazed groups, ignored Keiser's orders that they defend themselves. Exhaustion, hunger, lack of sleep, and shock had left a battle-toughened regiment broken and afraid. A solitary man was returning the Chinese fire: a sergeant who had unloaded an 81-mm mortar from a truck, set it up in the road, and begun bombarding the enemy forces commanding the southern exit.

The general saw what needed to be done. Infantry attacks must be mounted along both sides of the pass, wrecking equipment brought in to clear the roadblock, and more air support called down before it grew too dark. He turned wearily back toward his jeep. On the way he tripped over the body of a GI sprawled across the road. The body sat bolt upright and said: "You damned son of a bitch." The general mildly apologized and went on.

Salvation lay among the latest arrivals at the pass—squads from 9th Infantry, staff clerks and cooks, ROKs and Turks—who were formed into assault groups by Brigadier General Sladen J. Bradley, Keiser's second-in-command. The newcomers were sent up the slopes to engage the enemy while two amphibious tanks bulldozed through the wreckage blocking the pass. Soon after dark, troops, trucks, and guns were breaking out beyond the dreadful confines of "The Gauntlet," past a burning village and across the Taedong River to the outposts of the 27th Commonwealth Brigade.

The British had spent an infuriating day butting vainly against heavy concentrations of Chinese. Hampered by lack of transport and artillery, they had arrived at the river to find the dominant heights already in enemy hands. Troops of the Middlesex Regiment made repeated bayonet charges up the mountain slopes, trying to cut a pathway to the trapped Americans. But without tanks or artillery support the Londoners were blasted back by mortar and machine-gun fire. At nightfall they were themselves being encircled by the still-advancing enemy.

The escape route was kept open, however, by the Australians. Troops of the 3rd Royal Australian Regiment, popularly known as "The Diggers," who were patrolling both banks of the Taedong, managed to block further infiltration.

General Keiser broke through about 1930 looking gray and grim. One battery of guns came after him, followed by part of another, but after that the traffic died away. From then on, most of those who escaped did so on foot. Some strode proud and tall, still eager to do battle; others wept on finding themselves in friendly hands. The Commonwealth soldiers had always questioned American lack of discipline. As the demoralized stragglers hurried in, an Australian sergeant snorted in disgust.

"Their cigar butts went by," he sneered later, "like tracer bullets in the night."

The Gauntlet,
Early evening,
November 30, 1950

They found Colonel Yang Shixian bleeding among the bodies. The explosion that occurred as his sapper attacked the U.S. half-track had blown Yang off his precarious perch. A fragment of rock had caught him square on the forehead. Splinters from the demolished half-track killed one of his sappers and wounded most of the others. Adjutant Lo, his spectacles smashed, managed to organize a follow-up satchel charge, which sent an approaching truck plowing into the half-track. A speeding jeep piled in behind, creating enough havoc to delay the enemy for hours. Helped by the mortarmen, covered by a rifleman firing the BAR, the adjutant then heaved the colonel up the hillside in search of medical attention. Air attacks had ceased with the onset of darkness; a mob of Chinese wounded was gathering among the uppermost rocks in a hollow shielded from the biting wind.

The colonel was regaining consciousness, tearing feebly at the bandages around his head. His first fuzzy recollection was of someone who resembled Lo leaning anxiously over him. "The pass?" the colonel remembered asking him. The adjutant was reassuring. It was not until the following day that they told him at least 2,000 Americans had managed to escape. Right now he was in no fit state to listen. Pain throbbed through his brain like hammer blows. A medic came over with a shot of morphine, part of the supplies looted from the ROKs, and the pain receded.

He dreamed of cruising up a broad, brown river like the Yangtse. Long islands of cut bamboo floated past, steered by ragged men in pale straw hats. The men waved to him as he passed, squinting in the silver sunlight; one of them looked remarkably like his father, who had been dead for more than 20 years. He leaned far over the rail trying to call his father, but the effort hurt and something cold came howling round his ears. It was the wind. Major Ma was bending over him. The flaps of the major's hat were drawn across his ears and his mustache was crusted with snow. Dawn was breaking. The battalion was being relieved, the major explained, and the regimental commander had sent congratulations. The 2nd Battalion would be recommended for some sort of revolutionary citation. The men were exhausted, their ammunition spent. Many were dead or wounded. The battalion would withdraw and re-form five kilometers from the pass. It would be quiet there and everyone could regain his strength.

The colonel tried to sit up. The ache had almost gone but giddiness restricted his movements. He had sudden fears of some undisclosed and awful wound. How many times he had seen a man recover consciousness to find he had lost a leg! The major set his fears at rest. A doctor came up to add reassurance. There was nothing a lot more sleep could not cure. A litter party moved him painfully across the slippery rocks, everyone anxious to convince him that the action in the pass had by no means been in vain. The delay had cost the Americans enormous casualties and most of their guns. "Their division has ceased to exist," Major Ma declared with relish.

The Sharp Swords were not so certain. The squad again wore captured ROK parkas, pretending to be Koreans, though they had no intention of repeating the bluff that worked so well at Unsan. Marching up as an organized body of sham puppets might have deceived a single careless sentry, but it would never work tonight on the Sunchon Road. The GIs defending the ambushed column were fully alert, shooting at anything that moved. At least they had been, up until nightfall. While it was still light enough to see, the quad-mounted guns on a half-track had cut great swathes across the Chinese positions. The half-track was still there, as far as Captain Lao Kongcheng could make out, more threatening to him than a whole battery of cannon, though lately it had ceased firing. Orders were to raid the column, knock out the half-track, and cause further blockage on the road. Any American rearguard units trying to make a run for it were to be trapped and halted.

The squad spread out, line abreast, across the frozen countryside. A broad strip of fallow rice field, bare of cover, stretched out ahead of them. Mortars and rifle fire erupted from left rear; the regiment was staging a diversion. Tracer slugs showered overhead like sparks from a giant anvil. Bombs from the mortar tubes exploded unseen on the far side of the road. A low whistle from the captain set the squad leaping forward, half-crouching and wary, snow stinging hands and faces, weapons at the ready. Big Ears Wong and Little Li both carried Thompson submachine guns, still sticky from storage in an ROK supply depot. The cook, Fat Belly Wu, was draped with satchel charges and brandishing a BAR. Captain Lao ran between them, his belt stuffed with stick grenades, wondering whether the snowy night would make his men harder to hit.

No matter how much Lao fought down his fears, terror seeped into his gut. The closer the squad came to the column the more certain he became that unseen marksmen had them squarely in their sights. One hundred meters, ninety meters, eighty meters . . . out of the murk loomed the inert mechanisms on the roadway, raised by an embankment two meters above the fields: any moment now, he told himself, there would be a crash of gunfire, the shock of metal thumping into his body. But on this occasion he was wrong. The Sharp Swords dashed unscathed through the rows of halted trucks, finding them silent and empty, their contents spilled and scattered to the wind.

Bivouac bags, tents, broken footlockers and ration boxes were ankle-deep across the road. Mixed in with the trash of battle were the bodies of men, as frozen and forgotten as their own forsaken baggage. Some of the squad quickly got down to looting, but the captain ordered them into defensive positions. They could be caught in an elaborate trap. Surrounding vehicles were cautiously checked out for signs of life. A jeep stood slewed across the road packed with American military policemen. The MPs were all dead and quite rigid, the blood on their parkas long congealed. Other men had been killed seated inside their trucks, jumping out or scrambling for safety underneath. One driver hung half out of his open cab, dangling arms gently swaying in the wind. The same wind rustled the snow-flecked hair of the boy who still manned the traverse on the half-track. He sagged awkwardly in his seat, helmetless, shot between the eyes.

Opium Li climbed up, coughing, to check the quadruple machine guns. He pushed the boy's body impatiently aside, took over the gun layer's seat, and jerkily worked the traverse. Approvingly he scanned the field of fire. The half-track was parked diagonally across the road, its hood pitted with bullet holes. The still-serviceable guns covered a wide arc of the surrounding fields and, more promisingly, the approach road from Kunu-ri. A gap in the column left room to rake the bend, one thousand meters distant, around which any latecomers would have to drive. A burning truck close to the bend provided a possible aiming point through the snow flurries.

"Sure you can work these guns?" Captain Lao inquired. Opium Li looked knowing. "Let the Yankees taste their own medicine," he said grimly. "But I'll need some help." Young Kung, the educated one, climbed onto the opposite seat, controlling the elevation. He tried not to look down at the dead gunner's body.

Things were going more smoothly than expected. The captain could not believe his luck. The troops who should have been shooting it out with them in this deserted section of the column must have made off in the darkness shortly before the Sharp Swords' raid. Were they waiting out there in the snow to launch a counterattack?

"They can't have just vanished," whispered Fat Belly Wu. He crouched uncertainly behind the half-track, peering beneath the irregular line of vehicles. The only movement anyone could see was a streamer of toilet paper flapping around the flattened tires of an empty jeep. Sticking strictly to orders, the captain sent half his squad well down the road to ambush any last-minute absconders from Kunu-ri. Sappers hid among stalled vehicles close to the bend, satchel charges at the ready. A burst of flames from another truck indicated that someone down there was making sure they'd have enough light to fight by. A runner went off to regimental headquarters with a message clarifying the situation. Their commanding officer might consider moving the main body's ambush positions nearer to the road. The rest of the squad split into groups searching surrounding trucks and ditches. Six men including Fat Belly Wu began prodding the bodies with their feet, on the off-chance of finding a few alive. Others gathered armfuls of food, weapons, and ammunition. Watches would come later. The search extended down the embankment. Numbers of bodies had rolled there into the tall tufts of brittle grass.

Cook Wu let out a yell. Two of the bodies leaped to their feet shouting. Little Li and Big Ears Wong almost mowed them down with their tommy guns. One of the squad's new replacements fled, thinking he was seeing ghosts. The captain ordered everyone to cool it. He beckoned the apparitions with his pistol. The two GIs climbed painfully up to the road, hands in the air.

"Who are you? Where are your comrades?" Captain Lao asked in his missionary-school English. The men looked at him in surprise.

"We're Americans," said one of them.

"Are you going to kill us?" asked the other.

"Where's your outfit?" the captain demanded. He ordered them to turn out their pockets while they told their story. The man called Woodstock came from Maine. He and Johnstone, a corporal from Arkansas, had been crawling for hours beside the road trying to grab a lift from passing vehicles. They had started the road-march riding on tanks but after the first shoot-out the driver had roared off without them. Their buddies had either fallen or slipped away southward over the hills. About an hour before the Chinese appeared more than a hundred men had quit this part of the column and made off in the dark. Their officers reckoned a British relief force was approaching.

"What made you stay behind?" Captain Lao was genuinely puzzled. Surely there was safety in numbers? Woodstock shook his head. He kept his hands up and nervously watched the burly, menacing figure of Big Ears Wong. They had hesitated to join the main party, Johnstone said, because they hoped another section of the column, including artillery, would still make a run for it. They did not fancy their chances legging it across open country teeming with gooks . . . er, enemy troops. When the Chinese came charging up they had decided to play dead.

Yellow flashes, the bark of guns, came from the direction of Kunu-ri. The American rearguard was throwing out its final barrage. Wong and Little Li shuffled irritably as their commander wasted precious time mumbling to these foreign barbarians. But Lao had always been fascinated by the men who fought him, even in the days when those men were Japanese. Weeks after the Japanese surrender he had watched their soldiers being marched away, unarmed, through jeering Chinese crowds. The people who jeered loudest had kept the quietest when the emperor's men wielded the sword. The sight of those soldiers, downcast and defeated, still awed him. The Americans were softer stuff, but he was curious to discover what had brought them to Korea. Neither of these prisoners could give a coherent answer, though both plainly disliked the place. Did they have orders to advance into China? No sir, they said; as far as they knew, U.S. forces were to halt on the border, on some river, darned if they could remember the name. The attack schedule should have had them sitting beside that river, right this minute, ready to pack up and go home. Questioned about unit numbers and dispositions, they were equally vague.

The captain told the GIs to relax. He presented them with cigarettes made from pungent Shandong tobacco, but warned them against lighting up in their present exposed position. He asked about their families. Woodstock produced a dog-eared picture of his wife and two children. The other man said he was not married, though he also carried pictures of the folks back home. They showed his parents posed outside a farmhouse, looking thin and worn; the last letter said Pa was feeling poorly. The letter had arrived less than a week ago. Captain Lao was impressed. He had not received a letter from his wife for three months; he did not expect one until the current campaign was over. The American rulers, despite their oppressive system, really looked after their soldiers.

The snow showers had lifted. A star or two peeked through the overcast. Young Kung called down from the half-track. He could see a green signal flare curling up from the rice fields. The regiment was warning them that more Americans were on the move. Members of the squad mounted worried watch on the road. The roar of engines came faintly from the valley. The men grew increasingly impatient with the captain's unintelligible conversation; Opium Li leaned angrily out of the half-track and shouted "Shoot them!" The GIs did not understand what he said, but caught the menace in his tone. Both looked appealingly to the captain.

"You two take off," Lao told them regretfully. There were many more things he wanted to talk about. "Make for the mountains and move parallel with this road. Try to get across the Taedong River. Good luck." The Americans backed away suspiciously, expecting a burst in the back. Then they fled into the darkness. "Tell your comrades we treated you well," the captain shouted after them. The last thing he wanted was prisoners. Opium Li shook his fist in the direction of the vanished foe. "Swine!" he screamed. "All stinking swine!" He turned grumbling back to feed the machine guns fresh belts of shells.

Something with pale sidelights crawled around the bend. Flames from the burning truck silhouetted the turret of a Sherman tank.

Close behind came huge trucks towing guns. Lao climbed excitedly into the half-track. "Don't waste your slugs on armor," he told Opium Li. Together they waited for the satchel bomb explosions. The detonators on those things were notoriously unreliable; at crucial moments they stubbornly refused to work. At last there was a flash, a loud thud, followed by another. As the tank's lights went out, a Chinese machine gun began spouting tracer. Then came smaller explosions, probably grenades. Lots of distant shooting. "Aim high!" the captain told his quad crew as Opium Li squeezed the trigger. The guns jammed, and from the lips of Li came a stream of poetic curses molded over the centuries by the Shandong dialect. All at once they cleared again, spewing out a long burst, shaking the half-track and deafening the bystanders. A cluster of glowing shells arced northward into the night, way wide of their target. Opium Li grappled desperately with the traverse. The captain started telling him to hold it, fearing they might be hitting their own troops, when the guns jammed again.

Making notes on the campaign a year later, Captain Lao Kongcheng could not help noticing how often his best-laid plans refused to work. The Unsan raid proved, in the end, an honorable exception. What followed in Seoul was probably predictable. But this skirmish on the road . . . if it had been one of his country's propaganda movies, his gunners would have wasted the Yankees. The column would have been halted. The Sherman tank would have gone up in flames. But here was his first big shock—to the squad's amazement, the tank was still moving. Its lights were out but its tracks were turning. And its main gun was firing straight into the ranks of the Chinese, caught perilously in the open. The artillery column came on behind the tank, picking a path down the littered roadway.

The Korean-speaker, Deng, came racing up. "Charges bounced off," he panted. "The stuff's not powerful enough." He snatched a spare satchelful of explosives from Fat Belly Wu and ran back toward the enemy. A gunflash froze him momentarily in mid-swing, the satchel charge about to leave his hands and sail against the tracks. The charge went off in the darkness with a hungry crunch, the tank shuddered but kept on coming, by now less than 200 meters from the half-track.

Captain Lao jumped down, ordering Opium Li and Young Kung to follow. No sense trying to take on a tank. But as he jumped, the half-track's machine guns cleared, and an inaccurate fusillade from Li flew high over the tank's turret. The tank's main gun swung deliberately toward the half-track; the Americans now knew it was in Chinese hands. The first shot exploded against the gun-mount, hurling the captain over the embankment. He fell heavily, and watched, dazed, as the tank crushed the jeepful of dead MPs and nosed the now-burning half-track off the road. It fell down the opposite embankment, out of sight, in a shower of sparks.

The next thing Lao remembered was Fat Belly Wu massaging his hands. "Better now, better now," the cook was saying tenderly. Lao ached and felt freezing cold. Wong and Li's faces appeared, followed by Deng looking as if he'd been in a fire.

"Some of the guns got by," Deng apologized. "We did our best. We've stopped them again now."

Captain Lao had difficulty speaking. His tongue was swollen inside his mouth. "Where's Opium Li and Young Kung?"

"We got Young Kung out of the half-track," Deng volunteered. "He'll be fine."

"How about Opium Li?"

Deng stayed silent.

The captain struggled into a sitting position. They had carried him to a sheltered spot several hundred meters from the road. The eastern sky was turning pink. The column looked toylike from this distance, stalled again with still more vehicles that would never reach Sunchon. Most of the new ones were ambulances. "Must be two hundred wounded in them," said Big Ears Wong. "All litter cases. Not a medic stayed."

"The drivers just ran," said Little Li.

"Our people can't help for a while," said Deng. "Regiment took a lot of casualties."

Lao's right leg was in a splint. It did not seem to hurt. He merely felt tired, immensely tired. He lay back propped against a low wall, watching the arrival of the first planes of the day. He enjoyed watching the planes, even though they belonged to the enemy. The sun was not yet up but its early rays transformed them into gilded arrowheads. Back and forth they weaved across the pale morning, embroidering the sky with fine white contrails. Birds as beautiful as these held no apparent hint of menace. Drowsily he admired their easy grace, so far detached from the realities of earth. For years he had wanted to become a pilot; back in the summer, before the regiment came to Korea, he had applied to join the new training squadrons being formed in Manchuria. There had been no acknowledgment of his application. Probably he was too old. The cook produced a mug of hot tea and some wheat crackers. He sipped and munched and watched the planes without permitting serious thought to intrude.

The squad was carting Lao away on a litter when the jets struck. He glimpsed them diving overhead, heard the thump of the napalm, the distant shouts and screams, saw looks of horror on his comrades' faces. The American pilots were only doing their job. They had orders to destroy all abandoned equipment. They were not to know these ambulances were full of their own wounded. The captain felt instinctively for his amulet. It was good to be alive. . . .

Lieutenant Colonel Melvin Blair was on the telephone in his command post back at Kunu-ri when Chinese troops burst through the door. The commanding officer of the U.S. 3rd Battalion, 24th Infantry Regiment, cut short his conversation and dashed out into the night. He managed to gather enough men together to make a fighting retreat. It was 0200, December 1. With the colonel's abrupt departure Kunu-ri was overrun. The regiment fought desperately all night. It was an all-black regiment in a still-segregated army. Its commander, Colonel John Corley, the most-decorated U.S. Army battalion commander of World War II—the man who had been talking to Blair on the other end of the interrupted line—tried hard to save the 3rd Battalion, but the Chinese had it virtually surrounded. Some of the black soldiers fled, some stood and fought, some died. Some were captured and sent back to their own lines. By morning the battalion had ceased to exist.

But the men of the 24th Infantry Regiment bought time for the rest of the rearguard. The bulk of the force left behind to cover the U.S. 2nd Division's retreat had already escaped, ironically, down the very road General Keiser spurned. The sensible routing change was decided by the man in charge of the rearguard, Colonel Paul L. Freeman, Jr., of 23rd Infantry. He considered his chances of barreling through the Sunchon Road dim indeed. Ignoring unverified reports of roadblocks on the alternative route through Anju, he ordered withdrawal to start at dusk on November 30.

Time was fast running out. Chinese pressure was steadily building. The three defending regiments that made up the rearguard were depleted and crumbling. There was no hope of saving the guns. Too many sharp bends needed to be negotiated in the dark. The gunners concentrated their fire around the village of Pugwon, down the main Huichon road, where large enemy forces were seen to be massing. Every last round, a total of 3,206 shells, was fired off in 20 minutes. Paint peeled off the howitzer tubes. Breech blocks turned black. The Chinese advance temporarily halted, and during that pause the Americans blew up their own guns with thermite, the remaining troops pulled back across the Chungchon, and the first vehicles streamed safely westward beside the ice-rimmed river. Had the entire division taken the same route the story would have been different. The Chinese would have been deprived of their ambush.

The retreat to Sunchon cost the Americans more than 3,000 casualties, half their guns, and much of their transportation. This was no worse than Washington's losses at Valley Forge in the winter of 1777. But the U.S. 2nd Division suffered most of them in a single afternoon.

12

The UN Withdraws from Pyongyang / Making Movies with Kim Il Sung / General Peng Resumes the Offensive.

Pyongyang,
North Korea,
December 3, 1950

> *Hear the pitter patter of tiny feet*
> *It's old Two Div in full retreat*
> *I'm movin' on . . . back to Inchon*
> *I'm buggin' out fast*
> *Afore they get my ass*
> *Yes, I'm movin' on . . .*

The U.S. 2nd Division was badly but not irreparably mauled. By the end of December it was back in action. The collapse of Eighth Army's right flank never became as dangerous as it should have been. The Chinese were simply not mobile enough to exploit their tactical advantage. Given resolute generalship, the UN rout could conceivably have been checked at Pyongyang, and a defense line established along the lateral road linking that city to the east-coast port of Wonsan. But General "Johnnie" Walker, who had been treating the

220

campaign thus far as a quail hunt, had lost all stomach for a fight. Convinced that the heirs of Genghis Khan were about to overwhelm the entire Korean peninsula, he sanctioned the longest, most disgraceful retreat in U.S. military history.

The world press cried havoc as his powerfully equipped army, perfectly capable of confronting the Chinese, ignobly quit the field, urged on by panic, rumor, and unnerving newscasts from its own radio transmitters. The age of the transistor had not yet arrived, but battery-powered portables were on sale in every PX and many GIs owned them. U.S. Forces' broadcasters put the fear of God into the listening soldiery with their reports of "bugle-blowing hordes" flooding down from Manchuria.

Two days after the ambush on the Sunchon Road a charging herd of vehicles 20 miles long was still bearing down on Pyongyang, desperate to escape across the Taedong River. Military police tried feebly to ease the traffic flow as ill-disciplined drivers broke column and unlucky ones broke down. Roadsides were littered with discarded vehicles all the way south to Seoul.

The commander of the British 27th Commonwealth Brigade, 43-year-old Brigadier Basil Coad, fought his way through a stream of tanks, trucks, and guns as the ten-minute drive to Sunchon took more than an hour. The brigadier was impatient to reach the headquarters of IX Corps. The strangest signals had been coming from the Americans during the past couple of days; by the morning of December 2 the brigade needed to know exactly what was going on. He found U.S. Corps headquarters poised for takeoff. Papers were being set on fire. In the command post there was hysteria and confusion. The IX Corps commander, Major General John B. ("Nervous John") Coulter, was engaged elsewhere. He was, as usual, "directing operations in the field."

Brigadier Coad told the rest of the story to his officers when he returned to his own camp, caked in yellow dust and shaking a puzzled head.

"What orders, sir?" demanded an eager aide.

"No orders at all," replied the brigadier in his drawling English accent. "All they said was to, er, *haul ass*."

The Commonwealth Brigade began a long and lonely walk back. Most of its transportation was useless. Daunting distances were covered on foot, trying to keep contact with Eighth Army. Defense of the army's rear was theoretically shared with the U.S. First Cavalry Division, but as nervousness increased and phantom Chinese popped up on every hilltop, the gap between the foot-slogging British and their motorized allies steadily widened. Something like 20 miles lay between them on occasion.

The Argyll & Sutherland Highlanders accepted the reverse with bigoted satisfaction. The Yanks were, naturally, to blame. "Call 'emselves sojjers?" the Scots chuckled as the last of the First Cavalry scuttled off down the road. "Them's naething but mithers' boys!" No American in the disappearing trucks made any more cracks about tea.

The Scots marched to the skirl of bagpipes, company by company in open file on either side of the road, with intervals of 50 yards between platoons. Halts were regulated by blasts on the adjutant's hunting horn—a typical regimental eccentricity—which echoed eerily down the gloomy Korean glens. Small, tracked Bren-gun carriers tailed along behind, forming a lightly armored rearguard. Their drivers claimed the enemy could be distinctly heard following them a few miles back. That set Sergeant Major Murray whipping in the laggards. "If you don't keep up with us," he bellowed, "the next man you'll find coming down this road will be Joe Stalin." He made no mention of Mao Zedong; few Scottish soldiers had ever heard of him.

Shortly after midday on December 3, Dwight Martin of *Time* magazine drove about Pyongyang to catch the closing act of the drama. A month ago his jeep had cost him a case of Scotch. Now jeeps were going begging—provided the fleeing Koreans didn't get at them first. He parked beside a line of stalled army trucks picked clean by looters. Lamps, dashboard fittings, even the tires had been taken. Any vehicle left unguarded for more than half an hour in this part of the country was likely to be stolen or cannibalized. The Koreans were desperate and determined to survive.

The vehicular flash flood had suddenly dried. The roads converging on the capital from Anju and Sinanju were ominously empty. A final dust cloud marked the progress of First Cavalry bouncing in their battered trucks to holding positions south of the Taedong River. Way after them came the British and Australians on foot, their pipers playing a jaunty tune. As the Scots strode past, the American correspondent caught a snatch of ribald song: "Oh, me Auntie Mary had a canary . . . up the leg o' her drawers . . ." One of the Australians shook his fist at Dwight Martin. "You barstards couldn't punch yer way out of a paper bag!" he jeered.

The last train chugged in slowly from the north festooned with people. The locomotive, the cab, the flatcars, and the coaches bulged with humanity held on, it seemed, by magnets. Following down the tracks, and down the now-silent roads, thousands of Korean civilians trudged stoically southward. The halt and the lame camped briefly in the back streets of Pyongyang. The majority clambered down a levee in the shadow of a quiet Buddhist temple, then picked their way across the Taedong on the slippery spans of a shattered bridge. Their fortitude was immortalized by Associated Press photographer Max Desfor in a Pulitzer Prize-winning picture.

The normal population of Pyongyang was 300,000. It was impossible to guess how many had chosen to remain. As soon as the news spread that the Americans would not attempt to defend the city, tiny North Korean flags appeared in windows of the old red-brick houses in Ocean Village, the comfortable, missionary-built compound where Kim Il Sung once lived with his Soviet advisers. Caretakers must have been smartening up the place for reoccupation. No one cared to drive in and find out.

The Pyongyang city hall had been packed, until lately, with mobs of hungry politicians. The gray granite building had been a seedbed of patronage from the moment South Korean President Syngman Rhee made a surprise appearance there on the second-floor balcony in October, shortly after the city's liberation. Today the balcony door creaked open unnoticed in the wind. The draft rustled the crumpled papers carpeting the empty offices. Outside, above the deserted street, the South Korean national flag with its Confucian trigrams had vanished from the staff. Uneasy policemen guarding the city hall's main entrance prepared to flee in a purloined truck.

One of the last officials to leave was Lee Keun Tae. Dwight Martin found the wispy civilian administrator struggling into his topcoat. He was planning to walk to Seoul with his wife and seven children. The Americans planned to evacuate some 1,500 officials, clergy, and others who had actively supported the occupation. Administrator Lee was not among them.

Scattered fires broke out throughout the city. They seemed to have been started by saboteurs. The firemen had long gone, packing families and belongings onto their fire trucks. Posters welcoming "UNNITTED NISHUNS LIBERALTERS" gave way to equally ill-spelt denunciations of "YANGEE IMPELIARISM."

Elders at the West Gate Presbyterian Church reverently removed the black wooden cross from above the altar. Others packed prayer books and Bibles. Christianity had been permitted in the north until the UN forces crossed the 38th Parallel—as long as priests or pastors did not take an anti-Communist stance. But those who professed the faith now feared repression.

Fifty-nine-year-old La Sung Duk explained that his congregation planned to carry the cross and Bibles back to Seoul. "Though even there, we may not be completely safe," he said. "Who knows where this retreat will end?"

The Argylls rallied to the rescue of the Indian Field Ambulance unit, stranded without means of moving its stores. The government of Prime Minister Jawaharlal Nehru had taken a decidedly neutralist view of the Korean conflict, but had no compunction about providing medical aid to the United Nations forces. Left behind in the rush south, the Indians found themselves fuming in a rail siding. They had three cars full of supplies but no locomotive. The Americans told them everything would have to be destroyed.

"That is quite fantastic!" the Indian commander exclaimed. "All my doctors will have nothing to do. We have six months' supply of everything."

The Scots found a locomotive in the Pyongyang train-yards. They filled its water tank bucket by bucket, cut kindling for the boiler (there was no coal), and built up a workable head of steam. Two soldiers who claimed to know how to drive a train took the Indians across the last rail bridge at four in the morning. An hour later the bridge was demolished.

Dwight Martin quit his quarters, a *kisaeng* house, with only minutes to spare. The elegant establishment, with its heated floors and accomplished hostesses, had been reopened when the North Korean troops fled. It had been *Time*'s base for more than a month. Martin had elected to leave by jeep. The last two girls of the house accompanied him, wedged among the liquor boxes and bundled in furs, trilling the new song he'd taught them.

> *See the pretty girl on the hill?*
> *She won't lay but her sister will*
> *I'm movin' on . . . down to Pusan*
> *I'm comin' on fast to where I shacked up last*
> *And I'm movin' on . . .*

The only Communist capital ever liberated by the West was abandoned at dawn on December 5. A mile-high pall of ochre smoke rose from Pyongyang's burning fuel dumps. The rest was silence. The British Commonwealth rearguard retreated across the Taedong River through light snow. The snowflakes drifted past the boarded shop fronts of Bell Street, the main thoroughfare.

Pyongyang, December 5, 1950

The Chinese were tired and hungry. They were triumphant, too. Their forward patrols pressed exuberantly through the vegetable gardens, orchards, and shattered greenhouses that cluttered the northern approaches to Pyongyang. An undistinguished place, it seemed, scarcely worth a war. Tier upon tier of humble houses sheathed the hills and riverside in grim, gray tiles. A cluster of taller buildings sprouted from the business area, some as high as three or four stories, the connecting side lanes filled with shuttered shops. Smoke billowed into the threatening sky, most of it from the airfield; otherwise, there were few signs of fighting. A small factory burned unattended on the outskirts. Peony Park was pitted with foxholes fresh-hewn from the frozen earth. An empty streetcar, exactly like the ones in Manchuria, was dappled with camouflage paint.

Young runner Jia Peixing had noticed the same housing—originally built for the Japanese—back in his native Fushun. The ruling Japanese technocrats had lived comfortably isolated from the Chinese. It must have been the same here until five years ago. Korea had been under Japanese control for a very long time.

Colonel Gu Dehua urged his men to watch out for trouble despite assurances that resistance had ended. The clandestine radio signaling from inside the city had announced the enemy's departure a little after dawn. The staff heard the monotonously repeated broadcast over the battered old set that kept contact with division. But the Korean liaison officer rambled on about "unpatriotic elements." He still thought it likely that suicide squads would somewhere be holding out. His predictions kept the flagging Chinese sprinting cautiously forward in the prescribed manner, each squad covering the other down the silent streets, squatting in doorways and keeping an eye open for snipers. Close behind trotted regimental headquarters, brought specially up from the rear to gain the earliest possible entry into the capital. The colonel had been goading them relentlessly these past two days to get in ahead of the two other field armies known to be racing for the prize. Hopes of being hailed as liberators kept the Chinese 358th Regiment jogging day and night through the piercing cold, pausing periodically to urinate and catch its breath, to chew dried beef and raw millet and swallow scooped-up snow.

Jia had gotten past the aches of thirst and hunger. Sleep was the only thing he wanted. The thought of stretching out on the warm *kang* at the family home, nestling into a feathered eiderdown smelling of herbs . . . he nodded off, tripped, and fell onto the chief signaler, who shook him like a rabbit.

"Keep awake, stupid!" the signaler yelled.

The runner wanted to plead fatigue and crawl away into one of the empty houses where he couldn't possibly be missed. But the chief signaler booted him from behind. The other members of the staff hauled him onward by the scruff of his neck.

"No stopping now!" the colonel barked.

Jia had been awake so long (three, maybe four days, he reckoned) that even when awake he felt asleep. Strangely disjointed pictures floated past his eyes: frost-rimed turnips, trampled to sludge by the marching feet; suburban gardens planted with straw-protected shrubs; a freight train left standing in a rail yard full of American tanks; a movie poster advertising a cowboy film that would never be shown; and now, coming toward them, a jeep filled with armed men. It was their first glimpse of life in a dormant city.

The Chinese held their fire. The men in the jeep were brandishing the North Korean flag and shouting through a bullhorn. The colonel waved them to the curbside with his pistol. The jeep was filled with young Korean civilians wearing red arm bands. All carried Soviet-made submachine guns. The men did not attempt to hide their irritation at finding none of their fellow countrymen among the liberating troops. One of the party, speaking broken Chinese, demanded to be taken to the nearest NKPA army unit. The colonel pocketed his pistol, highly embarrassed. Other field armies, notably the 50th, coming down from Sinanju, were bringing token North Korean battalions to march in for the cameras—as soon as the Chinese tidied things up. But the colonel's regiment, indeed the whole 40th Field Army, which had made better time, contained no more than a handful of North Korean liaison officers.

Fortuitously, the chief commissar, a man called Han, arrived with Major Lee, their senior-most Korean, who worked closely with the political department. They spoke to the jeep-borne youths, who assured them that resistance had ceased. The NKPA major agreed to discard his padded *Chinese* jacket, despite the cold, and board the jeep. A chestful of bronze medals clanked across his tunic. The jeep drove off, leading the liberation and saving North Korean face.

The regiment formed column to march deeper into Pyongyang. People began emerging from their houses. They were gathered into sidewalk claques by the ubiquitous young men with arm bands, given small paper flags, and urged to cheer with feeling. Many of the older folk openly wept. Outside an important-looking building, which must have been City Hall, the Chinese stood at the salute while a civilian ran out the national flag. The man went off into a long speech nobody could hear, but the crowd cheered obediently on cue and the chief signaler tweaked Jia's ear to prevent him from falling asleep.

Military dispositions were completed by early afternoon. A defense line was set up overlooking the river. The Taedong was filled with wreckage. Every bridge was destroyed. Ferrymen rowed Chinese patrols to the southern bank. Regimental headquarters staff settled into a high school not far from the university. The signals group camped in the basement, where engineers were trying to restart the boiler. There was little coal. Several of the drooping runners, groaning with tiredness and complaint, were sent out scavenging to the rail yards. Jia was given a packet of papers for divisional headquarters. There would be hot food when he got back, the chief signaler assured him, and the chance to sleep.

It was only a short run up the road. But to Jia it seemed like a marathon. Chinese troops in their shaggy fur hats stood guard on every corner, while army telegraphists strung loops of wire from the street poles. A curfew was supposedly in force but Pyongyang was rapidly reviving. Power supplies were coming back and large numbers of people flitted about the back streets, avoiding the major roads. Jeeps and trucks roared around decked with North Korean flags, manned mainly by yelling youths firing rifles into the air.

The Chinese street patrols watched these carousing Koreans with wary reserve. Cold, hunger, and exhaustion pinched the soldiers' faces. The North Koreans looked well-fed and relaxed. Who, Jia wondered, had actually won this victory? A pretty girl tapped on a window as he passed. She coyly opened the double glazing and gave him a large green apple. The inner, heated air carried the smell of cooking. An older woman appeared from nowhere and slammed the windows. The runner ate the apple, core and all, feeling much revived.

On the way back to his quarters Jia watched a film crew preshooting footage for the official liberation parade scheduled in a few days' time. The crew took close-ups of the weeping old folk, tearful as ever, on the sidewalk. These shots would be intercut later with pictures of North Korean soldiers goose-stepping smartly. (The soldiers themselves would be filmed the day of the parade.) Women were next persuaded to burn an American flag, fresh out of the props department, and stand on the street corner selling first editions of the party newspaper, as yet unprinted, still in dummy form, displaying a full-size front-page picture of Kim Il Sung.

The whole thing was meticulously staged, the young runner noted. Shots were retaken several times until the director was satisfied. Four American flags went up in flames before the demonstrators got it right. The women were chosen for their looks and smart dress. The people who lined up meekly to receive their dummy copy of the newspaper, complete with photograph, were supposed to look both prosperous and ecstatic. Propaganda was obviously a more intricate art form than he had ever suspected.

Close to regimental headquarters Jia heard a burst of gunfire. The sound was much more purposeful than the euphoric volleys from the revelers' trucks. Across the road from the high school, spread-eagled upon the steps of a church, three old men lay dead. Blood soaked their traditional white robes and trickled into the gutter. The books they had been salvaging from the church lay scattered across the sidewalk. A mob of young Koreans hovered over the bodies. They wore red arm bands and carried Soviet-style submachine guns.

"Looters," declared one the youths in his strange-sounding Chinese. "We caught them stealing books."

Jia examined the books. They were expensively printed, gilded at the edges, with a gold cross on the covers.

A Chinese patrol ran up. The sergeant in charge was furious. "Who did this?" he demanded. The vigilantes shrugged insolently. "We did," said the Chinese-speaking North Korean.

"We do the shooting around here," snapped the sergeant.

"Not any more," said the Korean. "This is Pyongyang, not Shenyang." They swaggered back to their jeep and drove off.

"Turtle shit!" snarled the sergeant. "What are we supposed to do with these?" He indicated the dead old men. Women had come out of the church and were wailing over the bodies. One of the women cut short her cries and spoke up in perfect Chinese. "With your permission," she said, "we will take them for Christian burial."

"Do it quick," said the sergeant. "Otherwise there'll be all sorts of inquiries. As for you"—he turned on Jia—"get back to barracks and mind your own damned business."

The liberation parade through Pyongyang was not as spectacular as the North Koreans would have liked. Threats of air attack precluded a march, complete with crowds, troops, war trophies, and even a few American prisoners, as originally demanded by Kim Il Sung. The North Korean leader was reluctantly persuaded to settle for a brief speech from the balcony of City Hall, an equally brief military review (North Korean troops *only*, out at the football stadium), and a still briefer visit to one of the Chinese field armies regrouped in the dispersal zones around the capital. The date of the celebration was twice postponed while the police reestablished control, top personages assembled, and settings were painstakingly arranged for the cameramen. Six Chinese and two Soviet film crews had come in just for the occasion.

There remained a shortage of North Korean troops, and of the transportation required to bring them in from distant sanctuaries. There was even a temporary shortage of people. Two-thirds of the urban population had fled. Those who remained were mostly old. Municipal buses drove out into the countryside to bring in peasants with promises of a pleasant day's outing and extra rations of food and cloth.

Major Han Liqun arrived on December 10, one day ahead of the Chinese delegation. He inspected the guest house in the large walled compound reserved for the North Korean leadership. Workmen were busy cleaning up the mess left by the Americans. A man called Kilroy had written his name everywhere. It was believed to be some kind of secret code. Next door was a houseful of Soviets, all in civilian clothes, who had apparently moved in two days after the liberation. They seemed to know their way around. Many of them spoke Korean. Most worked in the embassy, others described their jobs as supply liaison or something equally vague.

Major Han spotted Captain Sergei Bolganoff, the Soviet interpreter from Shenyang, ice-skating on the small ornamental lake, gliding expertly around in a long leather coat. The Russian appeared not to notice the major struggling among the Chinese staff to carry in the advance luggage.

General Peng telephoned from Anju. The Chinese commander was fully recovered from his bout of pneumonia and in the highest spirits. The situation was looking most promising. He had spent the past few days touring the western battlefields, although heavy snowfalls had prevented him from spending as much time as he would have liked inspecting the ambush site on the Sunchon Road.

The general arrived by truck on the afternoon of December 11. It was one of the new Soviet trucks, named after Molotov, Stalin's foreign minister, and there was a heater in the cab. Peng swore he had never been more comfortable. Staff officers who rode in the back were less enthusiastic. They climbed out numbed with cold. One of them was Commissar Tang, who, Major Han remembered, would come in handy if the Russians started drinking again.

"The old boy never sleeps," Tang complained, nodding toward Peng. "Ran us all into the ground, he did."

That was a relief, thought Han. Ten days ago he'd been worried. The general needed every bit of vitality he could get. The pressure was on to abandon caution and continue the pursuit. That view was freely expressed by the delegation from Peking. It was led by Guo Moro. Guo, a minister and revolutionary poet as well, had made part of the journey by train, and the remainder by car. Enemy bombing was steadily puncturing the Korean rail network.

"Premier Zhou, and of course the Chairman, are delighted at your successes, Comrade Peng," said Minister Guo. "They hope to hear any time now of a revision of your plans."

In other words, "Get moving," Major Han thought to himself. They were closeted in a guest house suite with a handful of senior staff officers, including Chief of Staff Xie Fang.

Minister Guo sat back expectantly, smoking a Western-style pipe.

He was making his second visit to Pyongyang in recent months; the first had been in August, when the Chinese opened their embassy. Much had changed since then. The Chinese found themselves in a position of unaccustomed influence. The situation nonetheless required plenty of diplomatic finesse. Friction could occur at any time with the Russians and with the ever-touchy North Koreans.

"Plans are under constant review," said Peng, quietly sipping his tea. "You are aware that we have had certain logistic difficulties?" The gaunt, bespectacled intellectual smiled wanly through the smoke clouds. "Are you suggesting that the transportation arrangements by the comrades in Shenyang are proving inadequate?" It sounded to Han like hints of internal political feuding. "Let's say our supply system requires further development," said Peng cautiously.

"I think it was the French general Napoleon who spoke about soldiers marching on their stomachs," said Guo, who prided himself on his fund of military anecdotes. "But here, thanks to your magnificent achievements, every tree has become a soldier."

He was referring to one of the most celebrated episodes of the Three Kingdoms period (220–280), when Fu Chien, leading an invading army, grew so unnerved that he mistook swaying trees and grass for engulfing enemy hosts. The invader fled, defeated.

"This time, Fu Chien will not escape," Peng promised.

The North Korean protocol officer called to invite Guo Moro to a welcoming ceremony outside. The minister was conducted to a platform inside the driveway where he was greeted by Kim Il Sung. Together they stood through the two national anthems and saluted as the Korean honor guard paraded past. The youthful North Korean leader was afterward handed a glowing fraternal message from Mao and his Chinese comrades, playing down the contribution the Chinese were making to the war. The Chinese military read it and shrugged.

That evening there was a reception in an adjoining hall once used for missionary meetings. Kim arrived resplendent in high-collared white jacket and blue pants. His fellow Koreans wore Soviet-style uniforms or single-breasted lounge suits of uniform gray. The Chinese looked shabby by comparison; the baggy blue Sun Yat Sen suit worn by Guo Moro (nobody had yet heard of "Mao jackets") had seen a lot of laundering. General Peng's best fatigues were frayed and worn. (The People's Liberation Army was four years away from designing dress uniforms.) The Soviets opted mostly for blue serge suits of elephantine cut. Their ambassador, Terenty F. Shtykov, a squarely built man with a doleful face, appeared peculiarly enlarged by his voluminous suitings. The macro look dominated Moscow tailoring throughout the fifties.

Kim Il Sung shook hands with Minister Guo, then with General Peng and Major Han, mumbling routine greetings, and sipping sparingly at his Soviet champagne. He kept pushing back a lock of black hair that fell persistently over his left eye. Always at his elbow was Kim Tu-bong, the frail, birdlike chairman of the Workers' Party presidium, and the brooding figure of Park Il Woo, minister of the interior and head of the secret police. Comrade Park had been working day and night these past few days *restoring governmental authority* to the liberated city. "When he's around," North Koreans would say, "even the dogs are afraid to bark."

No one would have thought, Major Han told himself, that the North Koreans had just suffered a staggering defeat. The southern half of their country, down to the 38th Parallel, was still in enemy hands, although the hasty American retreat was turning it into no-man's-land. Premier Kim had put out a statement while holed up at Kanggye blaming the debacle on "improper organization of the Korean Communist Party and failure to understand and apply the principles of communism." Yet here he was, perfectly at ease among his foreign saviors, acting the gallant conqueror. It was as if his genius, and his alone, had snatched this last-minute victory.

"I can tell what you are thinking," a voice said in Han's ear. The major turned to confront Captain Bolganoff. The Soviet interpreter was munching a caviar canapé. He licked his fingers, squinting quizzically at the Chinese. "You're thinking the Middle Kingdom has a new vassal state"—he indicated the Koreans—"but you're wrong."

"That wasn't at all what I was thinking," Han answered, genuinely indignant.

"If you weren't," said the Russian, "you soon will be."

Ambassador Shtykov bustled over, grinning hugely, to renew acquaintances with General Peng. They had met the previous year in Peking. The two men embraced effusively. Relations between the Communist giants had never been warmer. Diplomatically the situation might be somewhat delicate, but militarily China and the Soviet Union stood shoulder to shoulder. Photographers clamored for a retake of their toasts, posing them before a large wooden cutout of the Korean peninsula flanked by red flags. Kim Il Sung joined in, leading Minister Guo by the hand. Arc lights flicked on, movie cameras began turning, and the North Korean leader launched into a lengthy speech translated periodically into Chinese and Russian. The gist of it was that fighting would not cease until Korea had been liberated down to the southernmost headland.

The guests applauded tirelessly while the cameramen swiveled their lights to pick up reaction cutaways. "March south!" the North Koreans chanted, clapping rhythmically. Kim acknowledged the cheers, nodding benignly at his supportive audience. The lights flicked off, leaving everyone half-blinded, the cheering died away, and the scramble began for the buffet. The Koreans handed out opened bottles of their musty-tasting gin. "March south!" they cried, clinking glasses with the Chinese. The Chinese nodded thoughtfully back, sipping orange juice.

Kim Il Sung's balcony appearance the morning of December 12 required infinite preparation. Liberation Day was the premier's first public appearance since early in the war. Nothing could be allowed to go wrong. Worried security men told Major Han they would have preferred a safer ceremony in the remote football stadium, but now that the puppet Rhee and his boss MacArthur had been filmed waving to the masses from City Hall, the Glorious Leader would settle for nothing less.

Peasants and townsfolk were marched into position at dawn. They were individually frisked for concealed weapons, after which the men were presented with rosettes and the women with plastic bunches of pink azaleas, the national flower. A man with a bullhorn rehearsed a few rounds of cheering. At every cheer the women were told to wave the azaleas. The Chinese and Soviet delegations arrived at 0845. They were loudly cheered. The azaleas vibrated wildly. In the reception room on the second floor uniformed men wearing green collar tags served tea and cake. The building was warmly heated, but out in the street the population was fainting from the cold. Despite the snow, no one was allowed to open an umbrella. The area was cordoned off, all adjoining buildings were evacuated, and sharpshooters shivered on the rooftops.

The premier's motorcade ploughed through a sea of seething pink plastic. The azalea women wept. Little boys with shaven heads and red neck scarves shrieked deliriously. Little girls threw rose petals. A troupe of heavily rouged dancers in billowing national costume solemnly gyrated with drums and fans. Kim Il Sung bounded out of his elderly Pontiac, beaming above the heads of the security screen, and swept inside City Hall. He hustled into the reception room with enormous gusto, greeting the foreign dignitaries as if he'd never seen them before. Under a theatrical cape he wore a general's uniform glittering with decorations. The long row of medals on both sides of his chest was supplemented by stars and decorations that looped diagonally down across the tunic. Klieg lights came on for a short investiture ceremony. Members of the underground received awards for their part in the resistance struggle. The majority of them were young civilians. A North Korean officer attached to one of the Chinese armies was given a medal for seizing an enemy jeep, driving ahead of the other forces, and *liberating* Pyongyang.

Mighty cheers welled up as Kim Il Sung then walked out onto the balcony. He stood nodding and waving to the multitude while snow whitened his long black hair; at a signal the noise stopped and Kim made a short speech in his youthful tenor voice pledging ultimate victory. He ended with the words "March south!" A band struck up the Soldiers' Song and the crowd joined in. Back inside the reception room the premier combed his hair, assumed a heavy fur hat, and bid his distinguished guests adieu. The parade at the football stadium was a purely North Korean affair.

General Peng drove in a captured U.S. jeep to 50th Field Army, encamped on the escarpment above Pyongyang. The general always showed intense interest in new forms of transport; the little American-made utility vehicle immediatcly caught his fancy. "When China moves on wheels," he told Major Han, "the world will tremble." They were greeted at the command post by Major General Zeng Zesheng and an honor guard one battalion strong. It was the token Chinese unit chosen for inspection by Kim Il Sung.

"I think he'll be another ten minutes," said Peng, glancing at his watch. He took the opportunity to inspect the front line of troops himself, stopping to speak to the men about their recent experiences. The 50th was made up almost entirely of former Nationalist troops who had defected to the Communists near Changchun in October, 1948. Their commanding general had been one of Chiang Kai-shek's most trusted officers; now he served the new rulers of China without demur.

The former Nationalist 60th Corps had been integrated into the People's Liberation Army for more than two years, but still retained some of its old parade-ground polish. There was a lot more saluting and heel-clicking. The commanding general, Zeng Zesheng, was a tall, round-shouldered veteran, deferential in manner, which was perhaps understandable, but respected by the Communists for his military know-how. His troops had given a good account of themselves in Manchuria before lack of food and ammunition forced them to surrender.

Soldiers questioned by General Peng said that so far they had seen little fighting. They were anxious to get into combat. The general checked over their winter clothing, put his fingers inside one man's boot. "Warm enough?" he asked. The man nodded doubtfully. "We must get urgent supplies," the general said to Major Han, "of heavier, quality winter boots. These things are made out of canvas. They'll be no good in wet snow."

A truck with red lights, a siren, and multiple radio antennas preceded the Kim Il Sung cortege into the camp. The premier was surrounded by a bevy of smartly clad officers from the North Korean general staff. Automatically he took the salute as a bugler sounded present arms and the regimental colors were lowered ceremonially to the ground. Kim then took a brisk walk down the open ranks (followed by the soldiers' slowly turning heads as he strode past), shook hands with the senior Chinese, and headed back to Pyongyang. The Chinese cameramen packed their gear and followed. The Soviets were still filming at the stadium.

Peng was eager to assess the morale of these men. It was extraordinarily high, General Zeng assured him, which was not surprising since the troops had so far seen little action. Most of their time had been spent marching up from the rear. They had been tired, cold, and hungry, but that's what soldiers had to expect.

General Peng turned and studied the wall map. The 50th Field Army staff officers watched attentively. "Tell me, general," said Peng, still studying the map, "how long will it take you to reach Seoul?" Zeng Zesheng eyed the floor, his lips moving in silent calculation. "I suppose a month," he said. "A month is too long," Peng snorted. "There's a vacuum down there"—he banged the area between Pyongyang and the 38th Parallel. "We have got to fill it while there's time." General Zeng mildly protested about the paucity of supplies. His men had marched the last two days of the advance on Pyongyang virtually without food. They now had three days' supplies. At present rates of resupply, ten days would be needed to stock up before resuming the advance. Peng tapped the wall map with his blunt peasant fingers.

"The first drum," he said, "makes courage." It was the Chinese way of saying "Strike while the iron is hot."

General Zeng nodded. Everyone knew the story. More than two thousand years ago a Chinese general had ordered his troops to stand silent while the enemy's drummers sounded their attack. Three times they rolled their drums. With each subsequent time the enemy's spirits sagged. After the third drum roll the waiting general ordered his own attack. The enemy fled.

"And I am sure you will recall," added Peng Dehuai, "that the same general was extremely circumspect. He pursued the enemy only after inspecting their chariot tracks. Those tracks proved to him that the enemy was in total disorder."

"When do we start?" asked General Zeng. "You have started," said Peng. "I will issue orders overnight."

Back in the guest house, Peng conferred with Chief of Staff Xie Fang and General Li Tianyu, commander of Thirteenth Army Group, the Chinese force assigned the task of flushing out the western flank of Korea. The original plan had been for General Li's troops to consolidate south of the Taedong River while the U.S. forces—made up largely of marines—on the northeastern coast were cut off and eliminated. But the enemy collapse on the western side of the peninsula had been quicker and more complete than the Chinese command anticipated. The favorable situation was not lost on the North Koreans—or on the leadership in Peking—and strident calls were coming in for Peng not to consolidate but instead to resume the advance south. The Chinese were tired, it was true; a few regiments had suffered severe casualties, and supply lines remained tenuous. More important, it was certain that the farther south the Chinese advanced, the more difficult their logistical problems would become. But there was no holding back. Orders were drawn up to resume the offensive. The first drum had struck.

PART THREE

BLOOD IN THE SNOW

13

The Chinese in New York, the British in Washington / An Army Drunk with Success / "When Are We Going to Eat?"

New York,
November 28, 1950

The Chinese were beginning to believe themselves invincible. Peking's heady, exultant mood following the victorious first offensive in North Korea quickly infected commanders in the field. Generals who should have been rectifying shortages of supplies and firepower, medical aid and winter clothing readily bowed to political demands for continued, headlong pursuit of the foe. China's plans changed overnight from limited advance to full-blown confrontation. No longer was it enough to halt the Americans, or even evict them from the north; within days of their initial onslaught, the Chinese Peoples' Volunteers were saddled with the far tougher task of driving the barbarians into the sea and unifying Korea under Communist rule.

This major revision of Chinese strategic policy—as fateful, in its way, as General MacArthur's decision to cross the 38th Parallel—was publicized in broadcasts from Radio Peking well before the fall of Pyongyang. The arbitrary boundary along the 38th Parallel was brusquely declared irrelevant, and the Seoul regime sentenced to

239

liquidation. Some Chinese leaders, notably Zhou Enlai, even expected to browbeat the West into granting their claims on Taiwan and a seat in the United Nations. Ambitions of such magnitude revealed the PRC's dangerous ignorance of the outside world. The Americans, shocked by their Korean setbacks, were seething with righteous indignation. The U.S. delegate to the United Nations, Warren Austin, truly reflected the public mood when he condemned the Chinese intervention in Korea as "blatant, criminal aggression." Any possibility that China might have cause for complaint was never seriously considered.

The arrival of a delegation from Peking to address the UN Security Council at Lake Success, New York, revealed the extent of the rift— the near-total lack of comprehension—that blighted relations between China and the United States. Nine Chinese diplomats checked into the Waldorf-Astoria in the early morning of November 24 at the end of an exhausting ten-day flight through Mongolia, across the Soviet Union, and on to New York from London by British Overseas Airways. Leading the seven-man, two-woman team was Ambassador Wu Xiuquan, 42, a Soviet-educated soldier-turned-diplomat. Earlier in the year Wu, a longtime, trusted confidant of Premier Zhou Enlai, had made considerable face in skillfully concluding China's first trade treaty with the Soviet Union. But here in the heartland of capitalism, stifled by the political hostility, he felt wary and apprehensive.

"A heavy responsibility had been placed on our shoulders," Wu wrote 35 years later. ". . . We had moved from the military battlefield to the debating platform to wage a face-to-face, tit-for-tat struggle against the then most powerful and arrogant imperialist state."

The Chinese found their ninth-floor hotel suite shockingly expensive, though they had to admit the accommodations were sumptuous. Each delegate was provided with a room and there was an office in the center. Callers were kept at bay by New York police bodyguards. The diplomats seldom ventured outside, except to confer in the privacy of a nearby park. They feared their rooms were bugged. "We often had the radio on in our suite and 'listened' to everything, whether news reports or advertising," wrote Ambassador Wu. "Actually we were less interested in the programs than in keeping up a constant din that might interfere with attempts to eavesdrop."

Nothing was done without clearance from Peking. Wu's main speech, 20,000 words long, had been written for him before his departure. Subsequent statements were cabled home for clearance, "after which we had to work round the clock to translate them into English and find a place to have them printed. . . . The hard work and the distasteful American food left us with a diminished appetite which we whetted with some Mexican chilli peppers that we bought, as well as fermented bean curd made by overseas Chinese."

Ambassador Wu was given the opportunity to speak only after prolonged and acrimonious debate within the Security Council. The United States bowed reluctantly to pressure from its allies, chiefly the British, in order that the regime in Peking be seen to enjoy the opportunity of defending itself against Western charges of aggression in Korea. A dwindling band of optimists in the Western camp hoped the Chinese appearance at Lake Success would somehow lead to cease-fire negotiations.

On the day that Wu's delegation flew out of Peking, General MacArthur still hoped to bring the boys home for Christmas. By the time the Chinese team reached New York, newspaper headlines were trumpeting tales of American defeat. The effect of such heady news on the Chinese leadership was described years later to the author by the chief adviser to the delegation, Qiao Guanhua. The tall, debonair, German-educated diplomat had been a key aide to Zhou Enlai during the civil war against the Nationalists.

Qiao claimed that although Premier Zhou started out anxious to avoid exacerbating international tensions, Chairman Mao insisted on a tougher line. The Chairman had leaned toward intervention in Korea from the start, as a way to re-establish China, overnight, as a military power. Caught up in the general euphoria of victory, Premier Zhou had given in to Mao's arguments. The Chinese switched to a diplomatic offensive. They decided to confront the United Nations with three resolutions of their own. The first condemned the United States for its "criminal acts of armed aggression against the territory of China, Taiwan, and armed intervention in Korea." The second demanded "a complete and immediate withdrawal by the United States government of its forces of armed aggression from Taiwan." The third called for the immediate withdrawal of U.S. and other troops from Korea.

"My job was to put China's case to the United Nations," Ambassador Wu told the author in 1986. "By that I mean China's complaints against continued American encroachment on our territory, U.S. support for the Kuomintang [Nationalist] regime [on Taiwan], and that sort of thing. Korea was a secondary consideration. The main burden of my speech to the General Assembly concerned the wrongs China was suffering at the hands of the Americans. I was more anxious to display China's indignation at the way the U.S. Seventh Fleet had been dispatched to protect Taiwan than with the situation on the Korean peninsula. The way I saw it, the Americans were directly interfering in China's domestic affairs. That, not Korea, was the all-important issue."

Three days after the Chinese delegation's arrival, members were invited to a session of the Political Committee of the United Nations. It was the visitors' sole opportunity to familiarize themselves with UN procedures.

The UN Political Committee was deep in debate when the Chinese filed in. Holding the floor was the head of the Soviet delegation, Andrei Vyshinsky, formerly the dreaded prosecutor at Stalin's 1930s' purge trials, who interrupted his speech to welcome the new arrivals. Ambassador Wu sat down at a desk bearing the plaque "People's Republic of China" in English. Next to him was the British minister of state at the Foreign Office, Kenneth Younger, and beyond him the glowering presence of John Foster Dulles, then special adviser to the State Department.

"It was actually very amusing . . . the distance between us was less than one meter," wrote Wu. "But Dulles, though he knew we were near him, strove to keep his composure and pretended not to notice our presence. I, however, had no such inhibitions and glanced at this poker-faced, prominent American figure who did not have the mettle to look at us. He sat there, looking ahead blankly from behind his glasses, with the corners of his mouth turned down in an obdurate way that was both annoying and funny."

Next day, November 28, came the big debate. The Yugoslavian chairman of the Security Council, Ales Bebler, invited Ambassador Wu to present the three Chinese resolutions. Yugoslavia, under Tito, had quarreled with Stalin and moved to a neutralist position between the East and West power blocs. They shared neutral India's eagerness to give China a fair hearing. As yet, though, they carried little weight; the massive inflow of uncommitted, developing nations to the UN was several years away. Ambassador Wu found himself seated at a U-shaped table opposite the representative of Taiwan, Tsiang Ting-fu. His seat was equipped with earphones and a switch to bring in simultaneous translation from linguists in booths on the upper floor; on the table before each seat stood a microphone. Wu went straight to the point.

"On the instructions of the Central People's Government of the People's Republic of China, I am here in the name of the Chinese people to accuse the United States government of the unlawful and criminal act of armed aggression against the territory of China, Taiwan—including the Penghu Islands."

Delegates shifted uneasily in their seats as this stranger with the bullet-scarred face launched into a two-hour tirade. Wu had sustained his facial wound during the latter stages of the Chinese civil war. The scar glistened under the television lights as he hunched over his voluminous notes, spitting out his words faster than the translators could decently follow, pouring out the pent-up shame and humiliation of a proud and ancient nation in a speech spiced with sarcasm and Marxist jargon.

"A documentary film of the meeting was later shown in China," wrote Wu. "My children said I looked 'ferocious,' like quite a different person when I spoke. Actually, I had not thought of giving an impressive performance. I had only felt that I was facing the imperialist state and its followers, and that they had invaded, bullied, and oppressed China for over a century. The memory of it was deep and bitter in my mind as well as in the minds of hundreds of millions of Chinese people. Only with great effort had we succeeded in expelling the foreign invaders and in defeating the KMT [Nationalist] forces, but now the American imperialists were deliberately scheming to subvert and annihilate New China. They had acted in such a reprehensible, such a vicious way that there was no need for consideration and courtesy on our part."

Americans watched the speech on television with stunned disbelief. The ranting intruder haranguing them from the tube could not *possibly* be speaking for the brave, embattled, Pearl Buck-fantasyland that evangelical America traditionally equated with China. Americans had a special affection for China. They had sent missionaries to China—not soldiers, gunboats, and opium. Secretary of State John Hay had actually refused, toward the end of the last century, to join the European powers in attempting to dismember the Chinese Empire, advocating, instead, the Open Door policy. The Chinese reacted at the time with undoubted gratitude. Yet here was this interloper from Peking daring to question U.S. altruism.

"The Open Door was in fact an aggressive policy," Wu told the tiers of upturned faces, ". . . aimed at sharing the spoils with other imperialists."

The American public believed U.S. aid for deposed Nationalist leader Chiang Kai-shek protected his Taiwan regime against a foreign-backed foe. It could scarcely be dismissed, editorials declaimed, as interference in Chinese internal affairs. How could anyone suggest, cried America's UN delegate, Warren Austin, that support for Taiwan constituted an act of U.S. aggression? But the Chinese Communists, embittered by their long struggle with Chiang, and eager to reunify their country, stuck to their contrary view. Nothing would shake their belief that "ruling circles" in the United States had vainly tried to shore up the Nationalists before the final flight to Taiwan and now planned to turn the island into an unsinkable aircraft carrier. According to Wu, U.S. deployments confirmed these fears. "Where . . . have the United States 7th Fleet and 13th Air Force gone?" he cried. "Can it be that they have gone to the planet *Mars*?

Not at all . . . they are now in Taiwan. . . . No sophistry, lie, or fabrication can alter a hard fact: United States armed forces have occupied China's territory [of] Taiwan."

Wu Xuiquan made no attempt to win friends among his hostile hosts. "Who has shattered security in the Pacific?" he cried, pointing a rhetorical finger. "Have Chinese armed forces invaded Hawaii? Or have U.S. armed forces invaded . . . Korea and Taiwan?" Desultory applause came from the Eastern bloc. "The real intention of the U.S.," he declared, "as MacArthur has confessed, is . . . to dominate every Asiatic port from Vladivostok to Singapore." But times were changing. "As a result of the victories of the great Socialist October Revolution of the Soviet Union, of the anti-Fascist Second World War, and of the great revolution of the Chinese people, all the oppressed nations and people of the East have awakened and organized themselves."

The Chinese spokesman turned the attack upon America's allies. Fifty-two UN members had voted to support the defense of South Korea. More than a dozen had provided troops. Brows puckered around the chamber as Wu warned against pulling "the chestnuts out of the fire for the U.S. because . . . you must bear the consequences of your actions."

Ambassador Wu's speech ended in predictable exhortation: "Regardless of the savagery and cruelty of the American imperialist aggressors, the hard-struggling people of Japan, the victoriously advancing people of Vietnam, the heroically resisting people of Korea, the people of the Philippines who have never laid down their arms, all the oppressed nations and peoples of the East will certainly unite in close solidarity. Yielding neither to the enticements nor to the threats of American imperialism, they will fight dauntlessly on to win the final victory in their struggle for national independence."

Throughout the speech, *Time* magazine reported, the official Chinese delegate, T. F. Tsiang, the Nationalist representative from Taiwan, "sat with the uninterested look of one who had known all along what was coming, and finally appeared to be dozing." Ambassador Wu saw it differently. Tsiang Ting-fu "kept his head down, supporting his forehead in his hands to avoid letting people see his face. . . . Perhaps he felt somewhat abashed and uncomfortable in front of the genuine representative of the Chinese people."

It was left to Warren Austin, on November 30, to slap the U.S. veto onto the three Chinese resolutions and press on, a week later, to railroad through the General Assembly his own resolution condemning Chinese aggression in Korea. The PRC delegation walked out of the UN in protest. It would be 21 years before another returned.

Orders came from Peking to settle up and leave. The problem was settling up. The delegation had brought and banked funds to cover expenses, including considerable purchases of encyclopedias and technical books. These funds were threatened shortly after passage of the condemnatory UN resolution by the U.S. government freeze on Chinese assets throughout the United States. Tipped off in advance, the delegates managed to get to the bank before it closed and draw everything out in cash. Checks given to some of the encyclopedia salesmen bounced, however, and the closely guarded suite in the Waldorf-Astoria was besieged by worried salesmen. Their dishonored checks were exchanged for cash.

Wu arrived home to a hero's welcome in Peking on New Year's Eve. "Everyone in our delegation had carried out a face-to-face struggle against the number-one imperialist state on its own turf," wrote Wu. "It was a rare chance for us to temper ourselves and to learn, and we all felt that it had been a rewarding visit."

Not so *Time* magazine. Its proprietor, Henry Luce, son of China missionaries and a fervent apologist for Taiwan, found that the debate confirmed his fondest beliefs. Appeasing Chairman Mao, the magazine warned, would be like "kissing a buzz saw." It would remain the common wisdom for the next two decades.

There was no question of appeasement as far as President Harry Truman was concerned. Early on November 28, at 0615, he braced himself for the worst. A call from General Omar N. Bradley, chairman of the Joint Chiefs of Staff, turned rumors of unexpected enemy resistance in North Korea into certainty. "A terrible message has come in from General MacArthur," the President told his White House staff. "The Chinese have come in with both feet." But later in the morning he called a special meeting of the National Security Council where it was agreed, after long and sobering discussion, that things might not be quite so bad as the newspapers led everyone to believe. A beachhead could yet be held. The service chiefs did not support MacArthur's pleas for interdiction raids against the Asian mainland. Use of the atomic bomb was discussed and rejected. It wasn't until two days later, at a Washington news conference, that the President was trapped into implying that the bomb remained an option. His off-the-cuff remark created a furor among America's allies, especially in London, where the House of Commons was caught in nervous mid-debate about the worsening world situation.

The British were unusually concerned. The optimum prize, in their view, was Western Europe with its vast industrial potential. The North Atlantic Treaty, drawn up the previous year after the Soviets tried to squeeze the Allies out of Berlin, required a long-term American military commitment to contain Stalinist encroachment.

The last thing the British wanted to see was American strength dissipated across the rice fields of Asia. They were prepared, at a pinch, to look the other way while the Chinese Communists took Taiwan and walked into the United Nations.

But the British were not doing this—as their critics have since alleged—to protect Hong Kong and the remaining United Kingdom assets in China. The ruling Labour government was unmoved by the plight of British business interests in China (whose assets had been seized anyway); and having given away, in 1947, India, the jewel of the imperial crown, the high-minded Attlee government was unlikely to make more than a token fuss over a place like Hong Kong, seized from the Chinese in shameful circumstances, since ravaged by the Japanese, and now apparently moribund.

Truman's A-bomb remark caused an uproar in Westminster because it reminded the British of how completely they had lost control of world events. Their own inability, as yet, to acquire atomic weapons further emphasized the extent of their decline. The presidential gaffe swung the pacifist, pro-Soviet Labour left into programmed attack on American warmongering, seen by the party's intelligentsia as the root cause of all the world's troubles. Jingoistic, reactionary Tories responded with plaintive pleas for reassertion of British influence. Tweedy spokesmen from the conservative shires upbraided the prime minister for not having conferred personally with the U.S. President since Potsdam.

The querulous tone of debate matched the mood of the nation. The British felt frustrated and exhausted. Five years after the bruising confrontation with Germany and Japan, the nation faced continued austerity, power shortages, and rationing. During the Christmas festivities of 1950 there would be no extra meat, a mere two shillings' worth for each adult every week, no more than had been available in 1945. Turkeys? You must be joking. The main concession to the holiday was a five-ounce bacon ration during Christmas week, three ounces of extra cooking fat, and a kiddies' bonus of six ounces of candy.

The British had fought two massive and debilitating wars in the twentieth century. Once more they felt themselves sliding into a conflict, possibly a nuclear one, whose course they could not contain. Parliamentarians quoted some of the scarier statements by American senators who wanted to bomb Manchuria and mount a naval blockade of the China coast. Their one hope was that Britain still carried sufficient clout to urge restraint on Washington. The suggestion was accepted by Prime Minister Clement Attlee, a modest little man "with plenty to be modest about," as Churchill once sourly remarked. The self-effacing Attlee, who had sat doodling during most of the debate, finally rose to his feet and announced that he would fly to Washington to meet Truman.

The news was received without enthusiasm in the White House. The President had quite enough to worry about without the British. Vicious 1950 mid-term elections, fought on foreign-policy issues, had just cost the Democrats precious seats in Congress. The Republican opposition, starved of power for 19 years, was baying for blood. A noisy knot of former isolationists, once dedicated to keeping the United States out of World War II, now called for war against China. Their clamor was sustained, none too subtly, by General Douglas MacArthur. The fallen idol was himself under unaccustomed attack for the fiasco in North Korea. Newspapers were unanimous in their condemnation of his "home by Christmas" offensive. The much-respected Homer Bigart, one of the New York *Herald Tribune*'s team in Korea, called MacArthur's battle plans "an invitation to disaster." Desperately bolstering his sagging image, the general gave a series of self-serving interviews to journalistic trusties in an attempt to shift the blame.

The facts were plain: the hero of Inchon had gambled again and lost. The general refused to admit this. He did not believe he had lost at all. He was simply being denied final victory. His warplanes had only to bomb supply bases and communications on the China mainland to bring the Communist offensive to a halt. He claimed the bombing raids were being prohibited by weaklings and temporizers in Washington intent on providing the enemy with safe refuge in Manchuria. The Supreme Commander was being forced to fight, he declared, under "an enormous handicap . . . without precedent in military history." Harry Truman was furious. The former artillery captain did not question MacArthur's right to disagree with Washington; what he objected to was the way this senior and experienced officer aired disagreements in the press. The general would have court-martialed any second lieutenant who dared do that, the President declared—"and rightly, too."

"I should have relieved General MacArthur then and there," Truman wrote afterward in his memoirs. "The reason I did not was that I did not wish to have it appear as if he were being relieved because the offensive failed. I have never believed in going back on people when luck is against them, and I did not intend to do it now."

Not for the first time the general was told to keep his mouth shut. The U.S. Army chief of staff, General J. Lawton Collins, was sent to Tokyo early in December to size up the situation for himself. The wild fluctuations in assessment from the Dai Ichi, flipping in little more than a week from high hopes to deep despair, cried out for judgment by an experienced outside observer. Even the Joint Chiefs of Staff, who had, until now, been handling their latter-day Caesar with a mixture of reverence and servility, began, too late, to assert a modicum of control.

Clement Attlee walked into the White House promptly at four o'clock on the afternoon of December 4, small and anonymous-looking in an unpressed gray suit. Truman's first impressions of Attlee during the Potsdam conference had not been particularly favorable; little transpired over the next four days to alter this view. The Americans tended to be skittish with their allies (traditionally they had managed to do without foreign entanglements), though now they needed a friendly UN figleaf to clothe their police action in Korea. Solemnly the President's advisers reaffirmed the U.S. commitment to the defense of Western Europe and the avoidance of war with China. The British were plainly delighted. On those two points alone their flight had been worthwhile. The Americans agreed that the forces in Korea should revert to their original policy of defending the country only as far as the 38th Parallel. Truman reassured Attlee in private conversation that he would consult with Britain in the unlikely event of ever requiring to use the atomic bomb.

Over mainland Chinese membership in the United Nations, how-ever, the Americans dug in their heels. Dean Acheson suavely demolished British appeals to treat the Chinese Communists as potential Titos. The Yugoslav dictator's refusal to accept Soviet hegemony in 1948 had been hailed in London as the first of many cracks to come in the Communist monolith. Though totally in agreement with such views only a year earlier, the U.S. secretary of state now found the very thought unthinkable in the prevailing political atmosphere. The British lamely backed down, promising for their part not to abandon Korea.

"We are in it with you. We'll support you," Attlee told Truman. "We'll stand together on those bridgeheads."

A communiqué was cobbled together satisfactory to all. The British departed cheerfully but with diminished status. Attlee's pledges of loyalty won him scant thanks from the Americans, most of whom wrote the British off as appeasers. Attlee's own supporters were equally ungrateful toward their leader. The following year the isolationists of the Labour left brought down the Attlee government for being too pro-American.

North Korea,
December 18, 1950

The work demon consumed General Peng. His staff would know no rest until the Chinese Peoples' Volunteers converged on Seoul. So far, no major unit had moved. This did not suit the restless leadership in Peking. The liberation of Pyongyang was two weeks stale, it was December 18, and precious days were wasting. Columns would have to be on the road within the next two days, the general swore, or senior commands would go begging. He postponed returning to Shenyang, daily pushing deeper into the Korean countryside aboard his Soviet-made truck, warm and comfortable in the cab, his shivering officers in the back trying to warm themselves around an iron *hibachi*. Showers of hot ash flew up in their faces each time the wheels went over an exceptional bump.

The general made it his personal business to burst unannounced upon laggard regiments, heckling the officers and galvanizing training details into frantic action. Or he would pull up at the roadside in a cloud of dust to cheer on the coolie columns stumbling southward with supplies. Sometimes Peng would take over a bamboo carrying-pole or a loaded A-frame, the typical Korean backpack, and trot off for a kilometer or two to the amusement of the coolies. "Man will always overcome machines," he would declare. Every man should be capable, Peng said, of a little manual labor. Major Han Liqun feared that any day the general would call on him to join them. But somehow it was always the hard-drinking Commissar Tang who got hauled into the act. And there were invariably roars of approval when he managed to hoist the most staggering loads.

There was of course an element of showmanship in all this, the major noted; a revolutionary peasant army appreciated and needed the general's glad-handing style. The way Peking was screaming for action, any amount of incitement could be helpful. The coolies were flattered. They had been treated in past wars like beasts of burden. Now they had hay-filled barns to sleep in, hot food kitchens, and medical care along the wayside. But it was indicative of the lack of effective staff structure and of the communications capable of projecting it that Peng himself was forced to forsake his distant headquarters, get out into the field, and set the offensive in motion with his own bare hands.

By now more than 300,000 troops were under Peng's command in Korea. They were divided into two main bodies. The Ninth Army Group, made up of three reinforced field armies totaling 120,000 men, was charged with the destruction of the American bridgehead in the northeast. The Ninth Army Group was under the command of General Song Shilun. The Thirteenth Army Group, composed of 180,000 men in six field armies, was now in pursuit of U.S. Eighth Army down the western side of the Korean peninsula. This army group reported to General Li Tianyu. Generals Li and Song reported in turn to Peng himself.

Peng was less concerned at this stage about Song Shilun's operations on the east coast. Heartening reports were coming in from the Chinese field commanders that—in spite of surprisingly tough resistance by the U.S. Marines—the enemy bridgehead there would shortly be liquidated. The lethal blow, the general kept emphasizing, would be struck by the Thirteenth Army Group in the direction of Seoul. The war would not be won until the U.S. Eighth Army was destroyed. One more mighty effort, delivered without further delay, would turn the enemy retreat into rout. Peng chafed at the time it took his foot-soldiers to follow through with their obvious tactical advantage. Given half the Americans' mobility, he grumbled, the Chinese would by now have reached Pusan.

Trucks, cars, and passenger buses had indeed been commandeered from all over northeast China to hasten the advance. The requisitions succeeded only in crippling urban communications in Manchuria without contributing greatly to the supply-lift to Korea. By mid-December some 6,000 Chinese-registered vehicles of all shapes, sizes, and conditions puttered along North Korean roads, the majority bedeviled by fuel shortages and breakdowns. Few of them were in mint condition. Drivers worked all day in camouflaged depots to keep their wheezing wrecks roadworthy during the work-night. Threat of air attack restricted daylight movement, although the cloudy, wintry weather had lately reduced the overall volume of enemy aerial activity.

Responsibility for west-coast road traffic was in the hands of the Chinese 42nd Truck Regiment, which organized fuel dumps at 60-kilometer intervals along the rutted mud tracks that passed for highways. Gangs of regimental mechanics, augmented by civilians from as far afield as Shanghai, did their best to maintain mobile repair services. They were handicapped by lack of recovery vehicles and spares. Batteries and antifreeze were particularly scarce.

Word went round the nightly planning conferences that the Soviets were coming to the rescue. Trucks and guns were being transported across the Trans-Siberian Railroad or delivered by freighter directly to Manchuria through the Soviet naval base at Port Arthur (now Lüta). Heavy artillery and tank units, together with whole new armies of Chinese troops, were being equipped with Soviet weaponry. The MIG-15, a new Soviet fighter aircraft equal to anything produced by the Americans, was being delivered in large quantities to Manchurian airfields, where the fledgling Chinese air force was staging its first successful sorties against U.S. Air Force intruders over the Yalu.

Soviet supplies could not solve their immediate problems, Peng was quick to point out. The Chinese had to move fast on their own stout feet. But things were looking good. The general paced restlessly around the Thirteenth Army Group's operations room at the Kim Il Sung University, gloating over the incoming signals traffic confirming the enemy's deflated morale, applauding each move as the blue markers pinpointing the U.S. Eighth Army crept closer and closer to Seoul. The Thirteenth Army Group commander, Li Tianyu, hovered close at hand mumbling comments to Peng in his atrocious southern accent.

Draperies in the operations room were carefully drawn. North Korean sentries were notoriously quick to shoot at lighted windows. So many scare stories were circulating these days about enemy spies and saboteurs. Sirens sounded nightly as American bombers thundered north on their long-range raids from Japan. Windows rattled to bursts of distant antiaircraft fire and the rarer rumble of bombs. One night an unexpected near miss brought plaster raining down from the ceiling. "They couldn't hit pig shit!" roared General Peng, still poring over the map of Seoul. His staff laughed nervously.

Final orders for what came to be known as the Third Campaign were distributed on December 19. The news was received with relief in impatient Peking. The first Chinese columns marched off the following day, December 20, flooding into the vacuum south of Pyongyang. Most of the southern part of North Korea was free of enemy troops, according to the intelligence reports; the American rearguard was preparing to evacuate Kaesong, close to the 38th Parallel. The North Koreans, urged on by the Soviets, were eager to restore their administration. Thirteenth Army Group was instructed to concentrate as unobtrusively as possible along the Parallel for a major drive to Seoul and beyond on New Year's Eve. Hopes were slim of repeating the staggering surprise of the recent counterblow, yet General Peng insisted on keeping the enemy guessing. Movement would be mainly by night, concealment discipline to be strictly maintained in the daytime.

The westernmost flank was given over to 38th Field Army, one of whose crack units was the Sharp Swords. They would ferry the Taedong River at Chinnampo, the port of Pyongyang, and swing down through the Ongjin peninsula to concentrate near Kaesong. The direct route south from Pyongyang would be cleared by the former Nationalist corps, 50th Field Army, backed by 39th Field Army, still re-forming after heavy involvement in the Sunchon ambush. The hard-marching men of 42nd Field Army, who had covered more territory than any other Chinese outfit—from the upper reaches of the Yalu all the way through the central Korean mountains—had orders to cut cross-country to the Imjin River valley and make for the town of Tongduchon–in on the alternative approach road to Seoul. The victors of the main offensive across the Chungchon, 40th Field Army, together with 66th Field Army, which had not yet been heavily engaged, were assigned to the central sector of the front. They would take the lateral road through Kumhwa, aiming finally for the road junction of Chunchon. Out on their left flank above the east-coast town of Kangnung were fragments of three North Korean divisions in a reconstituted North Korean II Corps.

The Chinese offensive would strike primarily at Seoul, thrusting on down the coastal highway to the Suwon-Osan airfields; secondarily, through the Pukhan River valley on the central front in the direction of Wonju. This forceful left hook against what was thought to be a lightly held sector had every chance of becoming an enveloping movement, if it moved fast enough, blocking the retreat of the American rearguard in much the same way as in the Sunchon Road ambush. One last heave after that should carry the advance past Chongju and deep into the southern recesses of the country, leaving the Americans no alternative but to depart with dignity through their Pusan beachhead.

The plans were greeted in Peking with uncritical approval. They fitted neatly into the strategic picture as perceived by the Chinese leadership. It was a rosy picture tempered by wishful hopes and considerable distance. But the PLA's commander in chief, Zhu De, a cautious man disinclined to gamble, came up with the most fulsome praise. A message from Prime Minister Zhou Enlai revealed that he was thinking of modifying the nationwide recruitment drive. Mao Zedong spoke confidently of rounding off hostilities in time for the spring festival (the Chinese lunar New Year), about six weeks away. A similar optimism infected the staff who had accompanied General Peng to the liberation ceremonies in Pyongyang. Officers spent their evenings musing nostalgically about steamy dumpling soups, newspapers, regular mail, heated quarters, and all the comforts of head-quarters life in Shenyang.

The only person harboring genuine doubts seemed to be General Peng himself. He had grown daily more confident since the clashes on the Chungchon. The American retreat had almost convinced him that the enemy was totally defeated. Seoul would probably fall without firing a shot. But he hesitated to share the leadership's wild exhilaration over the Chinese victory. He complained quietly to the major that "the Schoolmaster"—Chairman Mao—was "getting drunk with success." His misgivings surfaced in private sessions with General Li

Tianyu and Chief of Staff Xie Fang. Peng never refrained from pointing out that their offensive against Seoul, and the still *more* tentative plans for a final drive to Chongju and the extreme south, depended on a supply system barely capable of sustaining the Chinese armies in their present positions a full 200 kilometers south of the Manchurian border. Problems had been eased for a time by widespread looting of American rations during the advance from the Chungchon. Even then, the forward troops were half-starved by the time they reached Pyongyang. What sort of state would they be in another 200, let alone 400, kilometers farther south?

General Zhou Chunquan, director of the Rear Services Department, produced soothing statistics promising that 180,000 men, women, and children would be mobilized for the supply-lift by the end of the year. Railroad troops were being brought in from China to keep the tracks repaired faster than the Americans could bomb them. Nightly freight services by train and truck, plus the loads carried on human backs, should initially guarantee the Thirteenth Army Group a daily thousand tons of food, munitions, and supplies. Each Chinese soldier required 4.5 kilos (10 pounds) a day, according to the estimates, or about 50 tons for each field army. That was one-sixth the amount the Americans "needed" in combat, but more than enough to see the Chinese through to Pusan. The North Koreans checked out the figures and agreed. They had tackled the supply problem, admittedly in summer and from nearer, better-prepared base areas, with variable success. Lack of artillery and tanks might actually prove a boon, they believed, in the ultimate stages of the campaign.

Peng went on worrying. Most generals were prone to suppose that events would go their way. They assumed the weather would be favorable, the terrain ideal, and the enemy obligingly compliant. But Peng had seen too many fatal miscalculations during the Chinese civil war by capable men incapable of reading their opponents' minds. And yet, this MacArthur was old and jumpy. His field commander, Walker, could think only of retreat. Eighth Army troops were too demoralized to fight. The Americans would need a miracle to avert the most crushing defeat in their history. As a practicing atheist, the general set no store by miracles.

Things began to go wrong as soon as the Chinese left Pyongyang. The snow set in, hard-driven by freezing winds. Their march pace slowed, thousands of feet dragging in the fresh-blown drifts, vision clouded by gusts of stinging flakes twisting off the hilltops onto the crowded roads. Men adjusted their face scarves, pinned the flaps of their fur hats tighter beneath the chin, and plodded patiently forward, heavily laden, into the storm. Sergeant Gu Wentu snatched a quick, furtive glance at his watch. Making a real show of rolling up his sleeve, peeling back his glove and examining the luminous dial was likely to attract attention, to remind his platoon that time existed. The men had enough to do right now without counting the hours to embarkation. The trucks waited seven kilometers ahead. At the usual pace they would have been there within the hour.

"Why march this far when we could ride?" It was Trooper Liu, the cocky one who always asked the awkward questions. "Something to do with dispersal," the sergeant shouted. His words whipped away on the wind. He fell in beside the trooper, heavily encrusted with snow.

"Something to do with dispersal," sneered Liu, mimicking the sergeant's Nanking intonation. "The Yankees won't send out planes on a day like this."

"Maybe our generals didn't know it was going to snow?" the sergeant suggested. He tried not to betray his lack of faith in the top brass.

"Fuck 'em, they should've known," said Liu. He pulled down his frosted face scarf and hawked noisily onto the road. They marched on in silence.

The Chinese sergeant cursed the snow. He cursed Korea. High hills and biting cold were the way he would always remember this asshole of a country. Winter was never this bleak in his own Yangtse valley. He glanced bitterly back at the long, dark columns snaking through the snow. What was he doing in this frozen wilderness of fallow fields, ruined villages, and uninviting women? Like everyone else in this vast column Gu was a onetime Nationalist soldier and a veteran of the anti-Japanese war. Today he belonged to the 2nd Battalion, 444th Regiment, 148th Division, 50th Field Army, the former Nationalist corps which changed sides abruptly in the penultimate year of the Chinese civil war. But he remained a soldier, tough and dedicated to his craft, and he remained his own man too. Floggings had not broken him in the old Nationalist days. Indoctrination failed to mold him now. Gu now marched against the Americans as he had marched against the Communists and, with more relish, against the Japanese before them; a soldier of peasant China, parroting new-found slogans, muttering half-forgotten prayers.

He accepted his fate without complaint. But for the Japanese he might still be happily in Nanking, toting luggage on the ferry, pocketing fat tips from foreign travelers, especially the Americans who came to gawk. The Nationalists had established the old walled river port of Nanking as their capital during the late twenties. The young and the brutal could scrape together a living of sorts there, fighting for the chance to grab some foreigner's bag and battling the bully-boys who tried to pocket the tip.

Then the Japanese had brought their typhoon of terror—raping, looting, and slaughtering. They killed more Chinese in two weeks, Gu later learned, than the atom bomb killed Japanese at Hiroshima. A Nationalist press-gang had found him, a 21-year-old orphan, wandering dazed and frightened far outside Nanking. He had run miles without remembering it. From then on the army had been his father, his mother, and his family: a bloodied brotherhood of submissive souls bending to the whims of leaders whom they had never seen, and whose notions they barely understood.

Sergeant Gu comforted himself with the stories he had heard about the slaughter at Hiroshima. Nothing he heard could make him sorry for the Japanese. Those bastards deserved everything they got, he thought as he marched through the snow. The thought of atomic vengeance searing the helpless city never failed to cheer him, and he suddenly laughed aloud.

"What's so damned funny?" It was Trooper Liu again. "Nothing you'd enjoy," Gu Wentu snapped sharply. The man made him uneasy; he saw too much.

"You wouldn't laugh if you knew what day it was," said Liu. "We've made an unlucky start. This is Saturday, December 23, by the new calendar. According to my reckoning, that's the first day of Tung Chih"—the 12-day period of the winter solstice—"and you never start a journey on Tung Chih. Most inauspicious." It was the sergeant's turn to sneer. "Where d'you learn that nonsense?" he asked. Liu was Manchurian, like most of these men. They harbored some peculiar superstitions. "It's not nonsense," Liu said stubbornly, "and you know it."

Sergeant Gu stayed noncommittally silent. True, he was not one of those dedicated revolutionary fighters who dutifully studied Marx and believed every word the commissars said. The Communists despised the ancient rituals, and with this Gu privately disagreed. Had his father and mother survived the Nanking massacre, he would have shown them the filial respect tradition accorded them. He carried their pictures at all times in a waterproof wallet. Nonetheless, Trooper Liu's words of ill omen did not depress him. Other men had said the same when marching orders first arrived. Cowards always sought the inauspicious. The sergeant did not care. What would be, would be. Nothing anyone could do would alter fate.

Sergeant Gu stared unblinking through the snow. The chimneys of Sariwon peered through the murk at last. The trucks should be waiting on the other side of town. Then they'd be off again, on a road with heaven knows what ending . . .

An officer rode up on horseback. It was their own Colonel Pang, commander of the regiment. "Move it, men! Move it!" the colonel shouted. His glass eye glared accusingly; in prerevolutionary days he would probably have laid about him with a riding crop. "You there, sergeant"—he pointed at Gu—"speed up this column. We're an hour behind schedule." "Yes, sir!" Sergeant Gu saluted smartly. The colonel might be an idiot but he was all they had. The stupid man had hung on so obstinately and so gallantly at Hengyang back in 1944, defending the Hunanese railroad station against waves of Japanese attacks, that it took the doctors six months afterward to pick shell-blast splinters out of his body. The sergeant had been injured by the same blast, though his wounds were fortunately less serious. Very fortunately: no Nationalist army doctor would have wasted that much time repairing a former coolie.

"A final blow against imperialism!" The regimental commissar, Pig-Snout Wu, was reciting a proclamation again and again as the column straggled past. He stood, caked with snow, at the entrance to Sariwon, bellowing through a battered tin megaphone. "Once more our glorious forces are destined to strike the foreign enemy. An assault on all fronts will *liberate* the puppet capital of Seoul and drive the enemy into the *sea*." The proclamation was signed by some general called Li Tianyu, who commanded their army group. As Sergeant Gu moved off down the street he heard the commissar begin the proclamation once more, like a cracked phonograph record.

"When are we going to eat?" groaned Liu. The trooper had run a noodle stall in Fushun before the army press-gangs grabbed him, and he could talk for hours about food. Sergeant Gu licked his wind-cracked lips. The battalion had been promised a hot meal in Sariwon before they boarded the trucks for the long drive down the southern highway. But here in this battered and deserted town he could see neither trucks nor field kitchens. "I told you there'd be a screwup," wailed Liu.

The battalion halted and fell out in a lumberyard. The officers moved into a windowless workmen's hut, leaving the men to find shelter as best they could. Some huddled inside the roofless sawmill. Others built cubbyholes among the piles of cut timber. Ponchos were pegged up with bits of sacking to stave off the wind. Enough dry shavings were found for a fire to boil some water. The men drank the hot water plain—"white tea," they called it—because their rations did not include much tea. Sergeant Gu went off in search of fellow sergeants to find out what was happening.

The regimental command post had been set up, as usual, in the town schoolhouse. Indecipherable slogans were painted on the outside walls in square-cut Korean script. Someone inside was doing a lot of shouting—it sounded like Colonel Pang. Inside the doorway, smoking a small-bowled pipe, sat the senior sergeant, "Sawtooth" Soong, puffing away complacently and oblivious to the commotion close at hand. "Radio won't work," said Sergeant-Major Soong as if this was nothing new. He pulled the pipe from between his broken teeth and hawked up phlegm out into the snow. "No trucks, no food." He gestured philosophically. "Looks like the Long March all over again."

"Not to worry, comrades," boomed a hearty voice. Commissar Wu, the pig-nosed one, emerged unexpectedly through the door, accompanied by a worried-looking quartermaster. "We will feed here off emergency rations." The sergeants all snapped to attention. Sawtooth Soong seemed almost to cringe. "With respect, sir, er, comrade commissar," he said. "Our orders insist no emergency rations should be touched for the next three days." The commissar slapped him familiarly on the shoulder. Soong winced: in the Nationalist army he might have been bashed on the jaw. "The plans are being amended," the commissar assured him. "Transportation and rations are waiting a further ten kilometers down the road. We move after the men have eaten."

Second Battalion dined gloomily off boiled millet taken from the sausage-shaped sack each man carried slung across his shoulder. It had weighed two kilograms. "Less to carry," said Sergeant Gu brightly. "Less to eat later," grumbled Trooper Liu, and glowered at the platoon huddled around their cooking fires. "If this is how we start," he whined, "how are we going to finish?" "Shut your big mouth," ordered the sergeant. "We'll get through the way we always do."

After eating, they marched another ten kilometers down the highway. It took six hours in the snow. The ditches were littered with rubbish discarded by the retreating enemy. Once they passed an abandoned tank. The snow blew steadily down on a moaning wind. The dried brown grass danced and rustled around them. Ice crunched underfoot. Their trucks were waiting in a fir forest. But there was no food.

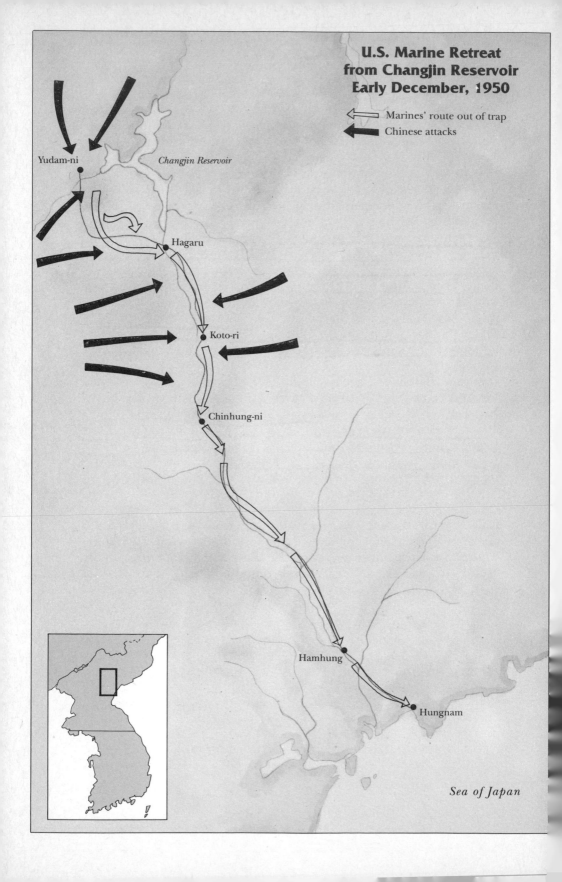

U.S. Marine Retreat from Changjin Reservoir Early December, 1950

⇐ Marines' route out of trap
⬅ Chinese attacks

Yudam-ni

Changjin Reservoir

Hagaru

Koto-ri

Chinhung-ni

Hamhung

Hungnam

Sea of Japan

14

The U.S. Marines Retreat to the Sea / Colonel Wong Among the Snowmen / Ah Lo Attends a Hate America Rally.

Changjin Reservoir,
North Korea,
First week of December, 1950

It looked as though the U.S. Marines were trapped. For three weeks their First Division had been inching out onto a limb. Beset by Korea's worst winter in a decade, and bedeviled by the mountainous terrain around the Changjin Reservoir, two marine regiments, the 5th and the 7th, had fought their way into Yudam-ni, a tiny huddle of clapboard huts 3,500 feet above sea level and girdled by mile-high peaks.

Seventy-odd miles from the coast, and linked by the slenderest of tracks to their port base at Hungnam, the marines were still attempting to reach the Yalu River when new orders arrived to strike *inland*, in the direction of Kanggye—home of the refugee North Korean government. It was a hopeless attempt to draw away Chinese troops attacking the U.S. Eighth Army on the far western side of the Korean peninsula. No sooner had the marines launched their drive on

November 27 than the isolated leathernecks were themselves encircled by Chinese armies that cut off their escape to the sea.

The full extent of the danger did not immediately occur to X Corps Commander Ned Almond—or to his impetuous patron in Tokyo. At an emergency meeting in the Dai Ichi on December 1, while MacArthur's puzzled staff tried to figure what had hit them, Almond kept assuring the Supreme Commander that a flanking attack from his bridgehead would certainly turn the Communist tide. As he spoke, the marines were beginning to retreat from Yudam-ni. General Almond was undoubtedly aware of a Chinese presence in the north, as was MacArthur, but both generals considered the threat exaggerated. The very day the Chinese launched their own offensive, Almond flew by helicopter to Task Force Faith, whose three battalions from the U.S. 7th Division were meeting "unexpected resistance" on the eastern edge of the Changjin Reservoir. He chided his soldiers for failing to press their advance.

"The enemy who is attacking you is nothing more than some remnants of Chinese divisions fleeing north," Almond declared, handing out decorations. "We're still attacking and we're going all the way to the Yalu. Don't let a bunch of Chinese laundrymen stop you."

That night the Chinese overwhelmed Task Force Faith. Its commanding officer, Colonel Don Faith, was killed by a grenade. Less than half his troops escaped. The Chinese attacked in squads, seeking weak points in the defense and exploiting any opening. They attacked at night, almost soundlessly, without preparatory bombardment by rockets or artillery.

But their prime target was not the army troops but the marines. The 5th and 7th Marine Regiments west of the reservoir had been specially earmarked for complete destruction. More than 100,000 Chinese troops were concentrated against these vulnerable intruders, and Radio Peking was soon announcing that "the annihilation of the United States First Marine Division is only a matter of time." Other prongs of the corps' advance—the South Koreans racing confidently northeast toward the short North Korean border with the Soviet Union; the 7th Division units, briefly ensconced beside the Yalu— were brushed smartly back toward the sea. The UN armada which had landed them little more than a month before had gathered again off the coast, and these troops were evacuated without trouble.

The marines had no such easy out, though the bind they were in was none of their choosing. For the first time in marine history, the best-disciplined, best-motivated fighting men in the American armed forces—the proud victors of Château-Thierry, Guadalcanal, and Iwo Jima—were operating under army command. Such a spirited elite was bound to accept Ned Almond's orders with healthy skepticism;

for put into practice, the X Corps commander's plans had indeed seemed crazy. Skirting the Changjin Reservoir meant overextending the division along the least negotiable route to the Yalu River, and trailing behind them a long, undefended supply line.

This might have been an acceptable risk, perhaps, as long as the enemy remained fragmented, but not when, as it now appeared, strong forces of Chinese were concentrating nearby. Fortunately for the marines their commander, Major General Oliver P. Smith, had refused to be rushed. Fortified base camps were deliberately and gradually established as the column ground up the winding mountain tracks: first at Chinhung-ni, which overlooked the seaport at Hungnam and the industrial complex of Hamhung; then at Koto-ri, a point overlooking the frozen Changjin River and halfway to the reservoir itself; and finally in the town of Hagaru, where river and reservoir joined. Each of these three base camps nestled behind well-sited perimeter defenses; all had airstrips.

A planeload of correspondents flew into Hagaru on December 4. Among them was Maggie Higgins. The marines were already streaming back from their final probe northwestward to Yudam-ni. They were frozen, exhausted, and had "the dazed air of men who have accepted death and then found themselves alive after all," she wrote. Their pullback was in no way a replay of the U.S. 2nd Division's debacle on the Sunchon Road. But it could have been. The wooded valleys, the narrow icy road, provided a ready-made trap. The Chinese had taken advantage of the high terrain around the Changjin Reservoir to maintain relentless pressure. The marines managed to keep column, however, through 14 fierce-fought miles, scaling the surrounding heights to avert ambush, and thrusting back repeated attacks until the last jeep-load of their wounded jolted painfully to safety in Hagaru.

The action added luster to a lustrous reputation; a disputed withdrawal has always been the trickiest maneuver in the book. Image-conscious as ever, the leathernecks refused even to admit it was a bug-out.

"Retreat, hell!" snapped General Smith, creating another corps legend. "We're not retreating. We're just advancing in a different direction!"

Said Lieutenant Colonel Raymond Murray, commander of the 5th Marine Regiment: "We're coming out of this as marines, not as stragglers. We're going to bring out our wounded and equipment. We're coming out, I tell you, as marines or not at all." The snow lashed hard at the raw faces of the officers gathered around him in subzero temperatures. The colonel glared at them harshly. "This is no retreat."

But retreat it was. After everything they had gone through, Maggie reported, the men took the withdrawal order hard. As the colonel spoke she watched their faces, "and their expressions were of deeply hurt pride."

The marines' fall-back position itself was endangered. Heavy Chinese assaults threatened the thinly defended Hagaru perimeter. Had the enemy concentrated completely on the perimeter, Colonel Murray observed, "we could never have gotten out of the trap. By trying to keep us consistently encircled, they dispersed their strength." The threat was so grave for a time that a scratch force 1,000 strong, commanded by a British lieutenant colonel and made up of British Marine Commandos, U.S. Marines, and U.S. soldiers, rushed up from Hungnam to flesh out the Hagaru garrison. This force was ambushed by one of the seven Chinese divisions now besieging the route, and less than half these reinforcements got through. The following day survivors of Task Force Faith also filtered in to bolster the Hagaru defenses, but only 385 of them were fit to fight.

Air power came once more to the rescue: fighter-bombers from the First Marine Air Wing, based at Yonpo Airfield in Hamhung, together with planes from the carriers *Leyte* and *Philippine Sea*, cruising in the Sea of Japan, blasted the Chinese throughout the dwindling hours of daylight. The darkening skies were thick with aircraft braving the snow clouds to smother Chinese-held hilltops, roadblocks, and supply columns with destructive firepower. Over Hagaru, red-and-yellow supply parachutes sprouted from the bellies of USAF Flying Boxcars, while down on the airstrip trusty old Dakotas flew 20-minute shuttles, bringing in food and ammunition from the coast, and evacuating more than 4,500 sick and wounded. A high proportion of these were frost-bite cases.

Winter was taking its toll. Temperatures of minus-20 degrees and below lowered human endurance; jammed rifles and carbines; and froze drinking water, medicines, and vehicles. Marines had to chip the ice off their mortars before they would fire. Candies and canned fruit were kept from freezing by being carried next to the body; the extra sugar from these helped restore energy. *Life* magazine photographer David Douglas Duncan found a marine patiently hacking a breakfast of beans from a frozen tin. The beans were encased in ice crystals, and more crystals had formed on the man's beard. Thinking ahead to the *Life* Christmas issue, Duncan asked the marine: "If I were God and could give you anything you wanted, what would you ask for?" The marine went on hacking at the beans. "Gimme tomorrow," he said.

The marines' final breakout from encirclement began Wednesday, December 6. The column fought off frenzied Chinese attacks as it crawled down the precipitous trail to Koto-ri. The enemy could see the prey was escaping. Hilltops swarmed with Chinese riflemen picking off the ragged, muffled marines shuffling past below. Mortar bombs swished in on the frozen roadway. There were costly delays while engineers ditched knocked-out vehicles, removed obstructions, and refilled holes. But throughout the march the column remained full of fight, and unafraid to tackle the toughest terrain or the strongest enemy resistance. Without care for casualties, hunger, or the bone-chilling cold, marine squads stormed across key ridges overlooking the canyon road. The ribbon of brown-clad humanity winding down the wind-whipped mountain face took 38 tortuous hours to cover 11 miles. The advance guard of the 7th Regiment was settling thankfully into the Koto-ri perimeter while men of the 5th, still at Hagaru, were fighting off furious night attacks that threatened to engulf them.

The saga was not yet over. Thick fog and snow suddenly masked the plateau. The ring of jagged peaks vanished in the murk. U.S. air support ceased, and the drone of planes gave way to a glacial silence over the hundreds of tents dotting the overcrowded camp. The Chinese could have wreaked havoc had they possessed artillery, but their heavily bombed horse-drawn guns were bogged down close to the Yalu. Their foot-soldiers continued to harass the escape route, destroying the bridge over the Funchilin Pass, a chasm midway down the escape route to Chinhung-ni. With the bridge gone, the Chinese assumed, the marines would be forced to abandon their vehicles and their guns. Reluctantly the UN forces decided to leave their dead, buried in mass graves dug from the rock-hard soil with explosives. The bodies were wrapped in ponchos. Some of the dead British marine commandos still wore their berets. The two main graves, containing more than 100 bodies, were marked by red and white surveying poles. Map references were recorded in case the Americans ever returned. The chaplain recited the 23rd Psalm, "The Lord Is My Shepherd," to a small audience of reporters and officers, but the bitter wind whisked away his words.

Maggie Higgins was not permitted to accompany the marines down any section of the road. It was considered too dangerous for a woman. Instead, as soon as the weather cleared, she flew to Koto-ri aboard one of the three marine fighter-bombers detailed to evacuate casualties. One plane burst a tire on landing. Another upturned on the inadequate runway. The third managed to fly out nearly 100 men.

There was an unmistakable difference in attitude, Maggie Higgins found, between the marines who had reached Koto-ri and the haggard men she had seen back at Hagaru. The new feeling seemed to be "If we've made it this far, we're bound to make the rest." She was also impressed to find a large number of Korean refugees who had followed the marines squatting stubbornly beyond the perimeter defenses out in the snowy fields.

"Our presence in Korea had brought destruction to their towns and death to their people," wrote Maggie. "Yet here were nearly a thousand people who had left their homes rather than remain and face the Chinese Communists."

Ten more miles remained to be covered before the base at Chinhung-ni and safety. But the wind was dropping and the Chinese were weakening. Dozens of their soldiers were creeping out of the snow with badly frozen hands and feet, begging to surrender. Other groups milled about in the distance not attempting to attack. Despite doubts about the stability of the weather, General Smith decided to move his troops out. On the afternoon of December 8, a protective shield of tanks was thrown around the perimeter, tents were struck, vehicles loaded, and the final salvoes fired. The 7th Marine Regiment set off to clear commanding heights above the road. Elements of 1st Regiment pushed up from the coast to meet them. The vital pass was rebridged with two-ton spans parachuted from eight Flying Boxcars and positioned ready for the bumper-to-bumper trail of trucks, tanks, guns, and half-tracks slithering and scraping down the face of the mountain. Fourteen thousand weary, bearded men reached the coast with equipment intact, just as Colonel Murray had promised; the Chinese could do nothing to stop them. The enemy was unable even to threaten the shrinking X Corps bridgehead once full-scale evacuation got under way three days later.

The send-off was witnessed by General Douglas MacArthur, making his last trip to the north. He praised the men's high morale without admitting the slightest flaws of generalship. Also present was *Time* correspondent Dwight Martin. There was no panic, he reported. No disorder. But as the perimeter contracted, the tempo of evacuation sharply increased. The black, mud-choked roads within the dock area were jammed with mud-spattered trucks grinding down toward the ships. They passed acres of gasoline drums, quarter-mile-long warehouses piled high with C rations, soap, lard, coffee, and fruit juices. American and Korean stevedores worked round the clock, pausing occasionally to casually hack open six-pound cans of pork luncheon meat to make sandwiches. Korean women walked out of a warehouse carrying off huge bags of flour. Some later found they had mistakenly looted sacks of fertilizer.

"We just got most of this stuff in here," groaned a transportation officer. "We're going to have to turn right the hell around and blow it up again. God help the taxpayers."

Blow it up they did, to prevent valuable materials from falling into Chinese and North Korean hands, but not before some 100 American,

Japanese, and Norwegian vessels had evacuated 105,000 troops and 91,000 Korean civilians from along the coast, and salvaged 350,000 tons of stores and 17,500 vehicles. They departed under the covering fire of an offshore naval support force that poured 35,000 rounds into the silent countryside.

The end came on Christmas Eve. Engineers had already destroyed the industrial complex at Hamhung. As the last UN ships pulled out to sea, hundreds of tons of high explosives shattered the already battered Hungnam waterfront. The irrelevant and misguided expedition had cost the U.S. Marines heavy casualties—718 dead and nearly 4,000 wounded—but the force survived to fight again. Its heroism took much of the sting out of the Korean debacle. The fact remained that the United States and its allies had suffered a humiliating defeat. There would be no further attempt to roll back communism in North Korea. For the moment at least, Chinese manpower had triumphed over American machines, exactly as Mao Zedong predicted—though the cost to China was terrible indeed.

Northeast Korea,
Late December, 1950

The snowmen puzzled Wong Lichan. The Chinese colonel first spotted them on the road from Kanggye to Chinhung-ni: humped-up mounds, human-shaped, first alone or in pairs, then in growing groups. Boys had made those sorts of things from ice and snow during his childhood in Manchuria. But who could be making them in these empty mountains? It was two days since he had seen a child. The truck stopped among a cluster of the figures, after a Korean came out of the trees signaling an air alert, and Wong realized with sickening shock that he was ringed by frozen, snow-coated Chinese corpses.

"There's hundreds like this, maybe thousands," his Korean driver said laconically. "Some of them coolies, most of them soldiers."

The two men crouched beneath white camouflage netting while American aircraft rumbled through the overcast sky. The cruel Siberian wind hissed about their ears, stirring up a mist of powdered snow that coated the rigid figures with further, merciful concealment. Colonel Wong hunched deeper inside his padded clothing, feeling distinctly sick and trying to silence his ever-chattering teeth.

"What do you expect with this weather?" the driver grumbled. "There'll be a dreadful stink round here next spring."

He walked over to one of the figures and tapped it irreverently with his foot. The corpse had frozen while kneeling beside a tree, as if sheltering from the cold.

"Like rock, see?" said the driver. With another tap the mask of snow slid off the face to reveal a gaunt, unshaven man with gaping mouth. The Korean was quite unmoved. A strange people, the colonel thought. "Nothing can survive long in this"—the driver waved a mittened hand around the frozen valley—"not without food, heat, or proper clothes." He squatted with his back to the truck, lighting a cigarette out of reach of the wind. Frost patches appeared on the Soviet-made submachine gun he carried round his neck. Colonel Wong was known to be carrying important papers and the driver had strict orders to guard him. "Korean troops are better prepared for this kind of winter," the man boasted, with a flash of the old national pride. "Better boots. Better coats. You've been with the NKPA long enough to know."

The Chinese liaison officer nodded miserably. He had seen more of the North Korean army than most foreigners since the start of this cruel war. Now he was being dragged all the way from Pyongyang—a city much mauled since he first arrived there with the embassy last summer—to establish liaison with a new North Korean army corps forming up in the northeast. A few battalions of this corps had backed the Ninth Army Group of the Chinese Peoples' Volunteers in its futile attempt to trap the American and puppet forces inside their coastal bridgehead. The Chinese pushed the invaders back into the sea but failed completely to destroy them. The Ninth Army Group had suffered such crippling losses that it would be out of the war for months. More than 40,000 troops were dead and thousands more laid low with wounds and frostbite. The army group commander, General Song Shilun, one of the finest soldiers in China, was offering to resign. And the man held directly responsible for the foul-up, General "Limp" Zhang Renchu, was said to have threatened suicide. Their former commanding officer, General Chen Yi, normally based in Shanghai, was hurrying in from China to Ninth Army Group headquarters to smooth things over.

The news of the crippling Chinese losses at Changjin so upset General Peng that he flew to Peking for a showdown with Mao Zedong. This much has been recorded in recent Chinese writings. Peng stormed into the Chairman's villa in Zhong Nan Hai one morning in late December, dragging him out of bed and creating an embarrassing fuss. Chinese troops in Korea were approaching exhaustion, Peng loudly proclaimed; their equipment, clothing, and logistics were entirely unsuited to a protracted, attritional campaign. The fiasco in northeast Korea showed that. The Third Phase offensive against Seoul would peter out disastrously, he predicted, unless the

Soviets stopped applauding from the sidelines, got off their backsides, and poured in equipment and supplies.

The newly formed Chinese air force might also consider taking a few more risks, striking south below the Yalu and, if necessary, attacking U.S. sanctuaries in Japan. Some of Peng's arguments mirrored those aimed by MacArthur at Washington. General Peng seems to have made his point, however; he returned, mollified, to command headquarters in Shenyang. Fresh Chinese armies prepared to enter Korea handsomely equipped with fresh Soviet weapons. Much of the output of Soviet arsenals would for the next three years be diverted to China. On payment, of course. The Chinese Peoples' Volunteers would emerge from the conflict equipped with heavy artillery, tanks, an expanded navy, and brand-new air force; the kind of weaponry that might have swung the balance had it been available earlier—during the final, crucial months of 1950.

The snowmen grew more numerous as Wong and his driver headed south. Whole platoons appeared to have perished, squatting in squad order, rifles on shoulders, kitbags on backs, all snow-sheathed, terrible. Gangs of coolies had frozen to death, pressed down by their heavy A-frames, and there were scatterings of North Korean refugees, women and children mostly, heaped hopelessly together in search of warmth. A few old men in tall Korean hats had chosen to meet their end sitting bolt upright, hands folded in laps, like Buddhas frosted by the snow. The white-painted truck passed through several checkpoints, manned by Koreans, but there were no more air alerts. Worn out by four days of travel, sickened at the sight of corpses, Colonel Wong felt grave forebodings. He'd had much the same feeling last summer in the battered North Korean command post at Kimchon, far to the south, when the NKPA was on the verge of victory. Or so it then seemed. The Chinese counterblow of recent weeks had effectively turned the enemy tide, negating most of the UN's gains since Inchon, but here, in this ghostly freezing ground, things had obviously gone badly wrong.

The colonel glanced warily up at the snowy sky. Still no planes around. He had never completely recovered from his near-fatal jeep journey on the way to observe at the NKPA Front. The driver told him not to worry. He knew this area, especially on the coast, like he knew his own face. Nevertheless an inner voice kept warning Colonel Wong that this was an inauspicious week to travel. His late father had always refused to leave home during the winter solstice. Generals in ancient days would never think of marching out their troops at this time of the year; the Book of Rights ordained Tung Chih a time for inspecting weapons, training recruits, and strengthening city defenses. For the ordinary folk in northern China it meant hibernation. The first of the cold nine seasons (lasting a total of 49 days) drove everyone indoors, set them busily blocking drafty cracks and repapering the windows, or huddling on top of the warm *kang* and rolling balls of boiling dough as offerings to the Door Gods.

Nothing but ridiculous superstition, Wong told himself, fondling the amulet around his neck. The revolution had killed off the gods. Man made his own fate. And man made his own irreversible mistakes. Periodically he thought of throwing the amulet away, but after the shot-up jeep, the bombed train, and that frightening interrogation . . . somehow the charm had helped. It might be worth keeping for a while. Certainly until the end of the war.

Colonel Wong pondered the mistakes that had led to this first Chinese setback against the Americans. It had to be recognized that the caliber of troops assigned to this part of Korea was nowhere near as high as those with whom Wong had served during the Chinese civil war: the elite Thirteenth Army Group fighters, who had smashed the American forces on the other side of the Korean peninsula, retaken Pyongyang, and now stood ready to capture Seoul. The troops comprising the Ninth Army Group, marooned here in the depths of winter, had been drawn from the Chinese Third Army. They were Chen Yi's men, charged until last summer with the invasion of Taiwan. The U.S. Seventh Fleet had put a stop to those plans by shielding the island immediately after the outbreak of the Korean War. Hurriedly re-assigned to attack the American bridge-head, Chen Yi's men had been given little time to switch themselves from amphibious to mountain warfare, especially considering these sub-arctic conditions; the 26th Field Army, "Limp" Zhang's command, had come straight off the trains wearing lightweight uniforms. Its companion field armies, the 20th and the 27th, lacked experienced junior officers, sergeants, and commissars. None had been prepared for the agonies of the frozen Koto-ri road at the Changjin Reservoir.

Wong's truck lurched into Chinhung-ni late on December 28. The rutted streets were filled with Chinese soldiers picking their way around the ruins. Some of the men wore bandages. The few surviving buildings were packed with wounded. A convoy of assorted vehicles, full of casualties, was leaving for the nearest intact railroad some 70 kilometers away. An oddly shaped building, probably once a church, had been converted into a medical station. Doctors inside were amputating frost-bitten limbs. One of them stepped outside for a smoke as Colonel Wong passed. He recognized the man, a surgeon whom he had last seen in Shanghai. The doctor was wizened with fatigue. "So many cases," he complained. "Nearly all frostbite. There's nothing much we can do." His surgical rubber apron was smeared with blood. "Got a drink?" he asked. The colonel fished out his emergency bottle of greasy Korean gin. "For my patients," said the doctor. "They need it more than you do."

The town schoolhouse had become Ninth Army Group headquarters. Before that the Americans had been there. Slogans in Western script were scribbled on the walls. The colonel could read a little English. There was the ubiquitous "Kilroy." Another word said "Tripoli," but it was years before he found out what it meant. The place was unusually quiet. The staff had boarded up the shattered windows and sat smoking silently around an old iron stove. The atmosphere was gloomy. Aides led the way to an outhouse where General Song Shilun was holding lonely vigil over the inescapable paperwork.

"The comrade from Pyongyang," he said when Colonel Wong entered the room. General Song was 43 at the time, a Hunanese like General Peng and Chairman Mao, a graduate of Whampoa Military Academy (same class as Lin Biao) and a veteran of the Long March. Tonight Song Shilun looked a tired old man, scarcely resembling the cocksure commander who had marched triumphantly two years before through the streets of surrendered Shanghai. Wong handed over his dispatches. The general dropped them absently on his desk. He turned to the wall map. "They've gone," Song said, tapping the Sea of Japan. "We could not stop them."

General Chen Yi arrived in Chinhung-ni the following morning, rotund and reassuring, his great moon face lit by a perpetual smile. He would still smile 15 years later when Red Guards hauled him out of his office in the Foreign Ministry and paraded him through the streets of Peking with a dunce's cap on his head. "You'll have to excuse me now," the Chinese foreign minister eventually told his tormentors. "I've got to go out to the airport and greet a delegation from Albania."

A conference was called with "Limp" Zhang, commander of the decimated 26th Field Army. The general hobbled into the schoolhouse, gray and dejected. With him was stocky little General Liu Fei, of 20th Field Army, which had also suffered along the Koto-ri road, and General Nieh Feng-che, whose 27th Field Army took severe punishment at Yudam-ni. They met behind closed doors and re-emerged in the late afternoon chattering amicably. Excuses appear to have been offered, face saved, and resolution reaffirmed. No record has ever come to light of the detailed discussions, but a summary circulated among the Ninth Army Group staff was shown to Colonel Wong.

The summary listed the weather, insuperable supply problems, enemy air attacks, and a serious lack of firepower as the four main factors hampering the Chinese campaign. The soldiers' clothing, especially the canvas boots issued originally for the Taiwan invasion, was totally inadequate for the weather encountered at the Changjin Reservoir. More men died of the cold, according to the summary, than from enemy bombs and bullets. A large proportion of the survivors suffered such severe frostbite that wholesale amputation was required of gangrenous hands and feet. The cold also killed off the coolies, sharply reducing supplies, until already-freezing soldiers starved and ran out of ammunition. Combat was constantly broken off in the last stages of the battle when attacking Chinese battalions ran out of rounds for their rifles and machine guns. Enemy air attacks further reduced supplies and made it difficult to concentrate for an all-out assault. The high, wide valleys favored the marines with their open fields of fire. Artillery could have proved crucial at several points in the campaign, notably at Hagaru, if the horse-drawn limbers had been able to negotiate the mountainous terrain. A terse self-criticism by General Song Shilun, appended to the report, admitted that overdispersal of his forces had robbed them of the opportunity to strike in force at key points along the marine retreat route. An attack was ordered on the marine base camp at Koto-ri, but for the reasons given the Chinese troops were unable to mount it.

Fires were still burning down on the coast when Colonel Wong drove off to find the North Koreans. He was forwarded to III Corps, a recently formed addition to the NKPA. Its command post was located close to the industrial center of Hamhung, now devastated by American demolitions. As his truck wove through the rubble-covered city streets of Hamhung, Colonel Wong marveled at the destructiveness of man. Clouds of smoke belched from one of the main chemical works. A tall concrete building sagged sideways on partially demolished foundations. Many areas were taped off behind bilingual warnings of mines. Wong's driver looked mildly surprised. "I used to live here," he said. He coasted through the ruins shaking his head in disbelief. "That was my school,"—a heap of splintered timber—"and out there I used to live." He paused beside a warning sign. Beyond it there were mines or unexploded bombs. The colonel could see nothing but rubble lightly covered with snow.

A long line of townsfolk waited outside a store. Soup was being doled out by a red-cheeked, pig-tailed girl, who stood beneath a portrait of Kim Il Sung. The Beloved Leader looked confident as ever. A loudspeaker played patriotic music. Wong's driver parked the truck, got out, and walked up and down the line asking if anyone had seen his family. People looked blank or tried to avoid his eyes.

He walked slowly back to his downcast passenger. "Gone," he told Wong. "All gone." They reached the hot springs spa where the North Koreans had set up their command post. Most of the buildings were flattened. "When we're through with this war," the driver said, "there won't be a great deal left." He showed no apparent emotion.

Andong, Manchuria, People's Republic of China, Late December, 1950

The children of Andong had never had such fun. Living on the Chinese side of the Yalu River, within sight of Korea, they had grown accustomed to the sound of air-raid sirens, the chatter of distant machine guns, and the occasional thud of bombs. Whenever the alarm went off they moved automatically and without panic into the kindergarten shelter. The whole thing would have been regarded as a game, a welcome break from toys and books, if the weather had not been so cold. There was no stove in the shelter, and the five-year-olds huddled together for warmth in spite of their padded coats, fur caps, and scarves. The principal, Miss Wu, a recognized authority on military affairs, peered out of the shelter door from time to time to watch the long white trails left by the airplanes high in the winter sky. Those were Chinese planes, she told the children, flown by brave airmen from bases close to the city. Daily they shot down the barbarian aircraft sent, she claimed, to destroy the cities of Manchuria. Several of the enemy were said to have crashed nearby, though no one had seen it happen.

Sometimes the guns would go off with a bang at the approaches to the bridge. This made them jump and set some of the smaller girls crying. Little Ah Lo did not cry. He knew they were perfectly safe. Father said so every time Mother started nagging him to send their son to Second Uncle in Shenyang. The matter had been raised less often lately because shopkeepers like Second Uncle were being put out of business. Father said they were becoming servants of the state.

Mother moaned more now about the lack of clothing at the new state store. Ah Lo was growing fast and needed another winter jacket, but there were not enough ration coupons. Everything on sale was the same color, a kind of darkish blue, and Mother hunted in vain for something brown or black in which to dress her little boy. The old man who used to do their tailoring had become a clerk in the state store. He bowed his head politely before Mother's stream of complaints, but the manager grew angry and told her to get out. Never had she been treated like this by a shopkeeper, Mother told other women in the street, and they agreed. So many things were in short supply. Needles and razorblades, for example. Father had never managed to find any glass to repair the bombed-out windows in their house. He had patched them up with opaque paper, which made the house darker and more drafty.

There wasn't quite so much to eat, either. Mother grew thinner and thinner on a bowl of rice a day, topped by bits of turnip and winter cabbage. Somehow she always found some scraps of chicken and some noodles for her menfolk. Father scolded her for eating so sparingly. Men needed more food than women, she replied, especially now that work at the cannery had stopped for the winter. The head of the block committee called one day to say the party could not bear to see Mother unemployed. She would be assigned to street sweeping during the heavy snows. Mother turned pale. Of course, if she ceased complaining in the streets and arousing the indignation of other women, the friendly comrade explained, he might forget the idea. Father was a good Party man with a heroic reputation as a onetime resistance fighter, and he assured the head of the block committee that Mother would make no further comments in public.

"These are hard times for everyone," the comrade said. "Our revolutionary forces are at war."

Ah Lo was still unsure what the war was all about. It went on, far away, beyond the reaches of the Yalu. The town of Sinuiju, on the opposite bank, had been destroyed. Several North Korean refugee children arrived at the kindergarten, but nobody could talk to them until they had picked up a smattering of Chinese. When asked what had happened they said, "Boom, boom," and covered their ears.

Since summer the barbarian bombers had knocked more spans out of the big steel bridges, but that was no loss because the river was frozen anyway. Nothing moved in the daytime, but every night there was frantic activity down on the ice itself. Trucks and coolies criss-crossed a regular route north of the bridges. Shortly before dawn people went out with brooms to sweep away the tire tracks.

Ah Lo snuck out one evening while his parents were away at a block committee meeting to watch the endless lines of Chinese soldiers marching off across the river to Korea. They left without the elaborate ceremonies of last October; no cheering children, no dancing girls or important-looking men in uniform came to give the troops a send-off; the brown-clad men in their big furry hats strode bravely away into the darkness without a word.

Most of the trucks arriving from Korea drove up to the station and unloaded litters onto waiting trains. The boy crept through the stationmaster's office and saw the litters lined up on the concourse. Nurses were attending men smothered in bandages. Some were so heavily bandaged that litter bearers had to light their cigarettes for them and hold them in their mouths while the wounded men smoked. Others were completely covered in sheets. These the nurses ignored. They did not load them on the trains. Ah Lo wondered what was wrong with them. He wanted to ask Miss Wu because she knew so much about the war, but he was afraid she would tell Father he had been out after dark.

Next day the children were drilling in the playground when Old Wong, the riverside drunk, came staggering past. He told Miss Wu the children looked silly marching around like little soldiers. He ignored the principal when she ordered him to be silent. Miss Wu affected a military-style uniform these days and never stopped talking about China's *splendid victories*. She ordered the old drunk not to defame the revolution.

Old Wong leered at her woozily. Hospitals all over North China were full of wounded, he claimed, because the war in Korea was proving a lot tougher than those fools in Peking had reckoned.

"Where are all the bands now?" he shouted at the children. "Oompa, oompa!" He pretended to be playing a trombone. The children laughed. Miss Wu went white with rage. She told Old Wong to go about his business before she called a militiaman. Old Wong started to reply, but changed his mind and walked off mumbling down toward the riverfront.

Ah Lo told Father what had happened. It was a pity, Father said thoughtfully. Old Wong had been something of a scholar before he started drinking. The man was perfectly harmless. And it was probably true what he had said about the wounded. Letters from the family in Shenyang said the hospitals there were full. Doctors were being drafted from all over China to help out. Ah Lo's family physician, an elderly man who had graduated in prewar Japan, left suddenly the following week. He came back months later refusing to talk about anything he had seen. Father said that was very wise. There were certain things nobody should talk about outside his home.

The Hate America campaign was growing steadily more strident. Miss Wu led the children to a rally on the riverside to hear several people on a platform make boring speeches. It was bitterly cold, the winter wind came whistling in across the ice, and some of the little girls began to cry again. Ah Lo felt so cold he wanted to cry as well, but Mother and Father were standing nearby, looking nearly frozen, and he could not cause them to lose face in front of all the neighbors. A fat man on the platform was denouncing foreign spies. Andong was *full* of spies, he shouted, *lick-spittles* of the imperialists and *saboteurs* of the revolution. Enemies of the people were circulating vicious rumors in an attempt to undermine the war effort and the *people's revolution*.

There was a gasp of surprise when Old Wong was hauled through the crowd, strangely sober, to confess to slandering the Chinese Peoples' Volunteers. The truth was that he secretly hoped for an imperialist victory, he shouted from the platform, firmly pinioned from behind by two stern-faced militiamen. Why, why? everybody yelled. *I am a bourgeois intellectual*, Old Wong admitted, and the tears ran down his unshaven face. He still read foreign books and received letters and money from two sons in America. Mention of the sons made him sound unusually guilty. "Traitor!" the crowd shouted, and he was led away. No one saw him again.

Miss Wu stepped forward. There were many more traitors, she declared, in Andong. Silence fell, people looked uneasily at one another. Who could be next? "Christian missionaries," shrieked Miss Wu, posturing like a general in the Peking Opera. The crowd looked puzzled. There were no missionaries here as far as Ah Lo was aware. Right in their midst there were foreign agents, Miss Wu went on, corrupting China with their alien religion. At that everyone loudly agreed. The running dog of these agents, cried Miss Wu, pointing an accusing finger, was Li Fulin, the little man who ran the Baptist chapel. Not many people went to worship there; lately they had been very few indeed. Soldiers plucked Mr. Li, trembling, from the crowd. He was a mild, balding man with spectacles, who spoke with a distinct stutter. Miss Wu confronted him, righteous and redfaced in her military uniform. To his face she accused him of sending signals to the American bombers. Poor Li tried to answer, but the words would not come. "Death to the traitor!" somebody yelled, and the crowd took up the chant.

Ah Lo glanced at his parents. Mother was crying and Father was comforting her. He wondered what she could be crying about. Mother was a devout Buddhist even if she no longer offered incense at the temple. Why should she care about a Christian traitor? Women were *always* crying. Mother was still sniffling when the boy got home. The air hung heavy with unspoken thoughts. Father sat on the *kang* and frowned. He started to say something critical of Miss Wu, saw his son listening, and changed his mind. Ah Lo asked: "When will they shoot Mr. Li?" Father did not answer. The air-raid sirens sounded. Ah Lo scampered off to the shelter singing "The Soldiers' March." He was learning it in class.

15

General Matt Ridgway and the Demolition of Al Jolson / General Peng Contemplates the Bitter Moon / The Sharp Swords in Seoul.

**South Korea,
Christmas, 1950**

There was no hope of holding Seoul. The U.S. Eighth Army faced a final, disruptive retreat south of the Han River estuary, following a tragic change of leadership. Midway through the morning of December 23, the highly polished jeep of Lieutenant General Walton H. "Johnnie" Walker smashed into a truck on a road northeast of Seoul. The jeep, with its shotgun rack, shiny metal rank flags, and whip antennas, bounced off into a telegraph pole. The 61-year-old general, hurrying to present a citation to the British 27th Commonwealth Brigade, had insisted on riding without his helmet. He received fatal head injuries.

It was a wretched, if timely, end. The stocky, rough-tongued Texan, a closely patterned protégé of the great Patton, had done his damnedest to defend Pusan, and done it well, during the earliest, most desperate days of the war. He had been still more in his element racing his road columns across North Korea, bagging a pheasant or two, pursuing the broken North Korean foe. But the massive Chinese offensive had paralyzed and unnerved him—as it unnerved MacArthur back in Tokyo—and touched off the longest withdrawal in

275

U.S. military history. Days before the accident, Walker's dismissal had been secretly discussed and a replacement named.

Choice fell on the Eighth Army's deputy chief of staff, 55-year-old Lieutenant General Matthew B. "Matt" Ridgway, whose considerable reputation stemmed from commanding airborne troops in the Normandy landings and in the Ardennes in the closing months of World War II. Ridgway was a big man, balding and brave; a sophisticated professional completely conversant with his craft, impatient of idiots, and meticulous over detail. Given less than 24 hours to leave Washington and assume his new command, he did not neglect to order his wife's Christmas present from the PX. Meeting MacArthur at the Dai Ichi on Christmas Day he was wearily told: "The Eighth Army is yours, Matt. Do what you think best." The Supreme Commander never interfered again in Korean field operations. Abolished forthwith was the system of divided command which put one general in charge of Eighth Army, leaving another, manipulated by MacArthur, running X Corps. The entire United Nations force, totaling 365,000 men, was placed under Ridgway's control.

Ridgway had no illusions about MacArthur. He held no brief for the cavalier way his famous superior was treating Washington. In his view, the Joint Chiefs should have brought the old man to heel long ago. Ridgway refused to accept the Supreme Commander's gloomy analyses of the still-mounting battlefront crisis and the apocalyptic solutions he was currently pressing on Washington. MacArthur was lobbying for an extra four divisions. Ridgway reckoned he could make do with what he had. He flew thoughtfully into Taegu, shivering in his mid-weight Pentagon battle blouse, determined to teach the Chinese a lesson. To MacArthur's discomfiture, he succeeded beyond belief.

First, Ridgway had to reassure the South Koreans. The ROK troops could hardly be expected to continue fighting as long as it was believed—and increasingly *widely* believed—that the Americans were planning to quit. There had been panic talk in the Dai Ichi of evacuating Korea. Ridgway went directly to Syngman Rhee and told him: "I'm glad to see you, Mr. President, glad to be here, and I mean to stay." Tears came to the old man's eyes. But some way had to be found of translating intent into action. It wasn't easy. Rushing around the country by jeep, light plane, and new-fangled helicopter, Ridgway was aghast at the state of military morale.

"There was too much of a looking-over-your-shoulder attitude, a lack of that special verve, that extra alertness and vigor that seemed to exude from an army that is sure of itself and bent on winning," he wrote 17 years later. "This was a bewildered army, not sure of itself or its leaders, not sure what they were doing there, wondering when they would hear the whistle of that homebound transport. There was obviously much to be done to restore this army to a fighting mood."

Much of the fault lay at the top. Heads rolled as Ridgway rooted out defeatism. The assistant chief of staff, Colonel John A. Dabney, right-hand man to Walker throughout the Korean campaign, handed his new commander plans to withdraw next spring to the old Pusan perimeter. Ridgway knew he would be forced to retreat at first, but this plan offered no possibility of eventual counteraction. It reeked of defensive thinking. Dabney was dismissed on the spot. Others stayed, on sufferance, provided they revised their tactics.

"I told the field commanders . . ." Ridgway wrote, "that their infantry ancestors would roll over in their graves if they could see how road-bound this army was, how often it forgot to seize the high ground along its route, . . . how reluctant it was to get off its bloody wheels and put shoe leather to the earth, to get into the hills and among the scrub and meet the enemy where he lived."

The Chinese traveled light, invariably at night, in the worst of weather, with none of the creature comforts so vital to Americans. But the "bugle-blowing hordes" were not invincible. The Americans could beat them. GIs would first have to abandon their road columns, along with much of the other labor-saving gadgetry of modern war, toil up to the mountaintops and fight there in disciplined fashion until properly concentrated firepower, of which they enjoyed such abundance, could be brought to bear on the engulfing enemy. The concept came to be known as the "meatgrinder." The defensive system, introduced by Ridgway, guards South Korea to this day. Ridgway used it as an offensive as well as a defensive weapon, confronting the Chinese with prohibitive losses in a protracted, attritional war they were in no shape to sustain. The Chinese armies were too lightly equipped, too poorly supplied, and too far from home base, Ridgway calculated, to aim for anything but quick victory. The trick would be to lure them into the killing ground he planned to spread across the snowbound countryside south of Seoul.

There was regrettably little time to reorganize. The Chinese were massing for the kill north and northeast of Seoul. A fresh offensive was expected at any moment. Plans were set afoot to move Eighth Army's main headquarters to Taegu, 150 miles south of Seoul. Ridgway declined to follow the bulk of his staff, and ended up camping behind I Corps' command post in the open fields away from towns and traffic. There he worked with only six men—two aides, plus an orderly, a driver, and two men to drive and operate his radio jeep. Two small tents were pitched end to end. One provided him a bedroom with camp cot, sleeping bag, and enamel wash basin; the other contained a small table, folding chairs, and a plywood panel mounting a relief model of the battle zone. Poring over this model for hours on end, and flying, driving, and walking across the countryside, he memorized large parts of the topography.

"Every road, every cart track, every hill, every stream, every ridge in that area where we were fighting or which we hoped to control—they all became as familiar to me as the features of my own backyard," he wrote. "Thus, when I considered sending a unit out into a certain sector, I knew if it involved infantrymen crawling up 2,000-foot ridges with their weapons, ammunition, and food on their backs."

The terrain in this south part of Korea favored the UN defense. The main mountain spine wandered toward the eastern coast, leaving wide tracts of reasonably flat farmland, intersected by ridges, sloping away westward from the upper reaches of the Han River to the sea; it was better suited to American tanks and artillery than the broken country farther north. The front was considerably narrower. UN forces were back at the 38th Parallel by the time Ridgway reached Korea. Supply lines were much reduced, and harried in places by North Korean guerrillas.

The left flank was held by Major General Frank W. Milburn's I Corps, just above Seoul; Major General John B. Coulter's IX Corps was assigned the center; to the east, the more easily defensible mountains were left to the weakened ROK II Corps and the newly committed, inexperienced ROK III Corps. They were shortly reinforced by ROK I Corps with the crack ROK Capitol Division. The U.S. X Corps, still under Ned Almond, was reorganizing in Pusan. The First Marine Division, detached from Almond's command, rested in reserve.

Matt Ridgway would have been happier with more information about the Chinese. All the intelligence experts could show him when he assumed command was "a big red goose egg out in front of us with '174,000' scrawled in the middle of it." The figure was close to the strength of the Chinese army group opposing the U.S. Eighth Army. But overall enemy strength was overestimated at 480,000 Chinese and North Koreans; in fact, no more than 280,000 were committed to the coming attack. Even less was known about the enemy's dispositions. Field commanders showed no inclination to probe forward and find out. Ridgway ordered active ground patrolling, supported by increased aerial reconnaissance. He personally flew aboard a T-bird jet trainer 20 miles into enemy-held territory at treetop level, to return marveling at the Chinese art of concealment. Nothing betrayed his enemy's presence: no campfire smoke, no wheel tracks, nor even trampled snow to indicate the passage of large numbers of troops.

Yet from this lifeless landscape, five days after Ridgway's arrival, the Chinese launched their New Year's Day offensive. Assault troops yelled "Kill GI!" as they leaped through the snow, hurling satchel charges and grenades. Squad after squad of determined brown-clad soldiery slipped through the U.S. defenses, spreading havoc in the rear. Nine Chinese divisions surged toward Seoul, supported, for the first time, by scatterings of their own artillery fire. Little could be done to stop them. The American meatgrinder was still in the planning stage. Ridgway's grit had yet to take hold among his troops. The defense line buckled and bent as the attackers bypassed Seoul. Enemy forward units crossed the Han River on either side of the city.

Driving north of Seoul on New Year's morning, General Ridgway was dismayed to see truckloads of South Korean soldiers streaming to the rear "without order, without arms, without leaders, in full retreat. They had just one aim—to get as far away from the Chinese as possible." He leaped out of the jeep waving his arms, knowing it was hopeless. The first few trucks shot past without slowing. Those that stopped failed to grasp what the American officer was saying. Ridgway ran vainly from truck to truck, a grenade pinned, showmanlike, to his shoulder webbing, urging the frightened men to turn back and fight. Roadblocks had to be set up, manned by American military police, to halt, reorganize, and rearm the fleeing rabble.

There was chaos, too, in the UN central sector. An all-too-familiar encircling movement began to develop as the Chinese punched their way toward the road-and-rail town of Wonju. An enemy swing westward from there could take the U.S. Eighth Army in the rear. Almond's X Corps was rushed into the gap, where the U.S. 2nd Division—the victim of the Sunchon ambush—was bracing itself once more for battle. By now Seoul was untenable. Its defenders were in danger of being cut off. Three days after the start of the offensive the South Korean government was advised to flee south.

Syngman Rhee's death squads had been at work all over the capital. Thousands of political prisoners, the majority arrested merely for daring to question the ruthless old man's dictatorship, were being executed by the police. On one occasion, British troops covering the north of Seoul were astounded to see a truck full of ragged, unwashed men and women pull up, escorted by the hated National Gendarmerie. The prisoners' hands were tied behind their backs with electrical wire. Said an indignant officer: "They made these poor sods kneel in the trench and then they shot them with automatic weapons through the backs of their heads."

The commander of the recently arrived British 29th Brigade, Brigadier Tom Brodie, personally intervened when South Korean military police launched a mass execution a few hundred yards from his command post. Twenty-three men and women were dead before the brigadier could stop the slaughter. The survivors were taken back to the Seoul prison. They were pursued by an indignant bunch of Commonwealth correspondents, who, bored with writing war stories, demanded to be allowed through the prison gates. One of them was BBC correspondent René Cutforth:

> A long column of prisoners was marching diagonally across the courtyard inside. At a sharp yelp from the warder they halted and knelt in the snow. What was so dreadful about them, I saw all at once, was that they looked like a company of clowns. They were bone thin, their hair stuck out golliwog fashion, their faces were green—the color of billiard chalk— and their noses were red with cold. . . . They coughed and shook as they knelt on the ground.

President Rhee promised to consider an amnesty. The longtime exile had hung onto office by foul means since his election in 1948. His shameless autocracy did not bear democratic scrutiny. But undue embarrassment was spared. The American campaign to protect ravaged South Korea had escalated over the past five months from police action to a crusade for freedom. Pressure mounted, first in the United States, later in Europe, to avoid overcritical examination of the repellent regime the West was forced to defend. One distinguished British journalist, James Cameron, resigned when his editor spiked his exposé of the political massacres in Seoul.

Following Brigadier Brodie's intervention in that mass execution, the South Korean minister of justice, Joon Kim Yung, announced swift review of all impending death sentences. A ministerial decree ensured that families would in future be notified of the date of executions and allowed to claim the bodies. Over the past six weeks, correspondents were blandly told, *only* 591 people had been convicted under the national emergency law. To date, 424 of these "criminals" had been executed. The shootings continued, rather more discreetly, and were soon forgotten in the mounting turmoil.

General Ridgway saw no point in wasting lives trying vainly to save Seoul. Manpower was worth much more than territory. Field commanders who issued dramatic orders to defend positions to the death were reprimanded. His aim, he kept emphasizing, was to tempt the

Chinese farther south into the mouths of the American guns. There, the decisive battle would be fought in superior combat country.

The immediate problem was withdrawing the UN forces safely across the Han River just south of Seoul. The riverbed is a mile and a half wide where it skirts the South Korean capital, shrunken behind sandflats and frozen in winter, but still strongly flowing beneath the ice. The Han was spanned by an old Japanese rail bridge, temporarily repaired, and by three frail floating bridges, whose pontoons sagged deep in the rushing water as British Centurion tanks crawled to new positions on the southern riverbank. Traffic grew so heavy the afternoon the evacuation began that orders were reluctantly given to close the floating bridges to the fleeing South Korean civilians; military policemen were posted at the riverside with the unenviable task of turning back the mobs of refugees clamoring to get out of the city. The MPs were ordered to shoot—to kill, if necessary.

Crowds fought to board the last train out of Seoul. Its big Japanese-built locomotive was smothered in people. They clambered onto the running plate, the boiler, and the buffers, clinging to every possible projection as well as to one another. The 34 covered cattle-cars were plastered with a patchwork quilt of brightly colored clothing where hundreds of women clutched perilously at the sides. Each roof was packed with refugees. A group of *kisaeng* girls, elegantly powdered, squealed pleasurably among a mournful clump of moon-faced peasant women. One old crone sat gripping a handrail, glowering stubbornly about her. She was still there, frozen to death, when the train arrived days later in Taegu.

Fires began to break out in the deserted city of Seoul. A quarter of a mile of wooden shops went up in flames in University Road. The market near the Nai Jai apartments became an inferno. Shadowy figures flitted in and out of the glare. Some were probably Communist sympathizers, bidding an arsonist's farewell to capitalism. Some could have been patriots denying the capital to the enemy. René Cutforth thought most looked like looters. The BBC correspondent, roaming the streets with cameraman Cyril Page, noticed the welcome signs were gone. In their place were freshly chalked hammers and sickles with slogans like AMERICANS GO HOME. When dawn broke on the morning of January 5, the red-starred flag of North Korea flew again over the capitol. Seoul was about to change hands for the third time in less than six months.

The BBC men waited on the south bank of the Han River to catch the demolition of "Al Jolson," the last of the three floating pontoon bridges. All other crossing points had already been blown. Most of the correspondents were gone. The BBC television team hung on to record this moment of high drama (without sync-sound or color), which they would ship for processing and censorship in Tokyo, then forward by airfreight to London, where the film would be aired with dubbed-in narration, music, and effects in about one week. Satellites were strictly the stuff of science fiction. Cameraman Page propped himself against the jeep, heavily muffled against the cold, his spring-wound 35-mm camera cradled in mittened hands. The last engineers walked backward down the pontoons unreeling drums of wire.

"The cold of the night had left a white sprinkling of ice crystals like a sifting of sugar on the dark green ice of the river," Cutforth noted. "On the far bank, Seoul towered up above the embankment in tip-tilted terraces. There were ice crystals glittering on them too, and all along the embankment down river from the pontoon bridge, a gaily colored multitude swarmed along the edge of the ice."

Thousands of Koreans were rushing out onto the frozen Han River in a final effort to escape. Women slipped and stumbled in the frantic crush, losing their bundles, and sometimes their children. A little lost girl stood five yards outside the mob, screaming in terror, but the refugees shuffled blindly past. Peasants goaded unwilling bullocks across the treacherous surface. Some of the animals fell, breaking their legs. They lay on their sides bellowing dismally. A loudspeaker plane cruised overhead, urging the refugees to turn back. Roads on the southern bank were so clogged with fleeing humanity that army convoys could not move. Orders went out to halt the exodus. American military policemen marched gingerly onto the ice, confronting the refugee columns, automatic weapons at the ready.

"The face of the youthful policeman nearest to me was a mask of distress," wrote Cutforth. "His conception of his role as liberator had included no such duty as he was now called upon to perform. First, they shot the bullocks, and that act was overdue; then . . . they slowly advanced, step by step, their guns pointing at the terrified people in front of them. These finally wavered and went back, wondering, step by step. And step by step, the policemen herded them, walking backward, towards Seoul. . . . A great wail broke out from the head of the column. Women acted frenzied appeals in dumb show, men shouted, gesticulating, children began to scream."

Families were separated. Mothers called hoarsely for vanished children. Fathers plodded unknowingly ahead, pushing their pathetic cart-loads of possessions, while a few yards behind, their wives were being driven back to the blazing city. When the river was cleared of crowds, mortar bombs broke up the ice. The floating bridge disappeared with a thunderous crash. Wreckage sailed high into the air. Ruptured pontoons sank in a swirl of water. Cyril Page got great pictures. Viewers back in Britain saw only the demolition; footage of the refugees never passed the censors.

Sariwon,
North Korea,
December 25, 1950

General Peng had started talking about the _Chinese_ end-the-war offensive. Officially it was dubbed the Third Campaign. Final plans were reviewed in the North Korean town of Sariwon. Peng had come down from Shenyang just for the conference. The commander of the Thirteenth Army Group, the swarthy General Li Tianyu, a much-admired tactician who would direct the crucial battle, drove up from his headquarters outside Kaesong. The North Koreans were represented by Lieutenant General Kim Ung. The North Korean entourage in their splendid uniforms predictably outshone the Chinese. They arrived in blue-lined brown capes worn over Soviet-style blouses glittering with decorations, while the shabby Chinese still seemed to be recovering from the Long March. The plain, threadbare jacket worn by General Peng carried no more than the standard red collar-stars. It was heavily patched at the elbows. The general's aide, Major Han Liqun, stood furtively smoothing the creases out of his crumpled pants. The four-day journey from Manchuria, partly by train, partly by road, had done nothing to improve staff turnout. The Spartan facilities so close to the front could not even cope with their laundry. Washed clothes froze into the weirdest shapes when drying out of doors.

The generals met in an ancient temple atop a high rock in the center of Sariwon. The complex of neglected wooden buildings, once said to house more than a hundred monks, was suitably remote and remarkably undamaged. During breaks in their talks officers stepped outside to admire a splendid view: orchards, hills, and rice fields merging mosaiclike southward toward the battlefront. At the distance of a brisk march beyond the last horizon-humps of misty hills the Chinese Peoples' Volunteers waited in concealment for the order to attack.

There was an enormous feeling of optimism throughout the conference, Major Han recalled; Peng was looking forward to ending the war. Confusion in the enemy ranks was obviously increasing. The man called Walker who commanded the U.S. Eighth Army had been killed—in a guerrilla ambush, according to Pyongyang radio—and his replacement, a little-known airborne general with no Asian experience, would hardly have had time to study his maps before the Chinese armies were upon him. The situation was so favorable that the generals were debating whether to swing more strength toward the central front instead of concentrating their main thrust on Seoul. The move was vetoed by the political leadership in Peking, urged on, no doubt, by the North Koreans, who demanded early capture of the puppet capital as the swiftest way of dealing a death blow to enemy morale. Seoul was bound to fall in two or three days. There would be *ample* time afterward to land a body punch elsewhere.

Chinese mobility was improving. The foot-soldiers had reached their jump-off points in a remarkably short time. Some, but by no means all, had made part of the journey by truck. Supplies were now pouring in from Manchuria. The Chinese logistics wizard, General Zhou Chunquan, produced tables to show how well the transportation was holding up. Truck convoys crept each night through Sariwon on their way to the front. Breakdowns had miraculously decreased. Major Han silently doubted whether this was *strictly* accurate; he had seen dozens of stalled trucks on his way down from the Yalu River. But General Zhou claimed his maintenance crews were keeping the majority of vehicles moving.

Thanks to the construction gangs, freight trains were getting through almost as far as Kaesong. Hardy comrades were removing whole sections of track in daytime to fool enemy aerial reconnaissance. The railroad disappeared outside Seoul, the general admitted, and the highways were mined and cratered. From there on the task of transporting food and ammunition farther south fell upon the coolie force conscripted from Manchuria and North Korea. This stage of their supply work was proving understandably difficult. It could only grow worse, General Zhou agreed, the farther the Chinese advanced.

Lieutenant General Kim Ung politely coughed. General Zhou corrected himself. "The farther the Chinese *and* their glorious Korean allies, the [North] Korean People's Army, advance . . ." General Peng Dehuai nodded approvingly. The northerners might play a minor role in this war, but face had to be respected. The North Koreans had in fact astonished the Chinese by the speed at which they had reconstituted their shattered forces. Three new North Korean corps reinforced the eastern flank for the coming offensive. They would be most welcome now that the Chinese Ninth Army Group was temporarily out of action. The cost of their futile encounter with the U.S. Marines at the Changjin Reservoir was the subject of endless rumor.

The conference went on for two days in the Temple of Lustrous Enlightenment. Staff officers gathered in a high-ceilinged hall with faded red pillars where monks had once assembled for instruction. A notice on the door forbad superstitious practices. A dust sheet coyly covered the big gilt Buddha above the northern altar. Beloved Leader Kim Il Sung had created many images—mostly of himself— but refrained from destroying old ones. Ranks of tall wooden bodhisattvas along the temple walls beamed benignly down on these atheist intruders, grouped around the relief model in the middle of the room. The model now showed only the southern part of the Korean peninsula.

General Peng often stayed staring at the model after the others had gone off for a meal. Major Han would slip out to the kitchen and fetch him a bowl of peppery noddle soup; the general sipped it absently, gazing attentively at the painted rivers, the plaster plains and mountains. The chief of staff, Xie Fang, joined him one lunchtime, and together they talked in low voices. Major Han sensed elements of doubt and hesitation shared between them, but failed to pinpoint the reason. Throughout the open discussions, Peng had never sounded more confident. The improved supply situation cheered him up no end. Reports of enemy disarray confirmed his every calculation.

"The imperialists will run like sheep," Peng told the final meeting on December 27. The staff applauded. "Our problem is not Seoul," he went on. "It is Pusan. Not taking it—just walking there!" Everyone laughed.

The general indicated troop dispositions on the model. The Thirteenth Army Group covered two-thirds of a front roughly equivalent to the 38th Parallel. ("The discarded frontier," Peng liked to call it.) The Chinese 38th Field Army, heroes of the Sunchon Road, waited outside Kaesong for the order to thrust straight at Seoul. The 50th Field Army was astride the main Seoul highway. Behind them massed the 39th Field Army, and, to the northwest, the 42nd Field Army, taking an alternate approach pass to Seoul. The 40th and 66th Field Armies, posted south of the Hwachon Reservoir, were ready to drive straight down the central highway through Chunchon to the road junction of Wonju.

"It is there at Wonju," Peng declared, tapping a gnarled finger on the model, "that the battle will be decided. A breakthrough at Wonju will carry us all the way to Taegu." He pointed farther down at the last important inland city south of Seoul. "If we maintain momentum we should be there midway through the Bitter Moon."

The staff applauded again, enthusiastically. The Chinese were moving into the last and bleakest month of their lunar calendar, the Twelfth or Bitter Moon. It was traditionally a time for the settling of accounts, usually of the financial kind, before the New Year festivities—the "spring" festival, as the Communists now preferred to call it. The four-day family celebration of the New Year was for most people in China their sole vacation. With Taegu taken, accounts with the imperialists would virtually be settled.

General Peng brooded on over the model long after the others had said their good-byes. Several times he picked up a pointer and traced imaginary movements. Enemy movements. Adjusting his glasses, he leaned closely across the miniature mountains toward the southern end of the peninsula. "Guerrillas," he muttered. The North Koreans had argued, most persuasively, that two of their divisions cut off after Inchon were tying down large numbers of enemy troops. They might even be able to stop reinforcements arriving from Pusan. General Xie Fang and Major Han watched patiently in the shadows. A high wind moaned outside, rattling the weathered fir trees. Melted snow ran down the paper windows.

"They won't fight," said Peng, almost to himself.

He snatched up his padded winter jacket and strolled slowly back to his room at the rear of the temple. The room had once been a monk's cell. It could not have been more bare as occupied by the general. A camp cot, a battered table, two chairs. A change of clothes in a canvas shoulder bag. Peng's only luxury was a pot-bellied stove whose rusted flue soared through a vent high in the wall. The floor was well swept. Major Han had made the ritual search for spiders. Across the passageway North Korean guards played martial music on the radio. It sounded like a victory march. A woman announcer broke in from time to time and said things in their peculiar language. She sounded immensely cheerful.

Peng called his chief of staff into the room and shut the door. As he did so, Major Han heard Peng say: "I still think we should reinforce the center." Han returned to the conference room to tidy up the papers. Sentries outside saluted smartly. The poor men looked frozen with the cold. They reminded Major Han of the guards outside the Shenyang arsenal when winter first set in. Since then there had been a lot of snow. Earlier in the week, while preparing to leave Shenyang for Korea, Han had noticed children building snowmen in the city streets. Before long housewives would begin preparing special dishes for the lunar holiday. The major leaned against the altar rail smoking a cigarette, thinking of family and home. He found the thought of snowmen cheering.

Seoul, South Korea, January 4, 1951

Seoul was so big. The Chinese had not expected anything like it. The Sharp Swords reached the ridge line overlooking the city shortly before sunset on January 4. They were surprised to see so many tiled roofs, penetrated in places by stumpy towers of brick and concrete, stepping down like a great gray staircase to the brink of the Han

River. Every place else in Korea, including Pyongyang, had been smaller-scale, mean, without much character. But here was one great whore of a city, historic and prosperous, somewhat like old Peking, with a handful of ancient palaces, handsome city gates, and networks of narrow back streets promising no end of unaccustomed delights. Hot food, perhaps a bath; the thought of something approaching civilization aroused the squad from its growing torpor. Big Ears Wong broke into a comic song, juggling three rocks in the air like a circus acrobat. His sidekick, Little Li, picked out a tune on his harmonica. They had found the instrument among the debris by the Sunchon Road. The other men gathered around, clapping and laughing.

Captain Lao Kongcheng was frankly relieved. The exertions of the past months had lately been undermining morale. No one was openly complaining, but the difficulties of bivouacking in a wintry countryside under constant camouflage, the lack of adequate sleep, and increasingly irregular meals had brought the troops to the point of exhaustion. The squad leader noted the growing silence, even sullenness, in the ranks, something he had often encountered in the past toward the end of a particularly demanding campaign. At least he hoped this *was* the end; the way the regimental commander was talking, the present Chinese offensive should just about wind up the war.

Sheer determination had carried Captain Lao through, thus far. There had been times when he feared he would never make it. He settled back in a hollow in the rock face, trying to ease his aching leg. The wound had not proved as serious as first thought and the medics had allowed him no more than a week in field hospital. A soldier had to be totally incapacitated these days to warrant much more attention. Only the worst cases—most of them amputees—were sent back to China. A leg wound like the captain's, sparing the bone but damaging the muscles, rated no more than week-long recuperation at 38th Field Army headquarters, to be spent hobbling around on a stick. Chinese casualties were inevitably mounting. There was a growing shortage of experienced junior officers, especially of men with the nerve and know-how to run commando squads like the Sharp Swords.

It had therefore been an unexpected pleasure to cover most of the advance by truck. They had traveled in motorized comfort down the Ongjin peninsula, then eastward to their start-point outside Kaesong, seldom setting boot to road. The Sharp Swords reckoned they were getting luxury treatment because their colonel wanted them well to the fore when the January 1 offensive jumped off. Many of the regular troops had to march the whole way. But for the last four frenzied days the squad had been solely on foot, fighting much of the way. The worst moment had been the machine-gun post at Munsan-ni manned by Americans who did not seem to know when to retreat. Three GIs with a belt-fed Point Five were shooting holes through the battalion until the squad crawled round and rushed the enemy from the rear. Two of their own men, one of them Young Kung, the would-be commissar, had been killed. The survivors now occupied the heights above Seoul, worn-out and hungry, awaiting orders to infiltrate the city.

Downtown Seoul had taken a nasty battering, though Captain Lao could make out little detail from this overlooking ridge and in the half-light. Fires were burning unchecked around the big domed building marked on his map as an important political objective. The fire-fighting services must have fled. The biggest bonfire by far was on the southern side of the river—possibly at the airfield—where the retreating enemy was indulging in the usual destruction. A single ball of bright orange flame sent up a column of smoke so dense that even the gusting wind failed to disperse it completely. The captain guessed the Americans were getting rid of their fuel reserves. The cost must be enormous. People would have to be immensely rich to stomach losses of that kind.

A letter from Second Aunt in Shanghai, full of patriotic fervor, which reached Captain Lao before the start of the latest offensive, referred—cautiously and obliquely—to the problems the Korean conflict was posing for the Chinese economy. The currency had not long been stabilized in the wake of runaway civil-war inflation. Industrial output was yet to recover from the shock of state takeover. The wages his aunt earned as a seamstress were equivalent to 22 dollars a month, but half would be deducted ("voluntarily," she hastened to add) because her workshop had joined the "Buy Bullets" campaign. Appeals were being launched nationwide to pledge donations toward ammunition purchases for Chinese soldiers at the front.

The captain smiled grimly to himself. Most of the rifle and machine-gun ammunition they had lately been getting—to say nothing of the food—came with the compliments of the U.S. taxpayer. Tons of supplies lay around for the taking in the littered wake of the retreating American army. Chairman Mao had for years been crowing at the ease with which his revolutionaries lived off the imperialists' own arsenals, but even he had not dreamed it could be this easy.

Second Aunt also reported big demonstrations against American imperialism; foreign missionaries were being arrested and expelled. "This is well-deserved," Auntie wrote. "It is common knowledge that missionaries are all spies." The captain was surprised at her tone. His elderly aunt had been converted years ago to Christianity. Maybe she was having second thoughts. He tried to picture the Reverend Browne picked up by militia and pushed across the border at Hong Kong, until he remembered that the poor man had died miserably in Japanese internment. He would be happy now, in the bosom of his God.

Fat Belly Wu, the Sharp Swords' cook, had managed to kindle a small fire behind a captured poncho. Lao thought it extraordinary the way he went on working, undetected, on the ridge top. When it grew dark Wu came around with bowls of chicken noodle soup, ready-made from ration crates in the abandoned American machine-gun post. The dead GIs did not need the food.

Now that the Chinese were advancing so fast, their own supplies no longer arrived. There was a rush to pilfer the small cardboard food boxes the Americans had left behind. These boxes sometimes contained candy bars. The other things inside were thrown away. The foreign soldiers' boots were big, but three of the squad each pulled on a pair. They were better, in this miserable weather, than Chinese-issue canvas sneakers. Newcomers scratched around for American sleeping bags, ponchos, and backpacks, all of superior quality. Ammunition pouches were generously replenished from the vast quantities scattered around. The enemy left untidy battlefields. The only disappointment was a mere three wristwatches. They were, moreover, not considered prime quality. Two went to Big Ears Wong, because he had closed in for the kill with his stick grenades. The other went to Deng, the Korean speaker, the first man to jump into the enemy position. He had not needed to use his bayonet.

It was snowing gently when a runner arrived from the battalion, one hour before dawn. Big wet flakes were settling and freezing on the lichen-covered rock face. Movement was becoming quite hazardous. The runner had fallen several times on the way from headquarters; his face was scratched and bleeding.

But the girl who trotted beside him seemed surer of her footwork. She leaped elegantly across the rocks in what looked like a homemade battle-blouse, a red band on her right arm and a well-oiled American carbine swinging around her neck. Her name was Comrade Li. Her job was to steer them safely into Seoul. The squad heartily approved of the idea. Their guide was a dainty little Korean, not more than 18 years old, with clean-scrubbed face and pigtails. She bowed farewell to the runner, shook hands with all 30 members of the Sharp Swords, and giggled modestly behind her hand in the most ladylike manner. Chatting to Korean-speaking Deng on the path down the mountain, she described herself as a university student whose father was also involved in the resistance. Nothing had been seen or heard of him for days. There were rumors that he had been snatched by the puppet South Korean police, but she still hoped he was alive. All this said in a brusque, matter-of-fact manner.

The Sharp Swords came on the first bodies in the northern suburbs of Seoul. The houses here were small but stylish, built clear of the ground on square stone piles amid miniature Japanese-style gardens. Stacked around a large stone lantern were the stiffened remains of some ten men and women, stretched out in the snow, their hands bound behind them. Comrade Li turned the bodies over tenderly. Identification was difficult. Shots through the back of the head can badly disfigure the face. The girl peered into the blood-stained features and shook her head. There was nobody she recognized. More corpses were lying around as they pushed deeper into the city, though some of these could have been looters. No citizens came out to explain. Anyone who still lived in this eerie urban sprawl was keeping carefully out of sight. Buses and streetcars stood stranded in the roadways exactly as their drivers had left them. There were a few autos, too, obviously the worse for wear. A sharp movement in a side street sent the squad leaping into doorways, rifles at the ready. Closer examination revealed an unfastened door, banging in the wind.

"They can't all have gone!" growled Fat Belly Wu. His hopes of finding a bathhouse heated up and ready to go were fading. Comrade Li explained through Trooper Deng's translation that most people had evacuated the northern part of the city because they feared there would be too much street fighting. The NKPA had desperately defended every meter, the Korean girl proudly declared, after the imperialists pulled off that dirty trick at Inchon. But the Yankees and their puppets had fled, like frightened children. The dreadful thing was—and now she spoke softly, with lowered eyes—the imperialists had kidnapped many of the inhabitants at gunpoint, *forcing* thousands south across the Han River into the freezing countryside, where most of them would doubtless die.

The Sharp Swords advanced through Seoul in two extended files, wary as wildcats. Softly they circled streets of burning houses. The wood was going up like tinder. No foe could survive such an inferno. And yet the blazing emptiness was charged with menace. Imaginary snipers lurked in every alleyway. A sound like pistol shots sent them ducking for cover but it was only glass windows shattering in the heat. "Nice to feel warm again," joked Big Ears Wong. Captain Lao, still slightly hobbling, read the exhaustion in the tall trooper's face.

The squad jumped nervously again when Comrade Li let out a tiny shriek The girl was pointing in the direction of the political building. The captain assumed it was some sort of party headquarters. On top of its dome, shimmering through the flames, flew a large North Korean flag. It was red, white, and blue with a red central star; the Chinese had been taught to recognize it in recent weeks. Surely that meant the downtown area must be secure? They were starting to head through clouds of smoke in the direction of the flag when the first North Korean resistance group appeared. These comrades came out of a tile-fronted office block carrying a larger-than-lifesize portrait of Kim Il Sung. The last few days, they said, had been spent hiding in a cellar. Several of the freedom fighters seemed to know Comrade Li, and there were guttural exchanges in the Korean language. The most important news was that the girl's father was safe. He had escaped the puppet gendarmerie and found sanctuary with a guerrilla group outside the city.

A burst of gunfire crackled overhead as the Sharp Swords entered the grounds of the domed building. Comrade Li ran boldly into the open, waving her arms and shouting. Men with red arm bands waved back from the big, broken windows. The girl led the squad to the front door, picking a delicate path through mounds of broken glass, and introduced them to a squarely built, middle-aged man who called himself the chairman of the revolutionary committee. The man delivered a short welcoming speech through Deng, acknowledging Chinese assistance in the liberation struggle but emphasizing that Seoul had for the second time been liberated by Korean patriots.

The Sharp Swords were ushered into an unheated, ransacked office and served bowls of a thin meat soup containing shreds of beef. There was no need to post sentries, the North Koreans declared, but Captain Lao insisted. He sent two men up the tower with his valuable binoculars, recalling how Young Kung would have enjoyed the chore. He had sat entranced for hours, watching the Sunchon ambush. But the young man who dreamed of becoming a commissar lay buried alongside Americans in the machine-gun post at Munsan-ni. The captain posted his own men alongside the resistance fighters at the windows. For all he knew, the Sharp Swords were the only Chinese troops inside the city. The time was 1100, January 5, and he sent one of the youngest squad members back with a Korean escort to advise the battalion commander about the absence of resistance.

Pretty Comrade Li stayed on in the building describing her adventures to awed members of the resistance committee. Big Ears Wong and Little Li, Fat Belly Wu and Korean-speaking Deng, together with other troopers not needed for immediate duty, slept soundly on the floor. Captain Lao dozed off, dreaming of the bathhouse the North Koreans promised to treat them to, as soon as life returned to normal. His leg was throbbing when he awoke.

People were beginning to stir in the street outside. A small crowd, fluttering paper flags, gathered in front of the building. The committee chairman addressed them through a bullhorn. The crowd grew. Columns of people came streaming up from the direction of the river conducted by resistance fighters wearing the now-familiar red arm bands. Many of the women carried bundles on their heads. These unfortunate people had been rescued from the imperialists in the nick of time, Comrade Li explained; most of them had been saved as they were about to be driven off across the frozen river. It was a wonderful deliverance. The women wept for joy. The enemy had tried to destroy Seoul and leave it uninhabited, but the plan had been foiled. The committee chairman said as much through the bullhorn. The people cheered. Many went on weeping.

Collaborators involved in this dreadful crime would be brought to justice, the chairman thundered—Deng whispering his translation into the captain's ear—and a flutter went through the crowd as people looked nervously at their neighbors. The Korean girl, Comrade Li, was introduced as a heroine of the resistance. She took the bullhorn in her giggly, modest way and shouted something that evoked more cheers. Deng stopped translating, looking surprised.

"Well, what did she say?" Captain Lao demanded impatiently. Their dainty little guide was prancing up and down brandishing her carbine, leading the crowd in a patriotic song.

"She said traitors must be killed like rats," said Deng. He hesitated. "It wasn't so much what she said. It was the *way* she said it."

A photographer popped up taking pictures. The chairman brought him back into the building, where the resistance fighters struck heroic poses, aiming their rifles through the windows. The Chinese were smilingly ignored. The crowds thinned again as the main body of 38th Field Army started pouring through the streets. The 1st Battalion, 347th Regiment, to which the Sharp Swords belonged, took over the domed building accompanied by a group of Korean officers. The North Koreans requisitioned all the least-damaged office space. The Sharp Swords were ordered out of the room they occupied, congratulated on showing exceptional initiative, and ushered into a large, empty house nearby. Too tired even to eat, the captain and his men slept away the night.

The squad awoke to find the floor they were lying on grown warm. Comrade Li could be seen outside with a small party of civilians stoking the furnace. Old women were arranging meat and vegetables for a meal. Fat Belly Wu cursed prodigiously. These people were encroaching on *his* prerogatives. But he soon came back in with Deng, plainly delighted. Their guide was preparing a feast, Korean-style, and a visit to the bathhouse down the street. The place had been specially opened on orders of the revolutionary committee. The troopers went off in two groups, scrubbed themselves down on little wooden stools, washed away the soap and dirt, and wallowed in the big central bath. Only when he began peeling off his uniform did the captain realize how filthy they had all become. He shaved and changed into his spare set of clean underwear, leaving the dirty laundry with the bath attendants.

Back at the house the North Koreans had prepared a bubbling casserole of dogmeat and turnips, which they served on low tables in a room strewn with cushions. The chairman of the revolutionary committee joined them for the meal and downed frequent toasts of fiery local liquor. It was the sort of drink that gave men renewed vigor. Each bottle contained a small, dead snake as testimony to its potency. Big Ears Wong grew redder and redder in the face. Comrade Li did not drink. She instead knelt at the captain's elbow, handing him his wine-cup between the fingertips of both hands. Most ladylike. Lao could not imagine those delicate fingers curling around a trigger. But small talk bored her. She only wanted to hear about combat. Pouting her pretty lips she begged the captain, through Deng, to retell the story of the Unsan action. His diffident description of the sneak attack on the cavalrymen's camp evoked squeals of the most unladylike delight.

Late afternoon, the runner arrived. The same slip-footed boy with the scratched face poked his head into the dining room, amazed to find it crowded with fellow soldiers lolling around the floor. "Some quarters!" he mumbled enviously. "Fuck off!" belched Fat Belly Wu. The cook was propped up against a paper wall-panel picking his teeth. "Captain Lao is wanted at the battalion command post," said the runner. "The commander says it's urgent."

Lao and the runner returned by truck through darkening streets. Troops and civilians were busy dousing the downtown fires. The worst was clearly under control, although much of the old shopping district seemed doomed. The sun had sunk into the growing smoke pall thrown off by the blazing dumps across the river. Above the ridge line sailed the slender crescent of the reborn moon—the Twelfth, the Bitter Moon—promising cold days, warm hearts, and new beginnings. Captain Lao hoped it would bring them luck. During the day, while the squad was cleaning and carousing, the 1st Battalion command post had moved out of the domed building into the old Japanese barracks at Yongsong, until recently the headquarters of the Americans. It was a two- or three-kilometer drive. The cold evening air cleared the captain's head. He felt rejuvenated by his bath and banquet. The battle must be going well, he told himself, and the advance was about to be resumed. The prospect both elated and daunted him. The men were worn out. But maybe the war could now be finished without much trouble.

"One last push," said the battalion commander. He was a new man brought in to replace their longtime colonel, who had been killed beside the Sunchon Road. "Got to keep advancing. Haven't any choice." He was a stout, shy man, gray-faced with fatigue, who spat out his speech in staccato bursts as if trying to make himself sound more convincing.

"We're ready to go," Captain Lao said gently. He thought of the squad, burping contentedly in the billet. "Tomorrow?"

"Tonight!" snapped the battalion comander. "Everyone's moving. We'll be right behind you."

He caught the look on the captain's face and strode over to the wall map. "Look, comrade, the enemy is on the run. If we follow through now we can keep the Americans off balance. Probably for good. We won't do it sitting on our backsides here. The high command, the party, the motherland, is appealing for one last great effort"—he thumped the plastic covering of the map—"across the river and down the coastal highway. Take Suwon and Osan"—he pointed out the towns, unsure how to pronounce the names—"and straight on to the south. Don't stop. You'll be in good company."

He beckoned Captain Lao closer to the map, which was covered with colored markings.

"Elements of 50th Field Army have already crossed the Han River east of here. The 39th is crossing to the west, between here and Inchon. We've got to keep up. Our crowd will go straight on down the Suwon highway. No problems. Should be all over by the spring [lunar New Year] festival."

The desk phone rang and a long argument ensued with the transportation regiment. The commander sat down rubbing his weary eyes.

"Supply troubles?" asked Captain Lao. Food had grown desperately short in the last stages of the advance on Seoul.

"Troubles," admitted the battalion commander. He shuffled nervously through his paperwork, eyes on the desk. "Emergency rations for a while. Take time to organize transportation south of the river." He looked up quizzically. "There'll be a lot more stuff abandoned, I suppose?"

"There'd better be," said the captain.

Two trucks transported the Sharp Swords to the Han riverbank. It was two o'clock in the morning and they were not in the best of spirits. Despite the hour, the battalion commander was waiting to see them off. He spoke a few comforting words about swiftly concluding the war. The men did not respond with their customary enthusiasm.

But they brightened up when they saw Comrade Li. The girl comrade gravely shook hands with each man. With a demure little bow she handed the captain a farewell present. He was surprised to receive a hand grenade.

"Throw it for me," she panted in an excited voice. Captain Lao managed a confused reply. He lead the squad out on the ice. The girl shouted after them. Deng shook his head in disbelief.

"She wishes she could come with us," he told he captain. "She thinks it would be fun."

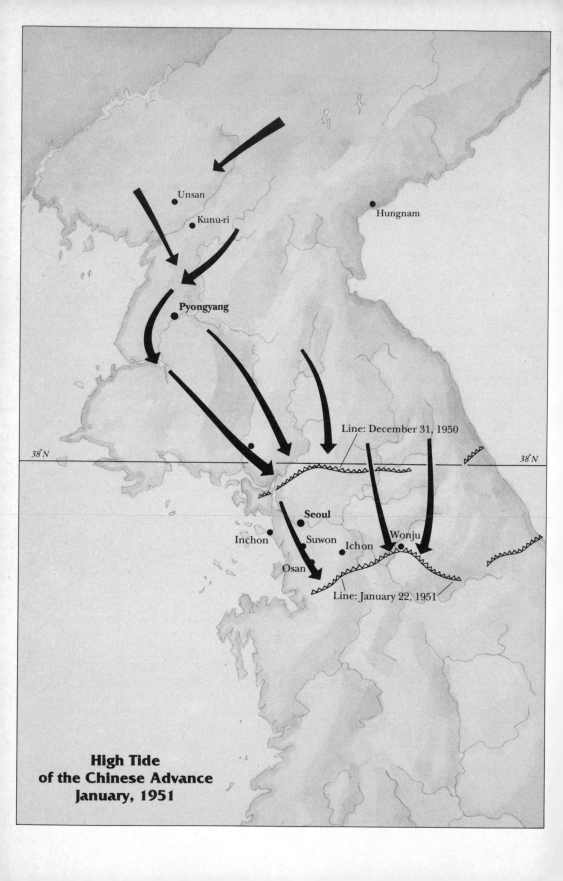

Unsan

Kunu-ri

Hungnam

Pyongyang

Line: December 31, 1950

38°N   38°N

Seoul

Inchon   Suwon   Ichon   Wonju

Osan

Line: January 22, 1951

**High Tide
of the Chinese Advance
January, 1951**

16

High Tide of the Chinese Advance / The Sharp Swords Meet the Meatgrinder /MacArthur Heads Home.

Outskirts of Wonju,
South Korea,
January 15, 1951

Jia Peixing sat down and cried in the snow. He was tired and hungry, though that was nothing new; the 18-year-old runner had seldom been anything else since his regiment launched its moonlight assault across the Chungchon River six weeks earlier. Life had dissolved into a series of forced marches, skimped meals, and sharp, periodic skirmishes that never quite destroyed the enemy. There were days when the young runner really wondered whether the generals knew what they were doing. The latest Chinese offensive at the beginning of January had convinced him the war was as good as over. Yet here they were, two weeks later, still blundering without apparent purpose all over the Korean countryside. It was rather like swatting flies. Some peculiarly agile survivors always evaded your best efforts. The same with the Americans: you hit out and off they hopped to a safe but tempting distance.

Entirely the wrong way of looking at things, admonished Colonel

Gu Dehua. The big man made patient efforts to keep his junior staff in touch with all developments in the field. But he was obviously feeling the strain. The colonel had lost a lot of weight. The bristle on his close-cropped head was completely white. Rumor had it he'd run out of hair dye; middle-aged Chinese often darkened their graying hairs.

Colonel Gu stoutly maintained the battle was going exceptionally well. Of course there were temporary supply shortages. The 40th Field Army had been ordered to undertake an arduous advance through the central part of South Korea. They had done so well that logistics could not keep up. Now the Chinese were bearing down on the town of Wonju, which stood astride the intersection of two important highways that roughly bisected the country. A swift turn to the west at this point, the colonel said, would carry them behind the U.S. Eighth Army, which was still regrouping after the loss of Seoul. The plan, so far, was working. Three Chinese field armies were pouring through the enemy's central defenses, with more men marching up to support them.

On January 13, the 120th Division, of which the 385th Regiment was part, passed through Hoengsong, or what was left of it, a farming town on the main highway some ten kilometers north of Wonju. From there on, for the next two days, the regiment had been staggering through snowdrifts so deep that each footstep became an effort. Rations ran out. And the Americans had begun to offer surprisingly stiff resistance. That afternoon, pushing through a gentle snowstorm, the regimental headquarters was caught by shell fire while crossing a shallow valley dotted with ruined farms. Several men were killed, including the second-in-command. The rest found whatever shelter they could as the earth shook and exploded around them.

The boy called Jia sat in midfield and cried. He'd had enough. The veteran of one year's soldiering and half a dozen battles wanted out of the Korean war. He wanted only to go home. Three weeks from today his family would be bidding farewell to the Year of the Tiger. There would be firecrackers and feasts to welcome the Year of the Hare. The lunar New Year was a time for family. He wanted to share the festival with Mother and Father, brothers and sisters, Venerable Grandmother, and Number One Uncle, and the distant cousin they had decided he should marry.

Fresh salvos showered the sobbing runner with dirt and biting pebbles. "Hit the ground!" someone shouted. Jia took no notice. He imagined himself back in Fushun preparing for the festival. Venerable Grandmother would be up to her usual tricks. She liked to hang a sign on the neighbor's wall saying "Prosperity to those living opposite."

Last year the block committee made her take it down. Father was sure to be relaquering the red front door, while Mother swept the bad luck out of the house. Then Mother would paste brightly colored portraits of the guardian gods on either doorpost. The custom was supposed to date back to the middle of the seventh century. Impish spirits had disturbed the dreams of the great emperor T'ai Tsung after his troops met military disaster in Korea. But two of his faithful generals volunteered to stand night guard outside the imperial bedroom until the conscience-stricken emperor slept peacefully. Paper likenesses of the generals had ever since guarded most Chinese homes throughout the festival.

The enemy shell fire switched to a battalion plodding forward in column farther down the valley. Troops scattered when the fountains of earth and snow erupted among them. The sound of the explosions thumped back on the wind, delayed, momentarily, by the distance. "Some swine's got us in his sights!" yelled the commissar. Colonel Gu looked back and nodded grimly. He saw Jia sitting upright in the snow and summoned a medic. A litter bearer loped over in the strangely crouched position men adopt under fire. The young runner wiped his tears. "It's a gut-ache," he said. His story was half true; for several days he had been suffering from diarrhea. "Not surprising with this shelling," said the medic sympathetically. "Keep your head down or your guts will be the least of your worries."

They camped at dusk in the shell of a nearby farm. The cook passed around mugs of boiling water made from the melted snow. Officers and men sat sipping their "white tea" and talking endlessly about food. The horrors of past famines were lugubriously recalled. Stories were told of starving Chinese peasants eating grass, tree bark, even boiled mud. "I think you can actually cook American boots," the commissar suggested tentatively. "I've heard the leather is quite edible if you simmer it long enough." The staff did not enthuse. Jia chewed on a webbing strap to stave off the hunger pangs. The medic gave him an herbal drink to ease his queasy stomach.

"Supplies should be up tomorrow," Colonel Gu brightly repeated. "We'll take Wonju. Transport will reach us there." He looked reassuringly around at the regimental staff, gathered for the assault briefing. Outside in the snow a burial detail was piling stones on the bodies of the second-in-command and the other three men killed in the afternoon shelling. The ground was too hard to dig graves. Jia could hear the stones clinking together on top of the corpses. Drowsily he caught the rumble of American artillery above the officers' muttered talk. The prospect of another battle depressed him. He was close to the breaking point but refused to acknowledge it. "We storm Wonju at moonset," said Colonel Gu, winding up the meeting.

"We should find plenty to eat there." He shook hands all round, as he always did, cheerful as ever, wishing each man good luck. The young runner he took aside.

"It's hard," the colonel said, and his face was grave. Many men were showing the runner's neurotic symptoms. "It's hard for us all. Tell me, are you homesick?" Jia denied it. "Wouldn't blame you if you were," said the colonel, patting him kindly on the shoulder. "I've a wife and four children. This is the time I miss them most. The children love the festival." He stared out across the moonlit landscape. The snowy hills glowed bright as day. The colonel examined them thoughtfully. "You'll get new strength," he said. "You will surprise yourself."

The divisional attack went in at 0200. Thousands of Chinese riflemen rose shouting to their feet, leaping through the snow in open irregular lines. The waning moon glinted on their bayonets. Bugles blew and whistles shrilled, and officers leaped to the fore yelling encouragement. The lines of men bunched up the farther they advanced; belief was spreading among the Chinese that in these dying days of war sheer weight of numbers would overwhelm the enemy. Star shells and parachute flares lit up the battleground, revealing the town ahead in wavering, silvery light. Mortar bombs dropped among the houses. A roof caught fire, and then another, and soon the whole town was blazing. But the enemy hung on, bouncing tracer into the approaching riflemen, calling down gusts of shells that blew great gaps in the encroaching lines. The snow was blood-stained now, heaped high with bodies, but still the Chinese waves kept lapping onward until assault troops with their satchel charges and grenades were well inside the burning streets of Wonju, shooting, bayoneting, grappling with half-seen shadows in house after burning house.

Colonel Gu kept well forward, in his customary way, tossing grenades through gaping windows and personally disabling a truck that tried to get away. A burst from his submachine gun set the engine steaming. Another burst cut down the occupants who tried to flee. They were Americans, sprawled grotesquely among the Chinese dead, some still alive and calling feebly for the medics. "Get their boots!" ordered the commissar, searching the bodies for ration packs. Hungry troops rifled the truck and found only ammunition. "Can't eat bullets," the colonel laughed, though he was clearly disappointed. "No matter. The supply train will get through tomorrow." He sounded so convincing that for the next two days Jia Peixing actually believed him.

The troops were disappointed to learn that the capture of Wonju did not wind up the war. The Americans did not bug out, as they had in the past; instead they fell back six kilometers in good fighting order to a low ridge overlooking the town. From there they fired air bursts over the burning rooftops into the triumphant Chinese crowding through the streets. Shell splinters showered among the jostling soldiery. Men ran, ducked, screamed, and fell. The enemy was making more lethal use of his artillery. Colonel Gu Dehua sheltered in a doorway shouting orders. A sliver of hot metal had cut his hand. Jia was sent off, his resolution temporarily restored, to prod 1st Battalion into further advance. Seizing Wonju had cost the Chinese plenty. The ridge would cost them still more. Picking a pathway across the snow-covered valley, past tangles of frosted corpses, the runner wondered where the regiment would find the manpower.

The men who had survived the moonset assault looked cold and miserable. Jia Peixing came across small clumps of Chinese riflemen and machine gunners shivering in the ditches and lifeless orchards. They seemed keener on keeping out of the wind than attacking the enemy. "Any sign of the rations?" all of them asked. Parties of shabby, unshaven men were picking through farmyards in the early morning light, hacking at rocklike vegetable fields, in hope of finding forgotten or unharvested crops. One man raised a cheer when he uncovered a handful of tiny, frost-bitten turnips.

Now that Jia could read a sketch map he had little difficulty locating the battalion command post. It stood in a roofless rice mill two kilometers to the east of Wonju. The building, needless to say, was bare of flour. Staff were sweeping the rubble-strewn floor in search of unhusked grain. The battalion commander sat before a pile of blazing lumber, sourly sipping hot water. He was the same small, schoolmasterly man the runner had first met across the Chungchon among the captured American guns. These past few weeks he had grown thinner, dirtier, and distinctly more ill-tempered.

"You might have brought some food," the commander grumbled as Jia delivered his message. The officer read it, crumpled the rice paper into a ball, and threw it onto the fire. "Amazing!" was all he said. Officers gathered around inquiringly. The commander glowered at them. "Regiment says to advance," he told them. Somebody groaned. "We're down to half strength, if that," said the man who seemed to be the acting second-in-command. "The troops are worn out," said a third man, who looked like a senior sergeant. The commander nodded gloomily. "I know, I know," he said, climbing heavily to his feet. It was then that Jia noticed the bloodstains on his jacket. "All the same, comrades, we have our orders. Battalion will advance after sunset."

Near Ichon,
Southeast of Seoul,
January 16, 1951

The men filling the gaps in the Chinese ranks were little better than cannon fodder. The colonel said so openly at divisional briefing. Other battalion commanders agreed. Only the smallest handful of recent replacements had gone through the assault school in the Lung Kang Mountains, not far from Tunghua in eastern Manchuria, where conditions were similar to those in Korea. Those who had gone through the assault course learned to march long distances over mountainous terrain, live rough in the open, and cope with the general rigors of a winter campaign. But the majority of the more recent recruits, the flood of volunteers signed up in the heat of the "Hate America" campaign, had emerged from three weeks' boot camp just able to march in step. Weapons practice was invariably skimped. It ate up too much time and ammunition. Men reported to their units unable to fire a rifle.

"It's downright ridiculous!" Colonel Yang complained to the divisional commander. He had spent two frustrating weeks trying to lick the latest replacements into shape. "Half of them have never seen an M-1 rifle," he declared. "They trained on Soviet rifles." The new armies being formed in northern China were handsomely equipped with Soviet arms. Unfortunately, none of this largesse had yet reached the Chinese Peoples' Volunteers.

Colonel Yang realized he sounded crotchety. The wiry little Hunanese had not fully recovered from the satchel-charge blast in the Gauntlet on the Sunchon Road. The stitches still shone white on his shaven scalp. The aftereffects of the concussion bequeathed him a constant headache. But he was determined to have his say.

Major General Wang Yang called for silence. This was a briefing, not a gripe session. "Manpower will triumph over machines," he soothingly intoned.

"Not if the men don't eat!" snapped Yao of the crack 347th Regiment. It was the regiment to which Colonel Yang's battered 2nd Battalion belonged.

The general looked pained, pausing in silent rebuke at this unseemly outburst. "Problems will be overcome." He spoke slowly and forcefully. "The advance so far has been magnificent. The Americans are fleeing in disorder." He held up one of the map cases every officer now carried. "Despite the weather, Ichon fell without difficulty. On our left, Wonju has already been taken. The brave comrades of 40th Field Army fought their way into the town yesterday morning. Farther east the puppet South Korean troops are collapsing. The situation is developing much as it did on the Chungchon River."

The general paced up and down in front of the wall maps, brandishing a pointer. Colonel Yang felt he was back in the village school. Any moment now the schoolmaster would beat him into an unhappy attempt at the Eight Characters.

"All available strength is being concentrated here in the center." General Wang indicated an area midway between Seoul and the eastern mountains. "It is here that our offensive is making the most important gains. The momentum of our advance must be maintained. There is talk of reaching Taegu. The war would then be over. Questions?" He silenced his audience before anyone had the chance to speak. "Of course I know about the supply, er, shortages. I am assured by 39th Field Army that supplies are on their way by road this minute."

He peered into his audience looking for Colonel Yang. The colonel stood up. "Old Yang," he said with measured politeness. "You and your men were all heroes on the Sunchon road. I fully understand your feelings about the latest replacements. I look to you to make *them* into heroes."

He pushed through the crush and shook the colonel's hand. "Problems will be overcome," he repeated. A politician to his fingertips, thought Yang. Orderlies moved among them with trays of hot tea. Real tea. "Supplies are on their way," said General Wang with a knowing look. "Soon we'll be joined by new Chinese armies, fully equipped by our Soviet friends and comrades."

"Unless we finish the war first," quipped Yao of the 347th.

"Of course, of course," chuckled General Wang, ushering them out the door. He seemed glad to see their backs. An aloof man and a hard one. The colonel left reluctantly. The command post at 116th Division, a commandeered farmhouse, was delightfully warm. Colonel Yang was beginning to forget what warmth felt like. Most days he was frozen to the marrow. Regimental commander Yao offered him a ride back in his brand-new Russian truck.

"Got a present with this truck," said Yao, the illiterate offspring of poor Shandong peasants. "Compliments of the Soviet aid mission. Supposed to be food. But do you know what I found? A big can of black fish eggs. Disgusting!"

"Some barbarians consider fish eggs a delicacy," Colonel Yang told him, remembering his days on the Yangtse steamer. "Russians especially like it."

"Like that cheese and butter they eat," sneered Yao. "Fucking barbarians!"

Quietly they compared notes about the state of the war, the state of the army. "I hear our 40th Field Army took a beating yesterday at Wonju," said Yao. He had higher access than Yang to classified signals traffic. "Their advance is stalled. The Yankees are still fighting.

Harder than ever, I'd say. All this talk of them running!" He looked into Yang's eyes, a crooked smile splitting his ugly face. "I'm glad you mentioned the replacements. It's scandalous."

"I'm glad you mentioned the rations," said Colonel Yang. "We can't go on like this forever." Yao dug the colonel in the ribs, waxing confidential. "Tell me, now. How do *you* think things are shaping up? All this bullshit about Taegu! With untrained replacements and damn-all food I'd say we aren't heading anywhere but back." The colonel sat silent. Morale was bad enough without officers indulging in defeatist talk. But the truth was hurtful.

Rations had arrived by the time Colonel Yang returned to 2nd Battalion. There was no great quantity—a few sacks of maize, some sugar, salt, tea, and canned fish—but it gave the riflemen new life. A convoy of trucks had negotiated the snowbound highway between Seoul and Ichon which led on, ultimately, to Wonchon and Wonju. More than 100 coolies followed next day with sadly depleted loads. The poor, frozen creatures had consumed as much as they delivered. After that, nothing arrived for a week.

By then the Chinese had fought themselves to a standstill. The 39th Field Army drove desperately toward Wonchon in the depths of the Korean winter. Snow drifted man-high. Temperatures fell to record lows. American artillery pulverized them in open country. Groping forward in waist-deep snow the riflemen found little shelter. The skirmishing line wavered and broke as the newer men fled the barrage. Shells tore into the snowdrifts, the underlying fields, destroying whole squads in bloody eruptions of cascading rubble. Yang's second-in-command, Major Ma, tried vainly to rally the fleeing men before he too fell beneath the shells.

Colonel Yang ordered the bugler to sound retreat. It was a long time since he'd had to do so. Some of the replacements did not even recognize the call. They huddled among the shell craters, too terrified to move. Sergeants had to kick them back onto their feet. Medics gathered up the walking wounded. The rest they would have to leave. The cold would kill them off fast enough. The battalion streamed back into a frozen gully beside the highway. Fewer than 200 men were still able to march. Among them was Commissar Wong Wiyu, wounded in the Unsan skirmish, and now blinded by a shell blast. The commissar leaned uncertainly on a medic, heavily bandaged, whimpering quietly. The colonel put his arm around him.

"Come along, Old Wong," Colonel Yang said gently. "Let's both of us walk back together."

Suwon,
South Korea,
January 20, 1951

Retreat did not unduly bother 50th Field Army. They had marched a mighty long way from the Yalu River, beating the better-equipped barbarians with acceptable losses. The final advance beyond the old walled city of Suwon had been the most punishing—the Americans hit hard with well-directed firepower—and the order to withdraw came as something of a relief. One regiment had been badly mangled in the open countryside, pitting rifles and machine guns against artillery and tanks. The Chinese end-the-war offensive was suddenly petering out south of the Han River.

"Taegu my ass!" groaned Trooper Liu, limping back along the highway on infected feet. A disease called trench foot was spreading alarmingly. The trooper tugged unhappily at his badly worn boots. "Next, you know," he grumbled, "we'll be defending Seoul."

Sergeant Gu Wentu nodded grimly. He understood what was happening. The Chinese Communists always outran their meager supply services. Their armies had persistently done so throughout the Chinese civil war; here in this empty, unfriendly land, faced with crucial shortages of food and ammunition, the Chinese tide was ebbing. They were being forced to pull back and regroup.

"We'll advance again," the sergeant said philosophically.

"You'll see me *dead* first," snarled Liu. Realizing he had uttered words of ill omen he snatched a talisman from his pocket and touched it to his forehead. Somewhere in his knapsack the trooper carried a slim packet of joss sticks—this the sergeant knew—and at the next halt he would sneak off and burn a couple for good luck. The practice was forbidden, of course, by the commissars, and not merely on superstitious grounds. It was lunacy to wander too far afield. The Americans had sown land mines everywhere. Two men had been blown to bits in recent days, creeping away for a quiet crap.

One-eyed Colonel Pang puffed past, an impressive figure even without his horse. His glass eye was frosted completely, giving him a glazed and ghoulish look. Snow speckled his mustache and eyebrows. He had aged a lot since his heroic stand at Hengyang, when the Nationalists had driven the Japanese out of the railroad station, then held on stubbornly for three more crippling days. That had been six or seven years ago. The action in faraway Hunan had been hailed during the anti-Japanese war as one of China's most significant victories.

"Get moving!" Pang barked as he bustled by swathed in coats and furs. Sergeant Gu had fought at his side in Hengyang, but the colonel never knew it. The old martinet recognized no names or faces below the rank of major. The sergeant preferred him still on horseback. Officers should ride at the head of their troops, he privately believed, not slog alongside carrying rifles like enlisted men. He felt sorry about that horse. The colonel had given him a slice of the sweet, barbecued flesh when they slaughtered the starving beast after bypassing Seoul. The battalion then found its commander a jeep picked up from an American airfield. He had driven it in style all the way to Osan until their gas supplies ran out. They had destroyed it, humanely, with a bullet through the engine.

"Doesn't it ever stop snowing?" moaned Trooper Liu. Other men took up the refrain. Give some of them the chance, the sergeant thought, and they would pack it in, here and now.

"Be thankful for snow," growled Sergeant Gu. "It blinds the Yankee airmen." Clearer weather would force them cross-country in the moonlight, not marching at midday, and in full column, straight up the road to Seoul.

The 444th Regiment began building a defense line at Kimpo Airfield. They were an unlucky bunch, the troops agreed; among Chinese the number *four* is extremely inauspicious. In some dialects it sounds uncannily like the word for *death*. Triple four was therefore three times as deadly, and recruits occasionally deserted rather than join an outfit so obviously doomed. But veterans were fatalistic. Soldiers were a despised breed anyway, no matter what their rank. Suffering and death were predictable. Lately some of the men had publicly referred to themselves as "The Three Times Dead."

This gloomy talk disturbed Regimental Commissar Wu, popularly known as Pig-Snout. "Do you think this regroupment has had any serious effect on morale?" the large-nosed commissar asked Sergeant Gu. The senior sergeants were supposed to have their fingers on the outfit's pulse. "Wouldn't worry too much," replied the sergeant. (He kept forgetting to say "comrade.") "These men will fight when they have to. It's just that we all hoped the war was over . . . comrade." The commissar nodded thoughtfully. The sergeant knew what was on his mind. They were all turncoats. These troops had surrendered once and could do so again. "Don't worry, comrade," said Sergeant Gu. "The 50th will fight."

Pyongtaek, South Korea, Mid-January, 1951

The high tide of Chinese advance touched the town of Pyongtaek, some 45 miles south of Seoul. Patrols of 38th Field Army reached the town's outskirts on January 13, after marching unopposed through Osan, past its blazing airfield, and on down the coastal highway.

First to infiltrate the outskirts of the empty town was the special duties squad of the 1st Battalion, 347th Regiment, also known as the Sharp Swords. Things had changed, they found. No pretty young resistance fighters appeared, as in Seoul, to guide them through the moonlight. The few civilians they encountered looked downright *hostile*. The Americans had stopped retreating. Their machine guns promptly pinned the squad down in a suburban cemetery. Artillery soon drove them out. The Chinese fell back into the frozen fields awaiting a prearranged regimental attack. It never materialized. A runner arrived instead, ordering a general withdrawal. The battalion was regrouping in Suwon. The army was clean out of supplies.

Captain Lao Kongcheng was more disappointed than surprised. It had been obvious since they crossed the Han River that the offensive was running out of steam. The same situation had arisen after the ambush on the Sunchon road. The entire field army spent nearly a month refurbishing before the drive on Seoul. At that time the Americans could not stop running. Now, however, they were determined to resist. Plenty of tough combat obviously lay ahead. The rumor was that fresh Chinese armies would be needed for the showdown. Present forces would fight a holding action in Korea until the reinforcements arrived.

"Surely we don't need *more* men?" asked Korean-speaking Deng. "With our present strength all we've got to do is piss together and wash the Yankees out."

"What's the good of men if you can't feed 'em?" replied Fat Belly Wu. It was a week since the squad cook had scraped together enough for a hot meal. They had lived mostly off the pickled Korean cabbage, *kimche*, which they sometimes found buried in jars in deserted farmyards.

"I could go another pig," said Big Ears Wong. "This cabbage gives me the shits." He was limping forward under the weight of the mortar base plate. Little Li carried the detachable mortar tube. Frostbite had nipped both men's hands and feet.

"We might bag a wild dog," Little Li said hopefully. Packs of dogs were scavenging among the thousands of refugee corpses scattered around the surrounding fields. The Sharp Swords had come across three dignified old men squatting, frozen, quite dead, beside a stream. The dogs had found them first.

"I don't mind dog, but not one of *those*," sniffed Deng. The thought of the old men still made him feel sick. He drew a scarf across his face to ward off the cutting wind. He turned the talk to pleasanter things. "It will be the festival soon," he said.

Chinese New Year, 1951, was to begin on February 5, according to the lunar calendar. Families would exchange gifts and lucky money in red envelopes and eat special foods—the squad thought only of food. "My mother makes a special kind of *do fu*," said Deng. "It's pink-colored, flavored with almonds."

"Pig," said Big Ears Wong. "I like roast pig."

They paused on a treeless hilltop, concealed by the long dry grass. American jets whistled high overhead. Enemy air activity had lately declined with the loss of their forward airfields. "But any plane you see," the Chinese told one another, "is bound to be theirs." The Soviet-supplied MIGs of the Chinese air force stuck close to their sanctuaries in Manchuria.

Captain Lao scanned the valley with his binoculars. Snow as far as the eye could see. Sparse trees, isolated farms, no signs of life. Directly below lay the town of Osan, roofless, empty; the black patch nearby would probably be the airfield. He made up his mind to reach the airfield by nightfall and rummage around for food before completing the withdrawal to Suwon.

Smoke rose from the hillside farm they passed on the way down. Curious, they poked around the farmyard. An iron pot stood boiling unattended over a smoldering fire. The farmers had fled. They searched the area and found several old women shivering in a ruined barn. The oldest woman pleaded with the Chinese not to take their food. The captain's offer to pay for it provoked cackles of cynical laughter. "You're all the same," the old woman shrieked at Deng in an uncharacteristic outburst. The Korean-speaking trooper patiently explained. The Chinese came to Korea as friends, liberators, supporters of the poor and the oppressed. The women fell sullenly silent.

Captain Lao led the Sharp Swords into Osan depressed and irritated. Throughout the Chinese civil war and the long struggle against the Japanese he had always been welcomed by the peasants. But here, it seemed, guerrilla fish no longer swam in rural water. He wondered how the North Korean partisans continued to operate, many thousands strong, farther to the south. It was difficult to understand these Koreans.

The Osan airfield was a wonderland of discarded technology. Hangars sagged twisted and blackened by the bonfires of denial set off by the American withdrawal. The squad camped overnight in the body of an abandoned aircraft. Many such wrecks lined the cratered runway. Stores that had escaped the blaze were looted bare, but sufficient ration cans could be found to provide an evening meal. Fuel for a fire came from an unexpected cache of gasoline cans. The squad threw nothing away, not even the tiny packets of paper found in waxed cardbox boxes. This was used by the GIs to wipe their backsides, Lao told his men; it was standard army issue. His men laughed in polite disbelief.

The sound of vehicular engines aroused them at dawn. They tumbled out into defensive positions, surprised to see an American mechanized column heading up the highway. The Americans were staging a comeback.

Wong and Little Li fired a few mortar bombs into the column. The machine gunner got a long burst into the foremost half-tracks, but the wicked quadruple machine-guns raked the frail Chinese positions, killing several members of the squad. Artillery rained in from nowhere, throwing chunks of torn aluminum up into the air. Captain Lao ordered his bugler to sound the retreat. Nothing happened: the bugler was wounded. The captain blew his whistle, directing the Sharp Swords to take cover in the countryside. It took more than an hour to round them all up. Eight men, including Fat Belly Wu, were missing. The mortar and machine gun were abandoned.

The Americans resumed their northward advance, blasting Osan as they went. Enemy infantry fanned out from the column, clearing the roadside on either hand. The Sharp Swords waited, crouched in a ditch, until the enemy had gone. There were not enough of them to offer serious resistance. It was a chastening reverse after their successes in North Korea.

Captain Lao crept back at dusk to look for wounded. Fat Belly Wu sat propped against an airplane wheel, an empty submachine gun gripped in his dead hands. Eight other men lay stiffened in the wreckage. Their bodies had been searched and looted. The captain gathered the dead together and doused them in gasoline. He stood well back, took the Korean girl's grenade from his pack, and hurled it at the remaining fuel cans. A fire flared up and burned for more than an hour. It could still be seen as the remaining Sharp Swords trudged back toward Suwon. The yapping of frustrated dogs followed them across the fields.

General Matthew B. Ridgway knew he had retreated far enough. His forces were hovering around the 37th Parallel; over the past six weeks the U.S. Eighth Army had withdrawn 275 miles. American soldiers had never fallen back so far. But now it was obvious that the Chinese were in difficulties. The punch had gone out of their offensive. Their threatening offensive in the center was quickly blocked. The re-formed U.S. 2nd Division, victim of the Sunchon ambush, redeemed itself outside Wonju by putting up magnificent resistance. The Chinese drive on Taegu and the outflanking move behind Eighth Army never got off the ground.

On January 15 Ridgway ordered a reconnaissance in force up the west-coast highway. Brushing aside minimal resistance at Osan, his armored columns ranged as far as Suwon. This proved to him that the enemy had shot its bolt. The Chinese were in no position to resist. This he pointed out to the chief of staff of the U.S. Army, General J. Lawton Collins, who came out to see things for himself. Satisfied that Ridgway had the measure of the invading hordes, Collins ignored MacArthur's clamor for extending the war to the Chinese mainland. The Supreme Commander kept calling for his big-bang solution, and openly courted support from Truman's Republican opposition, but the Joint Chiefs of Staff were no longer listening.

MacArthur maintained pressure on the Truman administration to end what he considered the tactics of stalemate. His plan called for the interdiction of Chinese supply routes to North Korea with air-dropped radioactive waste, followed by a massive drive into Manchuria itself. The UN's troops would be reinforced, if possible, by Chinese Nationalist forces from Taiwan. This plan would at least provide "answer to the obscurities," the Supreme Commander claimed, "which now becloud the unsolved problems raised by Red China's undeclared war in Korea."

It would indeed. It would also draw the United States far deeper into an Asian war than the Truman administration was willing to go. The president was in the process of issuing peace proposals, drafted three months before with British Prime Minister Attlee, which offered to suspend any UN advance back into North Korea pending negotiations.

MacArthur got wind of these proposals and threw out a public bombshell of his own, calling contemptuously upon China—whose "military weaknesses," he said, "have been clearly and definitively revealed"—to head off "imminent military collapse" by coming hat in hand to the negotiating table. The Chinese indignantly refused. America's allies nervously protested MacArthur's unasked-for comments; Truman himself found the general's *pronunciamento* to be a direct challenge to the Presidency, and ultimately to the concept of civilian control over the military.

"By this act MacArthur left me no choice," Truman later wrote. "I could no longer tolerate his insubordination."

But before the president could act, MacArthur had fired off yet another pronouncement, this time in reply to a letter sent him by House Republican minority leader Joe Martin, a longtime isolationist. In his message of reply MacArthur derided the government's policy of according defense priority to Western Europe.

"It seems strangely difficult," the general wrote, "for some to realize that here in Asia is where the Communist conspirators have elected to make their play for global conquest, and that we have joined the issue thus raised on the battlefield; that here we fight Europe's war with arms while the diplomats there still fight it with words; that if we lose this war to Communism in Asia the fall of Europe is inevitable; win it and Europe most probably would avoid war and yet preserve freedom. As you have pointed out, we must win. There is no substitute for victory."

Martin read MacArthur's letter aloud on the floor of the House of Representatives on April 5, 1951. On the next morning, Truman sought his closest advisers' opinions. Privately, however, he had already made up his mind on the matter in question: no matter what the political cost, MacArthur had to go. There was, in fact, reluctant agreement from the advisers, backed later by the Joint Chiefs of Staff. The orders dismissing MacArthur and turning over his commands to Ridgway were released to White House reporters at 1 A.M. on the morning of April 11. Owing to a communications foul-up, combined with the peremptory way in which Truman acted, the first MacArthur learned of his own dismissal was at a Tokyo luncheon, through a tearful call from his aide de camp Sid Huff, who had heard the news on a radio bulletin. "Jeannie," the general told his wife, "we're going home at last."

The old soldier returned to the U.S. mainland to an hysterical welcome. Twice the tonnage of ticker tape that had rained down on the aviator hero Lindbergh greeted MacArthur in a seven-hour New York parade attended by millions. Politicians wept openly when he addressed a joint session of Congress. "In war there is no substitute for victory," he intoned. "There are some who, for varying reasons, would appease Red China. They are blind to history's clear lesson, for history teaches, with unmistakable emphasis, that appeasement but begets new and bloodier war . . ."

The public's response to his speech, as to his return, was astounding. Yet the general had spoken true when he wound up his Congressional address with the words: "I now close my military career and just fade away—an old soldier who has tried to do his duty as God gave him the light to see that duty. Goodbye." For within two years—after the parades, speeches, and tours—he was virtually forgotten by the general populace.

MacArthur's gloomiest prognostications about appeasement notwithstanding, Ridgway had already turned the tide of the war in January of 1951 by launching a series of attritional campaigns. His first general offensive started on January 25—well before MacArthur's dismissal. The aim was less to regain territory than to wear the enemy down. The UN forces swept forward under the old U.S. Army slogan:

"Find 'em! Fix 'em! Fight 'em! Finish 'em!" The Chinese counterattacked desperately on the Korean central front. Bloody fighting raged for the tiny village of Chipyong-ni, a few miles northwest of Wonju. When the fighting there had ceased, Ridgway flew over the battlefield. The snow-covered hills were littered with Chinese dead.

Epilogue

The UN offensive resumed in March of 1951. Seoul fell once again
to UN forces on March 14. The Chinese, by now thoroughly alarmed,
poured fresh armies into Ridgway's meatgrinder. They tried to retake
Seoul in April, overwhelming a battalion of the British regiment, the
Gloucesters, and attacked once more in May, in massive strength, on
the central and eastern sectors. Both attacks were held. Ridgway
returned to the offensive, mauling the Chinese so badly that thousands
of their fleeing, demoralized troops surrendered; late in June, peace
feelers were put out by the Soviet delegate to the United Nations.
Armistice talks dragged on for two more years, punctuated by
sporadic fighting, until a cease-fire agreement was signed on July 27,
1953.

Chinese losses were so appalling that even today the figures are
unmentionable. The Korean wing of the military museum in Peking,
with its charts and weapons and photographs of leading generals,
contains ample claims of American and other casualties. Inquiries
about the numbers of Chinese dead are met with the polite shrugs
that hide so many of China's secrets. A total of 900,000 has been
bandied around in the past, but present-day Western estimates put
it nearer 450,000.

All the Chinese field armies that crossed the Yalu River in the fall of 1950 suffered crippling casualties. The former Nationalist corps, the 50th Field Army, was virtually wiped out in the final battle for Seoul. Taiwan propagandists claimed the turncoat troops were deliberately sacrificed. This was untrue. The 50th stood and fought, and fought well, as Sergeant Gu Wentu had promised; he was one of the few survivors. One-eyed Colonel Pang died leading a mass charge at Uijongbu. Trooper Liu, predictably, deserted.

The 38th Field Army also took frightful punishment in actions near the South Korean capital. Captain Lao Kongcheng, commander of the Sharp Swords, lost most of his close comrades during the next two months. Trooper Wong, known as Big Ears, was killed by napalm in April of 1951. His sidekick, Little Li, died of burns the following day. The captain was permanently retired two months later, severely wounded, and became an English-language instructor after taking a degree in Shanghai. He now lives abroad.

Colonel Yang Shixian, commander of the 2nd Battalion, 347th Regiment, 116th Division, 39th Field Army, lost an arm in combat on the central sector in March of 1951. He was invalided back to China and continued to work as a military analyst in Peking until his death in 1984. The battalion commissar, Wong Wuyi, died of wounds in February of 1951.

The 18-year-old runner Jia Peixing, attached to the headquarters of the 358th Regiment, 120th Division, 40th Field Army, recovered his nerve despite the death in February at Chipyong-ni of his revered commander, Colonel Gu Dehua. Jia served throughout the Korean war, was promoted to captain in the field, and became a writer for many years for the army newspaper, *Liberation Daily*. He lives in retirement near Peking.

Colonel Wong Lichan served as liaison officer in North Korea until 1956. He was sent to obscure units in western China for the remainder of his career. In 1979 he joined a son living in Macao.

General Peng Dehuai relinquished command of the Chinese Peoples' Volunteers after the Korean armistice was signed in 1953. He returned home a hero. The People's Liberation Army was reorganized two years later and he was among the ten marshals then created, second only in seniority to the archveteran Zhu De. But the megalomania addling Mao Zedong in his later years led to the absurdities of the Great Leap Forward, an ill-considered attempt to hustle China down the road to socialism. The leap fell flat, causing widespread famine, and Peng felt it his duty to protest. His mildly worded exhortation to Mao was dismissed as mutinous. Marshal Peng was stripped of command and sent to a labor unit in Sichuan province. There his agony continued. Chairman Mao launched a larger, bloodier extravaganza than the Great Leap Forward during the mid-sixties. The campaign was given the curious name of the Cultural

Revolution, a term intended to embrace all the ingredients of civilization. Its pretext was condemnation of an allegorical play criticizing Peng's dismissal. Its real objective was the seizure of state power in order to remold China to fit the Chairman's more utopian fantasies. Red Guards got their hands on the unfortunate marshal and subjected him to cruel inquisition. The outcome is told by the editorial committee which published Peng's memoirs in Peking in 1982.

> Peng Dehuai's refusal to admit any crime infuriated his interrogators. They kicked him until his ribs were fractured and lungs injured. Beatings sent him unconscious to the floor.
>
> He fought to the last. It is said that the noise he made banging on the table and shouting at his investigators shook the house.
>
> "I fear nothing; you can shoot me!" he roared. "Your days are numbered. The more you interrogate, the firmer I'll become."
>
> Peng Dehuai was interrogated until he was bedridden. He was deprived of the right to sit, to rise up, to drink water, to go to the toilet or to turn over in bed. By the time he died on November 29, 1974, he had gone through over 130 interrogations.

This Chinese hero of the Korean War was rehabilitated in 1980. His place in military history has lately been reappraised. There is no doubt that the campaigns Peng directed restored China's credibility as a power in Asia. Lack of equipment, especially of logistics, prevented exploitation of his most brilliant successes. It may also be true, though this is learned by inference, that political judgments in Peking were allowed to override the field commander's customary caution.

Major Han Liqun returned to China with General Peng Dehuai. He too suffered during the Cultural Revolution, as did many other staff officers, and it was not until 1978 that he was brought back to Peking from a pig farm. He was permitted to leave China two years later, and lives with relatives in Hong Kong. His full memoirs will not be published until 25 years after his death.

Little Ah Lo of Andong, who watched the Chinese crossing the Yalu, grew up to be a Red Guard. He repented, left China in the mid-seventies, and now works for an export firm in Bangkok. Other characters interviewed, but not quoted, live in Taiwan.

The United States and China remained sworn enemies until President Nixon's visit of 1972. The two countries' mutual enmity was by then beginning to look ridiculous. The Maoist economic system was patently unworkable; the hardworking Chinese people had taken to sitting on their hands. The Chinese Communist movement itself was harshly divided. The outbursts of scalding xenophobia thrown up by the Cultural Revolution had provoked an armed clash between the Chinese and the Soviets on the Manchurian border in February of 1969. The strength of the Soviet reaction scared Mao into making overtures to Richard Nixon, himself beset by disaster in Vietnam. The rest is history.

Matt Ridgway won remarkably little recognition for his performance in Korea. Many American military men never forgave him for achieving a compromise settlement. They ignored—and resented—his admonitions against involvement in Vietnam. Some of his most distinguished colleagues thirsted for a replay of Korea, only this time the United States would go for a win. Ridgway's warnings were no more welcome than Cassandra's.

The British came out of the struggle looking like sniveling appeasers, as far as right-wing America was concerned, blamed for luring the U.S. into a botched-up peace. The fact that this peace has ever since persisted failed for many years to assuage the critics. British pretensions to world power vanished in 1956 in the wake of the Suez disaster; from there on it was down, down, down into unimaginable obscurity.

Korea came out of it all a ruin. Two million people are believed to have died. The awful sacrifices brought an armed peace, but little freedom, to the Land of the Morning Calm. The peninsula remained divided close to the old administrative frontier; to the south, heavy-handed army generals kicked out the wicked old patriot, Syngman Rhee, and replaced one form of dictatorship with another. But by harnessing the vast energies of the South Korean people the new rulers conjured an explosion of industrial free enterprise that continues to astonish the world.

To the north, the Soviet-installed survivor, Kim Il Sung, presides to this day over a hermit-state beholden entirely to himself. Effigies abound of the Beloved Leader, Ever-Victorious Captain of the Korean People. The biggest effigy of them all beams down from the hilltop overlooking a rebuilt Pyongyang, in front of the museum devoted solely to the extraordinary cult of his personality. The section devoted to the Korean War—or the Great Patriotic Struggle, as the guides call it—takes one whole day to tour. Hidden among the models, the maps, and the theatrical statuary perpetuating the myth of the great man's generalship throughout the three-year struggle, it is possible to find one small, fuzzy photograph. It shows Chinese troops crossing a bridge.

"Well, yes," the guides agree. "We did have a little help from China, too."

APPENDIX

Abbreviated Command Structure, Chinese Peoples' Volunteers

Abbreviated Command Structure, Chinese Peoples' Volunteers

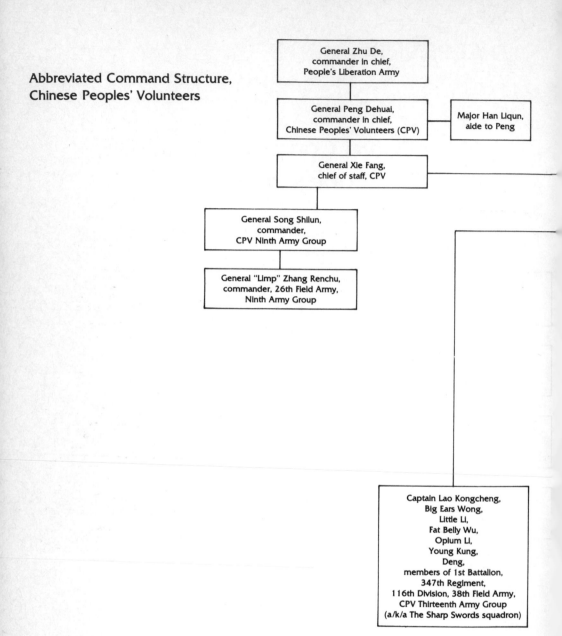

General Zhu De, commander in chief, People's Liberation Army

General Peng Dehuai, commander in chief, Chinese Peoples' Volunteers (CPV)

Major Han Liqun, aide to Peng

General Xie Fang, chief of staff, CPV

General Song Shilun, commander, CPV Ninth Army Group

General "Limp" Zhang Renchu, commander, 26th Field Army, Ninth Army Group

Captain Lao Kongcheng, Big Ears Wong, Little Li, Fat Belly Wu, Opium Li, Young Kung, Deng, members of 1st Battalion, 347th Regiment, 116th Division, 38th Field Army, CPV Thirteenth Army Group (a/k/a The Sharp Swords squadron)

Note: This chart omits the positions and ranks of personnel not playing a significant part in the narrative.

318

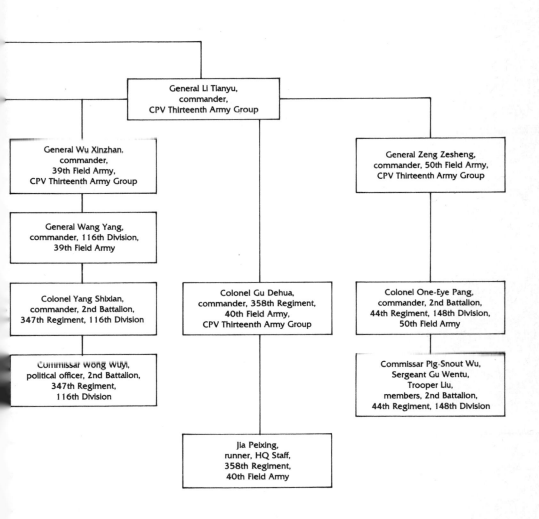

General Li Tianyu,
commander,
CPV Thirteenth Army Group

General Wu Xinzhan,
commander,
39th Field Army,
CPV Thirteenth Army Group

General Zeng Zesheng,
commander, 50th Field Army,
CPV Thirteenth Army Group

General Wang Yang,
commander, 116th Division,
39th Field Army

Colonel Yang Shixian,
commander, 2nd Battalion,
347th Regiment, 116th Division

Colonel Gu Dehua,
commander, 358th Regiment,
40th Field Army,
CPV Thirteenth Army Group

Colonel One-Eye Pang,
commander, 2nd Battalion,
44th Regiment, 148th Division,
50th Field Army

Commissar Wong Wuyi,
political officer, 2nd Battalion,
347th Regiment,
116th Division

Commissar Pig-Snout Wu,
Sergeant Gu Wentu,
Trooper Liu,
members, 2nd Battalion,
44th Regiment, 148th Division

Jia Peixing,
runner, HQ Staff,
358th Regiment,
40th Field Army

Bibliography

ACHESON, DEAN. *Present at the Creation.* New York, Norton, 1969.
———*This Vast External Realm.* New York, Norton, 1973.
ALEXANDER, BEVIN. *Korea: The First War We Lost.* New York, Hippocrene, 1986.
APPLEMAN, ROY E. *South to the Naktong, North to the Yalu.* Washington, D.C., Department of the Army, 1960.
BARCLAY, C. N. *The First Commonwealth Division.* Edinburgh, Thomas Nelson, 1954.
BARNETT, A. DOAK. *China & the Major Powers in East Asia.* Washington, D.C., Brookings Institute, 1977.
BEECH, KEYES. *Tokyo and Points East.* New York, Doubleday, 1954.
BRADLEY, OMAR, and CLAY BLAIR. *A General's Life.* New York, Simon & Schuster, 1983.
BUESCHEL, RICHARD M. *Communist Chinese Air Power.* New York, Praeger, 1968.
COLLINS, J. LAWTON. *War in Peacetime.* Boston, Houghton Mifflin, 1969.
CORR, GERARD H. *The Chinese Red Army.* New York, Schocken, 1974.
CUMINGS, BRUCE. *The Origins of the Korean War.* Princeton University Press, 1981.
CUTFORTH, RENÉ. *Korean Reporter.* London, Wingate, 1952.

DEUTSCHER, ISAAC. *Stalin*. London, Penguin, revised edition, 1966.

FEHRENBACH, T. R. *This Kind of War: A Study in Unpreparedness*. New York, Macmillan, 1963.

FIELD, JAMES A., JR. *US Naval Operations, Korea*. Washington, D.C., Department of the Navy, 1962.

FUTRELL, ROBERT F. *The United States Air Force in Korea*. New York, Duell, Sloan & Pearce, 1961.

GEORGE, ALEXANDER L. *The Chinese Communist Army in Action*. Columbia University Press, 1967.

GITTINGS, JOHN. *The Role of the Chinese Army*. New York, Oxford University Press, 1967.

GOULDEN, JOSEPH C. *Korea: The Untold Story of the War*. New York, Times Books, 1982.

HIGGINS, MARGUERITE. *War in Korea*. New York, Doubleday, 1951.

HIGGINS, TRUMBULL. *Korea and the Fall of MacArthur*. New York, Oxford University Press, 1960.

HOPKINS, WILLIAM B. *One Bugle No Drums*. Chapel Hill, North Carolina, Algonquin, 1986.

HOYT, EDWIN P. *On to the Yalu*. New York, Stein and Day, 1984.

KAHN, E. J. *The Peculiar War*. New York, Random House, 1951.

LIE, TRYGVE. *In the Cause of Peace*. New York, Macmillan, 1954.

MACARTHUR, DOUGLAS A. *Reminiscences*. New York, McGraw Hill, 1964.

MALCOLM, G. I. *The Argylls in Korea*. London, Thomas Nelson, 1952.

MANCHESTER, WILLIAM. *American Caesar*. New York, Dell, 1978.

MAO ZEDONG. *Military Works*. Peking, Foreign Languages Publishing House, 1965.

MARSHALL, L. A. *The River and The Gauntlet*. New York, William Morrow, 1953.

MCALEAVY, HENRY. *The Modern History of China*. London, Wiedenfeld & Nicolson, 1967.

MCGOVERN, JAMES. *To the Yalu*. New York, William Morrow, 1972.

MESSENGER, CHARLES. *The Art of Blitzkrieg*. London, Allan, 1976.

MONTROSS, LYNN, and NICHOLAS A. CANZONA. *U.S. Marine Operations in Korea: Vol. III Chosin Reservoir Campaign*. Washington, D.C., Marine Corps, 1957.

MORISON, SAMUEL ELIOT. *The Two-Ocean War*. Boston, Little Brown, 1963.

MORWOOD, WILLIAM. *Duel for the Middle Kingdom*. New York, Everest House, 1980.

PANNIKAR, K. M. *In Two Chinas*. London, Allen & Unwin, 1955.

PENG DEHUAI. *Memoirs of a Chinese Marshal (1898–1974)*. Peking, Foreign Languages Publishing House, 1984.

PERRETT, BRYAN. *Lightning War*. London, Granada, 1985.

REES, DAVID. *Korea: The Limited War*. New York, St. Martin's Press, 1964.

RIDGWAY, MATTHEW B. *Soldier*. Westport, Greenwood Press, 1956.
——*The Korean War*. New York, Doubleday, 1967.

RIGGS, ROBERT B. *Red China's Fighting Hordes*. Harrisburg, Pennsylvania, Telegraph Press, 1951.

ROVERE, RICHARD H., and ARTHUR M. SCHLESINGER. *The General and the President*. New York, Farrar, Straus and Young, 1951.

SCALAPINO, ROBERT A., and CHING-SIK LEE. *Communism in Korea*. University of California Press, 1972.

SHNABEL, JAMES F. *U.S. Army in the Korean War*. Washington, D.C., Department of the Army, 1972.

SHRAM, STUART. *Mao Tse-tung*. London, Penguin, 1966.

SMITH, ROBERT. *MacArthur in Korea*. New York, Simon & Schuster, 1962.

SPANIER, JOHN W. *The Truman-MacArthur Controversy and the Korean War*. Cambridge, Massachusetts, Belknap Press, 1959.

STONE, I. F. *The Hidden History of the Korean War*. New York, 1952.

SUN TZU. *The Art of War*. New York, Oxford University Press, 1963.

THOMPSON, REGINALD. *Cry Korea*. New York, White Lion, 1951.

TRUMAN, HARRY. *Memoirs, Vol. 2 . . . Years of Trial and Hope*. New York, Doubleday, 1956.

WHITING, ALLEN S. *China Crosses the Yalu*. Stanford University Press, 1960.

WHITNEY, COURTNEY. *MacArthur*. New York, Knopf, 1956.

WHITSON, WILLIAM W. *The Chinese High Command*. New York, Praeger, 1973.

WILLIAMS, HARRY T. *The History of American Wars*. New York, Knopf, 1981.

WILLOUGHBY, CHARLES A. *MacArthur 1941–1951*. New York, McGraw Hill, 1954.

INDEX

Index

About the Author

An Englishman by birth (born Ilford, Essex, 1922), peripatetic author RUSSELL SPURR is the son of a sea captain and a mother born in the Australian gold fields. During World War II he left his job as an apprentice reporter to join the Argyll & Sutherland Highlanders (whose exploits play a role in *Enter the Dragon*). Soon, however, he was transferred to the Royal Indian Navy, and served in motor gunboats through most of the Burma campaign. Returning to home and journalism after the Japanese surrender, he first worked for the BBC Overseas News Service, then flew out to India to run the Calcutta bureau of a small news-features agency. He became Far East correspondent for the London *Daily Express* in 1952, with a beat that included the Korean and Indochina Wars.

After three years in Canada as a feature writer, Mr. Spurr returned to India, and in the 1960s began freelancing for the British public-affairs television program "This Week." He subsequently became producer of another television program, "World in Action," and a producer of documentaries for the BBC. Working with television news agency Visnews, he covered the ground-breaking "ping-pong diplomacy" between the West and China, including President Nixon's historic journey to Peking. From 1974 to 1979 he was deputy editor of the *Far Eastern Economic Review* in Hong Kong. Following this he became ABC Radio Correspondent for China and began hosting the television talk show "Focus."

His first book, *A Glorious Way to Die: The Kamikaze Mission of the Battleship* Yamato, *April 1945*, was published by Newmarket Press in 1981 to worldwide acclaim. It has been translated into several languages, including Japanese. Mr. Spurr now resides in Sydney, Australia, with his wife, Rosemary, and is the father of three sons. *Enter the Dragon* is his second book.